ECONOMICS AND YOUTH VIOLENCE

Economics and Youth Violence

Crime, Disadvantage, and Community

Edited by Richard Rosenfeld, Mark Edberg,
Xiangming Fang, and Curtis S. Florence

NEW YORK UNIVERSITY PRESS
New York and London

NEW YORK UNIVERSITY PRESS
New York and London
www.nyupress.org

References to Internet websites (URLs) were accurate at the time of writing.
Neither the author nor New York University Press is responsible for URLs
that may have expired or changed since the manuscript was prepared.

Library of Congress Cataloging-in-Publication Data
Economics and youth violence : crime, disadvantage, and community /
edited by Richard Rosenfeld, Mark Edberg, Xiangming Fang, and
Curtis S. Florence
pages   cm
Includes bibliographical references and index.
ISBN 978-0-8147-8930-8 (hardback) — ISBN 978-0-8147-6059-8 (pb)
1. Youth and violence—Economic aspects. 2. Violence in adolescence—
Economic aspects. 3. Juvenile delinquency—Economic aspects.
4. Business cycles.   I. Rosenfeld, Richard, editor of compilation.
HQ799.2.V56E26 2013
303.60835—dc23   2013001059

New York University Press books are printed on acid-free paper,
and their binding materials are chosen for strength and durability.
We strive to use environmentally responsible suppliers and materials
to the greatest extent possible in publishing our books.

Manufactured in the United States of America

c   10 9 8 7 6 5 4 3 2 1
p   10 9 8 7 6 5 4 3 2 1

CONTENTS

1

Introduction

RICHARD ROSENFELD, CURTIS S. FLORENCE,
XIANGMING FANG, AND MARK EDBERG

Scholars, policymakers, and the general public have long been interested in how economic conditions such as poverty, unemployment, inflation, and economic growth affect public problems, including the level and types of youth violence in a community or society, the focus of the current volume. The connection between macroeconomic factors and youth violence has been referenced or alluded to in much of the literature on this issue. But significant research gaps remain, and opinion is far from settled with respect to the economic factors that are most important and how their impact is manifested in children, adolescents, and their families, schools, and communities. As the United States and other nations continue to confront the economic problems brought on by the 2008–9 Great Recession, these issues remain of utmost importance to researchers, policymakers, and citizens.

In the fall of 2008, the National Center for Injury Prevention and Control (NCIPC) at the U.S. Centers for Disease Control and Prevention (CDC) awarded a contract to the Development Services Group (DSG) to review the research literature on the relationship between macroeconomic conditions and youth violence in order to develop recommendations for future research and evidence-based intervention and prevention strategies. DSG convened a panel of research scholars to initiate the literature review. The panel consisted of experts in criminology, sociology, anthropology, economics, public health, and psychology (see appendix). All of the panelists have conducted research on youth violence, aggression, and crime and are research leaders in their areas of specialization.

The panelists and colleagues at the CDC began work on a series of papers based on the literature review and on their own related research programs. Over the next year, the papers were presented and revised at panel meetings and eventually became the chapters of the current volume. In this introductory chapter, we briefly describe the analytic framework used to guide and organize the literature review and the major conclusions of the review. We then discuss the organization of the current volume, summarize the objectives and results of each of the chapters, and consider the implications of the volume for future research on the causes and prevention of youth violence.

Analytic Framework and Literature Review

During the 1990s, Brooks-Gunn and colleagues developed an analytic framework connecting macro-social conditions such as segregation and labor markets to individual developmental outcomes, including physical and mental health, personal efficacy, interpersonal relations, and criminal behavior (Brooks-Gunn, Duncan, and Aber 1997). The framework specifies two key intervening domains that link macro conditions to individual development: neighborhood characteristics and family responses to neighborhood conditions. The framework has proven to be a durable foundation for subsequent basic and applied studies in what has come to be termed the "neighborhood effects" tradition in social research.

We used the Brooks-Gunn framework as a starting point for our own literature review and for shaping the chapters in the current volume. Our first task was to develop an analytic framework to guide our inquiries along the lines of that developed by Brooks-Gunn et al. (1997), but our framework is both narrower in scope and more elaborate in content. In keeping with the objectives of our project, we narrowed the range of macro-social conditions to focus on economic conditions such as poverty, unemployment, economic growth, and wealth inequality. We also narrowed the outcome of concern to violent offending and victimization of children, adolescents, and young adults. But we expanded the mediating domains linking macroeconomic conditions to youth violence to encompass the community (comparable to "neighborhood" in the Brooks-Gunn schema) and situational contexts of youth violence. The situational domain includes family structure and functioning as a major component but also incorporates other relevant micro environments affecting youth violence, such as schools, street gangs, illegal markets, and access to firearms (see table 1.1).

Our framework consists of a temporal dimension (long-term versus short-term impacts of economic conditions on youth violence) that is cross-classified with the intervening domains through which the impacts of macroeconomic factors are manifested: societal, community, situational, and individual. The temporal dimension distinguishes economic conditions on the basis of whether they change gradually or rapidly over time. Some macroeconomic factors, such as levels of wealth inequality, change relatively slowly over time, and their impact on youth violence may occur over many years or decades. Such effects are best captured by studies of long-term changes in economic conditions and violence or by cross-sectional studies that reflect the accumulated changes in economic conditions and violence captured at a single point in time. Alternatively, some factors may have an impact on youth violence only when they reach a critical threshold level, and the effective level may differ across communities. Other macroeconomic conditions, such as unemployment, inflation, or consumer confidence, change more rapidly over time, and their effects on violence can be examined in time-series studies covering shorter time periods.

The second dimension of the framework specifies the domains through which economic factors may influence youth violence, over both the short and long run. Broad economic phenomena, such as a

Table 1.1. *The Impact of Economic Conditions on Youth Violence: A Multilevel Explanatory Framework*

	Society	Community	Situational	Individual	Youth violence
Short-run factors and impacts	Cyclical economic change Reduced social spending Change in economic inequality (e.g., due to technology gap, wealth concentration)	Job loss from local business closings Public budget cutbacks—drop in social services and school resources Cyclical unemployment Reduction in after-school activities Increased incidence of violent behavior as a characteristic of the community environment	Increase in drug market volatility Increase in market for stolen goods Fluctuations in access to firearms Increased youth gang membership and prevalence	Increased likelihood of low-wage, unstable employment Economically induced stressors Increase in dysfunctional coping (e.g., drug, alcohol abuse) Increased truancy, decreased school participation, dropout Negative attitudes toward school Change in individual calculation of risk, resulting in more risk behavior Increased firearm carrying	Increased incidence of violent behavior Increased firearm use
Long-term factors and impacts	Job loss from international competition and outsourcing Unbalanced levels of global unemployment and poverty, leading to cross-border migrations Deindustrialization High economic inequality Media marketing of violence and violent models	Chronic joblessness for youth and families Concentrated poverty Poor housing, exposure to environmental toxins and pollution Physical degradation of neighborhood Lack of access to health care Secondary labor market Family disruption and instability Outmigration of better-off residents Low collective efficacy Low community attachment Immigrant enclaves	Lack of plausible, attractive, and stable job paths Few prosocial adult models—high salience of violent or negative models Ineffective parenting History of family problem behaviors (e.g., drug abuse, criminality) High levels of family violence, abuse, neglect Limited adult supervision Disorganized school climate Limited social capital outside of street environment Violent street code—prevalence of attitudes and beliefs (among adults and peers) supporting violence Easy access to firearms	Chronic unemployment for youth and families Educational deficits Low expectations with respect to mainstream economic and social roles High expectations with respect to gains from street economy Low perceptions of personal safety Decreased reliance on family for support Cognitive-behavioral deficits resulting from violent victimization, prenatal drug exposure, environmental toxins	Chronically high levels of community violence Chronically high levels of family violence, abuse, neglect Persistence of violent street codes—prevalence of attitudes and beliefs (among adults and peers) supporting violence

Differential Impacts of and on Race and Ethnicity

national or global recession, may affect entire societies (column one in the figure). Others, such as concentrated poverty or chronic jobless-ness, affect some communities more than others (column two). Eco-nomic conditions also may influence the situational context of youth violence by, for example, affecting firearm ownership and carrying, the salience of street gangs, and markets for illicit drugs (column three). Finally, the economy may affect individual youths in ways that heighten their risk for violence, for example, through its impact on family func-tioning, community support resources, illicit drug use, or dropping out of school (column four). The short- and long-run impacts of eco-nomic conditions are likely to ramify across multiple domains and may differ depending on the race, ethnicity, or immigration status of the affected youth.

If nothing else, the analytic framework depicted in table 1.1 should convey the complexity of the manifold connections between economic conditions and youth violence. The panel, in order to make its task manageable, decided to focus its attention on four key subdomains through which the impact of economic conditions on youth violence is manifested: families, schools, community resources, and street markets. These intervening contexts were not intended to exhaust the possible connecting links between economic conditions and youth violence, but they do constitute major pathways through which economic factors are likely to influence levels and patterns of youth violence.

The analytic framework proved to be useful for organizing the review and motivating the studies contained in this volume. We recom-mend continued use of this organizing schema or closely related ones in future reviews intended to summarize prior research and to guide future research on youth violence. The literature review culminated in the following general conclusions:

(1) The research literature on macroeconomic factors associated with youth violence is dominated by cross-sectional studies. Further, results from cross-sectional investigations often are not replicated in exist-ing longitudinal research. Perhaps the best example of such divergent results involves the relationship between unemployment and crime. Cross-sectional research reveals a robust, positive relationship between the unemployment rate and crime, whereas the findings of longitudi-nal studies are mixed, with some studies finding a negative relationship,

others a positive relationship, and others no relationship, particularly between unemployment and violent crime (e.g., Pratt and Cullen 2005). The difference in results could signal a corresponding difference in the short- and long-term impact of unemployment, with cross-sectional studies reflecting the impact on crime and violence of enduring or chronic joblessness and longitudinal research reflecting short-term cyclical effects or their absence. But the greater consistency of the cross-sectional findings also may be attributable to the absence of controls for other conditions that affect both the level of unemployment and violence. In other words, the relationship between unemployment and violence found in cross-sectional research may to some degree be spurious. Future research should adopt both a cross-sectional and longitudinal framework, as in pooled time-series or panel analyses, which may help to better identify the causal consequences of unemployment and other economic conditions for youth violence, across places and over time (see, e.g., Arvanites and Defina 2006; Raphael and Winter-Ebmer 2001; Rosenfeld 2009).

(2) The analytic framework directs attention to a range of potential pathways between macroeconomic factors, the mediating domains, and youth violence. Most of the literature reviewed, however, focuses on the relationship between mediating factors and youth violence (proximal linkages), rather than between macroeconomic factors and the mediating domains (distal linkages) or linkages spanning the full spectrum from macroeconomic factors to youth violence. Greater research attention to how economic conditions affect families, schools, community resources, street markets, and other mediating contexts of youth violence is clearly needed.

(3) The literature under review points to several individual and family-level risk factors for youth violence and to interventions that show promise in modifying those factors. Much less attention, however, has been devoted to interventions at the community level that may reduce rates of youth violence. Moreover, the research literature strongly suggests that the effect of individual and family factors cannot be separated from the surrounding community-level socioeconomic conditions in which they are embedded, supporting a conclusion that individual or family-level interventions, even if "best practices," will have limited effects unless they are combined with broader community interventions.

The Current Volume

Overall, the literature review constitutes a rich resource for the research community by summarizing the major results of, as well as deficits in, recent research on linkages between macroeconomic conditions and youth violence. It also served as a foundation for the current volume, which reviews prior research and introduces new results pertaining to youth violence across multiple domains of influence and over time. We asked the contributors to address important outstanding research issues that emerge from the literature review and to bring new data and insights to bear on these issues from their own research. The volume is organized in three main parts. The three chapters in part 1 focus on the relationship between changing economic conditions and general crime, violence, and youth violence trends over varying time periods. The chapters in part 2 examine patterns of youth violence and its control in relation to community socioeconomic conditions. Part 3 directs attention to how economic conditions influence individual and family factors implicated in youth violence. The final chapter derives policy and prevention implications from the research overviews and the new findings presented in the previous chapters.

Part 1 opens with a chapter by Shawn Bushway, Philip Cook, and Matthew Phillips that presents new research results on the relationship between short-run fluctuations in economic conditions and changes in homicide, property crime, and suicide rates over a 76-year period. The results replicate and extend those of a now classic paper by Cook and Zarkin (1985). The authors find that economic downturns result in increases in burglary, robbery, and suicide rates; decreases in motor-vehicle theft; and no significant change in homicide rates. An analysis of age-specific arrest rates since 1963 shows basically the same results, except for robbery, which is not significantly related to changes in age-specific arrests. The analysis of arrests indicates that the "procyclical" pattern (crime decreases coincide with economic downturns) for motor-vehicle theft is specific to offenders under the age of 18; no significant results are found for older age groups. The authors view the mechanisms linking cyclical economic change and crime as a "black box" to be filled in by other researchers. The remaining chapters begin to peer inside the black box.

Eric Baumer, Richard Rosenfeld, and Kevin Wolff present new results on how levels of inflation moderate the impact of unemployment on property crime and age-specific homicide rates for a sample of 82 American cities over the period between 1980 and 2009. Controlling for other influences, they find that the effect of unemployment on property crime rates is stronger during periods of high inflation; in fact, no relationship exists between unemployment and property crime during periods of below-average inflation rates. The authors report similar results for the effect of wage levels on homicide rates. These results may hold a clue for why crime rates did not increase during the 2008–9 recession, when inflation rates were at historically low levels. Contrary to expectations, the authors do not find evidence that the level of unemployment insurance benefits or a measure of drug market activity moderates the effect of economic adversity on crime rates. They conclude their chapter with the recommendation that future research on the relationship between macroeconomic conditions and crime rates move beyond simplistic assessments of "main effects" and consider the role of inflation and other conditions in moderating the relationship between crime rates and economic conditions such as unemployment and wages.

Janet Lauritsen, Ekaterina Gorislavsky, and Karen Heimer also present new research findings in their chapter on the relationship between changing economic conditions and rates of serious violent victimization among adolescents and young adults between 1973 and 2005. They compare the effects of unemployment, poverty, and consumer sentiment on rates of youth violence by the gender and race-ethnicity of victims. They find that increases in youth violence are generally associated with increases in poverty and growing consumer pessimism, but not with increases in unemployment. The effects of poverty and consumer sentiment, however, differ somewhat for males and females and youth of differing ages and race-ethnic groups. Like the previous results presented by Baumer and colleagues, these findings indicate that the relationship between macroeconomic conditions and youth violence is not simple and is conditioned by the age, gender, and race-ethnicity of victims.

In part 2 of the volume on the community context of youth violence, Xiangming Fang, Richard Rosenfeld, Linda Dahlberg, and Curtis Florence report new results from a cross-sectional study of the relationship between neighborhood socioeconomic disadvantage and self-reported violent offending among a nationally representative school-based sample of adolescents. They find that the relationship between disadvantage and adolescent violence is nonlinear: Adolescent violence is relatively low in the least disadvantaged neighborhoods, peaks in more disadvantaged areas, and falls off somewhat in the most disadvantaged areas. The authors recommend that policymakers consider these nonlinear patterns when devising interventions to control youth violence.

Robert Crutchfield and Tim Wadsworth present results from their research on youth and adult employment patterns in disadvantaged communities, school performance, and delinquency in a nationally representative sample of adolescents. An important result of this study is that neighborhood socioeconomic disadvantage conditions the effect of school performance on delinquency. Among students who live in disadvantaged areas, better grades in school are associated with *higher* delinquency rates, a pattern opposite to that found for students from more advantaged areas and suggesting that the relationship between school performance and violence involvement is conditioned by the neighborhood opportunity structure. This finding should concern policymakers and violence-prevention specialists and echoes the conclusion from the literature review that interventions to prevent youth crime and violence should be multivalent, encompassing the community as well as the families and schools of disadvantaged youth.

The following chapter by Mark Edberg and Philippe Bourgois considers how the exposure of adolescents to street market contexts (e.g., gangs, drug markets) shapes the connection between violence and identity development—thus increasing the likelihood of violent behavior by youth. Prior research has explored normative aspects of these contexts, particularly a violent "code of the street" (Anderson 1999). The authors, however, focus on the interaction of the street market context as embedded in structural inequality and the adolescent developmental phase of identity formation, concluding that violence comes to represent socially valued personal qualities, which strengthens its connection to positive identity models. The authors also conclude that interventions focusing on the risk factors that contribute to youth involvement in street markets do not sufficiently address the *generative* dynamic that exists once they are involved—as exemplified by the identity development process. Interventions utilizing a *substitution principle* are offered as one alternative.

In the final chapter of part 2, by Jeffrey Fagan and Valerie West, attention turns to the response of the criminal justice system to neighborhood violence. To what extent, they ask, do persistently high levels of incarceration depress economic well-being and human capital in disadvantaged and racially segregated communities? In a panel analysis of New York City neighborhoods between 1985 and 1996, a period in which the city's violent-crime rates both rose and fell sharply, the authors find evidence that high incarceration rates reduce income growth, educational attainment, and work experience in disadvantaged and racially segregated neighborhoods. They recommend targeted micro investment and housing development in such areas to break the connection between incarceration and economic and educational disadvantage.

The two chapters in part 3 of the volume address the interconnections among economic conditions, families, child development, and youth violence. Nancy Guerra employs a lifecycle approach to describe different kinds of links between macroeconomic factors and violent behavior that occur across the developmental continuum. She argues that such linkages must be viewed—for both theoretical and intervention purposes—in connection to developmental stage and as a *cumulative process*. Poverty increases early child exposure to fetal toxins, nutritional deficiencies, trauma (through violence exposure), and family/parenting difficulties. Such exposures set in motion a process that is exacerbated up the developmental chain by other factors connected to poverty and the macroeconomic context, including neglect; a lack of economic resources, educational support, and access to health care; and continued exposure to community violence and its social context. Intervention strategies must therefore be linked across developmental stages to have a chance of interrupting this process.

The chapter by Jennifer Matjasko, Sarah Beth Barnett, and James Mercy describes a cyclical dynamic between macroeconomic factors and families affecting child outcomes. Both short- and long-term economic strains disrupt the ability of families to provide a nurturing and positive developmental environment. Drawing on the family stress and the family investment models, the chapter shows how long-term and short-term economic strains can differentially (1) increase irritability, anger, depression, substance use, harsh parenting, family conflict, and other problems within families, potentially leading to adjustment and academic problems among children; and (2) affect decisions families make about resources they can (and cannot) provide for educational and developmental support. Further, Robert Agnew's general strain theory (2006) suggests an additional family stressor from a general frustration created by resource deprivation. Matjasko and colleagues propose a model capturing the cyclical dynamic that predicts different family—and thus youth—outcomes by type of economic strain, with implications for intervention.

The final chapter by Curtis Florence and Sarah Beth Barnett considers the implications for policy and prevention raised in the preceding chapters. The authors discuss three preconditions for the prevention of youth violence through improvements in economic conditions. First, a strong relationship between youth violence and economic conditions must be established, net of other influences. Second, prevention programs should target the specific economic conditions that affect youth violence, and their effectiveness in improving those conditions must be demonstrated. Third, the economic improvements must be sufficiently large to lead to reductions in youth violence.

With respect to the first question, several of the chapters in this volume report statistically significant relationships between economic conditions and crime, including youth violence, but some conditions appear to be more important than others. None of the analyses, for example, shows a direct relationship between unemployment and youth violence. The authors recommend that the impact of youth, adult, and family income levels on youth violence should be given high priority in future research intended to inform prevention policy and programs.

The second precondition for policy-relevant research requires that prevention efforts effectively ameliorate the particular economic conditions that influence youth violence. That will mean paying close attention to how economic conditions affect families, schools, and neighborhoods—the more proximate contexts in which youth violence emerges. Finally, the authors maintain that the demonstrated effects of prevention programs must be sufficiently large and sustained to result in appreciable reductions in youth violence. Some of the most effective

prevention programs focus on developmental processes in early childhood. The research challenge is to show that the beneficial effects of
early-life interventions persist into adolescence and young adulthood.

Outstanding Issues

The research reported in this volume offers new and important insights
regarding the relationship between macroeconomic conditions and
youth violence. To take only a few examples, we learn from Baumer
and colleagues' study that the relationship between unemployment and
property crime may be conditioned by the level of inflation: a significant relationship exists during periods of high inflation, while little or
no relationship exists during periods of low inflation. Lauritsen and
colleagues' research indicates that the impact of macroeconomic conditions on youth violence differs by race and ethnicity, with stronger
effects for minority youth. Crutchfield and Wadsworth report the dis-
turbing result that high-achieving students in disadvantaged neighborhoods may be more likely than other youth to engage in violent behavior. Edberg and Bourgois argue that, for some youth, a violent persona
fulfills otherwise positive identity needs and, as a result, may be difficult to modify without substituting prosocial identities that fulfill the
same needs. These and the other chapters highlight the complexities
in the relationship between economic conditions, youth violence, and
the community and situational contexts in which their connections are
forged. They also prompt questions that should guide future research
on the causes and prevention of youth violence.

We consider six questions to guide future research. We recognize
that many others could be added to this list and encourage readers to
identify other outstanding issues raised (or neglected) in this volume.
But we believe that the following six questions merit serious consideration in the design of future studies of youth violence and research on
policy and prevention:

1. Is macro-level research on youth violence sufficient in and of itself to
   address important questions about the causes and control of youth violence, or should all future research focus on the interplay of macro-,
   micro-, and individual-level conditions and processes?

2. What are the *disaggregated and interactive* effects of macroeconomic conditions on youth violence and its community and situational antecedents?

3. How do *social institutions* influence the level and types of youth violence observed at specific times and places?

4. What is the role of *property crime* in the generation of and risk for youth violence?

5. To what extent is research on youth violence biased by *selection effects*?

6. Are data and information on youth violence detailed and timely enough to adequately inform policy responses to youth violence?

Is Macro-Level Research Sufficient?

The first question invokes longstanding philosophical and disciplinary debates regarding the adequacy of macro-level theories and research for addressing important questions about human behavior (for an excellent treatment, see Jepperson and Meyer 2011). The debates are framed by two metatheoretical positions: methodological individualism and sociological holism. Methodological individualism, arguably the more dominant orientation in contemporary social science,[1] holds that cultural formations, institutions, and social structures are manifested only in the behavior of individuals and that, as such, explanations of human behavior must be grounded in research on individuals. The opposite holistic position, by contrast, posits that supraindividual conditions and processes (e.g., the nuclear family system, market economy, globalization) are sufficient to explain important social outcomes without invoking strong assumptions about the biological characteristics or psychological states of individuals.

We have stated these positions in their extreme form, which few social scientists adopt without some qualification. A common response in modern social science to the individualistic-holistic debate is to promote "multilevel" theorizing and research that incorporates macro, micro, and individual properties in the explanation of individual behavior. But the very emphasis on individual outcomes privileges the individualistic position and, by implication, rejects single-level macroscopic explanation as untenable.

We fully endorse multilevel theory and research in the study of youth violence and much else—indeed, the analytic framework underlying this volume explicitly invokes multiple levels of analysis (macro, community, situational, individual) in the explanation of youth violence. But the outcomes of interest are not limited to individual behavior, and the framework is intended as an analytic device to bring some order and clarity to the diverse research traditions and disciplinary perspectives that characterize the study of youth violence. Given the current state of knowledge about the causes and prevention of youth violence, social scientists would be ill advised to limit scholarly inquiry to studies that focus only on individual outcomes or to reject a priori single-level research, whether macro level, individual level, or somewhere in between.

The question of the appropriate level(s) of analysis for the study of youth violence ultimately depends on the explanatory purposes at hand. Consider the study by Bushway and colleagues of the relationship between the business cycle and youth crime and violence. They address a macro-level question: do rates of youth crime and violence rise and fall in systematic fashion during economic recessions and recoveries? Their research reveals relationships between the business cycle and property crime and robbery, but they leave it to others to interpret those relationships in terms of neighborhood or family or individual attributes.

The chapters in part 3 of this volume specify family and individual attributes that may increase the vulnerability of some youth, at particular points in the developmental process, to macroeconomic fluctuations of the sort Bushway and colleagues examine. More broadly, individual- and micro-level theory and research alert us to differential exposure to risk factors that explain why some youth are more likely than others to engage in violent behavior or are at greater risk for violent victimization. But such research does not, by itself, fully explain why *rates* of violence change over time or why some communities have persistently higher rates of violence than others. Those are macro-level issues that require macro-level theorizing and research designs or multilevel designs capable of studying aggregate and not simply individual outcomes (for extended discussion, see Rosenfeld 2011).

Elaborating Macro-Level Research

If macro-level research on youth violence remains viable and necessary, it also should be expanded and elaborated in at least two ways: greater attention should be directed to explaining the impact of macroeconomic conditions on demographically disaggregated rates of youth violence and to how economic conditions interact in their effects on youth violence. Lauritsen and colleagues provide a useful point of departure for research on disaggregated violence rates in their assessment in this volume of the impact of poverty, unemployment, and consumer sentiment on race- and ethnic-specific rates of violent victimization. Bushway and colleagues find that the impact of the business cycle on motor-vehicle theft differs according to the age of the offender (measured by arrests). Baumer and colleagues provide an important example of how some economic conditions (inflation in their study) moderate the influence of other economic factors (unemployment and wages in their study) on youth crime and violence. These results offer a more nuanced view of the relationship between macroeconomic conditions and youth crime and violence than is afforded by research limited to explaining variation in aggregate rates and the additive (versus interactive) effects of multiple macroeconomic conditions.

Social Institutions

"Macro" social conditions are not limited to the aspects of social structure and culture that are emphasized in most prior research on crime and violence (e.g., labor markets, poverty, inequality, violent conduct norms). Social institutions also matter. Social institutions are the enduring complexes of values, beliefs, organizations, positions, and roles that define a social system and set it apart from others (see Jepperson and Meyer 2011; Messner, Rosenfeld, and Karstedt 2011). The relationship between macroeconomic conditions and rates of youth violence and the effects of the economy on individual youth are likely to vary across differing institutional contexts. Indeed, the very concepts of "youth violence" and "adolescence" as a distinct phase of the developmental process are institutionally determined (see Felson 2002). Neither criminological nor public health research on youth violence has devoted sufficient attention to the role of institutions in shaping the cultural, structural, and individual contexts in which youth violence develops and is sustained and altered (for important exceptions, see Eisner 2001; Gartner 1991; LaFree 1998; Pampel and Gartner 1995; Roth 2009). Historical and comparative research is essential for understanding the institutional forces—and transformations—that give rise to youth violence and the possibilities for its prevention.

Property Crime and Youth Violence

Property crime (burglary, theft, receipt of stolen goods) has been largely neglected as a risk factor for youth violence in both the criminological and public health research literature. Criminologists tend to view the empirical association between property and violent crime as spurious, that is, the result of other individual or social factors such as self-control or criminal opportunities (see Rosenfeld 2009). Public health researchers evidence some interest in general delinquency as a risk factor for violence but have devoted little attention to how the dynamics of property offending may increase violent offending and victimization. Yet there are good reasons for suspecting that property crime and the exchange of stolen goods in underground markets pose specific risks for violence.

The lifestyle and activity patterns of property offenders bring them into contact with violent youth and adults. Violence is used to settle disagreements, to enforce compliance, and to punish wrongdoing among persons who lack access to formal dispute-resolution mechanisms and agents of social control such as the police, courts, and schools. The legal vulnerability of property offenders makes them attractive targets for street robbers and other predators. These risks have been documented in research on illicit drug markets (e.g., Jacobs 2000), but they exist wherever persons are engaged in illegal activity and cannot rely on formal authorities for assistance or protection.

Recent research indicates that the risks of property crime elevate rates of serious violence, including homicide, among youthful offenders (Loeber and Farrington 2011). Further, much research has shown that economic conditions have stronger and more consistent effects on property crime rates than on rates of violent crime (see Bushway et al.

in this volume). This suggests that property offending may be a significant intervening domain linking the economy to violence. Investigating the *causal* consequences of property offending and other forms of criminal involvement for youth violence, and the indirect influence of economic conditions on youth violence through property crime, should be high on the future agenda of youth-violence researchers.

Selection Effects

Perhaps no other issue has bedeviled contemporary research on the community context of youth violence more than that of *selection bias* (see Duncan, Connell, and Klebanov 1997; Sampson, Morenoff, and Gannon-Rowley 2002). The selection problem is part of a broader class of issues affecting the derivation of causal inferences from nonexperimental data. In the classic experiment, some subjects are randomly allocated to a "treatment" condition and others to a "control" condition. In principle, randomization ensures that the treatment and control subjects are similar on all conditions affecting the outcome, except for the treatment. Randomization is difficult to implement in field research on human behavior, however, and in many instances is simply not possible —especially in the study of risky or violent behavior. It is neither ethical nor practical, for example, to randomly expose children and adolescents to differing levels of poverty, abuse, or neglect to investigate the effects of such community and family conditions on violent behavior. Violence researchers are usually left with few alternatives to the use of *observational data* in the study of youth violence, that is, observations of violence and its hypothesized antecedents as they naturally occur in real-world environments. The reliance on observational data raises the problem of selection bias.[2]

Individuals and families are not randomly allocated across communities of different types; they make choices about where to live and, within limits, where to attend school, work, shop, and spend their leisure time. That is, individuals are selected into (and out of) social environments, and those observed in a particular environment may differ in all kinds of ways from those observed elsewhere. If those individual differences are correlated with a specific outcome we want to explain, such as violent behavior, and also with characteristics of the environment itself (e.g., the degree of poverty or racial segregation), how can we be certain that the outcome is caused by the environment and not by the attributes of the individuals in the environment? Failure to take adequate account of how individual attributes affect violent behavior can, therefore, lead to invalid causal inferences concerning the effect of social environments on violence by either overestimating or underestimating the hypothesized environmental effect (Duncan, Connell, and Klebanov 1997).

Researchers have long recognized the problem of selection bias in community-level research and have addressed it in essentially three ways: through single- or multi-level cross-sectional research designs that incorporate statistical controls for potentially relevant individual effects; through longitudinal designs that follow the same individuals and communities over a sufficient length of time to establish the temporal sequence between hypothesized causes and effects; and, more recently, through propensity-score models that match or otherwise equate individuals on those characteristics, other than the hypothesized "treatment," thought to affect the outcome (the classic statement is Rosenbaum and Rubin 1983). Each of these approaches can reduce selection bias, but none eliminates it, especially selection on "unobservables," that is, relevant individual attributes that the investigator is not aware of or cannot measure. So long as researchers must rely on observational data for studying youth violence and other significant individual and social outcomes, selection bias will remain a threat to causal inference, and causal claims—including those in this volume—must be viewed with caution.

Policy-Relevant Data

A final question that should inform future research on youth violence, especially applied research that has the potential for informing prevention policy and practice, concerns the quality and timeliness of the available data on youth violence and its correlates. To address problems of crime and violence *as they develop*, researchers and policymakers must have access to detailed, comparative, and timely data. Ideally, violence data should be available at the incident level and include information on date and time of occurrence, victim and (if known) suspect characteristics and relationship, and features of the event, such as its connection to other crimes and weapon use. Few violence data systems contain this level of detail, and those that do are not nationally representative (e.g., the FBI's National Incident Based Reporting System) or omit an important type of violence (e.g., the Bureau of Justice Statistics' National Crime Victimization Survey, which omits lethal violence). Triangulating data across systems is made difficult by the use of differing definitions and reporting jurisdictions. Researchers, policymakers, and the nation would be best served by a single nationally representative violence surveillance system that combines criminal justice and public health data on violent incidents, both lethal and nonlethal, enables comparisons across jurisdictions of varying size, and disseminates the data in small time increments (months or quarters) on a timely basis.

NOTES

1. For example, Jepperson and Meyer observe, "The idea that structural arguments are at best explanation sketches, to be resolved into and replaced by more adequate individual-level explanations, is now relatively commonplace" (2011, 66).
2. Selection bias and related methodological problems that compromise valid causal inference also occur in randomized field experiments in criminology and other social sciences (Sampson 2010).

REFERENCES

Agnew, Robert. 2006. *Pressured into crime: An overview of general strain theory*. New York: Oxford University Press.

Anderson, Elijah. 1999. *Code of the street: Decency, violence, and the moral life of the inner city*. New York: Norton.

Arvanites, Thomas M., and Robert H. Defina. 2006. Business cycles and street crime. *Criminology* 44:139–64.

Brooks-Gunn, Jeanne, Greg J. Duncan, and J. Lawrence Aber, eds. 1997. *Neighborhood poverty*, vol. 1, *Context and consequences for children*. New York City: Russell Sage Foundation.

Cook, Philip J., and Gary A. Zarkin. 1985. Crime and the business cycle. *Journal of Legal Studies* 14:115–28.

Duncan, Greg J., James P. Connell, and Pamela K. Klebanov. 1997. Conceptual and methodological issues in estimating causal effects of neighborhoods and family conditions on individual development. In Jeanne Brooks-Gunn, Greg J. Duncan, and J. Lawrence Aber, eds., *Neighborhood poverty*, vol. 1, *Context and consequences for children*. New York City: Russell Sage Foundation.

Eisner, Manuel. 2001. Modernization, self-control and lethal violence: The long-term dynamics of European homicide rates in theoretical perspective. *British Journal of Criminology* 41:618–38.

Felson, Marcus. 2002. *Crime and everyday life*. 3rd ed. Thousand Oaks, CA: Sage.

Gartner, Rosemary. 1991. Family structure, welfare spending, and child homicide in developed democracies. *Journal of Marriage and the Family* 53:231–40.

Jacobs, Bruce A. 2000. *Robbing drug dealers: Violence beyond the law*. Piscataway, NJ: Aldine.

Jepperson, Ronald, and John W. Meyer. 2011. Multiple levels of analysis and the limitations of methodological individualisms. *Sociological Theory* 29:54–73.

LaFree, Gary. 1998. *Losing legitimacy: Street crime and the decline of social institutions in America*. Boulder, CO: Westview.

Loeber, Rolf, and David P. Farrington. 2011. *Young homicide offenders and victims: Risk factors, prediction, and prevention from childhood*. New York: Springer.

Messner, Steven F., Richard Rosenfeld, and Susanne Karstedt. 2011. Social institutions and crime. In Francis T. Cullen and Pamela Wilcox, eds., *Oxford handbook of criminological theory*. New York: Oxford University Press.

Pampel, Fred N., and Rosemary Gartner. 1995. Age structure, socio-political institutions, and national homicide rates. *European Sociological Review* 11:243–60.

Pratt, Travis C., and Francis T. Cullen. 2005. Assessing macro-level predictors and theories of crime: A meta-analysis. In Michael Tonry, ed., *Crime and justice*, vol. 32, *A review of research*. Chicago: University of Chicago Press.

Raphael, Steven, and Rudolf Winter-Ebmer. 2001. Identifying the effect of unemployment on crime. *Journal of Law and Economics* 44:259–83.

Rosenbaum, Paul R., and Donald B. Rubin. 1983. The central role of the propensity score in observational studies for causal effects. *Biometrika* 70:41–55.

Rosenfeld, Richard. 2009. Crime is the problem: Homicide, acquisitive crime, and economic conditions. *Journal of Quantitative Criminology* 25:287–306.

Rosenfeld, Richard. 2011. The big picture: 2010 presidential address to the American Society of Criminology. *Criminology* 49:1–26.

Roth, Randolph. 2009. *American homicide*. Cambridge: Harvard University Press.

Sampson, Robert J. 2010. Gold standard myths: Observations on the experimental turn in quantitative criminology. *Journal of Quantitative Criminology* 26:489–500.

Sampson, Robert J., Jeffrey D. Morenoff, and Thomas Gannon-Rowley. 2002. Assessing "neighborhood effects": Social processes and new directions in research. *Annual Review of Sociology* 28:443–78.

PART I

Trends in Macroeconomic Conditions and Youth Violence

2

The Net Effect of the Business Cycle on Crime and Violence

SHAWN BUSHWAY, PHILIP J. COOK, AND MATTHEW PHILLIPS

Introduction

The business cycle has a pervasive effect on economic activity, employ-ment, and household income, as well as consumption patterns, school enrollments, mortality rates, and a variety of other social indicators.[1] It is reasonable to believe that the business cycle also has an effect on crime rates. In particular, conventional wisdom asserts that crime is countercyclical—trending up during recessions and down during eco-nomic expansions—because it is a substitute for legitimate sources of income. That view has been endorsed by numerous reports in the pop-ular media since the onset of the "great recession" of 2007 but is less securely anchored in systematic analysis.

One of the few scholarly studies of the association of business cycles and crime found mixed results—strong evidence that burglary and robbery are indeed reliably countercyclical but that auto theft tends to be procyclical and murder acyclic, being as likely to turn down as up during the recessions that have occurred between 1933 and 1981 (Cook and Zarkin 1985). The authors interpreted these results as causal rather than simply descriptive, adopting the view that each complete business cycle is a trial in a sort of natural experiment. Of course, this "experiment" has a very complex "treatment." A number of other scholarly analyses of aggregate data have attempted to unpack the business cycle, with its various causal channels, and to statistically isolate the effect of unemployment or some other single causal agent. But in practice it may be impossible to identify the effect of a single agent, given the considerable collinearity among time-varying characteristics of the aggregate economy.

Therefore, our goal here is a more humble one of analyzing the overall net effect of the business cycle and, more generally, of short-term fluctuations in economic activity (measured four different ways) on various measures of crime and violence. We do not attempt to identify the particular causal mechanisms by which economic conditions affect crime. Our analysis replicates that reported in Cook and Zarkin (1985) with the addition of 26 years of data including four complete business cycles. We also expand the analysis to include new outcome measures. First, we analyze suicide rates. Second, we analyze family violence, using both female and child homicide victimization rates as proxies. Third, we distinguish among different age groups of crime perpetrators, using arrest data by age group for the crimes of murder, robbery, burglary, and motor-vehicle theft. We also break down suicide rates by age.

We believe that our results provide transparent answers to simple questions of the form, Do recessions cause an increase or reduction in the rate of some types of crime or violence? And more generally, do fluctuations in macroeconomic activity have contemporaneous effects on rates of crime and violence? If so, how large are the effects? The answers are suggestive of the relative importance of the various channels by which economic conditions influence crime, but any interpretation along those lines is speculative. It is useful to know whether to expect higher crime and violence rates during a recession even if we lack a view into the black box that connects them.

The chapter begins with a discussion of causal mechanisms link-ing economic conditions to crime and violence, both overall and for youths. We then investigate the effect of short-term fluctuations in eco-nomic activity on crime using the quasi-experimental analysis of the last 13 business cycles (beginning in 1933). Subsequent sections explain our second approach to analyzing short-term fluctuations, a regression analysis on detrended data, and report the results. The regression analy-sis conveys more statistical power and thereby supports analysis of a variety of outcomes even when available time-series data are of limited duration. The final section concludes.

The Economy's Influence on Crime and Violence

The history of all advanced economies has been characterized by sec-ular economic growth with an overlay of short-term fluctuation, re-ferred to as "cycles" (despite their lack of regularity or predictability). A nonprofit organization, the National Bureau of Economic Research (NBER), assigns quasi-official dates to peaks and troughs in the eco-nomic cycle. Each cycle includes two periods, trough to peak (the "expansion" phase) and peak to trough (the "contraction" phase, usually labeled a "recession"). The typical pattern since the 1930s has been of a sustained expansion followed by a relatively short contraction (table 2.1). The NBER's Business Cycle Dating Committee has this to say:

> During a recession, a significant decline in economic activity spreads across the economy and can last from a few months to more than a year. Similarly, during an expansion, economic activity rises substantially, spreads across the economy, and usually lasts for several years.
>
> The Committee does not have a fixed definition of economic activ-ity. It examines and compares the behavior of various measures of broad activity: real GDP measured on the product and income sides, economy-wide employment, and real income.[2]

There has been extensive study of business cycles, in part to determine the degree of synchrony between various indicators of economic activi-ties. Gross domestic product (GDP) and employment are coincident with the cycle, while the stock market averages tend to be "leading indicators," turning down before the peak of the cycle and up before the trough. The unemployment rate typically continues to increase for two or three quarters following the trough—it is thus a slightly lagging indicator of the cycle. But the close linkages among the various markets that make up the private sector ensure that the overall trend is broadly shared, both in the product markets and the markets for factors of production such as labor—figuratively akin to another cyclical phenomenon, the ocean tides.

The plausible mechanisms relating the business cycle to crime include at least the following four (Cook and Zarkin 1985):

1. *Legitimate opportunities.* Recessions may tend to increase property crime rates by reducing access to a legitimate means for achieving a desired standard of living. Recessions may increase *both* property and violent crime rates by reducing the opportunity cost of time spent in connection with criminal activity (including time in jail or prison). On the other hand, school enrollments tend to be countercyclical (since the opportunity cost of attending school falls during recessions when the labor market is weak), and it is possible that youths who are attending school will be less exposed to certain kinds of criminal opportunities than they would be otherwise.

2. *Criminal opportunities.* Recessions may also affect the quality of criminal opportunities directly. Potential burglary victims are more likely to be home (and thus serving as guardians for their property), and robbery victims will be carrying less cash and "bling" and are perhaps more inclined to defend what they have. Prices for fenced merchandise may well go down. As a result of such changes, property crime will likely be less profitable in bad times than good.

3. *Drugs and alcohol.* Alcohol consumption goes down in recessions (Cook 2007). To the extent that intoxication plays a role in crime, especially violent crime (both victimization and perpetration), then we would expect fewer assaults. The cyclical pattern of drug use is less clear.

4. *Police and corrections.* Recessions reduce state and local tax collections, which may result in cuts in policing and corrections. The result may be some attenuation of the effects of the criminal justice system on crime via deterrence, incapacitation, and rehabilitation.

Even this incomplete listing of possible linkages suggests that social scientists should have no trouble providing an explanation for most any sort of empirical finding relating the business cycle to crime. And social scientists have been analyzing the data on this issue for a long time, at least since the mid-19th century (Bonger 1916). Fortunately the empirical findings are quite consistent for some types of crime.

Thorsten Sellin's *Research Memorandum on Crime in the Depression* (1937) quotes a review of the literature written by Joseph Van Kan in 1903, as follows:

> Crimes against property find in large measure their indirect causality in bad economic conditions; their direct causality in acute need and even more in chronic misery. . . . Material well-being generally exalts the vital instincts, increases alcohol consumption, and therefore increases crimes against morals. All our literature confirms this fact. . . . As for the question of the extent of the influence of economic factors on offenses against persons, the answers are less uniform. (Quoted in Sellin 1937, 23)

Similarly, Dorothy Swaine Thomas's classic study *Social Aspects of the Business Cycle* (1927) reports correlations between detrended crime measures and an indicator of business conditions for Britain, 1857–1913, finding strong negative correlations for burglary and robbery and no effect for crimes of violence. These findings have stood up quite well over the ensuing century.

One modern analysis focuses on the effects of US business cycles per se. Cook and Zarkin (1985; hereafter "CZ") utilized annual time series for four types of FBI Index crime for the period 1933–1982, using each of the nine cycles during that period as a "trial" in a natural "experiment." Also reported are simple-regression results on postwar data adjusted for short-term trends (three-year and five-year moving averages). Two measures of economic conditions were used: the unemployment rate and the employment-population ratio.[3] Both the nonparametric "natural experiment" study and the regression analyses confirm that burglary and robbery are countercyclical, and homicide rates are not influenced (on balance) by the business cycle. The most surprising result is for auto theft—it is strongly *procyclical*.[4] These analyses are replicated with a longer time series in what follows, but the basic results remain the same.

Most of the modern literature has been somewhat more ambitious, seeking to identify the separate effects of one or more causal mechanisms associated with the business cycle. Cantor and Land (1985) utilize postwar national time-series data in an attempt to estimate the separate effect of criminal opportunity (which they proxy by the contemporaneous unemployment rate) and criminal motivation (which they proxy by the change from the previous year in the unemployment rate). They present a variety of estimates and conclude that "the relationship between unemployment rates and crime rates can be positive, negative or null, depending on the type of crime and on whether one focuses on the effects on criminal opportunity or criminal motivation" (330). They do not take direct account of other potential mechanisms mentioned earlier, such as the effect of alcohol consumption or the effect of changing expenditures on police and corrections, and one can question the proper interpretation of their two indicators.[5]

Perhaps the most persuasive effort to distinguish among causal mechanisms is Raphael and Winter-Ebmer (2001). They analyzed a panel of annual state-level data on the seven FBI Index crimes (1971 to 1997), using a two-way fixed effects specification to account for national trends and persistent differences in crime rates among states. The main independent variable of interest is the unemployment rate, but they attempt to account for other mechanisms by including as covariates alcohol consumption, the poverty rate, income per worker, and the number of prisoners. They report that "a 1 percentage point decrease in the unemployment rate causes a 2 percent decrease in burglary, a 1.5 percent decrease in larceny, and a 1 percent decrease in auto theft" (273). In contrast, the authors deemed findings for violent crimes unreliable, since they are sensitive to the specification.

A similar approach was implemented by Rosenfeld and Fornango (2007) and Rosenfeld (2009). The former, for example, analyzes annual data for a panel of census regions for the period 1970–2003. The main independent variable of interest in this case is the Index of Consumer Sentiment (ICS), entered both contemporaneously and with a lag of one year. ICS is a leading indicator of the business cycle (Gelper, Lemmens, and Croux 2007). The authors control for the number of police and the prison population and in one version also control for other business-cycle indicators, namely, the unemployment rate and GDP per capita. The dynamics of their preferred specification is complex, to say the least, since it is estimated in first-difference form with both contemporaneous and lagged ICS, a trend term, and the lagged dependent variable all included.

The problem, to put it colloquially, is that in aggregate time-series analysis everything be correlated with everything else, including variables that cannot or are not measured and included. There inevitably is great uncertainty about the proper regression specification when the goal is to isolate the causal effect of a particular variable, such as unemployment or consumer sentiment. It is not only a question of which covariates to include in the specification but also whether to include trend indicators or a lagged dependent variable and how best to account for serial correlation in the error terms. Given the statistical tangle of causal mechanisms that are related to fluctuations in economic activity, generating reliable estimates of their separate contributions from aggregate data appears to us to be beyond reach.

That skeptical conclusion takes us back to the simpler task that we set for ourselves, to measure the overall (net) effect of the business cycle on various sorts of crime and violence. The causal ordering is clear, since it is implausible that a change in the crime rate would induce a recession. But in the absence of a structural model, the economic fluctuations that we observe are something of a "black box." There is no guarantee that the mix of relevant ingredients remains similar from cycle to cycle. As a result, the effect of economic fluctuation on crime may change over time, and the magnitude of the estimated effect therefore depends on the period under consideration. That serves as a caveat with respect to what is otherwise a well-defined goal.

Youth Crime and Violence

The effects of the business cycle on crime and violence may be moderated by the age of the perpetrator or the victim. For example, in the case of motor-vehicle theft, we can speculate that adolescents will be less influenced by the market for stolen cars than will adults to the extent that adolescents steal for the purpose of joyriding rather than sale.[6]

In one comprehensive review of the effect of macroeconomic factors on youth violence, the authors suggest that the influence of economic factors is mediated by four institutions: the family, schools, illicit street markets, and local government agencies (Edberg, Yeide, and Rosenfeld 2010). That framework is suggestive of what is certainly a complex set of causal pathways. For example, a weak labor market may mean that adults in the household are more likely to be home when adolescents return from school, which would provide some degree of added social control—but would also reduce family resources, leaving youths more to their own devices to acquire the funds for discretionary expenditures. School may serve as another source of social control, and the fact that school enrollment is countercyclical suggests that there is more control during recessions than in good times. On the other hand, the "incapacitative" effect of school on youth crime appears to be limited to property crimes—violence, especially minor assaults, tends to be higher when school is in session than otherwise (Jacob and Lefgren 2003; Luallen 2006). Of particular importance with respect to serious violence is the effect of economic conditions on illicit street markets and the opportunity to engage in very dangerous activities such as dealing drugs in public. Presumably the business cycle has an effect on illicit markets, but how much and of what sort is unexplored territory.

In studying youth crime and violence, we proceed in the same spirit as in our analysis of overall crime rates. We recognize the complex set of mechanisms potentially linking to economic conditions, and rather than attempting to sort out the effects of individual mechanisms, we seek only to estimate the net overall effect.

Nonparametric Results

There were 13 complete business cycles, as defined by the National Bureau of Economic Research (NBER), between 1933 and 2008. On average, the contraction or recession period of the cycles lasted less than one year, while the expansion or boom period lasted five years on average. Through this period, the recessions have stayed roughly constant in length, while the average expansion has increased from four and a half years from the period from 1933 to 1969 to over five and a

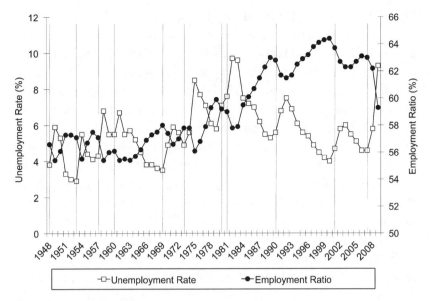

Fig. 2.1

half years since 1969. This increase reflects the longest expansion in the postwar period, a ten-year expansion from March 1991 to March 2001.

The up-and-down nature of the business cycle can be illustrated through an examination of two economic indicators, the employment ratio (the ratio of the population employed to the total population) and the unemployment rate (the percentage of people in the labor market who are not working), during this period. Figure 2.1 provides a description of the unemployment rate and the employment ratio from 1948 to 2008. The bars mark the peak years of the business-cycle expansions during this time period. (Since we are working with annual data, the peak *year* with respect to GDP/capita is not necessarily the same as the year of the peak month.) These two statistical trends are telling similar stories—unemployment increases when employment decreases—in close connection with the trough-peak-trough pattern of the business cycle.

Followers of crime trends will know that crime in the United States is not cyclical in this same way but rather tends to exhibit long swings.

Figure 2.2 provides the trends for two crimes, murder and robbery. While all crimes have unique characteristics, most crime types share a downward shift from 1933 until the war, followed by a sharp acceleration beginning in the mid 1960s, leading to a peak around 1975, followed by two peaks around 1981 and 1991. This last peak has been followed by the longest and deepest crime drop in the postwar period. The contrasting nature of the crime trends and the business cycle means that anyone searching for the main causes for crime trends should consider other processes besides the business cycle. But this strong conclusion does not mean that the business cycle cannot have a causal impact on the short-term changes in the crime and violence rates that accompany the longer-term swings.

To test this basic hypothesis that the business cycle can affect short-term changes in crime, tables 2.1 and 2.2 present the average annual rate of growth between each trough and the subsequent peak (the expansion period) and the percentage change to the subsequent year (the contraction period) for homicide and suicide (table 2.1) and then for murder, robbery, burglary and auto theft (table 2.2).[7] These four crimes were chosen because their measurement has remained relatively constant over the time period in question. Each cycle is considered as a separate event, occurring in its own unique criminogenic context. If recessions cause crime to increase, then we would expect the annual

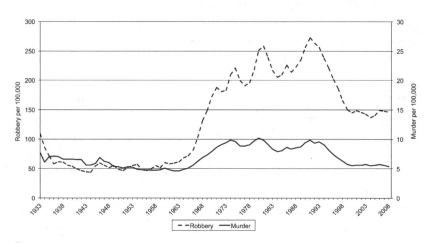

Fig. 2.2

Table 2.1. Vital Statistics Homicide and Suicide Movements over 12 Business Cycles

Reference cycle dates		Trough-to-peak interval used in calculations	Homicide			Suicide		
			Annual growth trough to peak (%)	Next year (%)	+	Annual growth trough to peak (%)	Next year (%)	+
Trough	Peak							
3/33	5/37	1933–1937	−5.9	−10.5		−1.4	2.0	+
6/38	2/45	1938–1945	−2.7	12.5	+	−4.4	2.7	+
10/45	11/48	1946–1948	−4.1	−6.9		−1.3	1.8	+
10/49	7/53	1949–1953	−2.9	0.0	+	−3.0	0.0	+
5/54	8/57	1954–1957	−2.1	0.0	+	−1.0	9.2	+
4/58	4/60	1958–1960	2.2	0.0		0.5	−1.9	
2/61	12/69	1961–1969	6.4	7.8	+	0.8	4.5	+
11/70	11/73	1971–1973	3.8	4.1	+	1.3	0.8	
3/75	1/80	1975–1979	0.0	7.0	+	−1.2	−1.7	
7/80	7/81	1980–1981	−3.7	−6.8		0.8	1.7	+
11/82	7/90	1983–1990	2.2	5.0	+	0.4	−1.6	
3/91	3/01	1991–2000	−6.0	18.3	+	−1.8	2.9	+
11/01	12/07	2001–2007						
Number of pluses			8			8		
			(p-value = .39)			(p-value = .39)		

Source: Vital Statistics 1933–2006
Notes: Number of pluses indicates the number of cycles in which growth in the crime rate from trough to peak was less than the rate of growth in the following year.
Vital Statistics data are not available for 2007–2008.

rate of growth to be higher during the recession than during the expansion period. Alternatively, if crime is procyclical, we would expect the rate of growth to be higher during the expansion period than during the subsequent recession.

Figure 2.3 provides a graphical description of this comparison. For each business cycle (and for each crime), we subtracted the average annual rate of change for the boom period from the average annual rate of change for the bust period. We expect this difference to be negative on average if recessions cause crime to increase and positive if crime increases during boom periods.

Murder is acyclical, with roughly equal numbers of business cycles in which the rate of change was higher during the recession and higher during the expansion. In contrast, the rates of growth were higher during the recession for most of the cycles for both robbery and burglary. Finally, auto theft appears to be either acyclical or slightly procyclical,

Table 2.2. UCR Crime Movements over 13 Business Cycles

Trough-to-peak inteval used in calculations	Murder — Annual growth trough to peak (%)	Next year (%)	+	Robbery — Annual growth trough to peak (%)	Next year (%)	+	Burglary — Annual growth trough to peak (%)	Next year (%)	+	Auto theft — Annual growth trough to peak (%)	Next year (%)	+
1933–1937	−2.4	−5.7		−13.2	−1.6	+	−6.9	0.8	+	−10.0	−13.3	
1938–1945	−1.6	16.9	+	−1.6	9.8	+	0.7	5.6	+	3.2	−9.7	
1946–1948	−6.7	−10.0		−6.6	5.8	+	−1.3	6.6	+	−15.7	−5.4	+
1949–1953	−0.9	−5.8		0.0	4.7	+	2.4	6.4	+	6.8	−6.3	
1954–1957	−1.4	0.0	+	−4.9	10.9	+	2.4	10.7	+	8.2	0.5	
1958–1960	3.1	−6.0		4.5	−3.2		6.9	2.0		4.1	0.4	
1961–1969	5.4	8.2	+	12.4	16.0	+	8.3	10.2	+	11.4	4.7	
1971–1973	4.5	4.3		−1.3	14.3	+	2.5	17.6	+	−1.9	4.4	+
1975–1979	0.3	5.2	+	−0.3	15.0	+	−0.3	11.4	+	1.6	−0.7	
1980–1981	−3.9	−7.1		3.0	−7.7		−2.2	−9.7		−5.6	−3.3	+
1983–1990	1.8	4.3	+	2.4	6.4	+	−1.2	1.6	+	6.2	0.5	
1991–2000	−6.2	1.8	+	−6.8	2.4	+	−5.8	1.8	+	−5.1	4.4	+
2001–2007	0.0	−4.4		−0.1	−1.1		−0.4	1.3	+	−2.8	−13.1	
Number of pluses	6 *(p-value = 1.0)*			10 *(p-value = .09)*			11 *(p-value = .02)*			4 *(p-value = .13)*		

Source: Uniform Crime Report 1933–2007
Notes: Number of pluses indicates the number of cycles in which growth in the crime rate from trough to peak was less than the rate of growth in the following year.

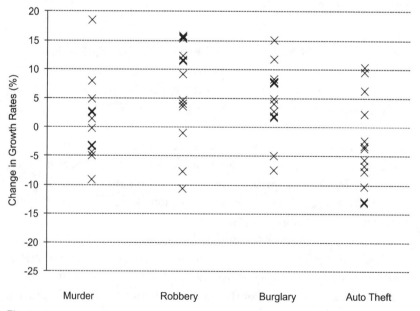

Fig. 2.3

with a tendency to have higher annual rates of change during expansions than during recessions.

CZ presented a novel way to make this test more precise by treating each of the business cycles as an experimental trial. A trial is given a plus if the postpeak rate of change exceeds the annual rate of change during the expansion and a minus if the postpeak rate of change in the crime rate is less than the annual rate of change during the expansion. If the business cycle has no impact on crime, then we would expect each result to be equally likely. In this case, each trial can be thought of as a coin toss, in which the coin has a 50% chance of being heads. Since multiple independent coin flips can be modeled using the binomial distribution, the null hypothesis that there is no relationship between the business cycle and crime can be tested using a binomial hypothesis test.

In CZ, there were 9 trials, and robbery and burglary both had 8 pluses, an event which would have happened only 2% of the time if there truly was no relationship between crime and the business cycle. Since we have no prior belief about whether the coin should land heads or tails, we actually report a two-tail test: 8 out of 9 with the same outcome occurs only 4% of the time by chance. Auto theft, with 7 out of 9 minuses, appeared procyclical, although this could have happened 18% of the time (two-tailed) even if there was no relationship.

As of 2010, we now have 13 trials, which gives us more power to test these same models. The results are presented in table 2.1. Murder has 6 pluses and 7 minuses, which is what we would expect if there were no relationship between homicide and the business cycle. Robbery, on the other hand, had 10 pluses (p-value of 9.2%) and burglary 11 pluses (p-value of 2.2%), suggesting that both are countercyclical. Auto theft is again weakly procyclical, with 4 pluses, which would only happen 13.3% of the time by chance.

The US Vital Statistics provide annual time-series data on homicide and suicide victimizations since 1933. These statistics are only available through 2006, so we only have 12 complete cycles. These tests are presented in table 2.1. Both homicide and suicide victimizations lean slightly toward the countercyclical, with 8 out of 12 cycles having higher growth during the recessions than during the expansions. With a p-value of 19.2%, there can be no firm conclusion on this matter.[8]

The nonparametric tests presented in this section are simple to calculate and have the advantage of speaking directly to the question of a link between the business cycle and crime with few assumptions. On the other hand, the tests do not allow us to assess the relative magnitude of the relationship. In the following section, we again follow CZ to estimate a parametric test of the causal relationship between the business cycle and crime.

Regression Specification

CZ sought a simple procedure for estimating the strength of the relationship between short-term movements in economic conditions and resulting short-term movements in crime rates. The major challenge was to generate estimates that are free from the possible biases introduced by secular movement in the underlying causes of crime. In standard time-series discussions, this potential for bias is referred to as a problem of nonstationarity.

The first task is to choose an indicator of economic conditions. Three indicators are widely used for this purpose: the civilian unemployment rate, the employment-population ratio, and the inflation-adjusted ("real") per capita gross domestic product. All three move nearly synchronously with fluctuations in business conditions (Leon 1981). Although CZ only used the first two measures, we have elected also to use GDP in our empirical work in part because Arvanites and Defina (2006) used GDP at the regional level and found stronger results than prior research using either unemployment rates or employment ratios. GDP and employment ratios are both used by the NBER committee when defining a business cycle.

A simple method for eliminating secular movements in the crime rate and the economic measures is to write each of them as a ratio of the contemporaneous value to a moving average. The actual specification used in our analysis is as follows:

(1) $\ln (C_t/\bar{C}_t) = a + b \ln (Q_t/\bar{Q}_t) + e_t,$

where C_t = crime rate in year t; Q_t = employment ratio or unemployment rate in year t; e_t = residual "error" term, assumed to be generated by a first-order autocorrelation process with $Ee_t = 0$; $\bar{C}_t$, $\bar{Q}_t$ = moving geometric means centered on year t. This specification eliminates secular movements in crime rates caused by trends in crime reporting, demographic structure, "culture," public policy, and so forth. It also eliminates secular trends in the business conditions indicators, which in recent years have been caused by changes in demographic structure, earlier retirement, the changing role of women in the labor force, and so forth (Leon 1981).

This approach accomplishes the same task as the first differencing seen in the work that follows in the tradition of Cantor and Land (1985). In those papers, researchers are attempting to create a stationary series. As discussed in detail by O'Brien (2001), first differencing to achieve stationarity can potentially eliminate the variation of interest to the researcher. In our case, we are interested in preserving the unique characteristics of the business cycle with its roughly five-year boom and then bust cycle while removing secular trends, something that can be achieved with our procedure but not with first differences (Paternoster and Bushway 2001). Appendix A provides a more elaborate justification for the specification.

We estimate these regressions using the Prais-Winston correction for serial correlation in the error term. Serial correlation exists when the error term for this period depends on past error terms plus a truly random error term. Prais-Winston assumes the error is first-order autoregressive and then uses generalized least-squares to estimate a transformed model.

Regression Results for Postwar Crime and Violence Rates

All regressions were run on data for the period between 1948 and 2008. Because we use the three-year geometric moving averages, the actual analysis begins in 1949 and ends in 2007. For that period, the three indicators of economic conditions are highly correlated with each other.[9] The correlation of GDP/capita (in ratio to the three-year geometric mean) with unemployment rate (also in ratio) is −.8507, and with employment it is .8211. The correlation between unemployment and the employment ratio is −.9243.

Equation (1) was estimated for the four types of crime (murder,

Table 2.3. Effects of Short-Term Fluctuations in Economic Activity on Crime and Violence Estimated Coefficients from Log-Linear Simple Regressions, 1948–2008

	Unemployment rate (S.E.)	Employment ratio (S.E.)	GDP/capita (S.E.)
UCR offenses			
Murder	−.022	.276	−.037
	(.026)	(.405)	(.221)
Robbery	.166[a]	−2.443[a]	−1.823[a]
	(.042)	(.654)	(.314)
Burglary	.121[a]	−1.657[a]	−1.301[a]
	(.029)	(.474)	(.221)
Auto theft	−.063[b]	1.066[b]	.092
	(.028)	(.450)	(.243)
Vital Statistics			
Homicide	.012	−.064	−.307
	(.027)	(.404)	(.231)
Suicide	.067[a]	−.857[a]	−.378[b]
	(.017)	(.265)	(.165)

Notes: Each coefficient is from a different regression. All variables are in natural log form, so coefficients are elasticities. Each variable is entered as a ratio to its three-year moving geometric average.
Estimation method: Generalized least squares with Prais-Winston correction for first-order serial correlation.
[a] Significant at .01 level
[b] Significant at .05 level
[c] Significant at .10 level

robbery, burglary, and auto theft) as well as homicide and suicide victims for the period between 1948 to 2008 (2006 for the victimization equation). The results are presented in table 2.3. These results are consistent with the quasi-experimental results presented in the preceding section. The relationship between murder and the macroeconomy is not significant for any of three measures of economic conditions, and the same null finding holds when we utilize homicide-victim data from the Vital Statistics in place of the Uniform Crime Reports murder data.[10]

The three measures of economic conditions also tell a consistent story with respect to robbery and burglary. All three of the coefficients are statistically significant at the 1% level for both crimes. The signs of the coefficients confirm the nonparametric results, namely, that robbery and burglary are countercyclical. Thus, robbery and burglary confirm the conventional wisdom.

The results for unemployment and employment are also remarkably similar to what CZ reported in 1985, despite the addition of almost 30 years of data. For example, the coefficient for unemployment rates in the robbery equation is .166. It was .17 in the CZ model. The coefficient for employment ratio and robbery is −2.443, and CZ report a coefficient of −2.79. The moderate magnitude of the elasticity with respect to unemployment is consistent with prior findings (Bushway and Reuter 2001). In this case, we estimate that a one-percentage-point increase in unemployment from 6% to 7% would increase robbery by 2.8%.

The story for auto theft is somewhat more complicated. Auto theft is significantly related to the unemployment rate and employment ratio but not GDP/capita. For each indicator, the magnitude of the point estimate is less in absolute value than that for burglary and in the opposite direction, suggesting that there is a weak procyclical relationship between the business cycle and auto theft. For example, an increase in unemployment from 6% to 7% would decrease auto theft by 1%.

Finally, the regression analysis reveals a consistent countercyclical relationship between suicides and all three measures of economic conditions, a relationship that was not evident in the quasi-experimental results. For a more complete treatment of this relationship with similar data, see Luo, Florence, and Quispe-Agnoli (2010).

Which of the three indicators is most highly correlated with the measures of crime and violence? In other words, which provides the best prediction for contemporaneous changes in crime? As it turns out, there is no clear winner. GDP/capita has the highest t-statistic for robbery and burglary, while the employment ratio does for auto theft and the unemployment rate for suicide.

Violence against Women

While our findings indicate that economic fluctuations have not had much effect on overall homicide rates, it is possible that they have had an effect on particular subsets of this diverse phenomenon. In particular, we might expect that domestic violence and related homicide rates would be influenced by the business cycle. Economic conditions have pronounced effects on household composition, family finances, child care arrangements, and substance abuse rates, each of which could affect the likelihood of serious domestic violence through plausible causal mechanisms.

Domestic homicide rates can be estimated directly from the FBI's

Table 2.4. Effects of Short-Term Fluctuations in Economic Activity on Femicide and Homicides with Children Victims. Coefficients from Log-Linear Simple Regressions, 1948–2005 and 1933–2005

	Unemployment rate (S.E.)	Employment ratio (S.E.)	GDP/capita (S.E.)
1948–2005			
Femicide	.005	.024	−.417
	(.036)	(.529)	(.314)

Notes: Each coefficient is from a different regression. All variables are in natural log form, so coefficients are elasticities. Each variable is entered as a ratio to its three-year moving geometric average.
Estimation method: Generalized least squares with Prais-Winston correction for first-order serial correlation.

Supplementary Homicide Reports (SHR), which provide data on circumstances and suspects. Unfortunately they tend to be incomplete and inconsistently reported by law enforcement agencies. As it turns out, however, there is an excellent proxy for intimate-partner homicide against women: the rate of homicide victimization for adult women (femicide rate). We compute the national time-series correlation between the femicide rate (using Vital Statistics data) and the SHR-reported intimate-partner female homicide rate to be .88 over the period 1980 to 2008.[11]

Regression results for female homicide victims are presented in table 2.4 for the postwar period. In no case are the elasticity estimates significantly different from zero. In this respect, the results are in line with our results for the overall homicide victimization rate.

Regression Results by Age

The focus of this volume is on youths under age 25 as victims and perpetrators. While we expect that youths respond to economic conditions much like adults, that is not necessarily the case. For adolescents in particular, the job market is likely to play little direct role, since they typically work part-time or not at all. Other institutions, including neighborhood, school, and, family, are more important in the lives of adolescents than for older youths, and these institutions may provide more social control during recessions than in good times.

The Vital Statistics provide homicide and suicide victimization rates by age during the postwar period, and we begin with those data. Table

2.5 reports regression results that mimic the approach in table 2.3, but now with the violence variable broken down into three age groups. We see that short-term variation in economic conditions have little effect on homicide victimization rates for people under 15 or over 24. One of our indicators (GDP/capita) has a strong negative association with homicide victimization for the group aged 15–24, and the estimated coefficients for the other indicators are suggestive of this countercyclical effect (although not significant). That anomalous finding bears further scrutiny. Since most killers of victims in this age range are also in this age range, the potential explanations incorporate processes that lead to either victimization or perpetration.

The suicide results are interesting, since they strongly suggest that while the overall rate is countercyclical (table 2.3), that is not true for youths under 25—and indeed, we find evidence that for those under 15, suicide is actually procyclical.[12] A possible mechanism in this case is guardianship. If adults spend more time with their adolescent children

Table 2.5. *Effects of Short-Term Fluctuations in Economic Activity on Homicide and Suicide Victimization, by Age Groups. Estimated Coefficients from Log-Linear Simple Regressions*

	Unemployment rate (S.E.)	Employment ratio (S.E.)	GDP/capita (S.E.)
Homicide: 1948–2006			
Age < 15	−.017	.436	.415
	(.042)	(.606)	(.365)
Age 15–24	.063	−.916	−1.267[a]
	(.052)	(.761)	(.434)
Age > 24	.003	.018	−.420
	(.039)	(.576)	(.338)
Suicide: 1950–2006			
Age < 15	−.313[a]	3.226[c]	1.177
	(.107)	(1.540)	(.991)
Age 15–24	.024	−.401	−.104
	(.031)	(.424)	(.269)
Age > 24	.067[a]	−.911[a]	−.439[b]
	(.018)	(.260)	(.168)

Notes: Each coefficient is from a different regression. All variables are in natural log form, so coefficients are elasticities. Each variable is entered as a ratio to its three-year moving geometric average.
Estimation method: Generalized least squares with Prais-Winsten correction for first-order serial correlation.
[a] Significant at .01 level
[b] Significant at .05 level
[c] Significant at .10 level

in recessions than in good times, that may provide for closer monitoring of their behavior and mood. For the middle age group, there is essentially no relationship with economic conditions, perhaps in part because of their relative insulation from the job market and the salutary effects of school enrollment (which is procyclical). In any event, these complex results remind us that the business cycle is not one thing but rather an intertwined bundle of causal processes.

To investigate national crime-commission rates by age group, we have little choice but to utilize Uniform Crime Reports (UCR) arrest data, which are available in consistent form since 1963. Arrest rates are an imperfect proxy for crimes known to the police (which are in turn an imperfect proxy for actual crime rates). Arrest rates are subject to distortion by possibly systematic effects of changes in police capacity and behavior over the business cycle.[13] In what follows we utilize arrest data broken down by age group but believe it is appropriate to view the results with some skepticism.

The first lesson from arrest data is that most burglaries and robberies are committed by youths. On average during the time period under study (1963–2008), 67.6% of robbery arrests and 72.3% of burglary arrests are of individuals under 25. Given the strong evidence that burglary and robbery rates are countercyclical (see earlier) and the predominance of youthful offenders for these crimes, it is reasonable to conclude that youthful rates of burglary and robbery are also countercyclical. That logical claim is a benchmark on which to assess results from the arrest data.

Table 2.6 presents regression results based on arrest rates by age group. The property crime arrest rates appear countercyclical, with the strongest evidence coming from the GDP/capita. The GDP/capita results for violent arrests also suggest that they are countercyclical, although that conclusion receives no support from the estimated coefficients for unemployment or the employment ratio. The latter pattern also appears in the results for murder and robbery. The lack of consistent support for robbery arrest rates as countercyclical is particularly surprising given the results on robbery rates based on crimes known to the police. Our inclination is to question the validity of the robbery arrest series as an indicator of actual crime-commission rates.[14]

The main theme of the age-group arrest results is consistency. The

Table 2.6. Effects of Short-Term Fluctuations in Economic Activity on UCR Arrest Rates, by Age Groups. Estimated Coefficients from Log-Linear Simple Regressions, 1963–2008

A. Total, Property, and Violent Crime

	Unemployment rate (S.E.)	Employment ratio (S.E.)	GDP/capita (S.E.)
Total			
All ages	.070[c]	−.497	−.848[a]
	(.039)	(.483)	(.254)
Age < 18	.010	−.296	−.522
	(.050)	(.603)	(.340)
Age 18–24	.077[c]	−.425	−1.052[a]
	(.045)	(.560)	(.285)
Age > 24	.091[b]	−.852	−.862[a]
	(.041)	(.508)	(.277)
Property crime, 1969–2008			
All ages	.116[c]	−.784	−1.502[a]
	(.064)	(.775)	(.383)
Age < 18	.027	.334	−.932[c]
	(.073)	(.866)	(.480)
Age 18–24	.212[a]	−1.844[c]	−1.984[a]
	(.076)	(.948)	(.483)
Age > 24	.171[a]	−1.637[b]	−1.836[a]
	(.065)	(.792)	(.388)
Violent crime, 1969–2008			
All ages	.041	.026	−.847[b]
	(.063)	(.753)	(.423)
Age < 18	.030	.232	−.741
	(.075)	(.881)	(.500)
Age 18–24	.045	.058	−1.038[b]
	(.073)	(.867)	(.485)
Age > 24	.035	−.006	−.680[c]
	(.058)	(.691)	(.395)

B. Specific Crime

	Unemployment rate (S.E.)	Employment ratio (S.E.)	GDP/capita (S.E.)
Murder			
All ages	.082	−.722	−1.237[b]
	(.078)	(.958)	(.515)
Age < 18	.089	−.146	−1.354
	(.129)	(1.580)	(.867)
Age 18–24	.072	−.691	−1.357[b]
	(.094)	(1.150)	(.628)
Age > 24	.218	−2.513	−1.239[b]
	(.135)	(1.649)	(.517)

(continued)

Table 2.6 (continued)

	Unemployment rate (S.E.)	Employment ratio (S.E.)	GDP/capita (S.E.)
Robbery			
All ages	.095	−.571	−1.464[b]
	(.084)	(1.038)	(.566)
Age < 18	.034	−.192	−.965
	(.106)	(1.286)	(.728)
Age 18–24	.107	−.542	−1.710[a]
	(.088)	(1.088)	(.580)
Age > 24	.129	−1.177	−1.484[b]
	(.081)	(.997)	(.556)
Burglary			
All ages	.138[b]	−1.008	−1.531[a]
	(.058)	(.743)	(.363)
Age < 18	.063	−.128	−.916[b]
	(.067)	(.828)	(.448)
Age 18–24	.236[a]	−2.111[b]	−2.308[a]
	(.065)	(.847)	(.382)
Age > 24	.178[a]	−1.538[b]	−1.730[a]
	(.059)	(.751)	(.377)
Auto theft			
All ages	−.116[c]	2.024[b]	.051
	(.068)	(.798)	(.479)
Age < 18	−.303[a]	4.561[a]	1.791[a]
	(.079)	(.840)	(.593)
Age 18–24	−.011	.657	−.757
	(.103)	(1.246)	(.726)
Age > 24	.006	.471	−.613
	(.080)	(.982)	(.555)

Notes: Each coefficient is from a different regression. All variables are in natural log form, so coefficients are elasticities. Each variable is entered as a ratio to its three-year moving geometric average.
Estimation method: Generalized least squares with Prais-Winston correction for first-order serial correlation.
[a] Significant at .01 level
[b] Significant at .05 level
[c] Significant at .10 level

three age groups tend to have a similar relationship to economic conditions for each of the crime types. The exception, and perhaps the most striking result from table 2.6, is auto theft. For that crime, arrest rates for juveniles are strongly procyclical, while arrest rates for the older groups are not influenced by economic conditions. This result, which we find in all three economic indicators, strongly supports the earlier suggestion by Paternoster and Bushway (2001) that the form of motor-vehicle theft associated with youths, joyriding, has a different etiology than thefts by older offenders and is procyclical.

A final observation involves the findings for robbery and burglary for youths under the age of 18. In all cases, the coefficients for arrestees under the age of 18 are substantively (if not significantly) smaller than the coefficients for older arrestees. This pattern achieves significance in the burglary regressions, where the coefficients for 18-year-olds are a fraction of the coefficients for the next-older age group. We found a similar pattern in results for all property crime (Part I) and forgery and fraud (Part II) arrests.[15] Although more work is clearly warranted on this topic, a preliminary conclusion is than juvenile arrest rates for property crimes are less sensitive to economic conditions than are arrest rates for adults. Whether that is an accurate reflection of offender behavior (rather than police behavior) is an open question.

Concluding Remarks

We set a modest goal for this analysis—determining the net effect of fluctuations in economic conditions on crime and violence. Other analysts have set a more ambitious agenda, going beyond estimation of the net effect to unpack the various causal processes that are brought to bear by the business cycle. The cost of ambition in this case is the loss of clarity, given that the various processes are highly correlated and difficult to distinguish on the basis of available indicators.

In this analysis, we have followed CZ in treating the business cycle, and short-term fluctuations in economic conditions, as a black box. Variations in the macroeconomy are inputs to the black box, and variations in the crime rate are outputs. In pursuit of our modest goal, we have analyzed four indicators for that "input" (the NBER cycle dates, the unemployment rate, the employment ratio, and real GDP/capita) and six "outputs" (homicide, suicide, and four Part I crime types). Our measures of crime and violence include the Vital Statistics public health data on suicide and homicide and the UCR data on crimes known to the police and on arrests. We provide a separate analysis of intimate-partner violence, as proxied by the femicide rate. We have also analyzed both Vital Statistics and UCR arrest data by age group to determine if the black box affects youths differently than adults.

Table 2.7 provides one simple summary of our results for UCR crime rates. We find very consistent results for robbery and burglary

Table 2.7. Summary of Significant Results (p < .10) for Alternative Tests of the Effect of Economic Conditions on Crime Rates

	Murder		Robbery		Burglary		Auto Theft	
Quasi-experimental, 1933–2008	0		C		C		0	
Regression: UCR crimes, 1948–2008	U	0	U	C	U	C	U	P
	ER	0	ER	C	ER	C	ER	P
	GDP	0	GDP	C	GDP	C	GDP	0
Regression: UCR arrests, 1963–2008	U	0	U	0	U	C	U	P
	ER	0	ER	0	ER	0	ER	P
	GDP	C	GDP	C	GDP	C	GDP	0

Sources: Tables 2.1, 2.3, and 2.6
C = countercyclical; P = procyclical; o = null effect; U = unemployment rate; ER = employment ratio; GDP = real GDP/capita

rates, which are strongly countercyclical by any measure. On the same basis, we conclude that murder is acyclical (the null finding cannot be rejected) and that auto theft is, if anything, procyclical. Our confidence in these conclusions is strengthened by the fact that they replicate CZ's results, with 26 years of additional data, four additional business cycles, and an additional economic indicator (per capita GDP). Table 2.7 also reports the results for the arrest rates, which with the partial exception of robbery are compatible with our other findings for overall rates. Although not shown in table 2.7, the results for the Vital Statistics homicide data are similar to the UCR murder data. The suicide results suggest that it is countercyclical, which corroborates recent findings by Luo, Florence, and Quispe-Agnoli (2010).

The magnitudes of the estimated effects are not large compared to the very large swings in crime and violence that the United States has experienced during the postwar period. According to our estimated elasticities, the most severe economic downturn since the 1930s—the recent "great recession"—increased the robbery rate by 7%–16%, the burglary rate by 5%–11%, and the suicide rate by 1%–5%, while reducing the rate of auto theft by as much as 7%. To be clear, these predictions are for changes relative to trend, not absolute changes.[16]

At every step in our analysis, we take as given the trends in crime and violence. Our qualitative analysis of 13 business cycles compares the growth rate during the expansion phase with the change in crime during the recession in the following year. Our regression specifications enter both crime and economic variables as ratios with the three-year moving average, assuring that the coefficient estimates are identified off of short-term variation from local trends. It is entirely possible—really inevitable—that secular changes in economic activity, including changes in technology, the standard of living, demography, and the labor market, influence the nature and volume of crime and crime control. Those secular changes are not our topic, and we warn against extrapolating our findings regarding GDP/capita. For example, it is quite possible that secular growth in GDP will have an effect on homicide rates, even though in the short term there is little or no effect.

In addition to analyzing the effect of economic conditions on overall crime and violence rates, we also explore the possibility that youths are affected differently than adults. The clearest example of this disparity is for suicide, for which we have data of high quality and a consistent set of results—namely, that the countercyclical effect of suicide is confined to adults over 24 year old and that the suicide rate for youths under 15 actually appears to be procyclical. The other example of interest is auto theft, which we analyze by use of a shorter time series on arrest rates. What we learn is that the procyclical pattern in auto theft (established from data on crimes known to the police) appears to be confined to juveniles under 18. Since juveniles have traditionally stolen vehicles for joyriding rather than for sale, it is something of a surprise that they (but not adults) are influenced by the economy. It is a reminder once again that variation in economic conditions conveys the possibility of a variety of causal mechanisms, which in some cases may cancel out.

For robbery and burglary, the elasticity estimates from age-grouped arrest data are much smaller for juveniles than for adults for all three economic indicators. That result could be accepted at face value, suggesting, for example, that reduced job opportunities during recessions have less effect on juveniles than on adults for these particular crimes. But we would warn not to take that sort of speculation too seriously, given the complexity of the relevant processes. It is also true that we are skeptical of the validity of arrest data as a measure of criminal offending over time. All of the robbery arrest results with respect to the unemployment rate and the employment ratio are null, despite the very strong effects estimated from the series on robberies known to police. That disparity reflects the low correlation between the "crimes known" measure of robbery and the arrest rate for robbery. The former is likely to be the more valid measure of true offense rates.

These findings also support the value of this relatively simple approach to the study of the business cycle. We submit that there now should be little doubt about the net effect of the business cycle on rates of robbery, burglary, and murder. Unfortunately we cannot provide a clear answer to why robbery and burglary are countercyclical or murder acyclical. What we are left with is a clear set of answers to a narrow question. Those answers provide a foundation for other, more ambitious explorations of economic conditions.

Appendix A

A more elaborate justification for equation (1) can be developed as follows. Define B as an intertemporally consistent indicator of economic conditions and X as an indicator of all other variables that influence the crime rate, weighted according to their relative importance. Then assume

$$(2) \quad C_t = aB_t^b X_t,$$

which implies

$$(3) \quad \bar{C}_t = a\bar{B}_t^b \bar{X}_t,$$

where the overbar indicates a geometric mean. Define ϵ_t such that

$$(4) \quad X_t = \bar{X}_t \epsilon_t.$$

Then dividing (2) by (3) and substituting (4) yields

$$(5) \quad C_t/\bar{C}_t = (B_t/\bar{B}_t)^b \epsilon_t.$$

If $e_t \equiv \ln \epsilon_t$ and $(Q_t/\bar{Q}_t)$ serves as a proxy for $(B_t/\bar{B}_t)$,[17] then

$$(6) \quad \ln (C_t/\bar{C}_t) = b \ln (Q_t/\bar{Q}_t) + e_t,$$

which is identical to expression (1) with $a = 0$.

The parameter b in equations (1) and (6) is equal to the elasticity of crime with respect to Q_t, which makes interpreting the magnitude of the relationship straightforward.

Appendix B: Vital Statistics Homicide and Suicide Movements over 10 Business Cycles, by Age Groups

A. Homicide

Trough-to-peak interval used in calculations	Age < 15 Annual growth trough to peak (%)	Next year (%)	+	Age 15–24 Annual growth trough to peak (%)	Next year (%)	+	Age > 24 Annual growth trough to peak (%)	Next year (%)	+
1946–1948	−0.004	−0.090		0.024	−0.033		−0.028	−0.065	
1949–1953	−0.047	0.086	+	−0.006	0.091	+	−0.021	−0.001	+
1954–1957	−0.020	0.135	+	0.018	0.091	+	−0.007	0.004	+
1958–1960	0.087	0.109	+	0.064	0.003		0.018	0.001	
1961–1969	0.051	−0.135		0.056	−0.043		0.049	0.077	+
1971–1973	0.086	0.035		0.004	−0.018		0.045	−0.018	
1975–1979	0.023	0.098	+	0.001	0.042	+	−0.012	0.045	+
1980–1981	0.066	0.033		0.066	0.282	+	0.066	−0.070	
1983–1990	0.023	0.067	+	0.043	0.115	+	−0.014	0.035	+
1991–2000	−0.026	−0.004	+	−0.037	−0.025	+	−0.052	0.278	+
Number of pluses	6 (p-value = .75)			6 (p-value = .75)			6 (p-value = .75)		

B. Suicide

Trough-to-peak interval used in calculations	Age < 15 Annual growth trough to peak (%)	Next year (%)	+	Age 15–24 Annual growth trough to peak (%)	Next year (%)	+	Age > 24 Annual growth trough to peak (%)	Next year (%)	+
1946–1948	−0.183	0.157	+	−0.027	−0.041		−0.006	0.027	+
1949–1953	0.136	−0.389		−0.020	−0.045		−0.037	0.019	+
1954–1957	0.194	0.089		−0.003	0.185	+	−0.006	0.096	+
1958–1960	0.064	−0.211		0.034	−0.011		−0.001	−0.011	
1961–1969	0.039	−0.027		0.050	0.105	+	0.001	0.024	+
1971–1973	0.096	0.216	+	0.068	0.025		−0.010	−0.002	+
1975–1979	0.000	−0.051		0.018	−0.003		−0.023	−0.035	
1980–1981	0.192	0.207	+	−0.008	−0.014		0.017	0.014	
1983–1990	0.036	−0.010		0.016	−0.011		−0.001	−0.013	
1991–2000	0.010	−0.092		−0.027	−0.024	+	−0.017	0.041	+
Number of pluses	3 (p-value = .34)			3 (p-value = .34)			6 (p-value = .75)		

Source: Vital Statistics 1946–2000
Notes: Number of pluses indicates the number of cycles in which growth in the crime rate from trough to peak was less than the rate of growth in the following year.

NOTES

1. This chapter was originally prepared for a CDC conference on the effect of mac-roeconomic conditions on youth violence, held May 13–14, 2010. The authors thank Erin Hye-Won Kim for her assistance in preparing tables and figures.

2. National Bureau of Economic Research, "Statement of the NBER Business Cycle Dating Committee on the Determination of the Dates of Turning Points in the U.S. Economy," http://www.nber.org/cycles/general_statement.html (accessed May 4, 2010).

3. The employment ratio is not just the complement of the unemployment rate. The denominators are different. The unemployment rate is defined relative to the labor force, which excludes people who are not working or looking for work. The employment ratio includes the entire adult population in the denominator, which, unlike the labor force measure, is not affected by the business cycle.

4. See Paternoster and Bushway (2001) for an analysis of cyclicality of auto theft by age.

5. Arvanites and Defina (2006) conduct a similar analysis but using panel data on states.

6. Joyriding is a dwindling component of motor-vehicle theft due to the growing sophistication of locking devices built in to new vehicles (Cook and MacDonald 2010).

7. Since we have annual crime rates and business cycles that end throughout the year, we identify peak years as those in which the real GDP/capita is maximized, whether that is the year that includes the peak month or an adjacent year.

8. Appendix B presents the same analysis with ten business cycles; the homicide and suicide data is broken down by age groups into less than 15, between 15 and 24, and over 25. None of the tests are significant at even the 10% level of significance.

9. In the next section, we report results on arrest rates, which are limited to the period 1963–2008. The GDP variable is somewhat less correlated with unem-ployment ($-.8227$) and the employment ratio ($.7536$) for that period than in the longer period.

10. Interestingly, when we extend the time series for the Vital Statistics data back to 1933, the elasticity estimates increase in absolute magnitude and are significantly different from zero for both the unemployment rate and GDP/capita, suggesting a countercyclical pattern. These results suggest that the homicide rate may have been influenced by macroeconomic conditions during the extreme economic hardships of the Great Depression and the subsequent wartime conditions.

11. According to SHR reports, intimate-partner homicides accounted for one-third of all femicides in 2005 (1,181 out of 3,545). The relationship data were missing in 35% of SHR reports. See James Alan Fox and Marianne W. Zawitz, "Homicide Trends in the U.S.," Bureau of Justice Statistics, http://bjs.ojp.usdoj.gov/content/homicide/homtrnd.cfm.

12. We would like to thank Feijun Luo for sharing the suicide data with us. The

data for homicides are available from 1940 to 2006, and for suicides, from 1950 to 2006.

13. Arrest data are also less reliable because police agencies are less likely to report to the FBI arrests than "crimes known" (Maltz 1999). Moreover, agencies report less consistently than for the overall crime rates, so annual trends for the United States will be based on a shifting pool of reporting agencies.

14. Arrests for robbery appear to be less correlated with offenses reported to the police ($r = .36$) than for burglary ($r = .62$). It is possible that the business cycle has more of an effect on police behavior with respect to robbery than to burglary (or vice versa).

15. These results are not reported in this chapter but are available from the authors.

16. In fact, the trend appears to have been sharply downward, with the net result that crime rates have actually decreased between 2007 and 2009.

17. Q represents the employment ratio, the unemployment rate, or the per capita real GDP, none of which is "an intertemporally consistent indicator of economic conditions" due to secular trends in the demographic composition of the labor force and other factors. For this reason, Q is not a good indicator for B, which is intertemporally consistent by definition. However, $(Q/\bar{Q})$ has a much stronger claim to being intertemporally consistent and a good indicator for $B/\bar{B}$.

REFERENCES

Arvanites, Thomas M., and Robert H. Defina. 2006. Business cycles and street crime. *Criminology* 44:139–164.

Bonger, William A. 1916. *Criminality and economic conditions*. Boston: Little, Brown.

Bushway, Shawn, and Peter Reuter. 2001. Labor markets and crime. In Joan Petersilia and James Q. Wilson (eds.), *Crime*, 3rd ed. Oakland, CA: ICS Press.

Cantor, David, and Kenneth C. Land. 1985. Unemployment and crime rates in the post–World War II United States: A theoretical and empirical analysis. *American Sociological Review* 50 (3): 317–332.

Cook, Philip J. 2007. *Paying the tab: The costs and benefits of alcohol control*. Princeton: Princeton University Press.

Cook, Philip J., and John MacDonald. 2010. *Public safety through private action: An economic assessment of BIDs, locks, and citizen cooperation*. Cambridge, MA: NBER Working Paper 15877.

Cook, Philip J., and Gary A. Zarkin. 1985. Crime and the business cycle. *Journal of Legal Studies* 14 (Jan.): 115–128.

Edberg, Mark, Martha Yeide, and Rick Rosenfeld. 2010. *Macroeconomic factors and youth violence: A framework for understanding the linkages and review of available literature*. Prepared for the Centers for Disease Control.

Gelper, Sarah, Aurelie Lemmens, and Christophe Croux. 2007. Consumer sentiment and consumer spending: Decomposing the Granger causal relationship in the time domain. *Applied Economics* 39 (1): 1–11.

Jacob, Brian, and L. Lefgren. 2003. Are idle hands the devil's workshop? Incapacitation, concentration, and juvenile crime. *American Economic Review* 93:1560–1577.

Leon, Carol Boyd. 1981. The employment-population ratio: Its value in labor force analysis. *Monthly Labor Review* 104:36–45.

Luallen, J. 2006. School's out . . . forever: A study of juvenile crime, at-risk youths and teacher strikes. *Journal of Urban Economics* 59:75–103.

Luo, Feijun, Curtis Florence, and Myriam Quispe-Agnoli. 2010. *Impact of business cycles on the U.S. suicide rates, 1928–2007.* CDC working paper.

Maltz, Michael. 1999. *Bridging gaps in the police crime data.* NCJ 176365. U.S. Department of Justice, Bureau of Justice Statistics. Washington, DC.

O'Brien, Robert. 2001. Theory, identification, operationalization, and the interpretation of different differences in time series models. *Journal of Quantitative Criminology* 17:359–375.

Paternoster Ray, and Shawn Bushway 2001. Theoretical and empirical work on the relationship between unemployment and crime. *Journal of Quantitative Criminology* 17 (4): 391–408.

Raphael, Steven, and Rudolf Winter-Ebmer. 2001. Identifying the effect of unemployment on crime. *Journal of Law and Economics* 44 (April): 259–283.

Rosenfeld, Richard. 2009. Crime is the problem: Homicide, acquisitive crime, and economic conditions. *Journal of Quantitative Criminology* 25:287–306.

Rosenfeld, Richard, and Robert Fornango. 2007. The impact of economic conditions on robbery and property crime: The role of consumer sentiment. *Criminology* 45 (4): 735–769.

Sellin, Thorsten. 1937. *Research memorandum on crime in the Depression.* Social Science Research Council Bulletin No. 27.

Thomas, Dorothy Swaine. 1927. *Social aspects of the business cycle.* New York: Knopf.

Van Kan, Joseph. 1903. *Les causes économiques de la criminalité.* Paris: A Storck & cie.

3

Are the Criminogenic Consequences of Economic Downturns Conditional?

Assessing Potential Moderators of the Link between Adverse Economic Conditions and Crime Rates

ERIC P. BAUMER, RICHARD ROSENFELD, AND KEVIN T. WOLFF

Introduction

In the wake of significant economic expansion and steeply falling crime rates for much of the 1990s, two notable economic downturns have served as bookmarks for the present decade: a significant contraction of the U.S. economy during the last half of 2001 and a major economic decline that emerged in different sectors in 2006 and 2007 and had by the end of 2009 morphed into one of the most severe economic recessions of the past century (National Bureau of Economic Research, 2010). The most recent of these economic downturns, dubbed widely as the "Great Recession," has stimulated renewed interest in, and speculation about, a possible link between economic conditions and crime rates. Numerous media reports in the first months of the Great Recession suggested possible links between increased crime rates and the foreclosure crisis, rising unemployment, mass layoffs, and depressed wages. Many accounts speculated that it was just a matter of time before those adverse conditions would yield a significant crime wave. More recently, the popular press has expressed surprise that crime rates did not increase significantly during or in the aftermath of the recession, despite an abundance of woeful economic reports and speculation about many possible collateral consequences. These stories often contrast the late 2000s spike in unemployment observed in many U.S. communities with reports that crime rates appear to have either remained surprisingly stable or have fallen (e.g., Yost, 2010; see FBI, 2010). Figure 3.1 illustrates these patterns for the sample of cities on which we focus in this chapter. More recent data for the nation affirm the basic pattern shown in figure 3.1; crime rates have shifted very little in the two years after the official end of the Great Recession, and in fact, they have declined slightly (FBI, 2011a, 2011b).

What are we to make of evidence that crime rates do not appear to have increased in response to the substantial economic decline that occurred in the late 2000s? More generally, should we expect crime

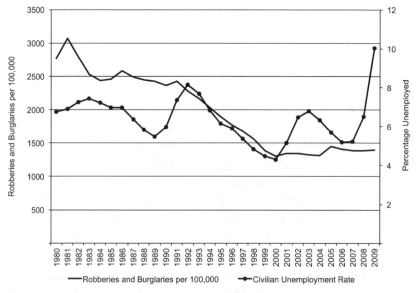

Fig. 3.1. Trends in rates of property crime and unemployment for 82 large U.S. cities, 1980–2009

rates simply to rise when economic conditions sour and to fall when they improve? Or are the consequences for crime of adverse economic conditions contingent on other prevailing factors, yielding increases in crime in some instances but not others? Economic perspectives point to rational assessments of opportunity costs associated with legitimate versus illegitimate economic pursuits and imply that a decline in legitimate income-generating opportunities is likely to yield increases in illegitimate income acquisition, such as robbery, burglary, and theft. However, as typically expressed in the research literature, economic perspectives may not be helpful in explaining why significant declines in the legitimate economy do not invariably produce the anticipated rise in instrumental criminal activity. This is a crucial empirical as well as theoretical issue, because the accumulated body of evidence on the relationship between crime rates and adverse economic conditions (e.g., rising unemployment and falling wages, GDP, and consumer optimism) suggests that sometimes significant downturns in the economy yield an increase in crime and sometimes they do not (e.g., Bushway, Cook, and Phillips, 2010; Chiricos and DeLone, 1992; Cook and Zarkin, 1985; Smith, Devine and Sheley, 1992). Indeed, a cursory glance at figure 3.1 reveals such a pattern for a common indicator of economic adversity: the unemployment rate.

The mixed or ambiguous empirical literature on macroeconomic conditions and crime rates sometimes is written off as a function of empirical misspecification (Greenberg, 2001; Raphael and Winter-Ebmer, 2001). However, another possibility is that adverse economic circumstances yield increases in crime (and good times yield decreases in crime) *only under certain conditions.* Cantor and Land (1985) drew attention to this idea, noting that increases in some adverse economic conditions, such as unemployment rates, may yield higher crime rates only to the extent that significant simultaneous or subsequent shifts in routine activities do not limit criminal opportunities. Yet several other plausible contingencies are also implied in the literature. For example, as we elaborate later in this chapter, the criminogenic consequences of the most often studied indicators of growing economic adversity—rising unemployment rates, falling wages, depressed economic output, growing consumer pessimism—may be conditioned by the presence of other economic conditions such as the level of inflation, by offsetting income-replacement government transfers, by levels of illicit drug involvement, or by the potential costs associated with participation in illegitimate activities (e.g., the likelihood of detection by the police or of incarceration once arrested).

In essence, the idea that increasing economic adversity should simply yield a linear increase in crime rates is unlikely to capture the full range of behavioral realities that may be observed. Not all economic downturns occur in the same broader economic or social context. In the United States, some have happened amid very high levels of inflation (e.g., the early 1980s recession), whereas some emerged during historically low inflationary periods (e.g., the two recessions of the 2000s). Some have occurred during periods when the gross probabilities of detection and imprisonment confronted by people contemplating illegal activity were high and rising significantly (i.e., the 1980s and 1990s), whereas others have progressed in an era of relatively stable incarceration rates and declining police forces (e.g., the most recent recession). Some economic declines have coincided with notable jumps in illicit drug involvement in America (e.g., the early 1980s and early 1990s), whereas others have come when significant levels of illicit drug use and drug market activity were much less noticeable (e.g., the 2000s). Finally, some of the contemporary economic contractions have been accompanied by relatively large and responsive outlays in unemployment insurance benefits (e.g., the most recent recession), whereas others have occurred during periods when such benefits were reduced dramatically (e.g., the early 1980s).

Most prior research has focused on the effects of adverse economic conditions on crime rates, irrespective of the broader context in which those conditions arise or play out. The primary objective of this chapter is to explore some of the conditions under which increasing economic adversity may be more, or less, likely to yield crime increases. Using data from 1980–2009 on property crime, age-disaggregated homicide, economic conditions, and other factors for 82 relatively large U.S. cities and the counties, states, and regions in which they are located, we evaluate the influence on crime rates of four common indicators of economic adversity: rising unemployment and consumer pessimism and declining wages and GDP. More specifically, we examine both the overall influence of these conditions on crime and the degree to which their effects on crime may differ depending on rates of inflation, unemployment insurance, illicit drug involvement, incarceration, and the size of the police force. We begin by outlining the theoretical rationales for our study and reviewing the relevant prior research. We then describe our data and methods and present a series of regression models that address our key research issues. We close with a discussion of the implications of our findings for crime theory, research, and policy.

Background and Research Questions

Although classic economic arguments about the rational assessment of perceived costs and benefits of legal versus illegal activities understandably represent the modal framework for linking economic adversity and increasing crime (Becker, 1968; Ehrlich, 1973; see also Bushway et al., 2010), several other perspectives are germane as well. Over time, economic hardships can increase crime and violence by fueling community disorder, reducing collective regulation of public spaces, and discouraging spending on the criminal justice system (Wilson, 1996; Edberg, Yeide, and Rosenfeld, 2010). Deteriorating economic conditions also can push low-income consumers into underground markets for stolen goods and may stimulate property crimes in response to growing demand (Rosenfeld and Fornango, 2007). Both processes have been linked to increases in lethal violence (Rosenfeld, 2009). Finally, the stress and frustration associated with job and income loss may lead to crime and violence as coping mechanisms (e.g., Agnew, 1999).

The rich theoretical landscape on possible connections between crime and the economy also reveals several possible contingencies that warrant attention when considering whether growing economic adversity is likely to result in increased rates of crime through one or more of the mechanisms just noted. Consideration of these contingencies has significant implications for the conclusions we draw from prior empirical studies, which almost invariably assume a linear, additive effect of economic conditions on crime rates.

One potentially important contingency in the link between changes in crime rates and changes in commonly studied economic conditions, such as unemployment rates and wages, is the level of inflation. Rising prices in legitimate markets may enhance the attractiveness of cheap stolen goods and thereby stimulate an increase in property crimes. They also may fuel violence indirectly by expanding the size and volatility of underground activity. Drawing on such logic, some research has evaluated whether crime rates are responsive to shifts in rates of inflation. The findings are somewhat mixed, but overall the evidence suggests that changes in inflation and crime rates covary significantly in the anticipated, positive direction, a pattern found across a variety of national contexts (e.g., Curtis, 1981; Devine, Sheley, and Smith, 1988; Fox, 1978; Gillani, Rehman, and Gill, 2009; Grant and Martínez, 1997; LaFree, Drass, and O'Day, 1992; Land and Felson, 1976; Ralston, 1999; Seals and Nunley, 2007; Tang, 2009; Tang and Lean, 2007). An additional hypothesis worthy of exploration is that high rates of inflation may aggravate the effects on crime of other economic conditions. As unemployment and consumer pessimism increase and wages and GDP decrease, the standard economic account predicts that growing numbers of individuals on the economic margins may consider illegitimate means to generate income. The economic pressures or incentives to engage in acquisitive criminal activity are likely to be stronger in a context of steep price increases than when prices are stable or falling. Displaced workers and others whose earnings have fallen should be more likely to turn to illegal markets to buy and sell goods during periods of high inflation because of the competitive price structure such markets offer, which may elevate rates of property crime and lethal violence (e.g., Rosenfeld, 2009). We explore this idea by testing for statistical interactions between changes in inflation rates and changes in unemployment rates, wages, GDP, and consumer sentiment. To our knowledge, the possibility that inflation levels moderate the effects of these factors on crime rates has not been examined in previous empirical research. This is a potentially important omission because substantial shifts in these economic indicators have occurred in very different inflationary regimes. The most vivid contrast during the contemporary era is between the early 1980s recession, when unemployment rates skyrocketed and wages, GDP, and consumer sentiment fell amid double-digit inflation rates, and the recession beginning in 2007, when similar movement in these common indicators of economic contraction occurred under stable prices in the legitimate economy.

Several other possible contingencies may help to clarify the empirical findings on the relationship between changes in macroeconomic conditions and changes in crime rates. One potentially relevant factor—the extension of unemployment insurance benefits—reflects government fiscal policy regarding how best to respond to economic crises, with an emphasis on easing the adversity of those who lose jobs and earnings. In theory, this type of government social spending can help to temper the criminogenic consequences of significant economic contractions by buffering families and individuals from the full brunt of market forces. This proposition is implied by Messner and Rosenfeld's (2007) institutional-anomie theory. The theory locates the genesis of motivations for crime in America's pronounced and universalistic cultural emphasis on the accumulation of wealth, in combination with differential access to legitimate economic opportunities (Merton, 1938). According to the authors, social institutions play a vital role in buffering citizens from the pressures that arise when the cultural and social structures are misaligned in this fashion. A key role of the polity is to provide protection, through income replacement and other means, from the full force of the free-market economic system, especially during significant economic downturns.

The provision of unemployment insurance benefits is a common way in which the U.S. government has attempted to soften the blow of significant economic contractions. As McMurrer and Chasanov explain, "The Federal-State unemployment insurance (UI) system, created in 1935, was designed to provide temporary wage replacement for unemployed workers . . . and to assist in stabilizing the national economy during cyclical economic downturns" (1995, 30). Some research has shown that government financial assistance can help to reduce crime rates and to reduce the criminogenic effects of high rates of poverty and inequality (e.g., Hannon and DeFronzo, 1998; for a review, see Messner and Rosenfeld, 2007), but we are aware of no prior research on the specific impact of unemployment insurance benefits on crime trends. Significant variation exists in the provision of unemployment insurance benefits during the past three decades, with historically low levels of support provided during the two recessions of the early 1980s and a much greater support during the early 1990s and the 2000s (McMurrer and Chasanov, 1995). We explore the potential implications of this variation in the present research by examining whether the effects on crime rates of unemployment rates, wages, GDP, and consumer pessimism are moderated by levels of spending on unemployment insurance.

Another consideration germane to a comprehensive assessment of crime trends during the past three decades, and specifically the possible contingent effects of adverse economic conditions, is the punishment risk faced by those who contemplate illicit activities. This is an essential ingredient in both classic economic and sociological theories of crime. Becker (1968) highlights the probability of conviction and punishment in his articulation of the factors that shape decisions to engage in illegal conduct. Also, an often overlooked component of Merton's (1938) anomie theoretical model is that illegitimate responses to significant economic adversity may be conditioned by assessments of the perceived costs of crime. As Merton suggests, when the social structure fails to distribute legitimate economic opportunities in sufficient volume, some persons view illegitimate income-generating pursuits as a viable option, and "there occurs an approximation of the situation erroneously held by utilitarians to be typical of society generally wherein calculations of advantage and fear of punishment are the sole regulating agencies" (1938, 682). This logic suggests that the effects on crime and violence of growing economic adversity may be conditioned by the objective risks to illegitimate actions, such as the probability of being detected by the police and the probability of incarceration. We consider these possibilities in the present research by testing whether the effects on crime rates of changes in unemployment rates, wages, GDP, and consumer pessimism are conditioned by changes in police force size and rates of imprisonment.

Finally, a key pathway through which growing economic adversity is theorized to yield higher crime rates is the expansion of illegal markets. As Rosenfeld (2009) notes, major economic downturns are likely to yield elevated levels of violence when such conditions generate vibrant illegal markets. Underground markets breed violence because disputes among market participants cannot be resolved by recourse to the police, courts, or other means of formal social control. The violence associated with markets for illicit drugs has been interpreted in this fashion (Blumstein, 1995). Although credible evidence indicates that alcohol consumption is reduced when economic conditions deteriorate, and some observers maintain that the demand for illicit drugs also may drop during such times (Bushway et al., 2010; Landers, 2008), others have emphasized the expansion of illicit drug economies that can occur when large segments of the population confront significant obstacles in the legitimate economy (Anderson, 1999).

Considerable evidence supports the connection between criminal violence and the emergence and proliferation of illicit drug markets (Baumer et al., 1998; Blumstein, 1995; Cork, 1999; Fryer et al., 2006; Goldstein, 1985; Messner et al., 2005; Ousey and Lee, 2007). Less frequently acknowledged, however, is the possibility that the presence of vibrant illegal drug markets can amplify the criminogenic consequences of a significant economic decline by serving as an arena in which increasing numbers of persons swept aside by the contraction of the legitimate economy become embroiled in activities that fuel instrumental property crimes and violence that are part and parcel to many drug markets. This suggests that the association between common indicators of economic adversity and crime rates may be especially strong when drug market activity is relatively high. We assess the merits of this argument by testing for statistical interactions between changes in illicit drug involvement and changes in unemployment rates, wages, GDP, and consumer pessimism.

In summary, a broad reading of the literature suggests that anticipating only main effects of economic adversity on crime rates may be overly simplistic. The link between macroeconomic conditions and crime rates may instead be highly contingent on the presence or absence of other factors, including levels of inflation, unemployment insurance benefits, police presence, incarceration, and drug market activity. Prior research rarely has assessed these possible conditional effects of adverse economic conditions. Instead, with some exceptions, the existing research has focused primarily on examining the main effects of economic conditions on crime rates,[1] and it has left a trail of mixed and inconclusive results. There is evidence that property crimes, including violent property crimes such as robbery, tend to rise during economic downturns and fall during periods of recovery (for a review, see Blumstein and Rosenfeld, 2008). Also, some prior research indicates that youth unemployment and wage levels are related to youth crime trends in the same fashion: adverse conditions drive crime rates upward (Gould, Weinberg, and Mustard 2002; Grogger 1998). But other studies

Table 3.1. Description of Variables Included in Analysis of Economic Conditions and Crime Rates (N = 82)

Variable	Variable definition and source	Mean	Overall SD	Within-city SD
Dependent variables				
Logged homicide rate	Homicides per 100,000 residents, logged (SHR)	2.155	.897	.423
Logged youth homicide rate	Homicides involving a victim under 18 per 100,000 residents under 18, logged (SHR)	.491	2.041	1.672
Logged young adult homicide rate	Homicides involving a victim age 18 to 24 per 100,000 residents age 18 to 24, logged (SHR)	2.427	2.061	1.518
Logged adult homicide rate	Homicides involving a victim age 25 and older per 100,000 residents age 25 and older, logged (SHR)	2.126	1.120	.692
Property crime rate	Robberies and burglaries per 100,000 persons (UCR)	1974.884	1022.149	719.775
Explanatory variables				
City unemployment rate$_{t-1}$	% of civilian labor force unemployed (BLS)	6.260	2.633	1.583
County average real wage rate$_{t-1}$	Mean real annual wage across all industries (BEA)	41940.95	7760.85	4146.99
State real GDP$_{t-1}$	State-level real gross domestic product (GDP) across all industries (BEA)	411915.70	426096.50	257195.90
Regional index of consumer sentiment$_{t-1}$	Summary index of consumer confidence and expectations (Reuters–University of Michigan)	87.730	11.898	11.856
Regional inflation rate$_{t-1}$	Percentage change in regional consumer price index (BEA)	4.098	2.831	2.829
County per capita unemployment insurance$_{t-1}$	Unemployment insurance compensation in real 2008 dollars (BEA)	133.807	91.3568	65.240
County per capita income maintenance$_{t-1}$	Income maintenance benefits (SSI, SNAP, Family Assistance) in real 2008 dollars (BEA)	526.369	267.303	119.488
City drug involvement rate$_{t-1}$	Residual drug arrest rate obtained after partialling out total arrest rates (UCR)	685.49	316.682	182.277
City police force size$_{t-1}$	Police officers per 100,000 residents (UCR)	202.480	83.823	24.410
State incarceration rate$_{t-1}$	Persons incarcerated per 100,000 residents (BJS)	342.620	167.045	142.598
City % age 15–24	% of population ages 15 to 24 (Census Bureau & SEER)	16.854	3.582	2.120
City % black	% of population who are black (Census Bureau & SEER)	19.641	17.631	2.815

Note: UCR = Uniform Crime Reporting Program; SHR = Supplementary Homicide Reports; BJS = Bureau of Justice Statistics; BEA = Bureau of Economic Analysis; BLS = Bureau of Labor Statistics; SEER = Surveillance Epidemiology and End Results; Reuters/University of Michigan = Reuters–University of Michigan Surveys of Consumers (http://www.sca.isr.umich.edu/)

yield the opposite conclusion (see Chiricos and DeLone, 1992; Baumer, 2008). The ambiguity in findings across studies in the role of adverse economic conditions may reflect differences in model specification or theoretical interpretations (e.g., Cantor and Land, 1985; Greenberg, 2001; Phillips and Greenberg, 2008). Another possibility, though, is that the effects on crime rates of such conditions are highly conditional, an issue we explore in depth later in the chapter.

The Present Study

We examine the main and interactive effects on crime rates of several economic conditions for a sample of 82 U.S. cities from 1980 to 2009. We integrated information from a comprehensive city-level database that contains annual indicators of a variety of relevant attributes for more than 100 large U.S. cities (those with 100,000 or more persons based on 2000 population figures) from 1980 to 2004 (Baumer, 2008) with more recent data from a variety of sources. Given the potential significance of the current economic downturn, we gathered data on crime counts for 2009 (such data were not publicly available as this study was under way) for as many of these cities as possible. Overall, we were able to obtain detailed data on homicide disaggregated by age, along with several key explanatory and control measures for 82 large cities. The average population of these cities in 2000 was about 375,000, ranging from just over 100,000 (Livonia City, Michigan) to just over eight million (New York City). Given the time-series panel nature of our data, the analysis is based on 2,460 observations (82 cities × 30 years per city).

Data and Methods

Table 3.1 lists the variables used in our analysis, providing definitions, sources, and descriptive statistics. Our key dependent variables represent rates (per 100,000 city residents) of property crime (robberies and burglaries), of total homicide, and of homicide disaggregated by age (under 18 years old, 18 to 24, and 25 and older). These measures were constructed using procedures described in appendix A, where we provide additional details about a variety of technical issues associated with our study that may be of secondary interest to many readers. The homicide measures exhibit significant skew, so we applied a natural logarithmic transformation and used the transformed values in the regressions described in the following section.

Our focus is on how these indicators of crime are affected by several economic indicators, including the city-level civilian unemployment rate, mean wage levels of the counties in which our cities are located, state-level real GDP, and regional levels of consumer sentiment. Aside from the unemployment rates, many economic measures are not generally available annually for a large number of cities for the period under investigation, but the data permit us to explore whether cities located in counties, states, and regions experiencing different economic trends exhibit different crime trends. We also emphasize the importance of developing well-specified empirical models, so we include in our regression models a variety of other factors shown in prior work to be associated with city crime rates. Several of the variables included serve both as important control variables and as potentially important moderators, as outlined earlier. The variables we consider include regional levels of inflation, city and state indicators of criminal justice sanction risks (police force size per capita, state incarceration rates), demographic attributes (age and race composition), and illicit drug activity. As described in table 3.1, we measure most of these indicators in a manner consistent with previous studies. One exception is the indicator of illicit drug activity, which represents the residual variation in drug arrest rates unaccounted for by total arrest rates. Further details about the construction of this measure are provided in appendix A.

Given the research issues addressed here and various features of the data used to do so, we estimate a series of two-way fixed-effects panel models of crime rates. We begin the analysis by estimating a baseline model for each of the crime types under consideration (i.e., property crime, overall homicide, youth homicide, young adult homicide, and adult homicide) that includes main effects for the explanatory and control variables. These models evaluate whether crime rates are influenced significantly by the indicators of economic adversity considered in the study. Subsequent models evaluate whether the role of economic conditions on crime is contingent on other prevailing conditions, including levels of inflation, unemployment insurance receipts, consumer sentiment, incarceration rates, and police force size. Pertinent statistical details of the models are elaborated in appendix A.

Results

The results of the baseline regression models are displayed in table 3.2. To better illustrate the magnitude of the observed relationships, we present the effects in the form of elasticities. Model 1 shows the findings obtained for property crime rates, and models 2–5 show the results for

Table 3.2. *Two-Way Fixed Effects Models of the Main Effects of Economic Conditions on Crime Rates (1980–2009, N = 82)*

Explanatory variable	Property crime (1)	Logged homicide (2)	Logged youth homicide (3)	Logged young adult homicide (4)	Logged adult homicide (5)
Property crime rate	—	.275*	.468*	.458*	.285*
		(.042)	(.136)	(.157)	(.057)
Drug involvement	−.011	.148*	.396*	.032	.171*
	(.017)	(.033)	(.144)	(.137)	(.051)
City unemployment rate$_{t-1}$	−.033	−.011	−.006	.415*	−.052
	(.028)	(.053)	(.201)	(.203)	(.087)
County average real wage rate$_{t-1}$	−.034	−.382*	−2.326*	1.470*	−.108
	(.100)	(.187)	(.543)	(.674)	(.212)
State real GDP$_{t-1}$	−.070*	−.112*	.053	−.196*	−.195*
	(.019)	(.028)	(.071)	(.092)	(.046)
Regional index of consumer sentiment$_{t-1}$	.051	−.936*	−5.374*	−1.119	−.976
	(.191)	(.473)	(1.584)	(1.467)	(.651)
Regional inflation rate$_{t-1}$	−.007	−.007	−.143	.199	.129
	(.033)	(.091)	(.335)	(.273)	(.129)
County per capita unemployment insurance$_{t-1}$	.021	−.044	−.076	−.114	−.052
	(.011)	(.024)	(.094)	(.096)	(.049)
County per capita income maintenance$_{t-1}$	.041	.052	.057	−.733*	.122
	(.050)	(.073)	(.303)	(.272)	(.135)
City police force size$_{t-1}$	−.091*	−.128	−.183	−.613*	−.263*
	(.044)	(.082)	(.316)	(.277)	(.131)
State incarceration rate$_{t-1}$	−.120*	−.338*	.057	−.354	−.273*
	(.046)	(.076)	(.215)	(.249)	(.094)
City % age 15–24	−.022	.219*	−.077	.780	.010
	(.051)	(.078)	(.426)	(.435)	(.135)
City % black	.228*	.190*	.186	.599	.193*
	(.054)	(.070)	(.341)	(.395)	(.092)
R–Squared	.795	.800	.327	.410	.628

* p < .05

overall homicide (model 2) and the age-disaggregated rates of homicide (models 3, 4, and 5).

Three notable patterns emerge from table 3.2. First, while not uniform across crime types, the indicators of drug involvement, property crime, police size, incarceration rates, and percentage of black residents yield the anticipated effects in many instances. In general, drug involvement is not associated with elevated property crimes, but consistent with substantial anecdotal evidence in the literature, it is positively and significantly related to homicide rates, with especially strong effects on youth homicide. As shown in recent research by Rosenfeld (2009), we observe a significant, positive effect of property crime on homicide rates. Nonetheless, our results for other indicators are not highly sensitive to whether we include property crime or drug involvement in the regression models, which suggests that (at least as measured) these dimensions of urban areas do not account for a sizable portion of the observed effects for factors such as adverse economic circumstances.

Second, with respect to the key variables of interest in our study, a general conclusion that emerges from an assessment of main effects is that the criminogenic consequences of adverse economic conditions are not limited to property crime. In fact, as illustrated in table 3.2, we observe more consistent evidence that these factors yield elevated crime rates in the homicide models.

Third, table 3.2 reveals several specific patterns that warrant some attention. One is that the indicator of overall economic output—state real GDP—exhibits the expected inverse association with each of the crime types considered, save for youth homicide. As GDP declines, rates of property crime, young adult homicide, and adult homicide increase. Another finding that emerges from table 3.2 is that the indicators of average wages and consumer sentiment yield an inconsistent pattern across the models. On the one hand, the results indicate that declining wages and growing consumer pessimism yield an increase in overall homicide and especially youth homicide. Yet, on the other hand, we see no relationship between trends in these economic attributes and property crime or adult homicide, and the results suggest a significant *positive* association between wages and young adult homicide. We also find that one-year lagged unemployment rates are significantly associated with only one of the crime types. Specifically, as shown in model 4, we observe that young adult homicide rates are significantly higher in contexts of higher unemployment, an important result given the comparatively high rates of homicide offending and victimization in this age group. This finding also demonstrates the utility of considering age-disaggregated homicide indicators, for if we were to look only at overall homicide rates, our conclusion would be that shifts in unemployment rates are not highly consequential for changes in lethal violence. Finally, we observe no evidence in these models of main effects that shifts in regional inflation rates are significantly associated with changes in crime rates, net of the other factors.

We now turn to the central question addressed in our study: are the effects on crime-rate trends of common indicators of economic adversity conditioned by other factors? We assessed this issue by reestimating the equations that form the basis of the results displayed in table 3.2 with the relevant interaction terms included. The resulting unstandardized regression coefficients and standard errors for the multiplicative models estimated in our study are presented in appendix B, with each table focusing on a different moderator variable (e.g., table 3.B1 shows results for the moderating role of inflation levels, 3.B2 shows results for the moderating role of unemployment insurance benefits, and so on). To more clearly capture the nature and magnitude of these results, we summarize the key patterns here by reference to a series of figures, which show the effects of selected economic conditions on crime rates at different levels of other factors. Further details about the model estimation procedures and the construction of the figures can be found in appendix A. Overall, three story lines emerge from this portion of our analysis.

First, while the influence of GDP and consumer sentiment on property crime and homicide appear to be invariant across levels of inflation, the effects of city unemployment rates and county wage levels depend on inflation levels in some instances. Figure 3.2 shows at different levels of regional inflation the estimated slopes for the effects of unemployment rates on property crime (panel A) and young adult (ages 18 to 24) homicide rates (panel B) and the estimated slopes for the effects of wage levels on overall homicide (panel C) and adult homicide (panel D). As panel A reveals, the effect of unemployment rates on property crime rates is highly contingent on levels of inflation in a manner consistent

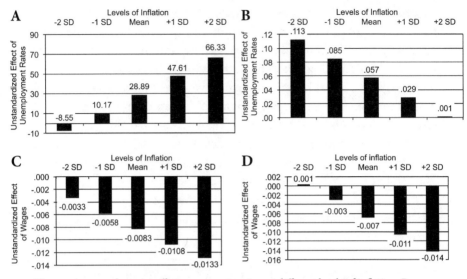

Fig. 3.2. *A*, unemployment effect on property crime at different levels of inflation; *B*, unemployment effect on logged young adult homicide rates at different levels of inflation; *C*, wage effect on logged homicide rates at different levels of inflation; *D*, wage effect on logged adult homicide levels of inflation

with expectations. Increases in unemployment are much more likely to yield elevated property crime rates when inflation levels are particularly high (e.g., above average). In fact, the estimated relationships between unemployment and property crime at below-average levels of inflation are not statistically significant in these data. This is an important finding, for it points to a possible explanation—below-average rates of inflation—for why we have not seen significant increases in property crime in the wake of the current recession, even amid striking increases in unemployment.

We see a similar pattern with respect to the relationship between wages and homicide, as illustrated in panels *C* and *D* of figure 3.2. Recall that, overall, we observed a significant inverse association between wages and logged homicide rates, indicating that falling wages are related to higher homicide rates (table 3.2, model 2). Our analysis of multiplicative relationships reveals that the magnitude of this association is significantly stronger when inflation levels are relatively high. Like the finding for unemployment and property crime, this suggests that high levels of inflation can amplify the adverse consequence of an economic downturn. An exception to this pattern, however, is displayed in panel *B*. Although inflation amplifies the degree to which rising unemployment rates yield increases in property crime, our estimations suggest that it *reduces* the effect of unemployment on homicide among young adults. The precise meaning of this pattern is unclear. It may be an artifact of measurement error or other features of our approach, but it is also possible that high inflation rates modify the routine activities of young adults in such a way as to reduce their exposure to situations conducive to lethal violence.

A second pattern that emerges from our results is that the level of objective risk appears to play a fairly important role in shaping how adverse economic conditions influence crime rates, though not always in ways we expected. Figure 3.3 shows that increases in unemployment rates (panel *A*) and decreases in GDP (panel *B*) are less likely to yield elevated property crime when the risk of incarceration is especially high. Stated differently, these results suggest that rising unemployment and falling GDP—two stalwarts of major economic downturns—yield increased property crime primarily under conditions of relatively low incarceration rates. This is consistent with the notion that the threat of custodial sanctions may mitigate the criminogenic consequences of adverse economic conditions, at least with respect to property crime and indirectly for homicide through property crime. But a different picture emerges for the direct effects on homicide and for the effects of wages. Contrary to the expectations outlined earlier, decreasing wages do not appear to have a weaker effect on crime when the risk of incarceration is high. In fact, we find just the opposite. As illustrated in panels *C* and *D* of figure 3.3, the inverse association between wages and both property crime and adult homicide is stronger when incarceration rates reach very high levels. Moreover, we observe a similar pattern with respect to the moderating role of police force size on the association between wages and property crime (panel *E*) and on the association between GDP and homicide rates (panel *F*).

Although contrary to our expectations, a possible implication of these patterns is that increases in wages for legitimate work yield larger reductions in crime when imprisonment levels are high because when wages rise, people immersed in illegal conduct might be more apt to discontinue that conduct if the risk of punishment also is relatively steep.

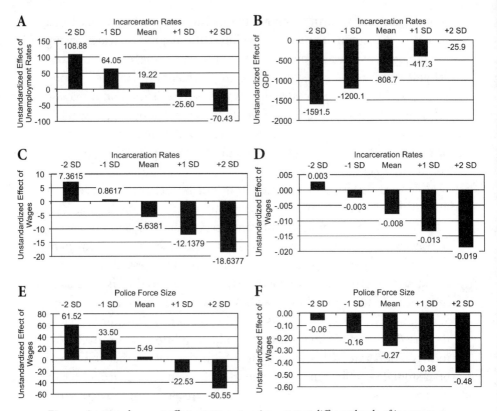

Fig. 3.3. *A*, unemployment effect on property crime rates at different levels of incarceration; *B*, GDP effect on property crime rates at different levels of incarceration; *C*, wage effect on property crime rates at different levels of incarceration; *D*, wage effect on logged adult homicide rates at different levels of incarceration; *E*, wage effect on property crime rates at different levels of police force size; *F*, wage effect on logged homicide at different levels of police force size.

A comparable rise in wages may not be as meaningful if the perceived costs of continued involvement in property crime are relatively low. This issue clearly warrants further investigation.

A third general finding that emerged from our moderator analysis is that the influence of economic adversity on crime levels is not highly sensitive to the provision of unemployment benefits (table 3.B2) or levels of drug involvement (table 3.B5). In each case, significant interactions with the economic indicators considered (city unemployment rates, county wages, state GDP, and regional consumer sentiment) were found in only one instance. Upon further investigation, the lone signifi-cant moderating effect of unemployment insurance (table 3.B2, model 2) is relatively small in magnitude and exhibits no significant simple slopes in the focal variable across various ranges of unemployment insurance. The statistically significant interaction between economic conditions and levels of drug involvement that emerged (see table 3.B5, model 3) was larger and substantively meaningful, suggesting that declining GDP yields increases in youth homicide only in the pres-ence of high levels of drug involvement. This is consistent with the idea that drug involvement may amplify the criminogenic consequences of adverse economic conditions. However, the general pattern observed is that levels of drug involvement as measured do not significantly con-dition the effects of economic conditions on crime levels. A measure that more directly captures illegal drug market activity may yield differ-ent findings.

Discussion

Much of the extant research on the link between indicators of economic downturns and crime rates has focused on estimating main effects, typ-ically evaluating the general hypothesis that declining economic con-ditions yield elevated crime rates. We propose that this was an overly simplistic approach. There are good theoretical reasons to anticipate the effects on crime rates of commonly examined economic factors to be conditioned by the presence or absence of other factors, and ignoring this possibility in prior research may help to explain why the empiri-cal evidence on the role of economic conditions is highly ambiguous. The primary objective of this chapter was to explore whether the effects of economic adversity on crime rates are conditioned by factors such as levels of inflation, unemployment insurance benefits, illegal drug involvement, and objective levels of sanction risk (police presence and incarceration rates). We pursued this objective with data from 1980 to 2009 on property crime, age-disaggregated homicide, economic condi-tions, and other factors for 82 relatively large U.S. cities and the coun-ties, states, and regions in which they are located.

Our analysis yields evidence that several commonly considered indicators of economic adversity do have effects on crime rates that differ depending on the rate of inflation and levels of objective risk. Most notably, we find that increases in unemployment are much more likely to yield elevated property crime rates when inflation levels are particularly high and, in fact, that unemployment is not significantly associated with property crime at below-average levels of inflation. We find a similar pattern with respect to the association between average wages and levels of homicide. These findings underscore the general need to consider conditional relationships when assessing the role of economic conditions on crime and to challenge simplistic views of the implications for crime levels of significant economic downturns such as the most recent recession, which has thus far been accompanied by relatively low levels of inflation and therefore may not yield substantial increases in crime, even with a doubling of the unemployment rate in many areas.

Incarceration rates and the relative size of police forces also serve a moderating role for presumed links between economic conditions and crime rates, although in this instance the patterns observed are mixed. Consistent with the idea that elevated incarceration rates reflect a heightened perceived cost to would-be offenders, we reasoned that economic downturns would be less criminogenic in the context of higher incarceration rates. We find evidence consistent with this logic in the effects of unemployment and GDP on property crime rates. Our results suggest that increases in unemployment rates and decreases in GDP are less likely to yield elevated property crime when the risk of incarceration is especially high. But other results are consistent with a different type of moderating role of incarceration and, to a lesser extent, police presence. In a few instances, we observe that increased wages yield larger reductions in crime when imprisonment levels are high. We speculated that this might reflect a tendency for crime desistence in response to rising wages (i.e., enhanced rewards) in an environment in which the risk of punishment is particularly high. Additional research is needed to explore this finding in greater detail.

We find very little evidence that the potential criminogenic consequences of economic decline are moderated by levels of unemployment insurance benefits. Drawing on institutional-anomie theory, we hypothesized that when benefits are more plentiful, economic adversity (perhaps especially rising unemployment) may be less likely to produce elevated crime rates. Our results do not bear this out. It may be that unemployment benefits are simply not of sufficient scale to yield the anticipated mitigating benefits. Higher levels of unemployment insurance or other social spending may be more successful in this regard. Indeed, Johnson, Kantor, and Fishback (2008), although they do not consider a moderating role for social spending, present persuasive evidence that the large-scale relief spending associated with the New Deal helped to keep crime rates low during and in the aftermath of the Great Depression. Additionally, Johnson et al. report that "work relief was more effective than direct relief in reducing crime" (2008, 2). Perhaps the partial income replacement provided by contemporary unemployment benefit programs is not the type of social spending that is likely to mitigate the potentially criminogenic consequences of adverse economic circumstances.

We also find little evidence that heightened involvement in illegal drug activity amplifies the effects on crime rates of economic conditions. This is inconsistent with our expectation that declining economic conditions may be more likely to elevate crime in the presence of expanding illegal drug markets. As noted earlier, although our measure of involvement in illegal drug activity partials out city differences in police activity, the measure may still lack the precision needed to test this argument satisfactorily. Even under the assumption that one can effectively purge the contribution of city differences in policing from the drug arrest indicator, one problematic aspect of the measure is that it likely captures some combination of city differences in drug use and drug market activity, and these two dimensions of drug activity may respond in divergent ways to an economic downturn. Specifically, while extant theory seems clear in suggesting that more people may turn to illegal drug markets to replace or augment lost employment and income in the legitimate sector—in other words, that illegal drug markets might grow in such periods—good evidence indicates that alcohol consumption declines as budgets tighten during a weakening economy, and the same may be true of illicit drug use. Thus, declining economic conditions may dampen demand for illicit drugs, even as it may increase the pool of drug sellers and grow illegal drug market participation. The latter mechanism would be expected to amplify the possible criminogenic consequences of adverse economic conditions, while the former may have the opposite effect. The null results for the moderating role of drug involvement may be due to the strong likelihood that our measure represents a combination of these two mechanisms with contrasting effects on crime.

In conclusion, our analysis suggests that future empirical research on links between the economy and crime should move beyond simple main effects and consider the possibility of theoretically informed conditional effects. Limitations of the data used for our study (e.g., the potential for significant measurement error in some of the key constructs, such as drug involvement, the high level of aggregation for some of our indicators, and the mismatch in levels of aggregation between the different measures employed (i.e., city, county, state, and regional measures) caution us from drawing strong conclusions about specific relationships. But one clear conclusion that emerges from our study is that the relationship between economic conditions and crime rates is complex. Simple assessments of the link between macroeconomic conditions and crime rates are likely to yield misleading results.

Appendix A: Elaboration of Data and Methods Used in Assessment of the Potential Conditional Effects of Economic Indicators on Crime Rates

Construction of Crime Rates

The dependent variables used in the study reflect the number of property crime and homicides (disaggregated by age of victim) per 100,000 city residents. Crime counts to construct these measures for 1980–2008 were taken from agency-level incident records produced by the FBI and distributed by the Interuniversity Consortium for Political and Social Research (ICPSR, 2010). We supplemented these publicly available data with primary collection from law enforcement agencies for comparable 2009 data. We obtained overall and age-disaggregated city population data from the decennial censuses that span our study period (1980, 1990, and 2000) and the annual versions of the 2005–2008 American Community Survey (ACS). We estimated population counts for the other years by using annual county data from the Surveillance Epidemiology and End Results (SEER) population database to compute rates of population change during the period in the counties in which our cities are located and applying those rates of change to the observed decennial points to interpolate annual city estimates.

Measurement of Illicit Drug Involvement

There are no systematic, direct measures of illicit drug use and drug market activity for American cities for the period under review (National Research Council, 2001). In response to this measurement gap, past research has relied on a variety of proxies, including emergency room drug mentions, drug-related mortality rates, arrestee and prisoner self-reports and drug-testing data, and drug arrest rates. Some research suggests that these indicators are strongly associated across cities and over time (Fryer et al. 2006; Rosenfeld and Decker 1999), and drug arrest rates, based in part on this evidence and their greater geographic and temporal coverage, have emerged as the most common measure employed to gauge differential illicit drug involvement across areas and over time (Blumstein, 1995; Ousey and Lee 2004). The expectation when doing so is that crime rates and drug arrest rates will be positively associated because the latter are thought to reflect differential involvement in illicit drug use and marketing. One limitation of this approach, however, is that the correspondence between drug arrest rates and underlying drug market activity and patterns of illicit drug use is imperfect, and in particular, it contains an unknown degree of error associated with city and temporal differences in police behavior. All else being equal, drug arrests likely will be more prevalent where the police are more productive or, in other words, where overall rates of arrest are higher. From a general deterrence punishment framework, higher arrest rates should yield less crime. Thus, in contrast to the logic just described about the anticipated positive association between crime rates and drug arrest rates (owing to an assumed link between drug involvement and criminal behavior), to the extent that higher drug arrest rates reflect more intensive policing, one might expect an inverse (not a positive) association with crime rates. To minimize the possible confounding effects of drug arrest rates (i.e., that they might be positively associated with crime to the extent that they reflect greater drug involvement and that they might be negatively associated with crime to the extent that they reflect broader police enforcement patterns), we incorporate a measure of illicit drug involvement based on drug arrest rates, from which we have partialed out city differences in overall arrest prevalence. Specifically, as documented in table 3.1, the measure we use reflects the residual variation in drug arrest rates unaccounted for by total arrest rates. We considered both this general measure and a parallel item based on the FBI category of cocaine/heroin arrests. The two were very highly correlated (> .90), and we use the broader measure because it better captures the full extent of changes in drug involvement over the period covered in our research.

Statistical Analysis Details

The econometric panel models estimated to generate the results presented in this chapter include fixed effects that control for stable unmeasured city attributes and temporal shocks that are shared across cities (Raphael and Winter-Ebmer, 2001; Worrall and Pratt, 2004). Consistent with previous research, the annual crime data examined in the study exhibited significant serial autocorrelation, which we accounted for by specifying first-order autocorrelation within panels and panel-specific AR(1) coefficients. Finally, preliminary analyses of the data indicated the presence of substantial cross-sectional correlation in disturbances across cities. Failing to account for these features of the data can lead to invalid inferences, so the models shown in appendix B report panel-corrected standard errors, which allow the disturbances to be heteroskedastic and contemporaneously correlated across panels (Wilson and Butler, 2007).

The multiplicative models estimated in appendix B (tables 3.B1–3.B5) build on the baseline equations displayed in table 3.2, adding to these equations the relevant interaction (i.e., product) terms. For example, to determine whether regional inflation levels moderate the effects on property crime and logged homicide rates (both overall and disaggregated by age) of city unemployment rates, county average wages, state GDP levels, and regional levels of consumer sentiment, we formed product terms between the inflation indicator and each of the other economic attributes and then added these product terms to the full equations shown in table 3.2. To minimize concerns about multicollinearity and to enhance the interpretability of the interactions estimated in our regression models, each predictor variable hypothesized to form multiplicative relationships was mean centered prior to computing the product terms (Jaccard and Turrisi, 2003). We present in appendix B only the most pertinent results for these models (the parameters for the main effects of the focus and moderator variables and the interaction terms). The models estimated also included all of the control variables and fixed effects (year and city) dummy variables, but to conserve space we omit these results. We computed the simple slopes implied in tables 3.B1–3.B5 using procedures outlined by Aiken and West (1991).

Appendix B

Table 3.B1. Two-Way Fixed Effects Models of the Moderating Role of Inflation on the Relationship between Economic Conditions and Crime Rates (1980–2009, N = 82)

Explanatory variable	Property crime (1)	Logged homicide (2)	Logged youth homicide (3)	Logged young adult homicide (4)	Logged adult homicide (5)
City unemployment rate$_{t-1}$	3.343*	−0.001	−0.001	−0.015*	0.001
X Regional inflation rate$_{t-1}$	(1.606)	(0.001)	(0.005)	(0.005)	(0.002)
County average real wage rate$_{t-1}$	1.020	−0.002*	0.001	−0.000	−0.003*
X Regional inflation rate$_{t-1}$	(0.582)	(0.001)	(0.002)	(0.002)	(0.001)
State real GDP$_{t-1}$	4.193	−0.013	0.010	−0.125	−0.005
X Regional inflation rate$_{t-1}$	(14.994)	(0.021)	(0.071)	(0.072)	(0.040)
Regional index of consumer sentiment$_{t-1}$	−0.877	0.001	−0.003	0.001	0.001
X Regional inflation rate$_{t-1}$	(1.071)	(0.001)	(0.006)	(0.004)	(0.002)
City unemployment rate$_{t-1}$	−7.133	−0.003	−0.0003	0.062*	−0.010
	(8.541)	(0.008)	(0.032)	(0.032)	(0.014)
County average real wage rate$_{t-1}$	−2.001	−0.011*	−0.054*	0.043*	−0.007
	(4.932)	(0.005)	(0.013)	(0.016)	(0.006)
State real GDP$_{t-1}$	−341.980*	−0.313*	0.144	−0.739*	−0.509*
	(87.963)	(0.075)	(0.227)	(0.252)	(0.135)
Regional index of consumer sentiment$_{t-1}$	1.678	−0.010*	−0.061*	−0.010	−0.011
	(4.231)	(0.005)	(0.018)	(0.016)	(0.007)
Regional inflation rate$_{t-1}$	−9.972	0.003	−0.045	0.054	0.032
	(16.360)	(0.023)	(0.085)	(0.070)	(0.032)
R-Squared	.798	.797	.327	.416	.632

* $p < .05$

Table 3.B2. Two-Way Fixed Effects Models of the Moderating Role of Unemployment Benefits on the Relationship between Economic Conditions and Crime Rates (1980–2009, N = 82)

Explanatory variable	Property crime (1)	Logged homicide (2)	Logged youth homicide (3)	Logged young adult homicide (4)	Logged adult homicide (5)
City unemployment rate$_{t-1}$	40.492	0.0542*	−0.001	0.093	0.074
X Unemployment insurance benefits$_{t-1}$	(29.614)	(0.0258)	(0.106)	(0.111)	(0.057)
County average real wage rate$_{t-1}$	−15.704	0.0343	0.025	0.006	0.037
X Unemployment insurance benefits$_{t-1}$	(20.266)	(0.0196)	(0.081)	(0.077)	(0.030)
State real GDP$_{t-1}$	−59.029	0.5387	2.199	−0.893	0.760
X Unemployment insurance benefits$_{t-1}$	(330.014)	(0.4448)	(1.364)	(1.569)	(0.783)
Regional index of consumer sentiment$_{t-1}$	1.699	0.0016	−0.049	0.054	−0.005
X Unemployment insurance benefits$_{t-1}$	(9.399)	(0.0107)	(0.038)	(0.041)	(0.019)
City unemployment rate$_{t-1}$	−8.734	0.0004	0.004	0.063	−0.006
	(9.036)	(0.0085)	(0.033)	(0.032)	(0.014)
County average real wage rate$_{t-1}$	−2.158	−0.0056	−0.051*	0.034*	0.001
	(5.359)	(0.0047)	(0.013)	(0.016)	(0.005)
State real GDP$_{t-1}$	−350.901*	−0.2707*	0.149	−0.478*	−0.467*
	(90.697)	(0.0681)	(0.164)	(0.217)	(0.111)
Regional index of consumer sentiment$_{t-1}$	1.006	−0.0098	−0.058*	−0.014	−0.010
	(4.440)	(0.0053)	(0.018)	(0.017)	(0.007)
County per capita unemployment insurance $_{t-1}$	103.615	−0.5994	−1.104	−0.578	−0.836
	(258.479)	(0.3187)	(1.214)	(1.233)	(0.536)
R-Squared	.787	.796	.328	.414	.622

* p < .05

Table 3.B3. Two-Way Fixed Effects Models of the Moderating Role of Incarceration Rates on the Relationship between Economic Conditions and Crime Rates (1980–2009, n = 82)

Explanatory variable	Property crime (1)	Logged homicide (2)	Logged youth homicide (3)	Logged young adult homicide (4)	Logged adult homicide (5)
City unemployment rate$_{t-1}$	−164.983*	0.049	0.284*	−0.158	0.053
X State incarceration rate$_{t-1}$	(42.923)	(0.031)	(0.114)	(0.122)	(0.051)
County average real wage rate$_{t-1}$	−40.544*	0.024*	−0.073	0.093	0.043*
X State incarceration rate$_{t-1}$	(16.936)	(0.011)	(0.039)	(0.050)	(0.020)
State real GDP$_{t-1}$	2,334.205*	−2.171*	−2.795*	−5.165*	−1.012
X State incarceration rate$_{t-1}$	(594.008)	(0.471)	(1.326)	(1.488)	(0.666)
Regional index of consumer sentiment$_{t-1}$	−0.411	−0.014	−0.009	−0.023	−0.018
X State incarceration rate$_{t-1}$	(7.202)	(0.009)	(0.028)	(0.030)	(0.013)

Table 3.B3 (continued)

Explanatory variable	Property crime (1)	Logged homicide (2)	Logged youth homicide (3)	Logged young adult homicide (4)	Logged adult homicide (5)
City unemployment rate$_{t-1}$	−13.820	0.003	0.016	0.077*	−0.007
	(8.896)	(0.008)	(0.031)	(0.031)	(0.014)
County average real wage rate$_{t-1}$	−0.368	−0.010*	−0.036*	0.018	−0.009
	(5.257)	(0.005)	(0.013)	(0.017)	(0.007)
State real GDP$_{t-1}$	−831.809*	0.241	0.850*	0.739	−0.276
	(161.053)	(0.139)	(0.382)	(0.435)	(0.217)
Regional index of consumer sentiment$_{t-1}$	1.050	−0.009	−0.060*	−0.003	−0.011
	(4.160)	(0.005)	(0.018)	(0.016)	(0.007)
State incarceration rate$_{t-1}$	−1,386.594*	−0.492*	0.710	−0.380	−0.358
	(256.534)	(0.224)	(0.655)	(0.730)	(0.326)
R-Squared	.816	.800	.332	.428	.626

* $p < .05$

Table 3.B4. Two-Way Fixed Effects Models of the Moderating Role of Police Force Size on the Relationship between Economic Conditions and Crime Rates (1980–2009, N = 82)

Explanatory variable	Property crime (1)	Logged homicide (2)	Logged youth homicide (3)	Logged young adult homicide (4)	Logged adult homicide (5)
City unemployment rate$_{t-1}$ X Police force size$_{-1}$	−151.516	−0.085	−0.069	−0.124	−0.075
	(79.209)	(0.066)	(0.246)	(0.257)	(0.090)
County average real wage rate$_{t-1}$ X Police force size$_{t-1}$	−225.684*	0.040	−0.101	0.078	0.001
	(47.554)	(0.033)	(0.121)	(0.116)	(0.040)
State real GDP$_{t-1}$ X Police force size$_{t-1}$	−989.839	−1.722*	−3.797	−6.457*	−1.939*
	(730.727)	(0.768)	(2.109)	(3.253)	(0.804)
Regional index of consumer sentiment$_{t-1}$ X Police force size$_{t-1}$	−10.950	−0.012	−0.003	−0.061	0.004
	(11.362)	(0.010)	(0.035)	(0.040)	(0.015)
City unemployment rate$_{t-1}$	−10.021	−0.002	−0.004	0.064*	−0.009
	(8.391)	(0.008)	(0.032)	(0.032)	(0.014)
County average real wage rate$_{t-1}$	−0.839	−0.009	−0.053*	0.039*	−0.002
	(4.073)	(0.004)	(0.013)	(0.016)	(0.005)
State real GDP$_{t-1}$	−615.588*	−0.373*	−0.211	−0.972*	−0.608*
	(104.278)	(0.075)	(0.208)	(0.276)	(0.107)
Regional index of consumer sentiment$_{t-1}$	2.686	−0.011	−0.063*	−0.010	−0.012
	(4.383)	(0.006)	(0.018)	(0.017)	(0.008)
City police force size$_{t-1}$	−722.504	−0.712	−1.006	−2.929*	−1.207
	(410.644)	(0.416)	(1.492)	(1.359)	(0.618)
R-Squared	.796	.796	.331	.409	.626

*$p < .05$

Table 3.B5. Two-Way Fixed Effects Models of the Moderating Role of Drug Involvement on the Relationship between Economic Conditions and Crime Rates (1980–2009, N = 82)

Explanatory variable	Property crime (1)	Logged homicide (2)	Logged youth homicide (3)	Logged young adult homicide (4)	Logged adult homicide (5)
City unemployment rate$_{t-1}$	−25.0538	0.0004	−0.0563	0.0792	0.0070
X Drug involvement$_{t-1}$	(18.8646)	(0.0147)	(0.0553)	(0.0500)	(0.0246)
County average real wage rate$_{t-1}$	−7.0431	−0.0045	0.0421	0.0012	−0.0120
X Drug involvement$_{t-1}$	(8.0793)	(0.0071)	(0.0272)	(0.0267)	(0.0105)
State real GDP$_{t-1}$	−98.9176	−0.0867	−2.0066*	−0.9209	0.4084
X Drug involvement$_{t-1}$	(122.3305)	(0.1686)	(0.5411)	(0.7634)	(0.2159)
Regional index of consumer sentiment$_{t-1}$	−3.4474	−0.0035	−0.0046	−0.0121	−0.0068
X Drug involvement$_{t-1}$	(3.0021)	(0.0024)	(0.0097)	(0.0093)	(0.0045)
City unemployment rate$_{t-1}$	−9.4739	−0.0024	−0.0004	0.0591	−0.0100
	(8.5420)	(0.0086)	(0.0324)	(0.0325)	(0.0137)
County average real wage rate$_{t-1}$	−2.8232	−0.0096*	−0.0539*	0.0343*	−0.0043
	(4.8233)	(0.0044)	(0.0132)	(0.0162)	(0.0051)
State real GDP$_{t-1}$	−363.0623*	−0.2961*	−0.1494	−0.6741*	−0.4058*
	(89.2775)	(0.0702)	(0.1929)	(0.2716)	(0.1140)
Regional index of consumer sentiment$_{t-1}$	1.6973	−0.0104	−0.0633*	−0.0126	−0.0107
	(4.2881)	(0.0054)	(0.0184)	(0.0169)	(0.0074)
Drug involvement	−16.9798	0.2106*	0.3125	−0.0727	0.3126*
	(45.3532)	(0.0546)	(0.2357)	(0.2499)	(0.0789)
R-Squared	.815	.800	.333	.413	.629

*p < .05

NOTES

1. One exception is a series of cross-national studies that explore whether levels of social welfare mitigate the criminogenic consequences of income inequality or high rates of poverty (for a review, see Messner and Rosenfeld, 2007). This issue also has been examined in U.S. studies (e.g., Hannon and DeFronzo, 1998).

REFERENCES

Agnew, Robert. 1999. "A General Strain Theory of Community Differences in Crime Rates." *Journal of Research in Crime and Delinquency* 36:123–155.

Aiken, Leona S., and Stephen G. West. 1991. *Multiple Regression: Testing and Interpreting Interactions.* Newbury Park, CA: Sage.

Anderson, Elijah. 1999. *Code of the Street: Decency, Violence, and the Moral Life of the Inner City.* New York: Norton.

Baumer, Eric P. 2008. "An Empirical Assessment of the Contemporary Crime Trends Puzzle: A Modest Step toward a More Comprehensive Research Agenda." In Arthur Goldberger and Richard Rosenfeld (eds.), *Understanding Crime Trends*. Washington, DC: National Academies Press.

Baumer, Eric P., Janet L. Lauritsen, Richard Rosenfeld, and Richard Wright. 1998. "The Influence of Crack Cocaine on Robbery, Burglary, and Homicide Rates: A Cross-City, Longitudinal Analysis." *Journal of Research in Crime and Delinquency* 35:316–340.

Becker, Gary. 1968. "Crime and Punishment: An Economic Approach." *Journal of Political Economy* 73:169–217.

Blumstein, Alfred. 1995. "Youth Violence, Guns, and the Illicit-Drug Industry." *Journal of Criminal Law and Criminology* 86:10–36.

Blumstein, Alfred, and Richard Rosenfeld. 2008. "Factors Contributing to U. S. Crime Trends." In Arthur Goldberger and Richard Rosenfeld (eds.), *Understanding Crime Trends*. Washington, DC: National Academies Press.

Bushway, Shawn, Philip J. Cook, and Matthew Phillips. 2010. "The Net Effect of the Business Cycle on Crime and Violence." Prepared for the Centers for Disease Control.

Cantor, David, and Kenneth C. Land. 1985. "Unemployment and Crime Rates in the Post–World War II United States: A Theoretical and Empirical Analysis." *American Sociological Review* 50:317–332.

Chiricos, Ted, and Miriam DeLone. 1992. "Labor Surplus and Punishment: A Review and Assessment of Theory and Evidence." *Social Problems* 39:421–446.

Cook, Philip J., and Gary A. Zarkin. 1985. "Crime and the Business Cycle." *Journal of Legal Studies* 14:115–128.

Cork, Daniel. 1999. "Examining Space-Time Interaction in City-Level Homicide Data: Crack Markets and the Diffusion of Guns among Youth." *Journal of Quantitative Criminology* 15:379–406.

Curtis, Lynn A. 1981. "Inflation, Economic Policy, and the Inner City." *Annals of the American Academy of Political and Social Science* 456:46–59.

Devine, Joel A., Joseph F. Sheley, and M. Dwayne Smith. 1988. "Macroeconomic and Social-Control Policy Influences on Crime Rate Changes, 1948–1985." *American Sociological Review* 53:407–420.

Edberg, Mark, Martha Yeide, and Rick Rosenfeld. 2010. "Macroeconomic Factors and Youth Violence: A Framework for Understanding the Linkages and Review of Available Literature." Prepared for the Centers for Disease Control.

Ehrlich, Isaac. 1973. "Participation in Illegitimate Activities: A Theoretical and Empirical Investigation." *Journal of Political Economy* 81:521–565.

FBI. 2010. "FBI Releases 2009 Crime Statistics." http://www.fbi.gov/ucr/cius2009/documents/pressreleaseciuso9.pdf.

FBI. 2011a. "FBI Releases 2010 Crime Statistics." http://www.fbi.gov/about-us/cjis/ucr/crime-in-the-u.s/2010/crime-in-the-u.s.-2010/summary.

FBI. 2011b. "Preliminary Semiannual Uniform Crime Report, January–June, 2011."

http://www.fbi.gov/about-us/cjis/ucr/crime-in-the-u.s/2011/preliminary-annual-ucr
-jan-jun-2011.

Fox, James A. 1978. *Forecasting Crime Data: An Econometric Analysis*. Lexington, MA: Lexington Books.

Fryer, Roland G., Paul S. Heaton, Steven D. Levitt, and Kevin M. Murphy. 2006. *Measuring the Impact of Crack Cocaine*. NBER Working Paper. http://www.nber.org/papers/w11318.

Gillani, Syed Yasir Mahmood, Hafeez Ur Rehman, and Abid Rasheed Gill. 2009. "Unemployment, Poverty, Inflation and Crime Nexus: Cointegration and Causality Analysis of Pakistan." *Pakistan Economic and Social Review* 47:79–98.

Goldberger, Arthur S., and Richard Rosenfeld, eds. 2008. *Understanding Crime Trends*. Washington, DC: National Academies Press.

Goldstein, Paul J. 1985. "The Drugs/Violence Nexus: A Tripartite Conceptual Framework." *Journal of Drug Issues* 15:493–506.

Gould, Eric D., Bruce. A. Weinberg, and David B. Mustard. 2002. "Crime Rates and Local Labor Market Opportunities in the United States, 1979–1997." *Review of Economics and Statistics* 84:45–61.

Grant, Don Sherman, II, and Ramiro Martínez, Jr. 1997. "Crime and the Restructuring of the U.S. Economy: A Reconsideration of the Class Linkages." *Social Forces* 75:769–798.

Greenberg, David. 2001. "Time Series Analysis of Crime Rates." *Journal of Quantitative Criminology* 17:291–327.

Grogger, Jeffrey. 1998. "Market Wages and Youth Crime." *Journal of Labor Economics* 16:756–792.

Hannon, Lance, and James DeFronzo. 1998. "The Truly Disadvantaged, Public Assistance, and Crime." *Social Problems* 45:383–392.

ICPSR. 2010. *Uniform Crime Reporting Program Data [United States]: Supplementary Homicide Reports, 2008*. http://www.icpsr.umich.edu/cocoon/NACJD/STUDY/27650.xml.

Jaccard, James, and Robert Turrisi. 2003. *Interaction Effects in Multiple Regression*. 2nd ed. Thousand Oaks, CA: Sage.

Johnson, Ryan S., Shawn Kantor, and Price V. Fishback. 2008. "Striking at the Roots of Crime: The Impact of the New Deal on Criminal Activity." Unpublished manuscript.

LaFree, Gary, Kriss A. Drass, and Patrick O'Day. 1992. "Race and Crime in Postwar America: Determinants of African-American and White Rates, 1957–1988." *Criminology* 30:157–188.

Land, Kenneth C., and Marcus Felson. 1976. "A General Framework for Building Dynamic Macro Social Indicator Models: Including an Analysis of Changes in Crime Rates and Police Expenditures." *American Journal of Sociology* 82:565–604.

Landers, Jim. 2008. "It's a Recession—in the Illegal Drugs Market." *Dallas News*, March 18. http://www.dallasnews.com/sharedcontent/dws/bus/columnists/jlanders/stories/DN-landers_18bus.ART0.State.Edition1.39aa1c4.html.

McMurrer, Daniel, and Amy Chasanov. 1995. "Trends in Unemployment Insurance Benefits." *Monthly Labor Review* 118:30–39.

Merton, Robert K. 1938. "Social Structure and Anomie." *American Sociological Review* 3:672–682.

Messner, Steven F., Glenn D. Deane, Luc Anselin, and Benjamin Pearson-Nelson. 2005. "Locating the Vanguard in Rising and Falling Homicide Rates across U.S. Cities." *Criminology* 43:661–696.

Messner, Steven F., and Richard Rosenfeld. 2007. *Crime and the American Dream.* Belmont, CA: Wadsworth.

National Bureau of Economic Research. 2010. "Business Cycles and Expansions." http://www.nber.org/cycles/cyclesmain.html.

National Research Council. 2001. *Informing America's Policy on Illegal Drugs.* Washington, DC: National Academy Press.

Ousey, Graham C., and Matthew R. Lee. 2004. "Investigating the Connections between Race, Illicit Drug Markets, and Lethal Violence, 1984–1997." *Journal of Research in Crime and Delinquency* 41:352–383.

Phillips, Julie A., and David F. Greenberg. 2008. "A Comparison of Methods for Analyzing Criminological Panel Data." *Journal of Quantitative Criminology* 24:51–72.

Ralston, Roy W. 1999. "Economy and Race: Interactive Determinants of Property Crime in the United States, 1958–1995: Reflections on the Supply of Property Crime." *American Journal of Economics and Sociology* 58:405–434.

Raphael, Stephen, and Rudolf Winter-Ebmer. 2001. "Identifying the Effect of Unemployment on Crime." *Journal of Law and Economics* 44:259–283.

Rosenfeld, Richard. 2009. "Crime Is the Problem: Homicide, Acquisitive Crime, and Economic Conditions." *Journal of Quantitative Criminology* 25:287–306.

Rosenfeld, Richard, and Scott H. Decker. 1999. "Are Arrest Statistics a Valid Measure of Illicit Drug Use?" *Justice Quarterly* 16:685–699.

Rosenfeld, Richard, and Robert Fornango. 2007. "The Impact of Economic Conditions on Robbery and Property Crime: The Role of Consumer Sentiment." *Criminology* 45:735–769.

Seals, Alan, and John Nunley. 2007. *The Effects of Inflation and Demographic Change on Property Crime: A Structural Time Series Approach.* Working Paper, Middle Tennessee State University.

Surveillance Epidemiology and End Results. 2010. *US Population Data—1969–2009.* http://seer.cancer.gov/popdata/.

Smith, M. Dwayne, Joel A. Devine, and Joseph F. Sheley. 1992. "Crime and Unemployment: Effects across Age and Race Categories." *Sociological Perspectives* 35:551–572.

Tang, Chor Foon. 2009. "The Linkages among Inflation, Unemployment and Crime Rates in Malaysia." *International Journal of Economics and Management* 3:50–61.

Tang, Chor Foon, and Hooi Hooi Lean. 2007. "Will Inflation Increase Crime Rate? New Evidence from Bounds and Modified Wald Tests." *Global Crime* 8:311–323.

U.S. Census Bureau. 2010. American Fact Finder. http://factfinder2.census.gov/faces/nav/jsf/pages/index.xhtml.

Wilson, James Q. 1996. *On Character: Essays by James Q. Wilson.* La Vergne, TN: AIE Press.

Wilson, Sven E., and Daniel M. Butler. 2007. "A Lot More to Do: The Sensitivity of Time-Series Cross-Section Analysis to Simple Alternative Specifications." *Political Analysis* 15:101–123.

Worrall, John L., and Travis Pratt. 2004. "On the Consequences of Ignoring Unobserved Heterogeneity When Estimating Macro-Level Models of Crime." *Social Science Research* 33:79–105.

Yost, Pete. 2010. "Crime Rates Down for Third Year, Despite Recession." *Los Angeles Daily News*, May 24. http://www.dailynews.com/news/ci_15152909.

4

Economic Conditions and Violent Victimization Trends among Youth

Guns, Violence, and Homicide, 1973–2005

JANET L. LAURITSEN, EKATERINA GORISLAVSKY,
AND KAREN HEIMER

Introduction

The purpose of this chapter is to describe previously unknown national trends in violent victimization among youth and to provide evidence about the association between these trends and national economic conditions. Information about long-term trends in youth violence has been primarily limited to the crime of homicide, which may not mirror trends in nonfatal serious violence. Data for short-term trends in nonfatal youth violence are available for more recent time periods, largely for the 1990s and beyond. However, such data exclude the major economic downturns that occurred in the United States during the 1970s and 1980s. By developing estimates of youth violence for the earlier period and linking these estimates to more recent data, we obtain more information about how national economic conditions are associated with trends in youth violence. Such data also can be used to assess whether the nature of the relationship between youth violence and economic conditions may have changed over time and whether findings about trends in serious nonfatal violence mirror those found for homicide.

In addition, we also disaggregate youth nonfatal violence trends by gender, race, and ethnicity to present previously unknown subgroup trends in youth violence. Like the work of Blumstein and Rosenfeld (1998) and others on homicide trends, recent research has demonstrated the importance of disaggregating nonfatal violence trends by key demographic characteristics of victims. For example, Heimer and Lauritsen (2008) show that the long-term trends in male and female violent victimization are not the same, resulting in declines in the gender gap in violent victimization during the 1990s to early 2000s. Their research also demonstrates that male and female homicide victimization patterns differ from those found for serious nonfatal violence. In subsequent analyses of trends in male violence, Lauritsen and Heimer (2010) show the importance of disaggregating rates by race *and* ethnicity. These results show that long-term trends in nonfatal violence are similar for Latino and non-Latino black males and that both series coincide with changes in national economic conditions as measured by the Index of Consumer Sentiment. In contrast, the trends for non-Latino white males were distinct from those of minority males, exhibiting fewer fluctuations that corresponded with changing economic conditions. This suggests that the relationship between economic conditions and violence may be contingent on an individual's race and ethnicity.

While such findings suggest that analyses of youth violence trends should be disaggregated by race, ethnicity, and gender of the victim, such trends currently are not available in the literature. Nor is it possible to develop long-term trends from existing homicide or mortality records because the ethnicity of the victim (i.e., Hispanic or Latino information) is not available for periods prior to the 1990s. However, such disaggregated rates can be estimated using existing data from the National Crime Survey (NCS) and National Crime Victimization Survey (NCVS). We present trends for serious nonfatal violent victimization, including victimization involving guns, for non-Latino black, Latino, and non-Latino white males and females ages 12–24 in the

United States for the period 1973–2005 and provide the first detailed examination of how these trends are associated with several indicators of national economic conditions, including consumer pessimism, poverty, and unemployment.

Previous Research

Aside from the research presented in this volume, there is relatively little work assessing how changes in economic conditions are associated with changes in youth violence rates. Nonetheless, there is a substantial body of cross-sectional research that has found a relationship between economic disadvantage and violence at various levels of analysis. Generally speaking, a strong and significant relationship between economic conditions and rates of violence has been found in studies of census tracts (e.g., Krivo, Peterson, and Payne, 2009), neighborhoods (e.g., Sampson, Raudenbush, and Earls, 1997), cities (e.g., Land, McCall, and Cohen, 1991), and metropolitan areas and states (e.g., Land, McCall, and Cohen, 1990). A recent meta-analysis of 153 studies has shown that there is a strong and stable relationship between poverty and violence in past research (Pratt and Cullen, 2005). The consistency of these cross-sectional findings suggests that changes in economic conditions should be associated with changes in youth violence in analyses of temporal patterns in both phenomena.

However, aside from the crime of robbery—an economically motivated form of violence—only a handful of studies have demonstrated a relationship between economic trends and changes in violence. State-level changes in unemployment or wages (Raphael and Winter-Ebmer, 2001) and in gross state product (Arvanites and Defina, 2006) have been found to be associated with state-level robbery trends. Rosenfeld (2009) found that changes in regional economic conditions, as measured by the Index of Consumer Sentiment, have an indirect effect on homicide through their effect on economically motivated crimes such as robbery, burglary, and auto theft. Rosenfeld's findings suggest that economic downturns can indirectly affect homicide rates by increasing the demand for stolen goods through underground or illegal markets, which are supplied by such acquisitive crimes. Increases in underground market activity can prompt increases in homicide because they create more situational transactions in which disputes may arise. Such disputes are not regulated by legitimate market practices, and because of this, they are more likely to result in violence (see also Rosenfeld and Fornango, 2007). Although it is beyond the scope of this chapter to examine how underground markets are related to youth violence trends, we extend this research by examining whether change in the Index of Consumer Sentiment is related to change in youth violence patterns.

Lauritsen and Heimer (2010) argue that if significant declines in the economy contribute to increases in violence, then trends disaggregated by race and ethnicity should reveal greater changes among minorities during periods of economic downturn because minority groups typically have been more susceptible to increases in poverty and unemployment during bad economic times. As noted earlier, this research found that the trends for Latino and non-Latino black male violence were associated with changes in the Index of Consumer Sentiment, while the relationships in the trends for non-Latino white males were substantially weaker. Such findings demonstrate the importance of distinguishing Latinos from non-Latino whites in analyses of trends in violence and economic conditions: these relationships are masked in aggregate violence trends and in "white" trends that do not exclude Latinos because such trends are dominated by the experiences of the majority group (i.e., non-Latino whites). Lauritsen and Heimer also found that the relationship between the Index of Consumer Sentiment and violence among minority males appears to break around 2001, at which point violence continued to remain relatively low as economic conditions began to worsen. Thus, it is also important to consider whether other historical changes might moderate a relationship between economic conditions and rates of youth violence.

The research by Lauritsen and Heimer (2010) was descriptive, using bivariate, first-difference correlations to portray the relationship between economic conditions and male violence. In one of the few studies that focused on trends in youth violence using a multivariate approach, Messner, Raffalovich, and McMillan (2001) examined racially disaggregated data to assess the relationship between changes in child poverty rates and changes in homicide arrests among black and white youth under age 18. They used national time series data for 1967–1998 to examine how changes in indicators of economic deprivation and intra-racial inequality affected changes in age-race-specific arrest rates. As measures of economic deprivation, Messner et al. included information on median family income and the percentage of children under 18 years of age living in poverty. Intraracial inequality was measured using the Gini coefficient, the interquartile income range, and the share of income received by the top 5% of households. Messner et al. found that changes in economic deprivation are positively associated with changes in juvenile offending as measured by UCR homicide arrest data. They also found that increases in unemployment had a lagged, negative effect on black and white juvenile arrest rates for homicide, a finding that was unexpected and in contrast with the influence of poverty. Intraracial inequality (but not interracial inequality) was shown to be associated with higher arrest rates for youths; however, these relationships were contingent on the type of measure and lag structure used. Messner et al. note that the complex findings about inequality and unemployment should be regarded with caution. They comment that there are "few clear theoretical guidelines in the literature . . . to govern the selection of specific measures" (2001, 605), and this caveat also is relevant to the findings presented in this chapter.

The analysis that follows shows how changes in economic conditions are associated with changes in violent victimization for non-Latino black (hereafter "black"), Latino, and non-Latino white (hereafter "white") male and female youth ages 12 to 24 in the United States. We begin by describing the data and estimation procedures we use for producing reliable long-term trends in youth violence, as well as the various national economic indicators used in our analysis. Our selection of economic indicators was informed by past research. Preliminary investigations of several sets of possible indicators determined which economic conditions would be the focus of subsequent analysis. Those that were found to be most strongly associated with the trends are displayed in figures to illuminate the nature of these relationships; however, we also include details about conditions that we found not to be related to the trends. Although these analyses are bivariate and descriptive in nature, they are the necessary first step toward understanding whether economic changes are associated with changes in youth violence.

Data and Measures

For the purpose of these analyses, we produce two sets of youth violence trends: gender by youth for age groups 12–17 and 18–24 and gender by race and ethnicity for youth ages 12–24. To estimate the trends in serious violent victimization and gun violence among males and females by age and by race and ethnicity, we compile data from the National Crime Survey (NCS) and the National Crime Victimization Survey (NCVS) for the period 1973–2005.[1] Descriptions of long-term trends in nonfatal violence for various sociodemographic subgroups must rely on data from the NCVS because no other monitoring system is capable of being used for this purpose. The national Uniform Crime Reports (UCR) data that are often used in criminological research do not include information about the characteristics of victims of nonfatal violence. Use of the NCVS also provides several important advantages over other aggregate data series: the data include crimes not reported to the police, allow for more refined disaggregations by victim characteristics, including measures of Latino ethnicity not available elsewhere, and provide important details about the incident, such as whether a gun was used by the perpetrator. In addition, the only changes to the methodology that affected violent victimization rates were those associated with the transition from the NCS to the NCVS in 1992. Because these changes were phased into the data-collection process, the effects of the new methodology on rate estimates can be assessed and adjustment weights can be used to make estimates from the NCS and NCVS comparable over time.

The NCVS and its predecessor, the NCS, have been used to gather self-report data about individuals' experiences with violence and other forms of victimization continuously since 1973. The data are gathered by the Census Bureau and sponsored by the Bureau of Justice Statistics. Using a nationally representative sampling frame, interviews are conducted with all persons age 12 and older in each sampled household.[2] The sample size of the NCVS has varied over time, ranging from approximately 275,000 interviews per year during the early 1970s to about 134,000 interviews per year in 2005 (Rennison and Rand, 2007).

Victimization experiences are measured through a series of cues and common-language questions, and the characteristics of the experiences are used to code the incident into crime types following the interview. We define *male serious violence* to include attempted or completed robberies and aggravated assaults, which are defined as attacks in which the perpetrator used a weapon or those that resulted in injury (Bureau of Justice Statistics, 2005).[3] *Female serious violence* includes attempted or completed rapes in addition to attempted or completed robberies and aggravated assaults. We also assess trends in *gun violence* for males and females by age and by race and ethnicity. *Gun violence* represents a subset of *serious nonfatal violence* and includes any form of violent victimization in which the victim reported that the offender had a gun.[4]

Race and ethnicity as well as *age* are measured using self-reports to questions created and used by the Census Bureau. Following Census practices, NCVS items on race and ethnicity have changed over time.[5] To create a set of consistent categories, we combine responses to the "race" questions with responses to the "ethnicity" question and code for the three largest race and ethnic groups in the nation: non-Latino blacks, non-Latino whites, and Latinos (persons of Hispanic origin or descent who may be of any race). Unfortunately, there are insufficient numbers of subjects to provide reliable annual estimates of youth violence for other race and ethnic groups.

For the purpose of these analyses, the key strengths of the NCVS data are that they permit custom estimations of subgroup rates of victimization, they include incidents not reported to the police, and the data have been available for more than 35 years. Aside from the redesign, there have been no methodological changes that would be confounded with observed changes in violence rates.[6] Nonetheless, these data are subject to concerns that affect all survey data, such as recall error and under- and overreporting. Potential sources of error in the NCVS have been studied extensively (Groves and Cork, 2008; Lynch and Addington, 2007; Penick and Owens, 1976), and two issues that may be relevant to the trends are noted here. First, the use of adjustment weights for the pre-1992 data assumes that the effect of the new instrument would have been the same had it been phased in at a different time point; however, available data cannot assess this assumption (Rand, Lynch, and Cantor, 1997). Second, the willingness of respondents to report violence to interviewers may have changed over time. This concern applies to all survey-based data gathered over time and derived from self-reports, and the magnitude of such changes and their potential effects on the trend estimates remain unknown.

We also estimate trends in *homicide* among male and female youths, using the FBI's Supplementary Homicide Reports (SHR) data for 1976–2005.[7] The SHR data permit age-by-gender trends beginning in 1976, which prohibits comparison with the NCVS serious-nonfatal-violence and gun-violence trends for the 1973–1975 period. Another limitation associated with the SHR data is that, although information on the race of the victim is available back to 1976, ethnicity information necessary for distinguishing Latinos from non-Latino blacks and non-Latino whites is not consistently available. The alternative data source on homicide is WISQARS, but it only provides information on ethnicity starting in 1990. Since those data miss the important recessions in 1970s and 1980s, they are of limited value to our purpose here. Thus, we restrict the measurement of trends by race and ethnicity to nonfatal violence using the NCVS, while our analyses of the homicide trends are limited to gender-by-age disaggregations.[8] We present the comparison of homicide, gun violence, and serious violent victimization by gender and age because it provides important information about whether increases in gun use were accompanied by increases in homicide across age and gender groups, and information about whether conclusions drawn from homicide trends are similar to those based on nonfatal violence.

As noted by Messner et al. (2001), there is no clear guidance in the existing literature about what specific indicators should be used in analyses of the relationship between changes in economic conditions and violence. To select our economic indicators, we consider a range of measures that have been used in prior research, including national levels of poverty and unemployment from the Current Population Survey (CPS), as well as subgroup trends in poverty and unemployment where available from the CPS. We examine subgroup trends in poverty for whites, blacks, and Latinos (Census Bureau, 2012b); for all youth ages 18 and under (Census Bureau, 2012a); and for white, black, and Latino youth ages 18 and under (Census Bureau, 2012a). We also examine subgroup trends in unemployment for whites, blacks, and Latinos; and for all youth ages 16 to 24 (Bureau of Labor Statistics, n.d.). Unlike the available poverty-trend data, the unemployment-trend data from the CPS do not distinguish non-Latino whites and non-Latino blacks from Latinos.

Following research by Rosenfeld and Fornango (2007), we also assess the Index of Consumer Sentiment (ICS).[9] The ICS is a summary measure derived from a longstanding and ongoing survey of U.S. adults that includes questions about personal finances, assessments of the economy now and in the short and long term, and consumers' willingness to purchase large household items. The ICS captures the "subjective experience of economic hardship and change" (Rosenfeld and Fornango, 2007, 740) and is used as part of the Index of Leading Economic Indicators (Conference Board, 2009). According to Curtin (2004), changes in the ICS predict changes in GDP and foreshadow the onset of recessions. In the current analyses, we reverse the scaling of the ICS axis so that the peaks represent greater levels of *consumer pessimism*. Unfortunately, it is not possible to get ICS trend data disaggregated for non-Latino white, non-Latino black, and Latino subgroups.[10]

Our choice of economic indicators focused on poverty, unemployment, and the ICS. We examined each of the trends just noted and, for poverty and unemployment, selected the one that was found to be most strongly associated with each of the violence trends to become the focus of our subsequent analysis.[11] To represent changes in poverty, we found that the *youth poverty* measure (i.e., percentage of youth ages 18 and under living below poverty) generally outperformed indicators of the overall poverty rate and the race/ethnic-group-specific poverty rates (when applied to their respective subgroup violence trends). Interestingly, the youth poverty trend also outperformed the race- and ethnic-group-specific youth poverty trends for each of the race- and ethnic-group-specific violence trends. In other words, greater subgroup specificity in economic indicators did not result in higher correlations, a finding consistent with prior analyses (e.g., Messner et al., 2001). We conducted a comparable set of analyses for our choice of unemployment indicator and found that the trend in *youth unemployment* (i.e., percentage of persons ages 16 to 24 who are unemployed) similarly outperformed the overall unemployment trend as well as the race- and ethnic-group-specific unemployment trends. Thus, the following analysis focuses on how trends in youth poverty, youth unemployment, and consumer pessimism are associated with each of the violence trends we produce.

Findings

We begin by showing how our national indicators of economic conditions are related to one another over time. Figure 4.1 displays the trends in the ICS, youth poverty, and youth unemployment along with U.S. recessionary periods as defined by the National Bureau of Economic Research.[12] As expected, this figure shows that increases in levels of consumer pessimism tend to precede the onset of recessions and that consumer pessimism tends to subside as recessions have ended. Trends and fluctuations in consumer pessimism also tend to precede changes in youth unemployment and poverty, although these changes appear to have become more contemporaneous around the 2001 recessionary period. The first-difference correlation between ICS_{T-1} and youth unemployment$_T$ is .51 ($p \le .05$, one-tail test), and between ICS_{T-1} and youth poverty$_T$ it is .41 ($p \le .05$, one-tail test). Changes in youth unemployment$_T$ and youth poverty $_T$ are strongly correlated (r = .76, $p \le .05$, one-tail test).

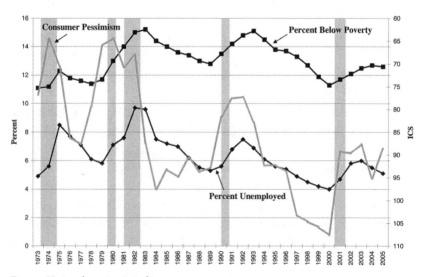

Fig. 4.1. National economic indicators, 1973–2005

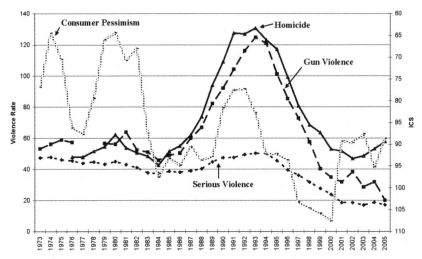

Fig. 4.2. Homicide (per 100,000), gun violence (per 10,000), serious violent victimization (per 1,000), and consumer pessimism: males ages 12–17

Trends in Homicide, Gun Violence, and Serious Nonfatal Violence by Age and Gender

Our first set of youth victimization trends examines the similarities and differences in male and female patterns of nonfatal and fatal violence for younger and older youth and compares these trends to changes in economic conditions. Figure 4.2 displays the trends in homicide, and our estimates of the trends in nonfatal gun violence and serious violent victimization for males ages 12–17. In this and all subsequent figures, we display our estimates of the annual rates in nonfatal violence using three-year moving averages to better depict the overall trends, and we use different base rates for the various forms of violence (i.e., per 100,000 for homicide, per 10,000 for gun violence, and per 1,000 for serious violence) to ease comparisons of the similarities and differences in the trends. In figure 4.2, the national trend in consumer pessimism is also superimposed. Changes in the consumer pessimism measure are presented in this figure, as opposed to the youth poverty or youth unemployment measures, because generally speaking, we found that the consumer pessimism measure was more strongly and consistently associated with these male violence trends (see table 4.1).

Table 4.1. First-Difference Correlations between Macroeconomic Indicators and Youth Violence by Gender, Age, and Type of Victimization

	Consumer pessimism		Youth poverty		Youth unemployment	
Males ages 12–17						
Homicide	**.48***	**(.38*)**	**.33***	**(.32*)**	.23	(.17)
Gun violence	.23	(.10)	**.45***	**(.42*)**	.18	(.19)
Serious violence	**.33***	(.09)	.29	(.27)	.06	(.00)
Males ages 18–24						
Homicide	**.49***	**(.49*)**	**.33***	**(.31*)**	.09	(.11)
Gun violence	**.42***	(.28)	.30	(.26)	.11	(.04)
Serious violence	**.57***	**(.38*)**	**.33***	**(.30*)**	.13	(.04)
Females ages 12–17						
Homicide	.29	(.19)	.07	(.03)	−.09	(−.08)
Gun violence	.10	(.02)	**.50***	**(.48*)**	.28	(.26)
Serious violence	.22	(.11)	**.57***	**(.55*)**	**.33***	**(.31*)**
Females ages 18–24						
Homicide	.21	(.19)	.15	(.16)	−.05	(−.02)
Gun violence	.05	(.07)	**.37***	**(.34*)**	.11	(.11)
Serious violence	.24	(.17)	**.34***	**(.32*)**	.01	(.01)

Note: Correlations for 1973–2000 period appear first, followed by correlations for 1973–2005 period in parentheses.
* $p < .05$ (one-tail). Significant correlations also appear in bold type.

For the same reason, all subsequent figures for male violence include consumer pessimism as the corresponding economic trend. In contrast, the figures for female violence include the youth poverty trend because we found that this measure was most strongly and consistently associated with the trends in female victimization. Youth unemployment indicators exhibited weaker and less consistent relationships with the male and female youth violence trends, and so they are not included in any subsequent figures. However, the magnitude and direction of all relationships are included in the tables that present the first-difference correlations between youth violence$_T$ and consumer pessimism$_T$, youth poverty$_T$, and youth unemployment$_T$.

The male violence trends for youth ages 12–17 in figure 4.2 show quite clearly that for this subgroup, rates of violence remained relatively stable during the 1970s and early 1980s but that rates of nonfatal gun violence and homicide grew dramatically beginning in the mid-1980s. There is some evidence of a comparatively small periodic increase and decrease in these forms of violence in the late 1970s to early 1980s. While gun violence and homicide grew dramatically from 1984 to 1993 (approximately 173% and 208%, respectively), rates of nonfatal serious violence were not increasing to the same degree (35%). In 1993, both homicide and gun violence began to decline at nearly the same rates that they increased, and at that time the rates of serious violence also began to decline. The decline in each of the violence trends ended around 2001–2002, and from then until 2005, only rates of homicide began to show some increase. Thus, the large increase in homicide for this subgroup during the 1984–1993 period was associated with a large increase in gun violence but does not appear to have been driven by a large increase in serious violence more generally.

The correspondence between these violence trends and economic conditions is somewhat complex. Increases in consumer pessimism exhibit somewhat similar patterns as increases in violence in the late 1970s and early 1990s, but it appears that the change in economic conditions was associated with a proportionately small change in male youth violence in the earlier period compared to the later period and that the increase in consumer pessimism in 2001 is not matched by a correspondingly large increase in violence from 2001 to 2005. The first-difference correlations between consumer pessimism and homicide (r = .48) and serious violence (r = .33) are statistically significant ($p \le .05$, one-tail test) for the 1973–2000 period, but the relationship for gun violence (r = .23) during this period is not large enough to reach statistical significance (see table 4.1).[13] When the correlations are estimated for the full 1973–2005 period, we find that only homicide (r = .38) remains significantly associated with ICS for males age 12–17 (but see note 13). Thus, we find some evidence that changes in violent victimization among males age 12–17 are significantly associated with changes in economic conditions as measured by the consumer pessimism index.

The trends in violence for males ages 18–24 in figure 4.3 exhibit patterns that are somewhat similar to those found for males ages 12–17. For the older males, there is a comparatively small periodic increase and decrease in homicide during the late 1970s to early 1980s, and as with the younger males, gun violence and homicide began to grow around 1984, while rates of nonfatal serious violence were not increasing to the same degree. Around 1993, both homicide and gun violence began to decline at roughly the same time that the rates of serious violence also

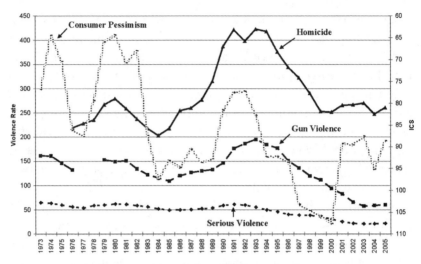

Fig. 4.3. Homicide (per 100,000), gun violence (per 10,000), serious violent victimization (per 1,000), and consumer pessimism: males ages 18–24

began to decline. The decline in homicide ended around 1999–2000, and the declines in gun violence and serious violence leveled off around 2002–2003. Like the younger males, the large increase in homicide for males 18–24 that occurred from approximately 1984 to 1993 (108%) appears to be associated with the increase (69%) in gun violence rather than with the increase (7%) in serious violence more generally.

The relationships between the violence trends and economic conditions for males 18–24 are stronger and more consistent than they were found to be among the younger males for gun violence and serious violence and are equally strong for homicide. Changes in consumer pessimism are significantly associated ($p \leq .05$, one-tail test) with changes in homicide (r = .49), nonfatal gun violence (r = .42), and serious violent victimization (r = .57) from 1973 to 2000 for older male youth. However, the relationships with gun and serious violence are reduced some to .28 (ns) and .38 ($p \leq .05$, one-tail test), respectively, when the full 1973–2005 period is considered (see table 4.1). Thus we find evidence that changes in homicide among males age 18–24 are significantly associated with changes in consumer pessimism and that for the period prior to 2001, all three forms of violence are significantly associated with changes in consumer pessimism.

The trends in violence among females ages 12–17 in figure 4.4 differ considerably from the corresponding trends for males. For younger females, there are comparatively smaller periodic increases and decreases both in nonfatal serious violence and homicide throughout the entire period 1973–2005. Serious nonfatal violence and homicide rates were quite steady during the 1970s and until the mid-1980s. Starting in 1983, both rates began to increase and continued to increase until 1993. After that, both serious violence and homicide exhibit steady decreases until 2005. The trends indicate that nonfatal serious violence and homicide trends among females ages 12–17 exhibit similar behavior throughout the period of interest, with the homicide rates fluctuating slightly more over the years. Gun violence for females in this age group was increasing slowly but steadily from the late 1970s to around 1990. Compared to the 1984–1993 increases in serious violence (57%) and homicide (44%), the increase in gun violence during this period was much higher (160%). From 1990 to 1993, the rate of gun violence exhibited a particularly dramatic increase, when it almost tripled in magnitude. All three violence rates declined steadily starting in 1993, with the exception of a few short-term increases in the homicide rate. It is important to note that compared to young males, the large increases in gun

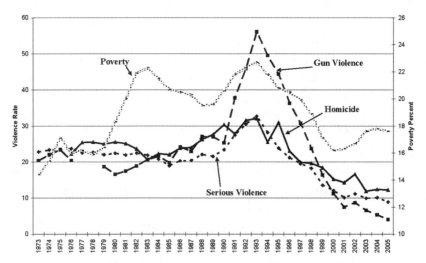

Fig. 4.4. Homicide (per 100,000), gun violence (per 10,000), serious violent victimization (per 1,000), and youth poverty: females ages 12–17

victimization against females ages 12–17 were not matched by comparably large increases in homicide.

The relationships between the violence trends for younger females
and economic conditions are no less complex than was observed among
males. Increases in poverty rates appear to correspond little with violence rates until the early 1990s. From approximately 1990 to 2003,
changes in youth poverty correspond more closely with changes in
homicide and nonfatal gun and serious violence. However, the higher
rates of youth poverty at the end of the series were not matched with
similar increases in any of these violence trends. Despite the ambigui-
ties in the figure, we find that for females ages 12–17, changes in youth
poverty are significantly associated ($p \leq .05$, one-tail test) with changes
in gun violence (r = .50) and serious nonfatal violence (r = .57) for the
period 1973 to 2000 and remain statistically significant with the inclusion of data for 2001 to 2005 (see table 4.1). However, the relationship
between youth poverty and homicide among females ages 12–17 is not
statistically significant, regardless of period. This suggests that the factors associated with changes in female youth homicide are somewhat
unique compared to males and compared to changes in nonfatal violence against female youth. Overall, we find that changes in economic
conditions as measured by youth poverty rates are significantly associated with changes in nonfatal violence for females ages 12–17, but no
comparably significant relationship is found for homicide.

Why the youth poverty measure produces larger correlation coefficients for female violence than the consumer pessimism measure does
is not clear, nor can it be easily interpreted given the current state of
research. We considered the possibility that the youth poverty measure
was simply capturing a lagged association between consumer pessimism and female violence; recall that the change in ICS at $year_{T-1}$ is
correlated .41 with the change in youth poverty at $year_T$. However, we
found that the first-difference correlations between ICS_{T-1} and female
$victimization_T$ were smaller in magnitude in almost all instances than
youth $poverty_T$. This suggests that youth poverty and consumer pessimism represent different aspects of economic conditions and that
the salience and relevance of these conditions varies some by gender.
Moreover, even though ICS_{T-1} has a slightly stronger correlation with
youth $unemployment_T$ (r = .51) than with youth poverty, the associa-

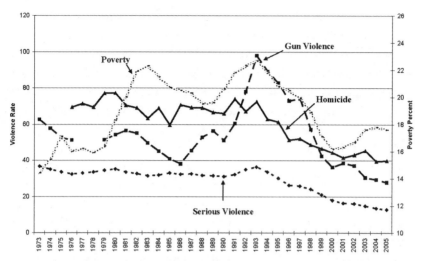

Fig. 4.5. Homicide (per 100,000), gun violence (per 10,000), serious violent victimization (per 1,000), and youth poverty: females ages 18–24

tions between violence$_T$ and youth unemployment$_T$ are generally much weaker than they are between violence$_T$ and consumer pessimism$_T$ or youth poverty$_T$. Thus, all three economic indicators appear to be capturing important but different aspects of economic conditions, and changes in some of these conditions are associated with serious violent victimization.

The trends in violence for older females in figure 4.5 are in many ways similar to the trends for the younger category of females. The trends in serious violence and homicide for the older females are also quite stable across the period, although in absolute terms they exhibit higher fluctuations than for younger females. Serious nonfatal violence for older females was very steady from 1973 to 1990, exhibiting a modest increase from 1990 to 1993, before declining until 2005. Homicide rates for this group of females have been similar to serious violence: very stable until the early 1990s, followed by general declines thereafter. The rates of gun violence have followed a different pattern compared with the other two groups of rates. Gun violence rates in the early 1980s appear to be similar to their levels in the early to mid-1970s, and then they decreased from approximately 1981 to 1986. In 1987, gun violence began to increase quite rapidly and peaked in 1993, similar to the pattern among younger females. From 1993 until about 2000, there was a comparable decrease in gun violence, and by 2005 the rate was even lower. Although the decreases in gun violence corresponded with decreases in homicide and serious violence, the increases in gun violence (117%) from 1984 to 1993 (the period of the large increases for males) were not matched with comparable increases in homicide (5%) or serious violence (14%).

The relationships between economic conditions and the violence trends for the older female youth are similar to those found for the younger females, though somewhat weaker in magnitude for non-fatal violence. We find that changes in youth poverty are significantly associated ($p \leq .05$, one-tail test) with changes in gun violence (r = .37) and serious nonfatal violence (r = .34) for the period 1973 to 2000 and remain statistically significant when the full 1973–2005 period is examined (see table 4.1). As with the younger females, the relationship between youth poverty and homicide among females ages 18–24 is not statistically significant, regardless of period. In other words, changes in economic conditions as measured by youth poverty are significantly associated with changes in nonfatal violence for females ages 18–24 but not with fatal violence among these young women. Together, these findings suggest that the impact of increases in gun victimization are less likely to result in the death of young females than they are to result in the death of young males and that female youth homicide may be associated with unique factors.

Trends in Gun Violence and Serious Violence by Race,
Ethnicity, and Gender

Our second set of youth violence trends examines the similarities and differences in male and female patterns of nonfatal gun violence and serious violence for youth ages 12–24 by race and ethnicity and compares these trends to changes in economic conditions. Despite the large sample, the NCVS data lack the statistical power necessary for producing estimates of these statistically rare forms of victimization for the separate age groups. As noted earlier, we do not include homicide in these comparisons because such data by race and ethnicity are not available prior to the 1990s. As with our previous graphs, the subsequent figures for male violence include consumer pessimism as the corresponding economic trend, while youth poverty is included with the female youth violence trends. Recall that measures of poverty and unemployment disaggregated by race and ethnicity (and by age, race, and ethnicity) did not provide a better fit to their respective subgroup trends than did the measures of consumer pessimism or youth poverty.

Figure 4.6 shows the trends in serious nonfatal violence for males ages 12–24, and table 4.2 displays the first-difference correlations between these trends and our economic indicators. Figure 4.6 shows that minority males experience higher rates of serious violent victimization, particularly during periods of economic downturns in which consumer pessimism is high. During periods in which consumer pessimism is low, the differences in male violence across these race and ethnic groups appear to be much reduced. Thus, what is apparent in these disaggregated violence trends that was not visible in the earlier figures are the differences in levels of risk by race and ethnicity, and the greater periodic fluctuations in the minority trends that coincide with periods of economic downturns. It is also the case that serious violence declined considerably during the 1990s for all three groups.

The relationships between consumer pessimism and the serious violence trends for black (r = .52), Latino (r = .39), and white (r = .39)

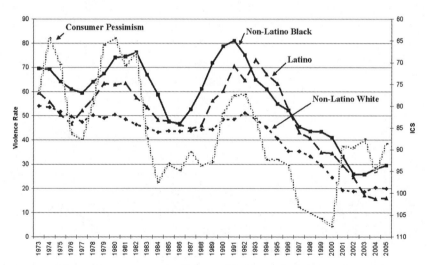

Fig. 4.6. Serious violent victimization (per 1,000) by race and ethnicity and consumer pessimism: males ages 12–24

Table 4.2. First-Difference Correlations between Macroeconomic Indicators and Youth Violence by Gender, Race and Ethnicity, and Type of Victimization

	Consumer pessimism		Youth poverty		Youth unemployment	
Males ages 12–24						
Non-Latino black						
Gun violence	**.37***	(.22)	.25	(.21)	.16	(.07)
Serious violence	**.52***	**(.34*)**	.25	(.22)	.16	(.07)
Latino						
Gun violence	**.39***	(.22)	**.33***	(.26)	.21	(.13)
Serious violence	**.39***	(.27)	.23	(.18)	−.03	(−.08)
Non-Latino white						
Gun violence	.16	(.12)	**.34***	**(.34*)**	.09	(.12)
Serious violence	**.39***	(.16)	**.33***	**(.32*)**	.10	(.04)
Females ages 12–24						
Non-Latino black						
Gun violence	.10	(.05)	**.48***	**(.47*)**	.30	(.28)
Serious violence	−.02	(−.06)	**.48***	**(.48*)**	**.36***	(.34)
Latino						
Gun violence	−.15	(−.23)	.13	(.12)	.03	(.00)
Serious violence	.06	(.01)	**.41***	**(.39*)**	**.33***	**(.31*)**
Non-Latino white						
Gun violence	.12	(.18)	**.38***	**(.33*)**	.10	(.13)
Serious violence	**.41***	**(.31*)**	.31	(.29)	−.02	(−.02)

Note: Correlations for 1973–2000 period appear first, followed by correlations for 1973–2005 period in parentheses.
*p ≤ .05 (one-tail). Significant correlations also appear in bold type.

males are statistically significant ($p \leq .05$, one-tail test) for the 1973–2000 period (see table 4.2). In addition, this relationship remains statistically significant for black males (r = .34) for the full 1973–2005 period. These results are similar to those reported by Lauritsen and Heimer (2010), which were based on a sample that also included males over the age of 24. However, those results did not show a significant association between consumer pessimism and serious violence among white males. The findings presented here indicate that the relationship between changes in consumer pessimism and serious violence among white males in prior research was masked by the differing age compositions of the race and ethnic groups. More generally, the analyses in figure 4.6 and table 4.2 show that changes in serious nonfatal violence among young males in each of these race and ethnic groups are significantly associated with changes in consumer pessimism for the period 1973–2000 but that this relationship appears to break from 2001 to 2005.

Figure 4.7 displays the trends in gun violence for males ages 12–24, illustrating important differences in level and peaks in this form of victimization across race and ethnic groups. These data show that young black males have consistently faced the highest risks of gun violence over time but that during the early to mid-1990s, Latino rates were nearly as high. In addition, the large increases in gun victimization for black and Latino male youth that appeared around 1984–1985 began several years prior to the increases for white male youth, which did not appear to increase until approximately 1989.

These trends also show that young minority males experience larger periodic increases in gun violence than do white males during times in which consumer pessimism is increasing, though missing gun data in 1977 and 1978 make it difficult to discern whether this was the case in the late 1970s. When consumer pessimism is low, the patterns are complex. During the mid-1980s, the level differences between blacks, whites, and Latinos in male gun violence were proportionately smaller than they were when consumer pessimism was at its lowest levels during the late 1990s. Nonfatal gun violence declined considerably during the 1990s for all three groups, and like other forms of violence considered here, these declines leveled off beginning in the early 2000s.

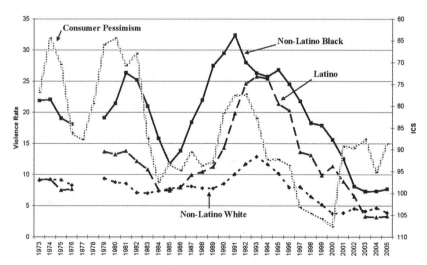

Fig. 4.7. Gun violence (per 1,000) by race and ethnicity and consumer pessimism: males ages 12–24

The relationships between consumer pessimism and the gun violence trends for young black (r = .37) and Latino (r = .39) males are statistically significant ($p \leq .05$, one-tail test) for the 1973–2000 period. However, this relationship is not significant for young white males (r = .16), and it is not significant for any of these race and ethnic groups when the period is extended to include the later years. In other words, changes in consumer pessimism are significantly associated with changes in minority rates of gun violence for males for the period 1973–2000, but these relationships appear to break around 2001.

Figure 4.8 shows serious violent victimization trends for females ages 12–24 by race and ethnicity. It is clear from this figure that young black females experience the highest rates of serious violence. Latinas and whites, by comparison, have lower rates of serious violent victimization that do not appear to differ from one another in a meaningful way. Among young females, there appears to be relatively little connection between serious violence and youth poverty rates in the early 1980s, but when youth poverty increased in the late 1980s and early 1990s, black female victimization rates spiked upward. There was a modest increase in white and Latina violence during this time; however, the Latina increase began somewhat earlier. As with males, serious

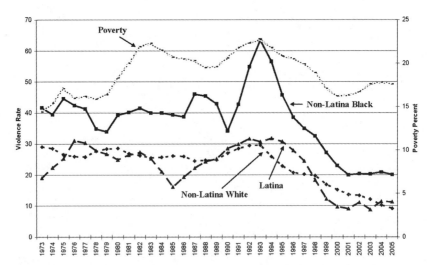

Fig. 4.8. Serious violent victimization (per 1,000) by race and ethnicity and youth poverty: females ages 12–24

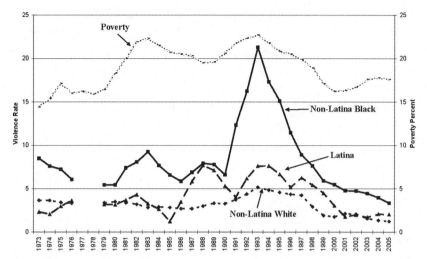

Fig. 4.9. Gun violence (per 1,000) by race and ethnicity and youth poverty: females ages 12–24

violence declined starting in the middle 1990s for all three race and ethnic groups. Among Latina and black females, the decline leveled off, but it continued for white females into the early 2000s.

The relationships between youth poverty and serious violence trends for black (r = .48) and Latina (r = .41) females are statistically significant (*p* ≤ .05, one-tail test) for the 1973–2000 period, and these relationships remain significant when the period is extended to include the later years (see table 4.2). However, this relationship is weaker and does not reach significance for white females, regardless of the time-period specification (r = .31 and r = .29). Thus, the findings about the relationship between changes in economic conditions and serious violence for young females by race and ethnicity are generally similar to the overall patterns found for young males.

Finally, figure 4.9 shows gun violence against young females ages 12–24 by race and ethnicity. The pattern is similar to that for young women's serious violent victimization. Young black girls and women experience consistently higher rates of gun violence victimization than do young white females and Latinas, although black-Latina differences vary more over time. During the 1980s, there is some increase in gun violence against blacks that corresponds with increases in youth poverty at the time, but this is not evident among Latinas or whites. The most notable pattern in the figure, however, is that black female gun violence increased substantially between 1990 and 1993 and then quickly began to drop off, showing a long-term decline from 1993 through 2005. This spike and decline corresponds with increases and decreases in youth poverty in the 1990s, particularly the decline after 1993. However, the increase in youth poverty after 2000 is not matched by an increase in black female gun victimization. The patterns among Latinas and whites are much less pronounced and less clear, and their levels are more similar. There is the familiar decrease after the middle 1990s among both Latinas and whites and some interruption in their declines after 2000.

The relationships between youth poverty and the gun violence trends for black (r = .48) and white (r = .38) females are statistically significant ($p \leq .05$, one-tail test) for the 1973–2000 period and remain significant when the period is extended to include the later years. However, this relationship is not significant for Latinas (r = .13), regardless of the time-period specification. These findings differ from those shown for males, in that Latino male trends are more similar to those of black males, while across the female trends, we find that Latina trends are more similar to white trends and their association with economic conditions is not significant. Table 4.2 summarizes this somewhat complex mix of findings across race and ethnicity for young females. Youth poverty is significantly associated with both gun violence and serious violence among black females, while Latina serious violence, but not gun violence, is associated with youth poverty. The findings are reversed among non-Latina whites; gun violence, but not serious violence, is correlated with youth poverty.

Discussion

This research has presented trends over time in youth violent victimization that heretofore have not been estimated or published. By using the combined NCS-NCVS data for the period 1973–2005, we shed light on long-term patterns in youth nonfatal violent victimization, and we compare these patterns to UCR homicide data for youth. The use of the NCVS allows for the examination of the "dark figure" of violence by capturing events that were not reported to the police. It also allows for refined disaggregation by victim characteristics that enables us to present rates of nonfatal violent victimization for Latino/a youth as well as non-Latino/a black and non-Latino/a whites. Our findings suggest that reliance on UCR data can mask important similarities between Latino and black males, as well as important differences between Latino and white males. Moreover, the NCVS data allows us to disentangle nonfatal violence involving guns from serious violence more generally, which allows for more detailed analyses of the relationships between fatal and nonfatal violence and the use of guns in violent crime incidents.

As described earlier, our findings reveal many differences and similarities in youths' exposure to violent victimization over time across gender, race, and ethnicity. Throughout our descriptions, we have examined correspondences between shifts in major indicators of the economy and youth violent victimization, in an attempt to uncover possible connections and to lay the foundation for subsequent research on the macroeconomic contexts of youth violence.

First, we observe that there is some association between economic shifts, as measured by consumer pessimism, and trends in youth violence by males, particularly homicide and gun violence. The increases in consumer pessimism in the early 1980s corresponded with modest increases in homicide and gun violence among males ages 12–17 and more substantial increases in homicide among males ages 18–24. Interestingly, the increases in consumer pessimism in the early 1990s —although at lower absolute levels than in the early 1980s—were associated with much larger upward swings in youth homicide and gun violence among males ages 12–17 and much greater increases in homicide among males ages 18–24. This suggests that while macroeconomic conditions are associated with male violent victimization, there was something unique during the late 1980s and early 1990s that also helped to drive the strong increases in homicide and gun violence. As suggested in past research, perhaps urban decay and the proliferation of crack-cocaine markets that also occurred at this time contributed to and magnified the effects of the broader economy. Certainly, previous research has connected the use of guns and crack markets with violence during this period (Blumstein and Rosenfeld, 1998; Blumstein and Wallman, 2006; Cook and Laub, 2002). Corresponding with the substantial decline in consumer pessimism after 1992, our data show a sharp decline in homicide and nonfatal gun violence. This decline leveled off in 2000, when consumer pessimism again increased, and consequently, its association with violence is stronger prior to 2000; we return to this issue later.

Female nonfatal violent victimization among females ages 12–17 and 18–24 also began to climb from the middle 1980s through the middle 1990s, with the most pronounced increase occurring in gun violence. Yet unlike males, this increase in gun violence exposure was *not* matched by proportionate increases in homicide. Female victimization was less strongly associated with consumer pessimism and more strongly associated with national youth poverty rates, and our data revealed that there was an association between both gun violence and overall serious violence and youth poverty across the series. This association in the trend lines appears to occur mostly because of the corresponding increases in youth poverty, gun, and serious violent victimization between the middle 1980s and middle 1990s and the subsequent decline in all three trends after the middle 1990s.

Female homicide is distinctive from nonfatal gun violence against females, particularly in the 18–24 age group. Indeed, female homicide does not appear responsive to economic conditions throughout the series, but rather in the case of the older age group, female homicide displays a long-term decline (see also Lauritsen and Heimer, 2008). This may reflect the proliferation of domestic and intimate-partner violence interventions over this period, which may have had greater consequences for female homicide than for nonfatal violence against women. Further development of trends by victim-offender relationship is necessary to examine this possibility. But this pattern may also reflect something about the willingness of the overwhelmingly male offenders in violent crime incidents to pull the trigger against male victims compared to female victims. It is possible that potentially lethal incidents that involve guns are less likely to result in a homicide when the victim is female rather than male because young women are viewed as less dangerous or threatening to the offender. If so, these findings suggest that the perceived dangerousness of male victims may change over time in ways that may be associated with economic changes, while the perceived dangerousness of female victims has remained relatively constant.

Our disaggregation of NCVS trends in youth violence by race and ethnicity, in addition to gender, produces some striking findings that at times parallel recent findings that were not disaggregated by age, published in our other work (Lauritsen and Heimer, 2010). First, young black males ages 12–24 have the highest rates of violent victimization over time. During the crime boom period of the late 1980s through early 1990s, however, young male Latino rates of both serious violence and gun violence approached the non-Latino black rates. Second, the rates of gun victimization in both groups of minority male youths show greater correspondence with consumer pessimism during this period than is the case for non-Latino white male youths, even though the rates of serious violence for all three groups are associated with changes in consumer pessimism. Moreover, unlike the trend lines for young males that were not disaggregated by race, serious violence and gun violence against both blacks and Latinos also increased in the early 1980s, again corresponding to trends in consumer pessimism. While we saw a modest association in the trends in violence and consumer pessimism when the data were not distinguished by race and ethnicity, the disaggregated data reveal a pattern that shows that the violent victimization of young minority males coincides somewhat more closely with macroeconomic conditions than is the case for white males. Lauritsen and Heimer (2010) argue that this may occur because minorities tend to be hardest hit during economic downtowns. However, we also note the greater increase in violence against minority males—particularly gun violence—during the 1990s crime boom. As discussed earlier, this may reflect a combination of economic factors, urban decay, and the growth in the crack-cocaine market that occurred during that period.

Among young females, by comparison, black females have the highest rates of both serious violence and gun victimization throughout the series, with a clear upward spike during the early 1990s, followed by a dramatic decline. Unlike the patterns for young males, Latina violent victimization is closer in level and pattern over time to white than to black victimization trends, indicating an important interaction between ethnicity and gender. For all three groups of females, fluctuations in economic conditions in the 1980s correspond much more weakly with

trends in victimization than is the case for males. Indeed, of most interest among young females are the parallel spikes in serious violence and
especially gun violence against black females. Again, it may be that during the 1990s, black female victimization may have been driven not only
by macroeconomic pressures but also by urban decay and the spread of
crack-cocaine markets. What is interesting is that Latinas, unlike Latino
males, did not experience increases in serious violence that were different from increases among whites. Latinas did, however, experience
higher rates of gun violence than did white females over the period
stretching from the late 1980s to the late 1990s.

In some of the series presented here, we saw a break between economic indicators and violent victimization rates after 2001. More specifically, we found that the association between male victimization and
consumer sentiment decoupled somewhat after 2000. The decoupling
of our economic indicator of youth poverty from victimization was less
evident for violence against young females. In fact, most of the first-
difference correlations between youth poverty and youth violence, for
males and females, changed relatively little when the time period was
respecified. This suggests that although poverty and consumer pessimism represent economic conditions, they represent different aspects
of economic circumstances. Perceptions of the economy by the public
may reflect concerns about well-being that go beyond actual and anticipated labor-market conditions, and poverty rates are affected by additional conditions, as they can be offset by social spending and child-
welfare supports, as well as by family social capital. Our finding that
consumer pessimism has a very limited relationship with female youth
victimization but that youth poverty rates tend to be associated with
both female and male youth violence in ways that are less contingent
on time specifications indicate the complexity of the potential meaning of various economic indicators. Consistent with previous research,
we find that the youth unemployment trend has the weakest and least
clear associations with the youth violence trends. Our interpretation of
these complexities is consistent with those of Messner et al. (2001) and
others; although changing economic conditions appear to be associated with youth violence trends, the theoretical mechanisms underlying
these relationships are not obvious. Clearly, more research is needed to
better understand these patterns.

The currently available data cannot tell us whether the decoupling in the male series will continue or whether the economic downturn that began in late 2007 will be associated with a subsequent increase in violent victimization. It is almost impossible to assess the cause of this break with the data presented here. It could be that this is to some extent a byproduct of the economic indicator that we use for males. We selected consumer sentiment (consumer pessimism here) for comparison with male victimization rates because it is the indicator most closely associated with violence against young males, whereas we compared trends in youth poverty among females. It may be that the consumer sentiment index was sensitive to the terrorist events of September 11 but that the dot-com economic recession of the early 2000s had relatively little impact on the life circumstances of the young males most exposed to violence; indeed, youth poverty rates increased some from 1999 to 2002 but then leveled off and even decreased slightly. Regardless, the association between consumer sentiment and male victimization became less strong after 2000, and better understanding the reason for this will require additional data.

The effect of the current economic crisis on youth victimization cannot be known or predicted with great accuracy. It appears that the economic crises of the 1980s and 1990s may have had different effects on youth violence, perhaps because of other time-bound contextual factors, including the proliferation of crack-cocaine markets, gang activity, and the pace of urban decay. It is also the case that government response varies across periods of economic decline and recession. The recent infusion of funds into government programs (such as extended unemployment benefits) and infrastructure may have had the effect of blunting some of the impact of the most recent recession, or it may be the case that criminal justice policies such as police practices have become more effective at deterring crime. These are important issues for future research. What our analysis offers is evidence that, over a long time series, there is an association between indicators of economic decline and violence against youth. However, careful theoretical development is necessary to understand the specific causal mechanisms underlying these relationships, and more research is needed to specify the precise nature of variation in economic effects across race, ethnicity, and gender.

NOTES

1. We used NCS and NCVS data made available through ICPSR (data sets 7635, 8608, 8864, and 4699). For more information, see http://www.icpsr.umich.edu/ NACJD/NCVS. Due to several changes in sample and methodology, data for the 2006 NCVS represent a "break-in-series" and should not be compared to data from 2005 or 2007 (see Rand, 2008). We estimated youth violence rates for 2007 and 2008 (using ICPSR data sets 24741 and 25461) and compared these rates to those for 2005 and did not detect any statistically significant changes. The average 2007–2008 rates for male and female youth violence were slightly lower than the 2004–2005 average rates. The reduced sample size of the NCVS in recent years and the use of small subgroups means that the changes in rates must be relatively large to be deemed statistically significant. Because we cannot link the 2006 data to either 2005 or 2007 and because the inclusion of 2007 and 2008 data does not alter the results reported here, we limit our analyses to 1973 to 2005.

2. Because the multistage cluster sample is developed by the Census Bureau in accordance with population information for the United States, the data do not contain the limitations that may be associated with sample selection in random-digit-dialing surveys. Persons in each sampled household address are interviewed either in person or by telephone once every six months over a three-and-a-half-year period.

3. The level of rape victimization reported by males is extremely low in the NCS and NCVS. The inclusion of rape victimization had essentially no effect on the disaggregated estimates provided here.

4. Due to unavailability of gun data in the 1978 and 1979 NCS files, we had to exclude these years from our series.

5. Prior to 2003, respondents designated their race by selecting one of the following categories: "white, black, American Indian/Aleut/Eskimo, Asian/Pacific Islander, or other." Beginning in 2003, respondents were permitted to select more than one race category, and the single race options included "white, black, American Indian/Alaska Native, Asian, and Hawaiian/Pacific Islander." Because the proportion choosing more than one race category in the 2003–2005 NCVS is small (approximately 1% of respondents), we restricted our analyses of those years to subjects who selected only one race category. Ethnicity questions also changed over time. Prior to 1986, multiple categories were available for the ethnicity item, including "German, Italian, Irish, French, Polish, Russian, English, Scottish, Welsh, Mexican-American, Puerto-Rican, Cuban, Central or South American, Other Spanish, Afro-American, and Another Group Not Listed." Beginning in 1986, the ethnicity categories were defined as "Hispanic" and "non-Hispanic." To create a consistent definition of "Hispanic" or "Latina/Latino" ethnicity over time, persons who selected "Mexican-American, Puerto-Rican, Cuban, Central or South American, or Other Spanish" were coded as "Hispanic" or "Latina/ Latino." An assessment of population estimates throughout the definitional

change period showed that the 1985 estimate of the Latino/Latina population was slightly lower than the 1986 estimate based on the "Hispanic" versus the "non-Hispanic" option—a finding consistent with population trends.

6. We found that no adjustments beyond those for type of crime were necessary (see Lauritsen and Heimer, 2010). For rates of serious violent victimization, we weighted NCS incidents of aggravated assault by 1.23 and rape by 2.57 (see Rand, Lynch, and Cantor, 1997). We found no need to adjust the NCS gun violence rates because the redesigned questionnaire did not result in increased reporting of these types of incidents.

7. For 1973–1979, we used the SHR data made available through ICPSR (study no. 4351, "Uniform Crime Reports [United States]: Supplementary Homicide Reports 1976–2003"). We generated the rest of the series using Easy Access to the FBI's Supplementary Homicide Reports: 1980–2006. For more information, see http://www.ojjdp.ncjrs.gov/ojstatbb/ezashr/.

8. SHR trends are correlated with the WISQARS estimates at .99 for the years that both series have in common (1981–2005).

9. A complete discussion of the ICS is found in Curtin (2004) and Rosenfeld and Fornango (2007). Rosenfeld and Fornango find that consumer sentiment accounted for a significant amount of the change in robbery and property crime independent of the effects of unemployment, GDP, age and race composition, and police and imprisonment. The ICS data are available at http://www.sca.isr.umich.edu.

10. The ICS data can be obtained to allow for "black" versus "nonblack" comparisons. Our analyses of the relationships between the black and nonblack ICS trends and the various race- and ethnic-subgroup violence trends showed that the black and nonblack ICS trends did not have a stronger relationship to subgroup trends in violence compared to the aggregate ICS measure.

11. We compared first-difference correlations for each of the trends and selected the economic indicator that produced the largest and most consistent set of associations with the violence trends.

12. The National Bureau of Economic Research (NBER) defines recessions as those periods in which there is a significant decline in economic activity across a variety of indicators including GDP, income, employment, industrial production, and retail sales (NBER, 2003). Recession periods begin when significant decreases in these indicators become evident and end when significant increases resume. Since 1973, the NBER has designated six periods as recessions: November 1973 to March 1975, January 1980 to July 1980, July 1981 to November 1982, July 1990 to March 1991, March 2001 to November 2001, and the most recent recession, which began in December 2007 (NBER, 2010).

13. This may appear odd because the patterns of gun violence and homicide are so similar. We find that for gun violence, the relationship is statistically significant ($r = .42$ for 1973–2000, and $r = .45$ for 1973–2005) if ICS at T–1, rather than T, is used.

REFERENCES

Arvanites, Thomas M., and Robert H. Defina. 2006. Business cycles and street crime. *Criminology* 44:139–164.

Blumstein, Alfred, and Richard Rosenfeld. 1998. Explaining recent trends in U.S. homicide rates. *Journal of Criminal Law and Criminology* 88:1175–1216.

Blumstein, Alfred, and Joel Wallman, eds. 2006. *The crime drop in America*. New York: Cambridge University Press.

Bureau of Justice Statistics. 2005. *Statistical methodology for criminal victimization in the U.S., 2005*. Available at http://bjs.ojp.usdoj.gov/content/pub/pdf/cvus/cvus05mt.pdf.

Bureau of Labor Statistics. n.d. *Employment status of the civilian noninstitutional population, 1940 to date*. LNS1400003, LNS1400006, LNS1400009, and LNS14024887. Available at http://www.bls.gov/cps.

Census Bureau. 2012a. *Poverty status of people by age, race, and Hispanic origin: 1959–2011 (Table 3)*. Available at http://www.census.gov/hhes/www/poverty/data/historical/people.html.

Census Bureau. 2012b. *Poverty status of people by family relationship, race, and Hispanic origin: 1959–2011 (Table 2)*. Available at http://www.census.gov/hhes/www/poverty/data/historical/people.html.

Conference Board. 2009. *The Conference Board Leading Economic Index (LEI) for the United States*. Available at http://www.conference-board.org/pdf_free/economics/bci/USLEItech_1209.pdf.

Cook, Philip J., and John H. Laub. 2002. After the epidemic: Recent trends in youth violence in the United States. In Michael Tonry (ed.), *Crime and justice*, vol. 28, *A review of research*. Chicago: University of Chicago Press.

Curtin, Richard. 2004. Psychology and macroeconomics. In James House, Thomas Juster, Robert Kahn, Howard Schuman, and Eleanor Singer (eds.), *A telescope on society: Survey research at the University of Michigan and beyond*. Ann Arbor: University of Michigan Press.

Groves, Robert M., and Daniel L. Cork. 2008. *Surveying victims: Options for conducting the National Crime Victimization Survey*. Washington, DC: National Academies Press.

Heimer, Karen, and Janet L. Lauritsen. 2008. Gender and violence in the United States: Trends in offending and victimization. In Arthur Goldberger and Richard Rosenfeld (eds.), *Understanding crime trends: Workshop report*, Committee on Understanding Crime Trends, Committee on Law and Justice, National Research Council, 45–80. Washington DC: National Academies Press.

Krivo, Lauren J., Ruth D. Peterson, and Danielle C. Payne. 2009. Segregation, racial structure, and neighborhood crime. *American Journal of Sociology* 114:1765–1802.

Land, Kenneth C., Patricia L. McCall, and Lawrence E. Cohen. 1990. Structural covariates of homicide rates: Are there any invariances across time and social space? *American Journal of Sociology* 95:922–963.

Land, Kenneth C., Patricia L. McCall, and Lawrence E. Cohen. 1991. Characteristics of U.S. cities with extreme (high or low) crime rates: Results of discriminant analyses of 1960, 1970, and 1980 data. *Social Indicators Research* 24:209–231.

Lauritsen, Janet L., and Karen Heimer. 2008. Gender and violent victimization, 1973–2004. *Journal of Quantitative Criminology* 24:125–147.

Lauritsen, Janet L., and Karen Heimer. 2010. Violent victimization among males and economic conditions: The vulnerability of race and ethnic minorities. *Criminology & Public Policy* 9:665–692.

Lynch, James P., and Lynn A. Addington, eds. 2007. *Understanding crime statistics: Revisiting the divergence of the NCVS and UCR.* New York: Cambridge University Press.

Messner, Steven F., Lawrence E. Raffalovich, and Richard McMillan. 2001. Economic deprivation and changes in homicide arrest rates for white and black youths, 1967–1998: A national time-series analysis. *Criminology* 39:591–614.

National Bureau of Economic Research. 2003. *The NBER's recession dating procedure, 2003.* Available at http://www.nber.org/cycles/recessions.html.

National Bureau of Economic Research. 2010. *Business cycle expansions and contractions.* Available at http://www.nber.org/cycles.html.

Penick, Betty K. E., and Maurice Owens, eds. 1976. *Surveying crime.* Washington, DC: National Academy Press.

Pratt, Travis C., and Francis T. Cullen. 2005. Assessing macro-level predictors and theories of crime: A meta-analysis. In Michael Tonry (ed.), *Crime and justice,* vol. 32, *A review of research.* Chicago: University of Chicago Press.

Rand, Michael R. 2008. *Criminal victimization, 2007.* Washington, DC: U.S. Department of Justice.

Rand, Michael R., James P. Lynch, and David Cantor. 1997. *Criminal victimization, 1973–1995.* Washington, DC: U.S. Department of Justice.

Raphael, Stephen, and Rudolf Winter-Ebmer. 2001. Identifying the effects of unemployment on crime. *Journal of Law and Economics* 44:259–283.

Rennison, Callie Marie, and Michael R. Rand. 2007. Introduction to the National Crime Victimization Survey. In James P. Lynch and Lynn A. Addington (eds.), *Understanding crime statistics: Revisiting the divergence of the NCVS and UCR.* New York: Cambridge University Press.

Rosenfeld, Richard. 2009. Crime is the problem: Homicide, acquisitive crime, and economic conditions. *Journal of Quantitative Criminology* 25:287–306.

Rosenfeld, Richard, and Robert Fornango. 2007. The impact of economic conditions on robbery and property crime: The role of consumer sentiment. *Criminology* 45:735–769.

Sampson, Robert, Stephen Raudenbush, and Felton Earls. 1997. Neighborhoods and violent crime: A multilevel study of collective efficacy. *Science* 277:918–924.

PART II

The Neighborhood Context

5

The Nonlinear Effect of Neighborhood Disadvantage on
Youth Violence

Neighborhood Effects on Youth Violence

XIANGMING FANG, RICHARD ROSENFELD, LINDA L. DAHLBERG,
AND CURTIS S. FLORENCE

Introduction

Youth violence is a serious public health problem that affects young people, their families, and communities across the United States. Homicide
is the second leading cause of death for young people between the ages
of 10 and 24 in the United States (CDC 2009).[1] In 2007, 5,764 young
people in this age group were victims of homicide, and more than
668,000 cases of violence-related injuries in young people aged 10 to
24 were treated in U.S. emergency departments (CDC 2009). In addition to causing injury and death, youth violence affects communities by
increasing health care expenditure, reducing productivity, decreasing
property values, and disrupting social services (Mercy et al. 2000).

One of the main emphases in contemporary youth violence research
is the influence of neighborhood/community disadvantage on fatal and

nonfatal violence involving young people. (e.g., Peeples and Loeber 1994; Elliot et al. 1996; Simons et al. 1996; Lauritsen 2001; De Coster, Heimer, and Wittrock 2006; Haynie, Silver, and Teasdale 2006). Previous research has proposed a variety of mechanisms through which neighborhood disadvantage may influence violent behavior. For example, social learning theory (Bandura 1977; Feshbach 1980) suggests that for youth living in disadvantaged neighborhoods, repeated exposure to violent attitudes and behaviors of adults and peers living in the same neighborhood may teach youth that violence and aggression are normal, acceptable responses, thereby increasing youths' potential to act aggressively. In addition, researchers often underscore the importance of formal and informal social controls as the mechanisms that mediate the effect of neighborhood disadvantage on youth violence. Social disorganization theory (Shaw and McKay 1942; Kornhauser 1978) hypothesizes that neighborhood structural characteristics, such as poverty, residential mobility, and ethnic heterogeneity, disrupt neighborhood- and family-level social controls, which in turn increases the risk of interpersonal violence among youth. Community social capital and collective efficacy have been emphasized as key intervening mechanisms (e.g., Bursik and Grasmick 1993; Sampson and Wilson 1995; Sampson, Raudenbush, and Earls 1997; Bellair 1997, 2000). According to this model, residents living in disadvantaged neighborhoods are less able to generate social trust and to enforce shared community values. Adults may be reluctant to supervise youth within the neighborhood, to socialize them with respect to conventional values, and to prevent them from becoming involved in violent activities. Another theoretical argument is that living in disadvantaged communities increases the chances youth will become involved in violent behavior by exposing them to a criminogenic street context (Anderson 1999; De Coster, Heimer, and Wittrock 2006).

Despite the growing number of studies documenting the impact of community disadvantage on youth violence, some researchers have argued that neighborhood effects could be simply an artifact of individual-level compositional effects or self-selection by families into particular neighborhoods (Duncan and Aber 1997; Manski 2000; Dietz 2002). Adjusting for compositional effects or self-selection bias is one of the most difficult tasks in contextual effects research. One way to address this problem is to control for individual- and family-level factors that may contribute to compositional differences among families and individuals within neighborhoods (e.g., race/ethnicity, family structure, social stratification) or are related to movement into or out of neighborhoods with differing characteristics. Obviously families are not randomly assigned to neighborhoods but make choices about where to live on the basis of factors such as education, economic status, and perceived characteristics of the neighborhood, or they confront barriers to moving to particular neighborhoods, especially on the basis of race/ethnicity or income (Massey et al. 1994; Elliott et al. 1996; South and Crowder 1997; Oakes and Rossi 2003; De Coster, Heimer, and Wittrock 2006). However, Sampson, Morenoff, and Gannon-Rowley (2002) warn that researchers should be careful not to overcontrol for factors that might mediate the link between neighborhood and youth behavior; otherwise, neighborhood effects could be underestimated.

Another complexity in examining the impact of community disadvantage on youth violence is the possibility of a nonlinear relationship between measures of disadvantage and violence (i.e., neighborhood effects on violence may not be the same across the entire range of neighborhood conditions). Researchers have pointed out that a high risk of social problems, including violence, appears only in the most disadvantaged communities (Crane 1991; Lauritsen 2003). Winslow and Shaw (2007) examined the impact of neighborhood disadvantage on early child behavior problems in a low-income, urban sample of 281 African American and European American boys and found the impact was nonlinear, reflecting a "threshold effect." A steep and significant slope was detected only for children living in underclass neighborhoods. Their findings suggest that a threshold of disadvantage has to be surpassed in order for neighborhood disadvantage to have a significant impact on child behavior problems. The results also imply that studies that use continuous measures of neighborhood disadvantage may underestimate neighborhood effects.

This study addresses the question of whether the effects of community disadvantage on youth violence are nonlinear. Using a nationally representative school-based sample of U.S. adolescents, we seek to establish whether neighborhood disadvantage is associated with violent behavior by youth, net of compositional and selection effects. Following the World Health Organization, violence is defined as the "intentional use of physical force or power, threatened or actual, against oneself, another person, or against a group or community, which either results in or has a high likelihood of resulting in injury, death, psychological harm, maldevelopment, or deprivation."[2] It includes such behaviors as physical fighting, serious assault, and the use of weapons to threaten or harm another person. We then address the question of whether any observed association with community disadvantage is linear or non-linear. The results may have important implications for both theory and public policy. Theories that direct attention to the impact of disadvantage on youth violence can be sharpened with more precise knowledge of how the prevalence of differing types of violent behavior varies across levels of community disadvantage. Of special interest is whether a threshold of disadvantage must be reached before violence is elevated. Lauritsen (2003) found such an effect for a nationally representative adolescent sample using tract-level data from the area-identified National Crime Victimization Survey. It is just as important to know whether community disadvantage has a "ceiling effect" on violence such that, after reaching a certain level, disadvantage no longer is associated with increased violence. Such knowledge, in turn, can help to improve the efficiency and effectiveness of targeting interventions and resources to those communities most in need of assistance. The current research builds on Lauritsen's (2003) important study by including multiple measures of violent behavior and additional controls for compositional and selection effects.

Data

Data for this study come from the National Longitudinal Study of Adolescent Health (Add Health), a longitudinal study following a nationally representative school-based probability sample of adolescents in grades 7 through 12 in the 1994–1995 school year. Systematic sampling methods and implicit stratification are used to ensure that the 80 high schools and 52 middle schools selected are representative of U.S. schools with respect to region of country, urbanicity, school size, school type, and ethnicity (Chantala and Tabor 1999; Udry 2003). In Wave I of the survey, used in the current study, 20,745 youths completed the in-home survey, which includes questions on self-reported vio-lent behavior. Of these, 18,924 have a sampling weight. When the sam-pling weights are incorporated into analyses, the results are considered nationally representative of students between the ages of 11 and 21 years (Chantala and Tabor 1999; Udry 2003). An additional 367 respondents are excluded because they are missing information on outcome vari-ables or main independent variables, resulting in a final study sample of 18,557 participants.

Add Health is particularly well suited for this study, due to several desirable features of the data. First, it includes data on individual- and family-level sociodemographic characteristics, census-based measures of neighborhood (tract-level) characteristics, and adolescents' self-reported involvement in violent behavior. The contextual-level data allow us to link individual violent behavior with a measure of neighbor-hood disadvantage and to examine the net effect of neighborhood dis-advantage on youth violence after adjusting for individual- and family-level sociodemographic factors. Drawing on a nationally representative sample of adolescents allows us to investigate the impact of neighbor-hood disadvantage on youth violence across a variety of neighbor-hood contexts and therefore affords greater generalizability of the study results. The sample of 18,557 adolescents is nested within 2,326 census tracts in 252 counties.

Measures

Dependent Variables

Our dependent variables, self-reported involvement in violent behav-iors, are taken from the Wave I in-home survey. We focus first on a dichotomous (yes/no) measure of general youth violence. Participants are categorized as engaging in violent behavior if they reported commit-ting *any* of the following offenses during the past 12 months: (1) engaged in a serious physical fight; (2) hurt someone badly enough to need ban-dages or care from a doctor or nurse; (3) took part in a group fight; (4) used or threatened to use a weapon to get something from someone; (5) pulled a knife or gun on someone; (6) shot or stabbed someone; (7) ever used a weapon in a fight. We then analyze two subcategories of the general violence measure: fighting and weapon-related violence. Adolescents are coded as engaging in fighting if they reported involvement in any of the first three acts of violence in the general violence measure during the past 12 months and as engaging in weapon-related violence if they reported any of the last four acts of violence.

To assess the robustness of our findings based on the dichotomous measures of youth violence, we repeated our analyses using variability indexes. For violent behavior in general, we first created a 0, 1 variable for each of the seven items, with 1 corresponding to engaging in that specific form of violent behavior at least once during the past 12 months and 0 corresponding to no involvement in the behavior during the past 12 months. We then summed across the seven forms of violent behavior to produce a violent behavior index (ranging from 0 to 7). The fighting index (ranging from 0 to 3) and weapon-related index (ranging from 0 to 4) were constructed similarly to the violent behavior index.

Neighborhood Characteristics

A longstanding debate in the multilevel literature concerns the boundary of neighborhood. While census tracts have been used extensively in multilevel analyses of neighborhoods (Krivo and Peterson 1996; Crutchfield, Glusker, and Bridges 1999; Peterson, Krivo, and Harris 2000; Lauritsen 2001; De Coster, Heimer, and Wittrock 2006), others have used the smaller units of census block groups (Caughy, O'Campo, and Patterson 2001; Diez-Roux et al. 2001). Studies of appropriate geographic units of analysis for neighborhoods have suggested that the use of census tract measures as a proxy for neighborhood does not produce substantially different results than the use of block-group data (Miethe and McDowall 1993; Gephart 1997; but see Hipp 2007). The present study uses 1990 census tracts to define respondents' neighborhoods and extracts tract-level information from census data to measure the neighborhood characteristics associated with the adolescent's residence in 1995, when Wave I in-home interviews were conducted.

Following previous research, we conducted principal-components analyses of many of the same census tract measures used in prior studies to identify the structural dimensions of U.S. census tracts. Similar to previous factor analyses of tract-level measures (Sampson et al. 1997;

Lauritsen 2001), three dimensions were found to describe the socio-demographic structure of U.S. census tracts: socioeconomic disadvantage, immigrant concentration, and residential stability.[3] The socioeconomic disadvantage index is a standardized and weighted index combining five variables which load highly on the disadvantage dimension (factor loadings are in parentheses): the proportion of nonelderly with income below the poverty line (0.89), the proportion of family households receiving public assistance income (0.89), the unemployment rate (.83), the proportion of family households that are female headed with children under 18 years of age (.79), and the proportion of the population aged 25+ without a high school diploma or equivalency (0.79).[4] Similarly, the residential stability index is a standardized and weighted index combining two variables: the proportion of individuals aged five or older who lived in the same house five years ago and the proportion of owner-occupied homes. The immigration concentration index is a standardized and weighted index combining the proportion of the tract population that is foreign born and the proportion that is of Hispanic origin. The residential stability and immigration concentration indexes are included in our analyses to control for other neighborhood attributes that may contribute to residual confounding bias when examining the impact of neighborhood socioeconomic disadvantage on violent behavior by youth.

Other Control Variables

To control for compositional effects, we include the following individual- and family-level characteristics in our models: adolescent's race/ethnicity, sex (1 = male, 0 = female), grade dummies (to capture cohort effects), whether the adolescent was foreign born (1 = foreign born, 0 = born in the United States), family structure, primary caregiver education, and the family's receipt of public assistance (1 = receipt of any public assistance, 0 = nonreceipt of public assistance). Respondents' self-identified race/ethnicity was grouped into six categories: White non-Hispanic, Black non-Hispanic, Hispanic, Native American non-Hispanic, Asian non-Hispanic, and other. We classified family structure into four categories: living with both biological parents, two-parent families in which one or both parents are stepparents, single-parent families, and no-parent families (in which neither parent of the adolescent lived in the household). The primary caregiver's (typically the mother's) education was divided into five categories: less than high school, high school graduate or equivalent, some college, college graduate, and postcollege. A considerable proportion of the data on primary caregiver education and family's receipt of public assistance was missing. Therefore, this study treated the missing data as a separate category for these two variables. To check the effect of the missing data on the results, we performed the statistical analysis with complete data only (i.e., limited to those who reported primary caregiver education and family's receipt of public assistance). The magnitude and significance of the coefficients obtained from the complete case analysis are similar to those obtained from analysis treating the missing data as a separate category. We also include controls for region, urbanicity (urban, suburban, or rural), school type (private or public), and school size (large: 1,001–4,000 students; medium: 401–1,000 students; and small: 1–400 students).

To further control for possible selection bias due to the fact that parents have some degree of choice regarding the neighborhoods in which the families live, we follow Haynie, Silver, and Teasdale (2006) and incorporate the primary caregiver's age (in years) and a measure of neighborhood selection. The primary caregiver's age may be related to neighborhood selection as well as the ability of caregivers to monitor adolescents. Parents may choose to reside in a particular neighborhood in part because of factors such as good schools, support from family or friends, and the level of crime. As in Haynie, Silver and Teasdale (2006), we created a dummy variable indicating parents' reasons for moving to their current neighborhood (gathered from the Wave I parent survey). This measure includes three responses: the availability of good schools, the proximity to family or friends, and low crime in the neighborhood. Adolescents whose parents indicated any of these reasons were coded as 1 on the selection variable and 0 otherwise. (See appendix A for a discussion of statistical methods and appendix B for all tables presenting results.)

Results

Table 5.1 presents descriptive statistics for the variables used in our analyses. After applying the sample weights, the distribution of the study sample by sex and race/ethnicity is very similar to that of the nation as a whole. About 43% of the sample reported participating in at least one of the seven acts of violent behavior during the past 12 months. Although about 41% of the sample reported engaging in fighting, only 10% reported engaging in weapon-related violence. The average age of participants in the study sample was 16 years old, 6.4% of the sample was foreign born, and 54% lived with two biological parents. In addition, there is considerable variation in the primary caregiver's education and the family's receipt of public assistance.

Logistic Regressions

Tables 5.2 and 5.3 present the relationship between neighborhood disadvantage and the dichotomous measure of general violence as blocks of covariates are added to the model sequentially. Model 1 in table 5.2 presents the relationships between the three contextual variables and general violence using the socioeconomic disadvantage index. Model 1 in table 5.3 presents the same relationships using the disadvantage quintile dummies, which allows for inspection of nonlinear effects. The linear relationship between the neighborhood disadvantage index and general violent behavior is positive and statistically significant in the specification shown in Model 1 of table 5.2. The results for the disadvantage dummy variables in Model 1 of table 5.3 indicate no significant relationship between general violence and less disadvantaged neighborhoods (second from the bottom quintile), when contrasted with the least disadvantaged areas (the bottom quintile). The coefficients for the remaining disadvantage dummy variables increase are positive, are significant, and increase in magnitude as the level of disadvantage increases. In both models, residential stability is negatively and significantly associated with general violence, and immigrant concentration has no significant relationship with general violence.

Model 2 of tables 5.2 and 5.3 adds region, urbanicity, school type, and school size to the neighborhood context measures. With the exception

of rural location in table 5.2, these variables are not significantly associated with general violence, and their addition to the models does not
substantially alter the effects of socioeconomic disadvantage and residential instability.

Model 3 adds individual characteristics. Males, racial/ethnic-minor-
ity youth (Black, Hispanic, and Native American), junior high students
(grades 7–9), and U.S.-born adolescents have higher involvement in
violent behavior compared to females, white youth, senior high students
(grades 10–12), and foreign-born adolescents. Although the linear relationship between disadvantage and general violence remains significant
(at $p < .05$), the inclusion of the individual characteristics results in a
39% decrease in the effect of the socioeconomic disadvantage index on
violent behavior (see Model 3 in table 5.2). By comparison, Model 3 of
table 5.3 shows generally small decreases in the magnitude of the coefficients on the disadvantage dummy variables, except for the coefficient
on the middle quintile, which is slightly larger than in Model 2. Adding
the individual characteristics induces small reductions in the effect of
residential instability on general violence.

Model 4 adds family characteristics. The family's receipt of public
assistance, lower parental education, and the youth's not living with
both biological parents are significantly associated with a higher risk for
engaging in violent behavior. After adding the family characteristics, the
significant linear relationship between neighborhood disadvantage and
youths' violent behavior disappears (see Model 4 in table 5.2). Model 4
in table 5.3 clearly indicates that the relationship is nonlinear. There is
little difference in risk for engaging in violent behavior for adolescents
living in the most disadvantaged areas compared to those living in the
next level of disadvantage (the fifth and fourth quintiles, respectively),
controlling for individual- and family-level factors. No difference in
violent behavior exists between the least disadvantaged and the less disadvantaged quintiles (the first and second quintiles, respectively). However, the effect of disadvantage on general violence increases markedly
from the second to the middle quintile of disadvantage. The negative
and significant relationship between residential stability and general
violence persists in Model 4.

In results not shown, we added the primary caregiver's age and the
neighborhood selection measure to Model 4 in tables 5.2 and 5.3.[5] Nei-

ther measure is significantly associated with adolescent reports of general violent behavior net of other individual- and family-level factors. Adding these two variables has little impact on the other results. The effect of neighborhood residential stability persists after the inclusion of the primary caregiver's age and the selection measure.

Tables 5.4 through 5.7 present the results for the dichotomous measures of fighting and weapon-related violence. These tables are formatted identically to tables 5.2 and 5.3, with covariates entered sequentially in blocks. The results for the fighting and weapon-related violence measures are, with few exceptions, similar to those obtained for general violence. Two differences are the nonsignificant effects of residential stability and the middle quintile of neighborhood disadvantage on weapon-related violence when the school, individual, and family covariates are added (see tables 5.6 and 5.7). Nonetheless, although the pattern of disadvantage effects on weapon-related violence differs somewhat from those found for general violence and fighting, we observe a nonlinear relationship between neighborhood disadvantage and weapon-related violence.

Spline Regressions

Spline regression offers another way to assess the nonlinear relationship between neighborhood disadvantage and violent behavior. Spline regression essentially partitions the relationship into meaningful and discrete linear segments. In other words, spline regression estimates different linear relationships between neighborhood disadvantage and violent behavior for different ranges of neighborhood disadvantage. Based on the logistic regression results presented in tables 5.2–5.7, we created three piecewise linear functions (the "splines") of neighborhood disadvantage using the two "knots" of the 40th percentile and 60th percentile on the disadvantage index. The results of the spline regressions, which are conditioned on all of the individual, family, and neighborhood control variables, are presented in table 5.8. We also graphically depict one of the regression results (general violence) to illustrate the nonlinear relationship (see figure 5.1).

For all three of the outcome measures, we find a significant effect (at $p < 0.01$) of area disadvantage on violent behavior only for adolescents

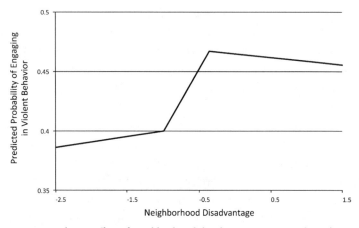

Fig. 5.1. Nonlinear effect of neighborhood disadvantage on general youth violence

in the middle quintile of the distribution of disadvantage. The effect of disadvantage is nonsignificant and negligible for those who live in the least to less disadvantaged areas (the bottom 40%) and for those in the more disadvantaged to most disadvantaged areas (the top 40%). These results suggest both a threshold and ceiling effect in the relationship between violent behavior and area disadvantage. As shown in figure 5.1, the predicted probability of general violent behavior increases by about 18% $(((.47 - .40) / .40) \times 100)$ for adolescents in the middle quintile of the disadvantage distribution compared with those in the bottom 40%. No further notable changes in the probability of general violence occur for adolescents in the top 40%. It appears, then, that a threshold of neighborhood disadvantage must be reached before disadvantage produces a marked increase in violent behavior. Beyond this threshold, additional increases in disadvantage are not associated with more youth violence.

Supplementary Analyses

To assess the robustness of our findings, specifically whether they are sensitive to the use of dichotomous measures of violent behavior, we repeated the analyses reported earlier using the three variability indexes of violence as outcomes, described earlier. These analyses were performed using negative binomial regressions due to the pronounced skew of the index measures. The results are substantively similar to those obtained using the dichotomous outcome measures and clearly indicate the same pattern of nonlinear relationship between neighborhood disadvantage and violent behavior. We report the results of the negative binomial regressions predicting violent behavior using the piecewise linear functions of neighborhood disadvantage in table 5.9.

Previous multilevel studies of community disadvantage and adverse individual outcomes, including violent behavior, have included interaction terms to determine whether the effect of disadvantage is conditioned by individual and family factors such as race and family structure. Significant cross-level interactions are often detected (e.g., Lauritsen 2003). We followed suit and tested for interaction effects on violent behavior of neighborhood disadvantage and adolescent race/ethnicity, family structure, and the family's receipt of public assistance. When the three interaction terms were entered in our models containing the continuous index measure of disadvantage (Model 4 in tables 5.2, 5.4, and 5.6), we found significant effects for the interaction between disadvantage and race/ethnicity and for the interaction between disadvantage and family structure for all three of the outcome measures but no significant effects for the interaction between disadvantage and receipt of public assistance. The significant results suggest that the relationship between disadvantage and violent behavior by youth is especially pronounced for whites and those living with both biological parents. However, in the piecewise linear spline regression models that account for nonlinear relationships between disadvantage and violent behavior by youth, the interaction terms for disadvantage and race/ethnicity and disadvantage and family structure are no longer significant. This finding suggests that some of the interaction effects previously detected may have resulted from treating the relationship between community disadvantage and adverse individual behaviors as if it were linear.

Discussion

Youth violence is a major public health problem in the United States and has been an important focus of research by public health researchers, sociologists, and criminologists. In recent years, researchers have turned their attention to the impact of community characteristics, especially community socioeconomic disadvantage, on youth violence. Several studies have found that youth violence and other problem behaviors are elevated in more disadvantaged communities, even when individual and family characteristics are controlled. Two challenges have been raised with respect to this line of research: failure to account for the effects of family self-selection into neighborhoods and failure to model the possible nonlinear effects of community disadvantage. The current study primarily addresses the second challenge, although we also attempt to account for some aspects of the selection problem.

Using a nationally representative school-based sample of U.S. adolescents, we estimated the impact of area socioeconomic disadvantage on a general measure of violent behavior, a measure of fighting, and a measure of weapon-related violence. Our models control for the effects of immigration to the community and community residential stability, school characteristics, family characteristics, and individual attributes, including year in school, sex, race/ethnicity, and whether the adolescent was foreign born. Net of the controls, we find strong and consistent evidence that the relationship between community disadvantage and violent behavior is nonlinear. Specifically, the results indicate the presence of both threshold and ceiling effects in the relationship between community disadvantage and individual violent behavior. The prevalence of adolescent violent behavior does not vary markedly for youth living in the least disadvantaged areas compared with those living in areas with somewhat higher levels of disadvantage. Together, these areas encompass about 40% of our sample of adolescents. Similarly, we find little difference in the prevalence of violence between youth living in the most disadvantaged areas and those in the next most disadvantaged areas, which together also encompass 40% of the sample. We did, however, find a significant and sizeable elevation in violent behavior among the remaining 20% of the adolescents in the sample who live in areas characterized by midlevels of disadvantage. These results are consistent across all three types of violence under investigation, withstand controls for compositional and neighborhood selection factors, and are robust to differing methods of modeling nonlinear effects and measuring the prevalence of violent behavior. Finally, a supplementary analysis suggests that the cross-level interactions between community disadvantage and individual and family characteristics found in prior research may be an artifact of assuming a linear relationship between disadvantage and violence and other adverse behaviors.

Our finding of a "step-up" or threshold effect of community disadvantage on violent behavior is consistent with the results of Winslow and Shaw's (2007) study of the effect of neighborhood disadvantage on boys' risk for early overt behavior problems and Lauritsen's (2003) study of adolescent violence. However, the detection of a ceiling effect in the current study differs from their results. For example, Lauritsen found a significant elevation in violence only for the 10% of adolescents living in the most disadvantaged areas. There are a number of possible reasons for the divergence in results, including the use of different methods of analysis and sets of covariates. The most important difference may be sample design. Lauritsen's study is based on a household sample, whereas the current research uses a school-based sample. Although both are national probability samples, school samples are likely to underrepresent the most violent youth because they have dropped out of school or attend irregularly. Assuming that many of these adolescents reside in highly disadvantaged neighborhoods, their underrepresentation could attenuate the relationship between violence and community disadvantage in the upper tail of the disadvantage distribution and thereby account, at least in part, for the ceiling effect we find. This is an important area for future investigation.

The underrepresentation of the most violent youth from school-based samples is part of the larger selection problem that has bedeviled cross-sectional multilevel research and even field experiments that have sought to randomly relocate families from high-poverty to low-poverty neighborhoods (see Sampson 2008). Families are not randomly assigned to neighborhoods but rather select neighborhoods based on a number of factors, including their income and what they can afford, the quality of schools, proximity to employment and other amenities, and proximity to family and friends. Although we controlled for several individual and family factors that may be related to the selection of neighborhoods, including a measure of the caregiver's reasons for choosing the neighborhood in which the family lives, other unmeasured family characteristics such as substance abuse and mental health, parenting behavior and support, and family functioning may be associated with neighborhood selection and also affect adolescents' violent behavior. We cannot rule out the possibility that selection bias related to unmeasured (or unmeasurable) factors could have affected our results.

Another limitation of the current research is the omission of other neighborhood characteristics that may be important but for which data were not available, such as collective efficacy and informal street norms, which prior research has shown to mediate the relationship between community disadvantage and violence (Sampson et al. 1997; Anderson 1999). Furthermore, the outcome measures used in the study are based on adolescents' self-reported involvement in violence and thus are subject to the possible biases and limitations inherent to this form of measurement, such as recall bias, social desirability, and reporting bias. These limitations suggest that our results should be replicated in research designs that (1) employ alternative methods and data to control for measurement bias and sample-selection bias, (2) provide extensive follow-ups of underrepresented subgroups, and (3) incorporate measures of key mediating factors in the relationship between community characteristics and individual outcomes. Future research should also continue to evaluate the nonlinear effects of community disadvantage on youth violence, especially when the results are used to design or evaluate the effectiveness of community-level prevention policies and programs on rates of youth violence.

If our results regarding the nonlinear effect of community disadvantage on youth violence are confirmed in future research, they can inform various housing programs, such as the U.S. Section 8 Housing Voucher Program, that enable families from highly distressed neighborhoods to relocate to more stable, less impoverished—and safer—communities (Katz, Kling, and Liebman 2001; Ludwig, Duncan, and Hirschfield 2001; Ludwig et al. 2008). A key question in such programs and the field experiments evaluating their impact concerns the nature of the new communities in which families are settled. Some research suggests that families participating in such programs typically move to communities with similar levels or similar pockets of disadvantage (Katz et al. 2001; Sampson 2008). Few families move to more prosperous communities with different structural and social characteristics.

This is not surprising given that local laws, public transportation issues, zoning restrictions, landlord preferences, and voucher program requirements themselves typically skew available options for families in these disadvantaged areas (Malpezzi 1996; Turner, Popkin, and Cunningham 2000; Turner et al. 2002). In addition, the strength of existing social ties to friends and families should not be underestimated in calculating the distances families will move to take advantage of better housing and opportunities. However, even if families moved to slightly better-off neighborhoods, the results of our study suggest a "step-up" in violent behavior in areas considered to be in the midrange of disadvantage, as illustrated in figure 5.1. Without knowing the characteristics of these communities, it is conceivable that these are largely transitional communities—either making the transition to more middle-class stability or slowly declining and showing signs of stress. These may be neighborhoods that are not poor or crime ridden enough to receive much in the way of state or federal funding but also are not stable enough to support their own initiatives, as is the case in more prosperous neighborhoods. The transitional nature and potential lack of cohesion in these types of communities also may make them less responsive to community members' needs and preferences. While our results suggest that moving from the midrange of disadvantage to more stable and prosperous neighborhoods may have a preventive effect on violent behavior, the mechanisms underlying such an effect constitute an important question for future research.

In terms of policy and program implications, there are at least three factors to consider. First, as evident in recent examinations of the impact of housing voucher programs, simply providing opportunities to move to better-off neighborhoods does not mean families will necessarily do so or that they will necessarily experience a range of positive outcomes as a result. Effort must also be made to address the constellation and cumulative nature of risk that characterizes impoverished families wherever they might end up and that is ultimately tied to violent behavior among youth. Even within highly disadvantaged neighborhoods, there can be quite a bit of variability in the offending patterns of youth (Gorman-Smith et al. 1998). Youths on a developmental trajectory toward serious violent and delinquent behavior often live in family environments that have a multitude of problems, including disruption, family conflict, poor communication and problem solving, parental criminality, antisocial attitudes, and substance abuse and mental health problems—problems that are not necessarily going to dissipate in a new setting.

Second, as suggested by Sampson (2008) and others (Elliott et al. 1996; Morenoff, Sampson, and Raudenbush 2001; Sampson et al. 2002), community-level social processes and contextual conditions matter. One of the more positive developments from research uncovering the importance of social processes and contextual conditions in the etiology of violent and delinquent behavior is the need for community-level interventions to effect change at the neighborhood level. Community-level intervention refers to modifying the characteristics of settings that increase the risk for victimization or perpetration. This includes modifying the social, environmental, and economic characteristics of settings. Measures aimed at modifying the social organization of neighborhoods, improving the economic landscape, altering the physical environment, and providing places, spaces, and opportunities to build and strengthen social relationships have the potential to shift communities away from disadvantage toward more thriving, safer, and more connected communities. Rather than simply moving families far enough away to where they might experience different labor markets or other social benefits (e.g., better schools, more green space, recreation and developmental programs for youth, better child care, more voluntary and civic organizations, or more supportive networks), there is much that could be done to alter the characteristics of disadvantaged communities and ultimately to disrupt the developmental effects and durability of disadvantage over time. From a public policy perspective, community-level interventions may also be more cost effective than those targeted primarily at individuals or families. Unfortunately, this is an area where little has been tried and tested.

Finally, in the absence of eliminating all risk, there is much more to be done to identify and evaluate strategies aimed at moderating or buffering against risk (i.e., to address protective factors). Protective factors are those factors that interact with risk (U.S. Department of Health and Human Services 2001). Research to identify protective factors is not as far along as research on risk factors; however, it is a crucial step toward developing and testing strategies aimed at moderating or buffering against risk. It is quite possible to conceive of a mixture of factors that moderate risk for youths and families in communities of disadvantage, either in highly distressed communities or in the midrange of disadvantage. In terms of the broader community context or neighborhoods themselves, it is also quite possible to conceive of a mixture of factors that are protective. Identifying and addressing protective factors as well as the tipping points for individuals, families, and communities may go a long way toward preventing violence and creating healthier, safer, and thriving communities.

Appendix A: Statistical Analysis

Logistic regression was used to analyze the relationships between neighborhood disadvantage and violent behavior by youth for the three dichotomous measures of violence: general violence, fighting, and weapon-related violence. To examine the presence of nonlinear relationships between violent behavior and neighborhood disadvantage, we estimated two separate models for each measure of violent behavior. The first model includes the socioeconomic disadvantage index as a continuous measure. For the second model, we divided the sample into quintiles based on respondents' scores on the socioeconomic disadvantage index and included the quintile dummies as separate independent variables. The same control variables, entered in blocks, are included in each model. We used piecewise linear spline regression models to further examine possible threshold and ceiling effects of neighborhood disadvantage on violent behavior.

To assess the robustness of our findings, we repeated our analyses using the three disadvantage variability indexes as the outcome measures. Because the indexes are strongly skewed, discrete variables with variances much greater than the means, negative binomial regressions were used in these analyses. The analyses were performed using Stata SE version 9, which allows for the control of survey design effects of individuals clustered within schools and stratification by geographic region. Poststratification weights were applied to generate nationally representative estimates.

Appendix B: Tabular Results

Table 5.1. Descriptive Statistics for the Sample (Adjusted for Sampling Design)

Variable	%	95% CI	Variable	%	95% CI
YV outcomes (dichotomous measures)			School size		
			Small (1–400 students)	17.6	11.0–24.1
General violence	42.8	40.9–44.8	Medium (401–1,000)	44.6	35.1–54.1
Fighting	41.3	39.4–43.2	Large (1,001–4,000)	37.8	28.0–47.6
Weapon related	10.1	9.1–11.1	School type		
Sex (male)	50.7	49.7–51.8	Public	93.3	89.4–97.2
Foreign-born	6.4	4.6–8.3	Private	6.7	2.8–10.6
Race/ethnicity			Region		
White	66.8	61.1–72.5	West	16.4	13.9–18.9
Hispanic	12.1	8.8–15.4	Midwest	31.5	27.0–36.0
Black	15.8	11.7–19.9	South	38.3	35.1–41.6
Native	0.8	0.3–1.2	Northeast	13.8	12.2–15.5
Asian	3.6	2.1–5.1	Urbanicity		
Other	0.9	0.7–1.2	Urban	26.3	18.4–34.1
Family structure			Suburban	58.4	48.8–68.0
Two biological parents	53.7	51.2–56.2	Rural	15.3	7.3–23.4
Two parents with ≥ 1			Neighborhood selection	69.5	67.3–71.6
nonbiological	16.8	16.0–17.7			
Single parent	27.5	25.2–29.8		**Mean**	**SD**
Other	2.0	1.5–2.4	Age	15.97	1.80
Parental education			Caregiver's age	41.3	7.2
< High school	14.0	11.7–16.3	YV variability indexes		
High school	28.6	26.6–30.7	YV in general	0.869	1.327
Some college	25.5	23.9–27.0	Fighting	0.703	0.982
College graduate	11.3	10.1–12.5	Weapon related	0.166	0.576
Above college	7.2	5.8–8.6	Neighborhood indexes		
Missing	13.5	11.9–15.0	(principal components)		
Parent receiving public assistance			Socioeconomic disadvantage	−0.001	1.959
Yes	21.7	19.1–24.4	Immigrant concentration	−0.002	1.369
No	66.1	63.4–68.8	Residential stability	0.001	1.214
Missing	12.1	10.7–13.6			

Note: YV = youth violence; CI = confidence interval; SD = standard deviation

Table 5.2. Logistic Regressions Predicting Youth Violence in General Using the Socioeconomic Disadvantage Index

Variables	Coefficient (Standard error)			
	Model 1	Model 2	Model 3[†]	Model 4[†]
Neighborhood context indexes				
Socioeconomic disadvantage	0.095*** (0.018)	0.090*** (0.018)	0.055** (0.017)	0.016 (0.017)
Immigrant concentration	−0.032 (0.024)	−0.040 (0.023)	−0.048 (0.031)	−0.043 (0.031)
Residential stability	−0.083*** (0.024)	−0.079** (0.025)	−0.068** (0.023)	−0.056* (0.022)
Region (reference category: West)				
Midwest		−0.081 (0.097)	0.004 (0.094)	0.018 (0.088)
South		−0.058 (0.089)	−0.059 (0.091)	−0.028 (0.091)
Northeast		0.047 (0.142)	0.102 (0.132)	0.077 (0.131)
Urbanicity (reference category: urban)				
Suburban		−0.071 (0.086)	−0.007 (0.088)	0.005 (0.081)
Rural		−0.194 (0.114)	−0.067 (0.106)	−0.083 (0.101)
Private school		−0.302 (0.178)	−0.220 (0.161)	−0.090 (0.149)
School size (reference category: small)				
Medium		−0.058 (0.120)	−0.015 (0.118)	0.003 (0.116)
Large		−0.191 (0.123)	0.029 (0.124)	0.057 (0.124)
Individual characteristics				
Sex (male)			0.879*** (0.041)	0.900*** (0.042)
Foreign-born			−0.436*** (0.072)	−0.429*** (0.072)
Race/ethnicity (reference category: white)				
Hispanic			0.538*** (0.101)	0.449*** (0.102)
Black			0.562*** (0.074)	0.488*** (0.071)
Native			0.732*** (0.205)	0.641** (0.205)
Asian			0.083 (0.109)	0.169 (0.111)
Other			−0.243 (0.248)	−0.299 (0.270)
Family characteristics				
Family structure (reference category: two biological parents)				
Two parents with ≥ 1 nonbiological parent				0.280*** (0.057)
Single parent				0.315*** (0.047)
Other				0.401* (0.171)
Primary caregiver education (reference category: < high school)				
High school				−0.101 (0.073)
Some college				−0.244** (0.078)
College graduate				−0.545*** (0.092)
Above college				−0.648*** (0.102)
Parent receiving public assistance				0.208*** (0.058)

[†] Regression results for grade dummies are omitted from the table.
* p < .05; ** p < .01; *** p < 0.001

Table 5.3. Logistic Regressions Predicting Youth Violence in General Using the Socioeconomic Disadvantage Quintiles

Variables	Coefficient (Standard error)			
	Model 1	Model 2	Model 3[†]	Model 4[†]
Neighborhood context				
Disadvantage quintiles				
Least (reference category)				
Less	0.068 (0.077)	0.039 (0.077)	0.071 (0.074)	0.015 (0.070)
Middle	0.267*** (0.074)	0.293*** (0.074)	0.308*** (0.074)	0.186** (0.070)
More	0.424*** (0.072)	0.430*** (0.080)	0.411*** (0.075)	0.249*** (0.074)
Most	0.602*** (0.095)	0.607*** (0.099)	0.473*** (0.095)	0.251** (0.097)
Immigrant concentration	−0.043 (0.025)	−0.057* (0.025)	−0.064 (0.034)	−0.057 (0.033)
Residential stability	−0.086*** (0.025)	−0.078** (0.025)	−0.064** (0.023)	−0.052* (0.023)
Region (reference category: West)				
Midwest		−0.104 (0.094)	−0.030 (0.089)	−0.015 (0.085)
South		−0.116 (0.088)	−0.127 (0.088)	−0.085 (0.088)
Northeast		0.061 (0.142)	0.102 (0.134)	0.075 (0.133)
Urbanicity (reference category: urban)				
Suburban		−0.071 (0.083)	−0.001 (0.085)	0.013 (0.080)
Rural		−0.233* (0.114)	−0.106 (0.121)	−0.105 (0.100)
Private school		−0.270 (0.178)	−0.166 (0.158)	−0.055 (0.147)
School size (reference category: small)				
Medium		−0.035 (0.124)	0.016 (0.121)	0.035 (0.120)
Large		−0.162 (0.130)	0.080 (0.131)	0.102 (0.133)
Individual characteristics				
Sex (male)			0.882*** (0.042)	0.901*** (0.042)
Foreign-born			−0.434*** (0.073)	−0.425*** (0.072)
Race/ethnicity (reference category: white)				
Hispanic			0.515*** (0.101)	0.434*** (0.102)
Black			0.537*** (0.081)	0.455*** (0.078)
Native			0.704*** (0.204)	0.614** (0.202)
Asian			0.066 (0.111)	0.152 (0.112)
Other			−0.278 (0.251)	−0.327 (0.273)
Family characteristics				
Family structure (reference category: two biological parents)				
Two parents with ≥ 1 nonbiological parent				0.271*** (0.058)
Single parent				0.303*** (0.047)
Other				0.375* (0.172)
Primary caregiver education (reference category: < high school)				
High school				−0.092 (0.074)
Some college				−0.222** (0.080)
College graduate				−0.511*** (0.093)
Above college				−0.607*** (0.104)
Parent receiving public assistance				0.189** (0.058)

[†] Regression results for grade dummies are omitted from the table.

* $p < .05$; ** $p < .01$; *** $p < 0.001$

Table 5.4. Logistic Regressions Predicting Fighting Using the Socioeconomic Disadvantage Index

	Coefficient (Standard error)			
Variables	Model 1	Model 2	Model 3[†]	Model 4[†]
Neighborhood context indexes				
Socioeconomic disadvantage	0.091*** (0.018)	0.085*** (0.018)	0.057** (0.018)	0.019 (0.017)
Immigrant concentration	−0.020 (0.025)	−0.023 (0.024)	−0.032 (0.031)	−0.028 (0.030)
Residential stability	−0.081*** (0.024)	−0.080** (0.024)	−0.068** (0.023)	−0.058** (0.022)
Region (reference category: West)				
Midwest		−0.060 (0.098)	0.018 (0.096)	0.032 (0.091)
South		−0.071 (0.090)	−0.070 (0.092)	−0.038 (0.093)
Northeast		0.059 (0.142)	0.111 (0.132)	0.087 (0.132)
Urbanicity (reference category: urban)				
Suburban		−0.061 (0.084)	0.006 (0.086)	0.018 (0.081)
Rural		−0.178 (0.112)	−0.052 (0.104)	−0.069 (0.101)
Private school		−0.314 (0.180)	−0.218 (0.168)	−0.093 (0.157)
School size (reference category: small)				
Medium		−0.066 (0.123)	−0.013 (0.121)	0.005 (0.120)
Large		−0.212 (0.126)	0.028 (0.131)	0.055 (0.131)
Individual characteristics				
Sex (male)			0.821*** (0.040)	0.839*** (0.041)
Foreign-born			−0.407*** (0.072)	−0.397*** (0.072)
Race/ethnicity (reference category: white)				
Hispanic			0.498*** (0.100)	0.413*** (0.102)
Black			0.484*** (0.073)	0.415*** (0.069)
Native			0.647** (0.221)	0.558* (0.217)
Asian			0.072 (0.113)	0.159 (0.114)
Other			−0.348 (0.259)	−0.397 (0.278)
Family characteristics				
Family structure (reference category: two biological parents)				
Two parents with ≥ 1 nonbiological parent				0.257*** (0.058)
Single parent				0.276*** (0.046)
Other				0.363* (0.178)
Primary caregiver education (reference category: < high school)				
High school				−0.088 (0.076)
Some college				−0.221** (0.079)
College graduate				−0.528*** (0.094)
Above college				−0.629*** (0.100)
Parent receiving public assistance				0.211*** (0.058)

[†] Regression results for grade dummies are omitted from the table.

* p < .05; ** p < .01; *** p < 0.001

Table 5.5. Logistic Regressions Predicting Fighting Using the Socioeconomic Disadvantage Quintiles

Variables	Coefficient (Standard error)			
	Model 1	Model 2	Model 3[†]	Model 4[†]
Neighborhood context				
Disadvantage quintiles				
Least (reference category)				
Less	0.056 (0.080)	0.023 (0.080)	0.056 (0.077)	0.002 (0.073)
Middle	0.257*** (0.075)	0.280*** (0.075)	0.296*** (0.076)	0.179* (0.073)
More	0.403*** (0.073)	0.411*** (0.080)	0.405*** (0.078)	0.248** (0.077)
Most	0.578*** (0.096)	0.577*** (0.099)	0.474*** (0.097)	0.262** (0.099)
Immigrant concentration	−0.031 (0.026)	−0.040 (0.025)	−0.048 (0.033)	−0.041 (0.032)
Residential stability	−0.084*** (0.025)	−0.079** (0.025)	−0.064** (0.023)	−0.053* (0.022)
Region (reference category: West)				
Midwest		−0.083 (0.096)	−0.014 (0.092)	0.000 (0.089)
South		−0.128 (0.089)	−0.137 (0.090)	−0.095 (0.091)
Northeast		0.074 (0.143)	0.113 (0.135)	0.087 (0.134)
Urbanicity (reference category: urban)				
Suburban		−0.059 (0.082)	0.012 (0.084)	0.026 (0.080)
Rural		−0.215 (0.111)	−0.089 (0.102)	−0.090 (0.100)
Private school		−0.283 (0.178)	−0.167 (0.164)	−0.060 (0.154)
School size (reference category: small)				
Medium		−0.041 (0.127)	0.019 (0.124)	0.038 (0.123)
Large		−0.184 (0.133)	0.078 (0.136)	0.099 (0.138)
Individual characteristics				
Sex (male)			0.823*** (0.040)	0.840*** (0.041)
Foreign-born			−0.405*** (0.073)	−0.394*** (0.072)
Race/ethnicity (reference category: white)				
Hispanic			0.475*** (0.100)	0.398*** (0.101)
Black			0.459*** (0.079)	0.384** (0.076)
Native			0.619** (0.214)	0.532* (0.213)
Asian			0.056 (0.115)	0.143 (0.116)
Other			−0.387 (0.260)	−0.428 (0.280)
Family characteristics				
Family structure (reference category: two biological parents)				
Two parents with ≥ 1 nonbiological parent				0.249*** (0.059)
Single parent				0.265*** (0.046)
Other				0.338 (0.180)
Primary caregiver education (reference category: < high school)				
High school				−0.079 (0.077)
Some college				−0.199* (0.081)
College graduate				−0.496*** (0.095)
Above college				−0.590*** (0.101)
Parent receiving public assistance				0.192** (0.059)

[†] Regression results for grade dummies are omitted from the table.

* $p < .05$; ** $p < .01$; *** $p < 0.001$

Table 5.6. Logistic Regressions Predicting Weapon-Related Youth violence Using the Socioeconomic Disadvantage Index

Variables	Coefficient (Standard error)			
	Model 1	Model 2	Model 3[†]	Model 4[†]
Neighborhood context indexes				
Socioeconomic disadvantage	0.114*** (0.018)	0.121*** (0.019)	0.054** (0.019)	0.023 (0.019)
Immigrant concentration	−0.063 (0.038)	−0.120** (0.041)	−0.107 (0.054)	−0.094 (0.053)
Residential stability	−0.094* (0.038)	−0.065 (0.041)	−0.059 (0.039)	−0.036 (0.038)
Region (reference category: West)				
Midwest		−0.119 (0.170)	0.012 (0.148)	0.039 (0.138)
South		0.040 (0.158)	0.051 (0.135)	0.104 (0.129)
Northeast		0.174 (0.178)	0.261 (0.150)	0.260 (0.146)
Urbanicity (reference category: urban)				
Suburban		−0.191 (0.110)	−0.157 (0.101)	−0.143 (0.096)
Rural		−0.322 (0.171)	−0.239 (0.149)	−0.232 (0.145)
Private school		−0.073 (0.187)	−0.093 (0.149)	0.018 (0.141)
School size (reference category: small)				
Medium		0.104 (0.135)	0.054 (0.120)	0.063 (0.118)
Large		0.167 (0.143)	0.129 (0.134)	0.138 (0.132)
Individual characteristics				
Sex (male)			1.126*** (0.082)	1.142*** (0.083)
Foreign-born			−0.727*** (0.156)	−0.715*** (0.153)
Race/ethnicity (reference category: white)				
Hispanic			0.667*** (0.134)	0.610*** (0.134)
Black			0.784*** (0.094)	0.639*** (0.094)
Native			1.186*** (0.284)	1.087*** (0.292)
Asian			0.225 (0.177)	0.311 (0.177)
Other			0.438 (0.344)	0.377 (0.344)
Family characteristics				
Family structure (reference category: two biological parents)				
Two parents with ≥ 1 nonbiological parent				0.403*** (0.083)
Single parent				0.521*** (0.083)
Other				0.985*** (0.206)
Primary caregiver education (reference category: < high school)				
High school				0.059 (0.113)
Some college				−0.088 (0.111)
College graduate				−0.136 (0.156)
Above college				−0.350 (0.180)
Parent receiving public assistance				0.203* (0.078)

[†] Regression results for grade dummies are omitted from the table.

* p < .05; ** p < .01; *** p < 0.001

Table 5.7. *Logistic Regressions Predicting Weapon–Related Youth violence Using the Socioeconomic Disadvantage Quintiles*

Variables	Coefficient (Standard error)			
	Model 1	Model 2	Model 3[†]	Model 4[†]
Neighborhood context				
Disadvantage quintiles				
Least (reference category)				
Less	0.022 (0.120)	0.032 (0.122)	0.035 (0.126)	−0.006 (0.126)
Middle	0.299* (0.133)	0.371** (0.125)	0.342** (0.125)	0.229 (0.123)
More	0.579*** (0.120)	0.652*** (0.126)	0.512*** (0.121)	0.378** (0.118)
Most	0.740*** (0.127)	0.876*** (0.133)	0.550*** (0.130)	0.358** (0.132)
Immigrant concentration	−0.082* (0.039)	−0.151** (0.044)	−0.131* (0.056)	−0.113* (0.053)
Residential stability	−0.100** (0.036)	−0.062 (0.039)	−0.053 (0.038)	−0.029 (0.038)
Region (reference category: West)				
Midwest		−0.156 (0.166)	−0.038 (0.144)	−0.009 (0.136)
South		−0.055 (0.157)	−0.039 (0.134)	0.022 (0.127)
Northeast		0.192 (0.173)	0.256 (0.147)	0.251 (0.145)
Urbanicity (reference category: urban)				
Suburban		−0.186 (0.105)	−0.140 (0.097)	−0.126 (0.094)
Rural		−0.370* (0.172)	−0.273 (0.154)	−0.250 (0.149)
Private school		−0.028 (0.190)	−0.020 (0.152)	0.071 (0.145)
School size (reference category: small)				
Medium		0.151 (0.135)	0.104 (0.117)	0.112 (0.117)
Large		0.226 (0.144)	0.205 (0.136)	0.207 (0.136)
Individual characteristics				
Sex (male)			1.127*** (0.082)	1.143*** (0.083)
Foreign-born			−0.723*** (0.155)	−0.706*** (0.152)
Race/ethnicity (reference category: white)				
Hispanic			0.630*** (0.136)	0.587*** (0.136)
Black			0.734*** (0.093)	0.591*** (0.095)
Native			1.136*** (0.278)	1.047*** (0.285)
Asian			0.208 (0.180)	0.291 (0.180)
Other			0.389 (0.349)	0.333 (0.348)
Family characteristics				
Family structure (reference category: two biological parents)				
Two parents with ≥ 1 nonbiological parent				0.392*** (0.084)
Single parent				0.509*** (0.083)
Other				0.959 (0.206)
Primary caregiver education (reference category: < high school)				
High school				0.071 (0.113)
Some college				−0.057 (0.111)
College graduate				−0.088 (0.155)
Above college				−0.294 (0.179)
Parent receiving public assistance				0.175* (0.079)

[†] Regression results for grade dummies are omitted from the table.

* p < .05; ** p < .01; *** p < 0.001

Table 5.8. Effect of Neighborhood Disadvantage on Youth Violence (Measured as Dichotomous Variables): Results of Piecewise Linear Spline Regressions

	Coefficient (Standard error)		
Variables	YV in general	Fighting	Weapon-related YV
Splines of neighborhood disadvantage			
Least to less neighborhood disadvantage[†]	0.037 (0.078)	0.021 (0.083)	0.056 (0.130)
Middle neighborhood disadvantage[†]	0.421** (0.137)	0.458** (0.145)	0.550** (0.202)
More to most neighborhood disadvantage[†]	−0.036 (0.021)	−0.033 (0.022)	−0.034 (0.028)

Note: YV = youth violence
[†] Estimates adjusted for individual, family, and neighborhood-level covariates.
* $p < .05$; ** $p < .01$; *** $p < 0.001$

Table 5.9. Effect of Neighborhood Disadvantage on Youth Violence (Measured as Variability Indexes of Youth Violence): Results of Piecewise Linear Spline Regressions

	Coefficient (Standard error)		
Variables	YV in general	Fighting	Weapon-related YV
Splines of neighborhood disadvantage			
Least to less neighborhood disadvantage[†]	0.043 (0.065)	0.051 (0.058)	0.015 (0.153)
Middle neighborhood disadvantage[†]	0.276** (0.096)	0.214* (0.088)	0.548* (0.220)
More to most neighborhood disadvantage[†]	−0.010 (0.014)	−0.006 (0.013)	−0.022 (0.029)

Note: YV = youth violence
[†] Estimates adjusted for individual, family, and neighborhood-level covariates.
* $p < .05$; ** $p < .01$; *** $p < 0.001$

NOTES

1. Disclaimer: the authors report no conflicts of interest. The findings and conclusions in this chapter are those of the authors and do not necessarily represent the official position of the Centers for Disease Control and Prevention.
2. World Health Organization, "Health Topics: Violence," 2012, http://www.who.int/topics/violence/en/. We do not address violence "against oneself," or suicide, in this study.
3. Similar to Lauritsen's (2001) findings, age composition (the percentage of the population less than age 18), which loads on the socioeconomic disadvantage index in Sampson et al.'s (1997) study, was found to be a single-item factor. However, this variable was not significantly associated with violent behavior, regardless of the measure of violent behavior and the specific regression model used, and is not included in the analyses shown.
4. The factor loading for the percentage of black residents is 0.55 and is not included in the disadvantage index reported here. We conducted analyses with percentage black included in the disadvantage index and obtained results nearly identical

to those reported. We also conducted analyses using the percentage black as a separate variable and found it to be unrelated to violent behavior regardless of the measure of violent behavior and the specific regression model used.

5. These and all other results not shown in this chapter are available from the authors by request.

REFERENCES

Anderson, Elijah. 1999. *Code of the street: Decency, violence, and the moral life of the inner city*. New York: Norton.

Bandura Albert. 1973. *Aggression: A social learning analysis*. Englewood Cliffs, NJ: Prentice-Hall.

Bellair, Paul. 1997. Social interaction and neighborhood crime: Examining the importance of neighbor networks. *Criminology* 35:677–703.

Bellair, Paul. 2000. Informal surveillance and street crime: A complex relationship. *Criminology* 38:137–167.

Bursik, Robert J., Jr., and Harold G. Grasmick. 1993. *Neighborhoods and crime*. New York: Lexington.

Caughy, Margaret O., Patricia J. O'Campo, and Jacqueline Patterson. 2001. A brief observational measure for urban neighborhoods. *Health Place* 7:225–236.

Centers for Disease Control and Prevention, National Center for Injury Prevention and Control. 2009. Web-Based Injury Statistics Query and Reporting System (WISQARS). Available at www.cdc.gov/injury/wisqars/index.html.

Chantala, Kim, and Joyce Tabor. 1999. Strategies to perform design-based analysis using the Add Health data. Carolina Population Center, University of North Carolina at Chapel Hill. Available at http://www.cpc.unc.edu/projects/addhealth/faqs/aboutdata/weight1.pdf/view.

Crane, Jonathan. 1991. The epidemic theory of ghettos and neighborhood effects of dropping out and teenage childbearing. *American Journal of Sociology* 96:1226–1259.

Crutchfield, Robert D., Ann Glusker, and George S. Bridges. 1999. A tale of three cities: Labor markets and homicide. *Sociological Focus* 32:65–83.

De Coster, Stacey, Karen Heimer, and Stacy M. Wittrock. 2006. Neighborhood disadvantage, social capital, street context, and youth violence. *Sociological Quarterly* 47 (4): 723–753.

Dietz, Robert. 2002. The estimation of neighborhood effects in the social sciences: An interdisciplinary approach. *Social Science Research* 31:539–575.

Diez-Roux, Ana, Sharon Merkin, Donna Arnett, et al. 2001. Neighborhood of residence and incidence of coronary heart disease. *New England Journal of Medicine* 345:99–106.

Duncan, Greg, and J. Lawrence Aber. 1997. Neighborhood models and measures. In Jeanne Brooks-Gunn, Greg J. Duncan, and J. Lawrence Aber (eds.), *Neighborhood poverty*, vol. 1, *Contexts and consequences for children*, 62–78. New York: Russell Sage Foundation.

Elliott, Delbert S., William Julius Wilson, David Huizinga, Robert J. Sampson, Amanda Elliott, and Bruce Rankin. 1996. The effects of neighborhood disadvantage on adolescent development. *Journal of Research in Crime and Delinquency* 33:389–426.

Feshbach, Seymour. 1980. Child abuse and the dynamics of human aggression and violence. In George Gerbner, Catherine J. Ross, and Edward Zigler (eds.), *Child abuse: An agenda for action*. New York: Oxford University Press.

Gephart, Martha A. 1997. Neighborhoods and communities as contexts for development. In Jeanne Brooks-Gunn, Greg J. Duncan, and Lawrence Aber (eds.), *Neighborhood poverty*, vol. 1, *Context and consequences for children*, 1–43. New York: Russell Sage Foundation.

Gorman-Smith, Deborah, Patrick H. Tolan, Rolf Loeber, and David B. Henry. 1998. Relation of family problems to patterns of delinquent involvement among urban youth. *Journal of Abnormal Child Psychology* 26 (5): 319–333.

Haynie, Dana L., Eric Silver, and Brent Teasdale. 2006. Neighborhood characteristics, peer influence, and adolescent violence. *Journal of Quantitative Criminology* 22 (2): 147–169.

Hipp, John R. 2007. Block, tract, and levels of aggregation: Neighborhood structure and crime and disorder as a case in point. *American Sociological Review* 72 (5): 659–680.

Katz, Lawrence F., Jeffrey R. Kling, and Jeffrey B. Liebman. 2001. Moving to Opportunity in Boston: Early results of a randomized mobility experiment. *Quarterly Journal of Economics* 116:607–654.

Kornhauser, Ruth. 1978. *Social sources of delinquency*. Chicago: University of Chicago Press.

Krivo, Lauren J., and Ruth D. Peterson. 1996. Extremely disadvantaged neighborhoods and urban crime. *Social Forces* 75:619–650.

Lauritsen, Janet L. 2001. The social ecology of violent victimization: Individual and contextual effects in the NCVS. *Journal of Quantitative Criminology* 17 (1): 3–32.

Lauritsen, Janet L. 2003. *How families and communities influence youth victimization*. NCJ 201629. Washington, DC: U.S. Department of Justice, Office of Justice Programs, Office of Juvenile Justice and Delinquency Prevention.

Ludwig, Jens, Greg J. Duncan, and Paul Hirschfield. 2001. Urban poverty and juvenile crime: Evidence from a randomized housing-mobility experiment. *Quarterly Journal of Economics* 116:655–679.

Ludwig, Jens, Jeffrey B. Liebman, Jeffrey R. Kling, Greg J. Duncan, Lawrence F. Katz, Ronald C. Kessler, and Lisa Sanbonmatsu. 2008. What can we learn about neighborhood effects from the Moving to Opportunity experiment? *American Journal of Sociology* 114 (1): 14–88.

Malpezzi, Stephen. 1996. Housing prices, externalities, and regulation in U.S. metropolitan areas. *Journal of Housing Research* 7 (2): 209–241.

Manski, Charles F. 2000. Economic analysis of social interactions. *Journal of Economic Perspectives* 14 (3): 115–136.

Massey, Douglas S., Andrew B. Gross, and Kumiko Shibuya. 1994. Migration, segregation, and the geographic concentration of poverty. *American Sociological Review* 59:425–445.

Mercy, James A., Alexander Butchart, David Farrington, and Magdalena Cerdá. 2000. Youth violence. In Etienne G. Krug, Linda L. Dahlberg, James A. Mercy, Anthony B. Zwi, and Rafael Lozano (eds.), *World report on violence and health*, 25–56. Geneva: World Health Organization.

Miethe, Terance D., and David McDowall. 1993. Contextual effects in models of criminal victimization. *Social Forces* 71:741–759.

Morenoff, Jeffrey D., Robert J. Sampson, and Stephen W. Raudenbush. 2001. Neighborhood inequality, collective efficacy, and the spatial dynamics of urban violence. *Criminology* 39:517–559.

Oakes, J. Michael, and Peter H. Rossi. 2003. The measurement of SES in health research: Current practice and steps toward a new approach. *Social Science & Medicine* 56 (4): 769–784.

Peeples, Faith, and Rolf Loeber. 1994. Do individual factors and neighborhood context explain ethnic differences in juvenile delinquency? *Journal of Quantitative Criminology* 10:141–157.

Peterson, Ruth D., Lauren J. Krivo, and Mark A. Harris. 2000. Disadvantage and neighborhood violent crime: Do local institutions matter? *Journal of Research in Crime and Delinquency* 31:31–63.

Sampson, Robert J. 2008. Moving to inequality: Neighborhood effects and experiments meet social structure. *American Journal of Sociology* 114 (1): 189–231.

Sampson, Robert J., Jeffrey D. Morenoff, and Thomas Gannon-Rowley. 2002. Assessing "neighborhood effects": Social processes and new directions in research. *Annual Review of Sociology* 28:443–478.

Sampson, Robert J., Stephen W. Raudenbush, and Felton Earls. 1997. Neighborhoods and violent crime: A multilevel study of collective efficacy. *Science* 277:918–924.

Sampson, Robert J., and William Julius Wilson. 1995. Race, crime, and urban inequality. In John Hagan and Ruth D. Peterson (eds.), *Crime and inequality*, 37–54 . Stanford: Stanford University Press.

Shaw, Clifford R., and Henry D. McKay. 1942. *Juvenile delinquency and urban areas*. Chicago: University of Chicago Press.

Simons, Ronald L, Christine Johnson, Jay Beaman, Rand D. Conger, and Les B. Whitbeck. 1996. Parents and peer group as mediators of the effect of community structure on adolescent problem behavior. *American Journal of Community Psychology* 24:145–165.

South, Scott J., and Kyle D. Crowder. 1997. Escaping distressed neighborhoods: Individual, neighborhood, and metropolitan influences. *American Journal of Sociology* 4:1040–1084.

Turner, Margery Austin, Susan J. Popkin, and Mary K. Cunningham. 2000. *Section 8 mobility and neighborhood health.* Washington, DC: Urban Institute.

Turner, Margery Austin, Stephen Ross, George Galster, and John Yinger. 2002. *Discrimination in metropolitan housing markets: Results from phase I of HDS2000.* Washington, DC: U.S. Department of Housing and Urban Development.

Udry, J. Richard. 2003. The National Longitudinal Study of Adolescent Health (Add Health), Waves I & II, 1994–1996; Wave III, 2001–2002 [MRDF]. Carolina Population Center, University of North Carolina at Chapel Hill.

U.S. Department of Health and Human Services. 2001. *Youth violence: A report of the Surgeon General.* Rockville, MD: U.S. Department of Health and Human Services, Centers for Disease Control and Prevention, National Center for Injury Prevention and Control; Substance Abuse and Mental Health Services Administration, Center for Mental Health Services; and National Institutes of Health, National Institute of Mental Health.

Winslow, Emily B., and Daniel S. Shaw. 2007. Impact of neighborhood disadvantage on overt behavior problems during early childhood. *Aggressive Behavior* 33:207–219.

6

Aggravated Inequality

Neighborhood Economics, Schools, and Juvenile Delinquency

ROBERT D. CRUTCHFIELD AND TIM WADSWORTH

One of the challenges of the scholarship connecting macroeconomic conditions to youth violence has been identifying the mechanisms that underlie the process by which individuals are influenced by the structural conditions in their communities.[1] While there has been much focus on labor markets and the impact of unemployment as well as employment in secondary sectors, a key theoretical connection has been missing. The people who have been directly influenced by unemployment and macro shifts in types of available employment (e.g., labor market restructuring resulting from deindustrialization) have been adults, while much of the violent crime is committed by adolescents or young adults who have not yet completed the transition to full-time work. This chapter addresses this issue by examining how concentrated disadvantage at the neighborhood level can both precede and condition the relationship between adolescents' attachment to school and their participation in delinquent behavior.

Here we focus on neighborhood disadvantage, a consequence of long-term macroeconomic patterns and one of three means by which the labor market may affect youth behavior. The other two, the evidence of which will be briefly reviewed later, are juvenile employment and the work experience of parents.

It is not hard to imagine that economic disadvantage may cause adults to engage in criminal behavior. Traditional sociological and criminological theories offer a variety of mechanisms connecting disadvantage and crime, and recent empirical work has debunked some and affirmed other hypotheses drawn from these theories (Fagan and Freeman, 1999). While popular conceptions of the role of unemployment in shaping criminal behavior often suggest that unemployed individuals engage in crime to provide or supplement their income, we know that the association between work and crime is neither simple, consistent, nor strong (Freeman, 1983; Cantor and Land, 1985; Parker and Horwitz, 1986; Box, 1987; Chiricos, 1987). As a result, researchers have sought more complete explanations of how employment is linked to adult criminality at both the individual and aggregate levels (Fagan and Freeman, 1999; Crutchfield and Pitchford, 1997; Uggen, 1999; Wadsworth, 2000, 2004; Gould, Weinberg, and Mustard, 2002; Grogger, 2006). These explanations focus on more nuanced relationships between individuals, communities, and labor markets.

Children's lives and their relationships to the labor market and the economy are even less straightforward. Their relationship to the economy is primarily through their parents, and their status is tied either to family socioeconomic status or to the unique hierarchy that is established among adolescents. Unemployment or low-quality employment, both of which are often viewed as more proximate predictors of crime for adults, mean something very different for adolescents. We suggest, however, that economic and labor market factors likely do influence children's criminality but that their effects are more indirect and contextual in nature. For example, instead of a direct effect of family poverty on children's crime, we believe that the influence may operate through three interrelated processes: children's own employment and educational experiences, their parents' labor market experiences, and the broader economic trends in the neighborhoods in which they live.

Juvenile Employment and Crime

The commonly accepted wisdom has long been that juvenile employment lessens crime by decreasing unsupervised time, instilling a work ethic, and providing for material needs and desires. The empirical findings concerning the role of work on adolescent crime, though, have been quite mixed. Some of the earlier research demonstrated a positive relationship between youth employment and delinquency (e.g., Greenberger and Steinberg, 1986; Wright, Cullen, and Williams, 1997). Others have not found a positive relationship between work and delinquency (Apel et al., 2006). Steinberg and Dornbusch (1991) found that students who worked long hours diminished their academic efforts, and students who worked had no advantages academically or behaviorally over those who did not. Apel et al. (2006) found that intensity of work did not matter. Generally the growing literature cautions us against simplistic notions of how adolescent employment influences delinquency.

Bachman and Schlenberg (1993), Ploeger (1997), and Paternoster et al. (2003) conclude that higher delinquency among working juveniles is a consequence of selection. Young people who are more prone to delinquent behavior are more likely to focus their attention on paid employment rather than school. When kids' backgrounds and educational success are included in statistical models, the observed positive relationship between work and crime is substantially attenuated. In examining different delinquency trajectories, Apel et al. (2007) found that youths who were involved in crime and drug use before they got jobs reduced these behaviors after they became employed. And Baron (2008) found that the relationship between work intensity and delinquency was mediated by anger over receiving minimum wages and low attachment to the labor market.

Warren, LePore, and Mare (2000) used juveniles' activity calendars to study the relationships between school, work, and behavior. They found that the amount and type of work being performed is central to understanding its relationship to juvenile misbehavior. Central to

Warren et al.'s argument is the degree to which an adolescent's employment interfered with his or her educational achievement and aspirations. They reported that juveniles who were already not attached to school and those who worked longer hours were more likely to be involved in delinquency (the selection argument made by others) but that those who had good grades and worked more modest hours were actually less likely to become involved in criminal behavior.

Warren et al.'s findings highlight an important approach to understanding the relationship between labor markets and delinquency: the role of education as a mediator between youth employment and delinquency, as well as between labor market conditions and delinquency. Indeed, Staff and Uggen (2003) found that work that "supports" school (employment cultures which stress or encourage academic success) leads to less delinquency and drug use, but jobs that are more "adult like" have the opposite effects.

Adult Employment and Juvenile Delinquency

As early as 1989, Sullivan reported in *Getting Paid* that the employment that was available to adults in communities was linked to the amount and type of delinquency in which young people there became engaged. Crutchfield, Rankin, and Pitchford (1993) found that marginal parental employment and local joblessness demonstrated small but significant indirect effects on delinquency, operating through the academic performance of children. Wadsworth (2000) found that this link was related in part to children's diminished academic expectations, their lower feelings of efficacy, and less adult supervision when the parent was employed in a marginal setting, and Bellair and Roscigno (2000) found that parents' low-wage jobs and unemployment led to children's problem behavior, which they attributed to resulting problems in families. Bellair, Roscigno, and McNulty (2003) reported that parents' labor market experience indirectly influenced their children's delinquency through their school performance.

These findings have been interpreted to mean that children invest less in education when the evidence in front of them, the work experience of parents, suggests that "playing by the rules"—or, to use Merton's (1949) term, "conformity"—offers little hope for advancement or material wealth. We expect that this influence extends beyond parents to other adults in children's social environment. For instance, children who grow up in an inner-city neighborhood where few adults are legally employed and those who are labor in low-paying, low-status jobs may be less likely to believe that getting good grades will really make a difference for their futures. While there are certainly young people who rise above this dismal image, it is not difficult to believe that children in this circumstance will have less faith in the power of education than will children whose parents' and neighbors' investments in education have more visibly paid off.

Connecting Labor Markets, Education, and Adolescent Crime

In *The Truly Disadvantaged*, Wilson (1987) argued that children growing up in underclass neighborhoods do not get to see most adults get up and go to work in the morning because so many of the local parents are without jobs. They do not witness the material fruits of employment because too many of the adults on their blocks are out of work or are scratching by in low-wage jobs that lead to few rewards. We propose that one important mechanism by which these kinds of contextual experiences translate into higher involvement in delinquency is by conditioning the relationship between school attachments and criminal behavior.

Over the past few decades, a sizable literature has developed which brings together research in labor markets (Gordon, 1971; Andrisani, 1973; Bosanquet and Doeringer, 1973; Rosenberg, 1975, Wilson, 1987, 1996), criminological theory (Crutchfield, 1989; Sampson and Laub, 1993), and empirical studies of crime and delinquency (Crutchfield, 1989; Crutchfield and Pitchford, 1997; Wadsworth, 2004, 2006). The general argument of this body of work is that the industrial restructuring, or deindustrialization, that began in the 1960s resulted in an expanded segmented labor market which offered fewer opportunities to less educated workers in urban areas. Individuals who once worked in well-paid, low- or semi-skilled manufacturing jobs found themselves unemployed or working part-time in retail stores, restaurants, and other service sector jobs that paid less, offered few benefits or promotional opportunities, and were less secure.

This process had a profound effect on both individuals and communities. Scholars have drawn primarily on social control theory to explore the effect this shift had on individuals, arguing that unemployment, as well as unstable or unrewarding work, diminished the "stakes in conformity" that deterred problematic and criminal behavior (Toby, 1957; Hirschi, 1969; Crutchfield, 1989; Sampson and Laub, 1993, Wadsworth, 2006). This negative consequence intensified when the destabilization of labor markets affected whole communities. When the number of people with no, or less rewarding, jobs reaches a critical level, a "situation of company" is created in which large numbers of occupationally unattached individuals, unconstrained by the requirements of a steady job, congregate in public spaces such as in bars and on street corners. Such situations, it has been suggested (Crutchfield, 1989), are often conducive to criminal behavior. Anderson (1999) has also suggested that such social processes can give rise to oppositional cultures which are more tolerant of, and at times encourage, deviant and criminal behavior. These connections between labor market segmentation and criminal participation have been empirically demonstrated at both the individual level (Crutchfield and Pitchford, 1997; Sampson and Laub, 1993; Uggen 1999; Wadsworth, 2006) and the aggregate level (Crutchfield, 1989; Krivo and Peterson, 2004; Wadsworth, 2004).

Determining that the quality of employment, and its location within the larger economic structure, influences the criminality of adults is an important contribution to the criminological literature. However, it leaves out a central piece of the puzzle. Many of the people who are directly affected by economic and labor market shifts are adults, while much urban crime is committed by juveniles. Most juveniles have not yet fully entered the labor market, and frequently the only jobs that are available to most of them are low-quality, secondary-sector jobs (the same types of jobs that may be criminogenic for adults). So, while there is evidence that unemployment, as well as low-quality and secondary-sector work, is positively related to criminal involvement for young adults (Crutchfield and Pitchford, 1997; Krivo and Peterson, 2004; Wadworth, 2006), things are less clear for kids. Despite the growing literature on adolescent employment that was reviewed earlier, we know less about how labor market patterns influence juvenile delinquency than we do about how they influence adult criminality.

Here, our central question is whether neighborhood economic and labor market characteristics condition the relationship between school achievement and delinquency. Do opportunities in the local labor market and the general economic climate of the neighborhood determine the degree to which an adolescent's attachment to, and achievement in, school acts as a buffer against delinquent behavior?

Data and Methods

For these analyses, we use data from two distinct surveys collected as part of the National Longitudinal Survey of Youth (NLSY79): the main respondent file and the file which includes responses from the children of the main respondents. The NLSY79 is a longitudinal survey that has been following a sample of 12,686 males and females, who were between the ages of 14 and 21 in the initial year of the survey (1979). The respondents were interviewed every year up to 1996 and every other year after that. The main file consists of three independent probability samples: a cross-sectional sample representative of the national population (N = 6,111), a supplemental sample that oversampled black, Hispanic, and economically disadvantaged nonblack, non-Hispanic youth (N = 5,295), and a military sample (N = 1,280). In 1986, the NLSY began conducting yearly surveys of all the children born to female respondents in the main file. The data we are using in the present analyses include the 1998 survey waves of both the female main respondents and their children. These data files were merged in order to combine information for both mothers and adolescents. For our purposes, the respondents are the children of the females in the original NLSY79 sample. We include all the children who were between the ages of 14 and 18 at the time of the 1998 wave of data collection. Information about their parents comes both from the children's survey data and the data that was collected from mothers.

Several features of the NLSY make it appropriate for our purposes. First, the data were collected to obtain detailed personal and work histories of the individuals in the samples. Second, the individual respondents are geocoded and thus can be linked to census data. By doing so, we can assess the macro forces that may affect work or crime. In previous research (Crutchfield, Rankin, and Pitchford 1993; Crutchfield,

1995; Crutchfield and Pitchford, 1997), county data were used to test the linkage between macro labor market forces, adult work experience, and crime. However, given the thesis being tested here, it would be more appropriate to use neighborhood rather than county data to examine macro effects. Census tract data for NLSY respondents are now available, albeit under very controlled circumstances. We use these data for our analyses. The Bureau of Labor Statistics (BLS) and the Center for Human Resource Research (CHRR) do not release the geocoded census tract information, even with the confidentiality assurances that they require with the county data. Their justifiable concern is that with the geocoded data, it would be possible to identify respondents. Clearly this concern is magnified when the aggregate data appended to individual respondents is at the tract level. Consequently these data could only be used by staff, on site at the CHRR in Columbus, Ohio, when these analyses were conducted.

We recognize that even census tract data are not ideal for our purposes because their boundaries are somewhat arbitrarily drawn and do not necessarily coincide with communities or neighborhoods as they are understood by local residents. However, while not perfect, census tracts are approximately the right size, the Bureau of the Census has endeavored to draw them so that they are as consistent to neighborhoods as possible, and these tracts provide the opportunity to study the multilevel influence of the labor market on crime (Elliot, 1999). By using census tracts as proxies for neighborhoods, we can study how neighborhood context influences the relationship between adolescent school achievement/attachment and criminal behavior.

Analytic Strategy

The analytic strategy was driven by our interest in linking individual or micro-level processes with those at the aggregate or macro level. The present research improves on earlier work by using census tract, rather than county-level, data. This is not to say that processes at the county level, such as the distribution of types of industries that characterize local labor markets, are not important; but counties can be quite heterogeneous, and such macroeconomic patterns influence some neighborhoods quite differently than others.

To work within the restrictions mandated by BLS, we used the individual-level data from the NLSY79 main and child files to construct scales and indices and to conduct preliminary analyses. We then sent to a research assistant at CHRR a list of individual (NLSY79) variables, along with tract-level variables from the 1990 U.S. Census and the SPSS syntax that was used to create new variables, to construct new scales and indices. The research assistant then created the new variables and merged the census tract data with the individual-level data set using the NLSY geocodes for each of the respondents. The research assistant then computed four sets of correlation matrices: a matrix for the full sample and matrices for respondents who lived within standard metropolitan statistical areas (SMSAs), those who resided in the central cities of SMSAs, and respondents who lived outside of SMSAs. The correlation matrices, in addition to descriptive data for the full data set and each subsample, were then sent to BLS for approval. BLS required final approval of all data output so that it could guarantee that the anonymity of respondents was maintained.

While this procedure was cumbersome, we felt that it was the best option because the census tract data provide a rich and important opportunity to examine how two important macroeconomic forces, labor market distribution and neighborhood disadvantage, affect individual-level delinquency. A central part of the labor stratification thesis is that when neighborhoods have relatively high proportions of marginally employed people, it negatively affects the community, which in turn increases the likelihood of individual criminality. This notion is consistent with the theoretical arguments of Wilson (1987, 1996) and research by criminologists (Sampson and Groves, 1989; Allen and Steffensmeier, 1989). Also, using census tract data permits us to study how neighborhood social-demographic composition influences adolescent criminality. These analyses can be conceptualized as nesting individuals' characteristics in neighborhoods' (census tract) characteristics, which in turn are nested in the larger settings of metropolitan areas, central cities, and nonmetropolitan areas.

Multilevel data structures are most often analyzed using hierarchical linear modeling (HLM) or other approaches which take into consideration the multilevel structure of the data. Given the significant restrictions in access to the data, we used ordinary least squares (OLS) regression instead (multilevel models cannot be run without access to the original data). However, aside from data limitations, there is another reason why using OLS regression may be more appropriate. In the Children of the NLSY data set, there are only one or two respondents per census tract.[2] As such, HLM would not be appropriate. Since these nonclustered data do not violate the assumption of data independence, using OLS is not a problem. That said, since a small number of tracts will have two respondents, we will take care to interpret results conservatively.

Variables

Our dependent variable of interest is an index of juvenile delinquent behavior. The following behaviors by respondents were used to create the index: skipped school without permission, damaged property of others on purpose, got into a fight at work or school, took something without paying for it, took something worth under $50 not from a store, used force to get money from someone, hit or seriously threatened someone, attacked someone to hurt or kill, tried to con someone, took a vehicle without permission of the owner, broke into a building or vehicle to steal or look, knowingly held or sold stolen goods, helped in a gambling operation, hurt someone enough to need a doctor, lied to parents about something important, and misbehaved so that parent had to come to school. For all of these items, respondents were asked if they had engaged in this behavior (yes or no) in the past year. The mean of respondents' answers to these questions was used as their delinquency score if values were available for at least eight of the questions.

Individual-level independent variables include gender, age, race/ethnicity (dummy variables indicating whether the respondent is black or Hispanic, with white as the reference), family composition (presence of father or stepfather), family's poverty status, mother's educational achievement, academic history (including grades, a scale measuring school attachment, and parental involvement in the school), respondent's employment status (whether the juvenile was employed at the time of the survey), and mother's employment status.

Census tract data including racial composition (percentage black and percentage Hispanic), percentage marginal work force (a combination of the percentage of adults unemployed and the percentage of adults employed in secondary-sector occupations), neighborhood disadvantage (a factor analysis combination of the percentage who are extremely poor, percentage on public assistance, percentage of population over 18 living in poverty, total percentage not married, and percentage who are in the workforce but unemployed), and high school dropout rate (the percentage of the population over 25 without a high school diploma).

Results

Table 6.1 presents the OLS analyses using the full sample. In Model 1, column one, respondents' delinquency is regressed on four background variables, sex (male = 0, female = 1), age, race (white = 0, black = 1), and ethnicity (non-Hispanic = 0, Hispanic = 1); two parental socioeconomic status variables, family poverty (below the poverty line = 0, above the

Table 6.1. Regression of Delinquency Index on Respondent, Parent, and Neighborhood Variables—Mothers and Children of the NLSY, 1998 Wave, Full Sample N = 1497: Standardized and Unstandardized Coefficients and Standard Errors

	Model 1	Model 2
Background variables		
Female	−.163***	−.165***
	−.225	−.228
	(.035)	(.035)
Age	−.035	−.036
	−.018	−.018
	(.014)	(.014)
Black	.007	.031
	.009	.043
	(.043)	(.054)
Hispanic	.003	.045
	.005	.074
	(.047)	(.059)
Father or stepfather present	−.030	−.026
	−.044	−.038
	(.039)	(.039)
Parental SES variables		
Family poverty	.080**	.079*
	.166	.165
	(.054)	(.054)

Table 6.1 (continued)

	Model 1	Model 2
Mother's education	−.051	−.052
	−.044	−.045
	(.023)	(.023)
School variables		
Attachment to school	−.182***	−.184***
	−.225	−.228
	(.032)	(.032)
Grades	−.067**	−.065**
	−.023	−.023
	(.009)	(.009)
Parental involvement in school	.022	.020
	.035	.032
	(.042)	(.042)
Youth work variables		
Employed	.013	.011
	.017	.015
	(.038)	(.038)
Mother's employment variables		
Mother employed	.002	.005
	.003	.007
	(.039)	(.039)
Neighborhood variables		
% black		−.058
		−.134
		(.097)
% Hispanic		−.083*
		−.262
		(.114)
Neighborhood disadvantage		.036
		.023
		(.029)
% marginal work force		.005
		.002
		(.015)
% of population over 25 with no high school diploma		.018
		.131
		(.203)
Constant	—	—
	.803	.822
	(.226)	(.228)
R Square	.080	.084

^ p < .1; * p < .05; ** p < .01; *** p < .001

poverty line = 1) and mother's education; respondents' school variables, attachment to school, grades, and parental involvement; whether the respondent was employed (no = 0, yes = 1); mother's employment (no = 0, yes = 1). Neighborhood variables (percentage black, percentage Hispanic, neighborhood disadvantage, percentage marginal work force, and the high school dropout rate) are added to the analysis in Model 2. It was our hope to more fully evaluate the nature of parents' work, but with too few fathers present in the homes of respondents, it was not possible to fully examine their work circumstance. And given the continued gendered nature of the workplace, we are not at all certain that a mother working in a secondary-sector job will have the same meaning for the household and for children as when a father is working in a marginal job. Many of the jobs traditionally occupied by women are considered secondary-sector jobs, especially for the women, disproportionately poor and working class, overrepresented in the NLSY samples.

To begin, we should note that the results are modest. The R^2 for Model 1 is .08 and goes up to only .084 when the neighborhood variables are added. We would note that frequently analyses of crime using the NLSY do not report large R^2s,[3] but there are significant results worthy of reporting. An important "nonfinding" is that juvenile employment is unrelated to delinquency when other factors, notably those having to do with school, are a part of the analysis. These results are consistent with those reported by others that were discussed earlier. That there is no measurable relationship between youth employment and delinquency when school attachment and grades are taken into account certainly questions the longstanding public argument that youth employment is a panacea for dealing with delinquency. Instead, it is school attachment and getting good grades, as has been reported by many others, which are important protective factors that inhibit delinquency.

Another nonfinding worthy of note is the absence of a direct relationship between mother's employment and juvenile delinquency. Contrary to some popular arguments, a working mother does not appear to increase the likelihood of delinquency. Presumably a lack of adequate supervision is a byproduct of maternal employment, resulting in juvenile criminal behavior. We cannot here measure the level of parental supervision, but the lack of a direct relationship between maternal employment and crime can be conservatively interpreted to mean that we might want to worry less about the effects of a mother's work and focus instead on the amount or quality of parental involvement (as well as the family's poverty status, as will be discussed later).

The central predictors of delinquency for the juveniles in this sample are, not surprisingly, family poverty and school attachment/performance. Both respondents' attachment to school ($b = -.225$, $p < .001$) and grades ($b = -.023$, $p < .01$) are significant predictors of delinquency. Neither of these results is surprising. Control theorists have long argued and demonstrated empirically that both of these factors lead to "school bonding," which makes it less likely that students with good grades and those who feel an attachment to school will become delinquents (Hirschi, 1969; Jenkins, 1997).

Family poverty also significantly predicts delinquency. Others (Tittle, Villemez, and Smith, 1978) have argued that delinquency is not related to socioeconomic status, especially when self-report data are used (Hindelang, Hirschi, and Weis, 1979). We do not think that our results are necessarily contradictory. Here we have found that children in poor families are more likely to be involved in delinquency. It may well be that the poor have higher levels of delinquency than others do but that there is not a linear relationship between crime and social class. Children living in solid working-class communities that have not been ravaged by deindustrialization are probably no more criminal than are children from the middle and upper classes. Perhaps only with the substantial disadvantage that comes from being poor is delinquency more likely.

It is no surprise that the neighborhood variables have little direct effect on delinquency. Others have found the same results. The only direct relationship is with the percentage of Hispanics in the census tract's population. In those tracts that have relatively large proportions of Latino residents, the respondents report less involvement in delinquency. This effect is small but statistically significant, and it is consistent with results reported by Desmond and Kubrin (2009), Sampson, Morenoff, and Raudenbush (2005), and Martinez (2002). Later, we more thoroughly explore the degree to which neighborhoods exert an important influence on juvenile delinquency by examining the interactions between individual and tract variables in tables 6.3 and 6.4.

Table 6.2 repeats the results for the full sample in column one to facilitate easy comparison with the subsamples. Column two contains the results of the regression for the subsample of respondents who lived within metropolitan areas, column three shows the center city subsample, and column four displays the results for respondents living outside of SMSAs. We have labeled these "rural" tracts for ease of discussion, but technically they may not all be completely rural areas. These respondents are simply not living within metropolitan areas. The results of the subsamples are very similar to the results from analyses of the complete sample. The smaller sample sizes for the subsamples likely account for respondents' grades dropping out as a significant predictor of delinquency in the SMSA and central city analyses. We do not believe that this insignificance should be interpreted to mean that grades are unimportant, because "attachment to schools," which is correlated with grades ($r = .064$, $p < .05$), remains significant even where the Ns are considerably smaller. Grades remains significant in the rural subsample, where it is a notably stronger predictor of delinquency ($b = -.047$, $p < .05$), than in the full sample ($b = -.023$), suggesting that

Table 6.2. Regression of Delinquency Index on Respondent, Parent, and Neighborhood Variables—Mothers and Children of the NLSY, 1998 Wave, All Four Samples: Standardized and Unstandardized Coefficients and Standard Errors

	Full sample N = 1497	In SMSA N = 1167	Central city N = 475	Rural N = 330
Background variables				
Female	−.165***	−.154***	−.173***	−.172**
	−.228	−.209	−.247	−.249
	(.035)	(.039)	(.065)	(.079)
Age	−.036	−.024	−.046	−.059
	−.018	−.012	−.024	−.031
	(.014)	(.015)	(.026)	(.030)
Black	.031	.049	.025	−.104
	.043	.068	.036	−.163
	(.054)	(.059)	(.107)	(.142)
Hispanic	.045	.042	.089	.054
	.074	.065	.143	.120
	(.059)	(.064)	(.118)	(.155)
Father or stepfather present	−.026	−.058^	−.090	.082
	−.038	−.083	−.130	.127
	(.039)	(.044)	(.070)	(.096)

Table 6.2 (continued)

	Full sample N = 1497	In SMSA N = 1167	Central city N = 475	Rural N = 330
Parental SES				
Family poverty	.079*	.063*	.071	.158*
	.165	.123	.103	.425
	(.054)	(.059)	(.093)	(.145)
Mother's education	−.052	−.055^	−.024	−.064
	−.045	−.042	−.021	−.062
	(.023)	(.026)	(.042)	(.058)
School variables				
Attachment to school	−.184***	−.159***	−.136**	−.284**
	−.228	−.197	−.178	−.351
	(.032)	(.037)	(.062)	(.068)
Grades	−.065**	−.045	−.024	−.114*
	−.023	−.015	−.008	−.046
	(.009)	(.010)	(.016)	(.022)
Parental involvement in school	.020	.004	.032	.065
	.032	.006	.051	.109
	(.042)	(.047)	(.079)	(.093)
Youth work				
Employed	.011	.019	.087^	−.041
	.015	.069	.125	−.059
	(.038)	(.043)	(.073)	(.085)
Mother's employment				
Mother employed	.005	.012	.034	.005
	.007	.018	.052	.008
	(.039)	(.044)	(.073)	(.084)
Neighborhood variables				
% black	−.058	−.105*	−.138^	.149
	−.134	−.224	−.265	.506
	(.097)	(.103)	(.146)	(.326)
% Hispanic	−.083*	−.108**	−.157*	−.047
	−.262	−.324	−.467	−.198
	(.114)	(.125)	(.198)	(.325)
Neighborhood disadvantage	.036	.045	.093	.005
	.023	.028	.049	.004
	(.029)	(.031)	(.042)	(.092)
% marginal work force	.005	.027	−.025	−.024
	.002	.012	−.011	−.014
	(.015)	(.017)	(.030)	(.043)
% of population over 25 with no high school diploma	.018	−.013	.026	.02834
	.131	−.092	.169	.203
	(.203)	(.231)	(.339)	(.445)
Constant	—	—	—	—
	.822	.819	1.013	.738
	(.228)	(.256)	(.427)	(.507)
R Square	.084	.076	.087	.177

^ p < .1; * p < .05; ** p < .01; *** p < .001

in these neighborhoods grades are in fact a better determinant of who is likely to become involved in illegal activity than they are in metropolitan settings.

There are two other modest but notable differences in the analyses of the subsamples from those of the full sample. The first is the weak negative relationship of mother's education (b = −.043, p < .1)[4] in census tracts that lie within SMSAs. The second is that family poverty is insignificant in the central city subsample. In that subsample, the coefficient (b = .145) is not appreciably lower than that from the analyses of the full sample (b = .166, p < .01) and is slightly larger than the coefficient for the metropolitan tracts (b = .127, p < .05), but with the much smaller sample (n = 475), this variable fails to achieve significance in the analyses of central city tracts. More importantly, family poverty is a much stronger predictor of delinquency in rural tracts than in metropolitan tracts when other factors are taken into account (b = .426, p < .01). This finding is at variance with popular images of impoverished inner cities being the spawning grounds of a subculture of poverty leading to delinquency. It is in nonurban places where poverty is more observable as a direct cause of crime. Of the aggregate variables, percentage Hispanic is joined by percentage black as weak negative predictors of individual criminality, but both are only significant in the SMSA and central city subsamples and not in the rural tracts.

Table 6.3 presents analyses of the same models just described but with the addition of an interaction term for grades and neighborhood disadvantage. The inclusion of this and other interaction terms in this analysis combines important individual-level characteristics with neighborhood characteristics in order to evaluate how the latter conditions the relationships of the former as predictors of delinquent behavior. The interaction terms selected for inclusion were constructed to test whether labor market marginalization and economic disadvantage in the neighborhoods condition the relationships between school variables and juvenile delinquency. We have displayed in the table only the analysis that includes the grades*neighborhood disadvantage interaction, but other interaction effects will also be briefly discussed.

The grades-disadvantage interaction is positively correlated with delinquency. In more disadvantaged neighborhoods, the effect of having grades as a protective factor against delinquency is muted. Presumably

Table 6.3. Regression of Delinquency Index on Respondent, Parent, Neighborhood, and the Interaction of Grades and Disadvantage—Mothers and Children of the NLSY, 1998 Wave, All Four Samples: Standardized and Unstandardized Coefficients and Standard Errors

	Full sample N = 1497	In SMSA N = 1167	Central city N = 475	Rural N = 330
Background variables				
Female	-.165***	-.154***	-.176***	-.171**
	-.228	-.209	-.252	-.247
	(.035)	(.039)	(.065)	(.079)
Age	-.037	-.023	-.039	-.065
	-.019	-.012	-.020	-.034
	(.014)	(.015)	(.026)	(.030)
Black	.029	.047	.030	-.101
	.041	.065	.043	-.159
	(.053)	(.059)	(.106)	(.143)
Hispanic	.044	.040	.092	.054
	.071	.062	.148	.120
	(.059)	(.064)	(.118)	(.155)
Father or stepfather present	-.029	-.064*	-.098*	.086
	-.042	-.091	-.141	.135
	(.039)	(.044)	(.070)	(.097)
Parental SES				
Family poverty	.080**	.063*	.069	.161**
	.166	.124	.132	.432
	(.054)	(.059)	(.091)	(.146)
Mother's education	-.049^	-.050	-.017	-.068
	-.043	-.042	.015	-.066
	(.023)	(.026)	(.042)	(.055)
School variables				
Attachment to school	-.182***	-.156***	-.133**	-.284***
	-.225	-.194	-.174	-.351
	(.032)	(.037)	(.062)	(.068)
Grades	-.077**	-.058^	-.074	-.124*
	-.027	-.019	-.026	-.050
	(.009)	(.010)	(.018)	(.023)
Parental involvement in school	.018	.002	.029	.064
	.029	.003	.046	.108
	(.042)	(.047)	(.079)	(.093)
Youth work				
Employed	.010	.017	.079	
	.014	.023	.112	-.056
	(.038)	(.043)	(.073)	(.085)
Mother's employment				
Mother employed	.004	.012	.038	.004
	.006	.018	.057	.006
	(.039)	(.044)	(.073)	(.085)

(*continued*)

Table 6.3 (continued)

	Full sample N = 1497	In SMSA N = 1167	Central city N = 475	Rural N = 330
Neighborhood variables				
% black	−.058	−.105*	−.149^	.144
	−.135	−.225	−.285	.489
	(.097)	(.103)	(.146)	(.328)
% Hispanic	−.081*	−.104*	−.155*	−.053
	−.256	−.314	−.459	−.224
	(.114)	(.124)	(.197)	(.328)
Neighborhood disadvantage	.181*	.225*	.328*	.098
	.117	.135	.173	.089
	(.050)	(.053)	(.075)	(.159)
% marginal work force	.006	.029	−.017	−.024
	.003	.012	−.008	−.014
	(.015)	(.017)	(.030)	(.043)
% of population over 25 with no				
high school diploma	.018	−.014	.016	.027
	.131	−.095	.108	.196
	(.203)	(.230)	(.339)	(.446)
Interaction terms				
Grades*neighborhood disadvantage	.158**	.197*	.258*	.095
	.020	.023	.026	.018
	(.009)	(.009)	(.013)	(.028)
Constant	—	—	—	—
	.811	.794	.887	.764
	(.228)	(.256)	(.430)	(.509)
R Square	.088	.081	.095	.178

^ $p < .1$; * $p < .05$; ** $p < .01$; *** $p < .001$

the negative social environment of these communities causes good students there to be more involved in delinquency than are good students elsewhere. Here, as we will see later, the quality of the neighborhood does matter. This effect is somewhat stronger in the SMSA subsample and is even more pronounced among central city neighborhoods. But we do not see a significant interaction effect in rural communities. Again the story of delinquency seems to be a bit simpler and more straightforward in nonurban areas.

These effects are graphically displayed in figures 6.1 through 6.4. In these figures, we have plotted the relationship of grades to delinquency for the mean level of neighborhood disadvantage and for one standard deviation above and one standard deviation below the mean level of disadvantage (with all other variables set to the mean). Figure 6.1 displays these relationships for the full sample, figure 6.2 for the SMSA subsample, figure 6.3 for the central city subsample, and figure 6.4 for the rural sample. Figure 6.1 clearly shows the deleterious effects of neighborhood disadvantage. While respondents who reside in the least disadvantaged communities and communities where there is an average amount of disadvantage do engage in less delinquency as school performance improves, this is not the case for children in the most disadvantaged circumstances. The economic and social disadvantage of these children mutes the positive effect on delinquency of doing well in school. Figures

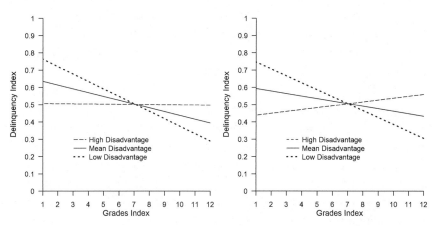

Fig. 6.1. Interaction of grades and disadvantage: in whole sample

Fig. 6.2. Interaction of grades and disadvantage: in SMSA sample

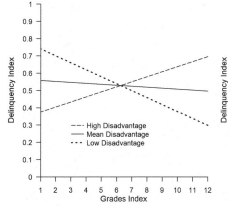

Fig. 6.3. Interaction of grades and disadvantage: in central city sample

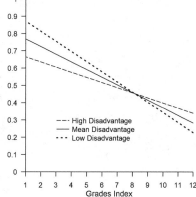

Fig. 6.4. Interaction of grades and disadvantage: not in SMSA (rural) sample

6.2 and 6.3 display the even bleaker realities experienced by some young people. In SMSAs (figure 6.2), for respondents who live in the most disadvantaged neighborhoods, getting good grades is positively associated with delinquency. And in central cities (figure 6.3), not only is there the same, but more exaggerated, positive association for respondents at the highest level of community disadvantage, but for those living in neighborhoods with the average amount of disadvantage, getting good grades does not offer protection from criminal involvement. The inequalities between these neighborhoods is exacerbated, or aggravated, when school performance cannot insulate children from delinquency. We will discuss the interpretation of these findings and patterns later. Figure 6.4 presents the patterns for rural tracts, but the interaction term is not significant. Getting good grades is an unconditioned protective factor for children outside of urban settings.

A similar set of analyses was also completed in which interaction terms are computed using grades and the percentage of marginal workers in neighborhoods (the sum of the percentage who are unemployed and the percentage who are employed in secondary-sector jobs), and grades and the percentage of the population without a high school diploma. These results are summarized in table 6.4. The effects are similar to those just described (for grades-disadvantage), but the interactions are significant only in the full sample and in the SMSA subsample. They are insignificant in the central city and rural tract subsamples, but the unstandardized coefficients are similar to those for the full sample, suggesting that they are insignificant because of small sample sizes. What is notable is the stronger effect of this interaction in SMSA tracts. Doing well in school does not insulate students from delinquency in those communities where relatively large proportions of workers are marginally employed or where more adults are without a high school education. Conversely, in neighborhoods that are not characterized by these problems, children who are not performing well in school lose some of the positive influences of living in nondisadvantaged neighborhoods where adults have more stable employment and are more likely to have finished at least secondary school.

The final two interaction terms focus on how the influence of parental behavior is conditioned by neighborhood context (summarized in table 6.4). Here the interaction term is computed by multiplying

Table 6.4. Summary of Additional Interaction Analyses—Mothers and Children of the NLSY, 1998 Wave, All Four Samples: Standardized and Unstandardized Coefficients and Standard Errors

	Full sample N = 1497	In SMSA N = 1167	Central city N = 475	Rural N = 330
Grades * % marginal work force	.137*	.178**	.123	.097
	.012	.015	.010	.012
	(.005)	(.006)	(.010)	(.019)
Grades * % of population with no high school diploma	.148*	.211**	.104	−.117
	.169	.229	.112	−.165
	(.086)	(.094)	(.172)	(.240)
Parental involvement * % of population over 25 with no high school diploma	.120**	.101*	.151^	.215*
	1.083	.897	1.935	2.045
	(.399)	(.445)	(.676)	(.854)
Mother employed * Disadvantage	−.050	−.069	−.154*	.104
	−.044	−.057	−.114	.114
	(.034)	(.036)	(.051)	(.105)

Note: The regression analysis for each of the interaction effects shown in this table included the same background, school, parental SES, youth work, mother's employment, and neighborhood variables that were included in tables 6.1 through 6.3.
^ $p < .1$; * $p < .05$; ** $p < .01$; *** $p < .001$

parents' involvement in their child's school by the percentage of the population without a high school diploma. Our results indicate that the positive effects of parental involvement are diminished when families live among more adults who have not successfully completed high school. Perhaps if the neighborhood undervalues education, the parents' efforts to be involved in their children's schools are less beneficial.

Finally, an interaction term that combines mother's employment and neighborhood disadvantage is added to the analyses (table 6.4). In initial analyses, our results suggested that mother's employment had an indirect positive association with delinquency because it seemed to be associated with lower grades (results not shown). This interaction term is not significant in three of the models, but there is a significant negative relationship between this term and delinquency among the central city respondents, meaning that in the urban core, just the opposite of the suggestion of a negative influence of mother's employment is the case. There, working mothers mitigate some of the negative effects of growing up in disadvantaged neighborhoods. This may indicate that urban households with working women seem to be a part of families that are striving, with some success, to overcome the difficult neighborhood situation in which they live.

In summary, neighborhood economic and labor market conditions have effects on juvenile delinquency, but they are indirect and conditional. Similar to much of the literature, we found that when other factors are taken into account, the employment of juveniles has no measurable effect on delinquency. Also consistent with previous work, the educational experience, most notably attachment to school and to a slightly lesser extent respondents' grades, does modestly predict who engages in illegal activity. Adolescents who report being more attached to school report less delinquency, and those who do not do as well in school are more likely to be law violators. Additionally, family poverty is positively related to delinquency. Most important, however, given the focus of this chapter, are our findings that school effects are conditioned by the social and economic character of the neighborhoods in which children live.

Discussion and Conclusions

The purpose of this chapter was to review and explore mechanisms by which macroeconomics influences juvenile delinquency. Juvenile employment may be beneficial, depressing criminality among some, but for most, it has little or no effect. The literature is quite clear: in general, children who perform better in school are less likely to become involved in crime. And parental unemployment and labor force marginality decrease children's school performance and as a consequence increase the likelihood of children's criminal behavior. Here we have presented new evidence that the positive effects of schooling are conditioned by levels of neighborhood disadvantage. At best, the positive effect of doing well in school is attenuated for children living in higher levels of disadvantage, but in urban areas, it is even worse. Within cities, children who live in the poorest neighborhoods are more involved in criminal behavior, and performing well in school does not insulate them from delinquency.

We titled this chapter "Aggravated Inequality" to play on the legal concept of aggravated crime (e.g., aggravated assault). The literature is quite compelling that social and economic disadvantage is injurious to children (e.g., Wilson, 1987, 1996; Massey and Denton, 1993; Anderson, 1990, 1999). Aggravated inequality calls attention to how these injuries are compounded when delinquency is considered. In most places, children's investment in their education not only has payoffs for their future but also pays off because it decreases the likelihood that they will become involved in criminal behavior, its dangers, and potentially dire justice system consequences. For children growing up in disadvantaged neighborhoods, where adult labor force participation is marginal and where adults have not done well in school, the delinquency protection of good grades is less likely to help them. And since we know that these children's school experience is less likely to have positive payoffs (Kozol, 1991; Lewis, 2003), it is fair to characterize this as aggravated inequality.

We at first wondered how to make sense of the positive association between getting good grades and delinquency in disadvantaged communities, but we now offer three post hoc explanations. First, good students who come to believe that their talents and hard work will not pay off in the legitimate labor market may turn, with some success, to the illegitimate market. This response would be classically in line with Merton's (1949) conception of "innovators," those whose route to the legitimately affirmed societal goals, the good life, is systematically structurally blocked. Young women and men in this circumstance would be just the kind of talented people who could succeed in the street life because their "smarts" would help them and make them attractive to old heads in "the life." Cloward and Ohlin (1960) long ago described those who could successfully take advantage of illegitimate opportunities, and children with academic skill in substantially disadvantaged neighborhoods are such people.

A second possible interpretation, which is certainly not exclusive of the first but does not require the imputed rational calculus of the former, is frustration. Children who strive but do not see people "like them," or people who come from where they live succeed may become frustrated and angry and as a result engage in not necessarily pecuniary crime. They are playing by the rules in school but cannot reasonably expect success to be theirs.

Our final interpretation is that children from tough, distressed neighborhoods who are doing well in school may feel the need to "represent." They may feel a need to show that they belong, that they can "hang with" others from the neighborhood, that they have "street cred." Delinquent behavior may give them the opportunity to express that they do well in school but that they are just like everyone else. This may be especially true for many of the relatively low-level delinquent behaviors represented in the NLSY. Being like "everyone else," as we all know, is terribly important for most teenagers. This interpretation too, is not mutually exclusive of the other two.

We also acknowledge the possibility that the most academically skilled among the NLSY respondents may answer questions differently. They may exaggerate; but on the other hand, they may answer accurately, while lesser performers may underreport their criminal involvement.

Finally a word is in order about our modest results. Nothing is more quintessentially sociological than social environmental effects on individual behavior, unless it is those effects on collective behavior. In recent years, a number of studies have sought to examine contextual effects, and generally little or nothing has been found. Yet we persist in developing theories that emphasize the importance of environment, probably because we expect, or even know, that the influence is there but is just hard to document. This study was a part of a larger effort that looked at the relationships between labor market participation, neighborhoods, and crime. That larger study also considered these relationships for young adults. We found no real neighborhood effects for the older group. However, an earlier study discussed earlier (Crutchfield and Pitchford, 1997) found that young adults who spent more time out of the labor force were more likely to become involved in crime when they lived in counties with higher rates of unemployment. How do we reconcile these results? It is our belief that when these studies are considered together, they point to unique environments of importance for children versus adults. For young adults, it is the local labor market, the county or metropolitan area, which is the important context in which their opportunities are realized or frustrated. Most adults find jobs not in their neighborhoods but rather in the wider community in which they live. Thus, their economic lives are more determined by that wider context. Children, on the other hand, are not as mobile. Their lives are more circumscribed, and thus influenced, by the neighborhoods in which they live. They cannot as easily transcend the spatial or social limitations of their immediate environment as can adults. It is this difference in influence across adults and children that must continue to be explored in order to gain a deeper understanding of the interplay between macroeconomic forces, social contexts—labor markets, disadvantage, poverty, and so on—and problematic outcomes.

NOTES

1. This work was supported by National Institute of Justice grant number 2000-IJ-CX-0026. The authors would like to thank the staff of the Center for Human Resource Research at The Ohio State University and the U.S. Bureau of Labor Statistics for assistance in obtaining the data used in this analysis. They also want to express their appreciation to Kevin Drakulich and members of the University of Washington Deviance Seminar for assistance, comments, and critiques of earlier drafts of this chapter.
2. This distribution was communicated verbally by Center for Human Development research staff.
3. The NLSY probably yields very modest results in criminological research for several reasons. The most obvious possibilities are that even though these are reasonably large samples, crime is a rare event; the crime measures are highly skewed; many of the theoretically important explanatory variables have significant numbers of missing cases (have been coded conservatively, usually imputing the mean); and as is the case with such surveys, the proximate causes of criminal events are not measured by the survey.
4. We felt that the small sample size justified using the less traditional, more liberal standard of significance of .1.

REFERENCES

Allan, Emilie Andersen, and Darrell J. Steffensmeier. 1989. "Youth, Underemployment, and Property Crime: Differential Effects of Job Availability and Job Quality on Juvenile and Young Adult Arrest Rates." *American Sociological Review* 54 (1): 107–123.

Anderson, Elijah. 1990. *Street Wise: Race, Class and Change in an Urban Community*. Chicago: University of Chicago Press.

Anderson, Elijah. 1999. *Code of the Street: Decency, Violence, and the Moral Life of the Inner City*. New York: Norton.

Andrisani, Paul J. 1973. "An Empirical Analysis of the Dual Labor Market Theory." Ph.D. diss., Ohio State University.

Apel, Robert, Shawn Bushway, Robert Brame, Amelia M. Haviland, Daniel S. Nagin, and Ray Paternoster. 2007. "Unpacking the Relationship between Adolescent Employment and Antisocial Behavior: A Matched Samples Comparison." *Criminology* 4 (1): 67–97.

Apel, Robert, Raymond Paternoster, Shawn D. Bushway, and Robert Brame. 2006. "A

Job Isn't Just a Job: The Differential Impact of Formal versus Informal Work on Adolescent Problem Behavior." *Crime and Delinquency* 52 (2): 333–369.

Bachman, Jerald G., and John Schlenberg. 1993. "How Part-Time Work Intensity Relates to Drug Use, Problem Behavior, Time Use, and Satisfaction among High School Seniors: Are These Consequences or Merely Correlates?" *Developmental Psychology* 29 (2): 220–235.

Baron, Stephen W. 2008. "Street Youth, Unemployment, and Crime: Is It That Simple? Using General Strain Theory to Untangle the Relationship." *Canadian Journal of Criminology and Criminal Justice/Revue canadienne de criminologie et de justice pénale* 50 (4): 399–434.

Bellair, Paul E., and Vincent J. Roscigno. 2000. "Local Labor-Market Opportunity and Adolescent Delinquency." *Social Forces* 78 (4): 1509–1538.

Bellair, Paul E., Vincent J. Roscigno, and Thomas L. McNulty. 2003. "Linking Local Labor Market Opportunity to Violent Adolescent Delinquency." *Journal of Research in Crime and Delinquency* 40 (1): 6–33.

Bosanquet, Nicholas, and Peter B. Doeringer. 1973. "Is There a Dual Labor Market in Great Britain?" *Economic Journal* 83:421–35.

Box, Steven. 1987. *Recession, Crime and Punishment*. Totowa, NJ: Barnes and Noble.

Cantor, David, and Kenneth C. Land. 1985. "Employment and Crime Rates in the Post–World War II United States: A Theoretical and Empirical Analysis." *American Sociological Review* 50:317–332.

Cloward, Richard, and Lloyd Ohlin. 1960. *Delinquency and Opportunity*. Glencoe, IL: Free Press.

Chiricos, Theodore G. 1987. "Rates of Crime and Unemployment: An Analysis of Aggregate Research Evidence." *Social Problems* 34:187–211.

Crutchfield, Robert D. 1989. "Labor Stratification and Violent Crime." *Social Forces* 68 (2): 489–512.

Crutchfield, Robert D. 1995. "Ethnicity, Labor Markets, and Crime." In Darnell F. Hawkins, ed., *Ethnicity, Race, and Crime*. Albany: SUNY Press.

Crutchfield, Robert D., and Susan R. Pitchford. 1997. "Work and Crime: The Effects of Labor Stratification." *Social Forces* 76:93–118.

Crutchfield, Robert D., Margaret Ann Rankin, and Susan R. Pitchford. 1993. "Inheriting Stakes in Conformity: Effects of Parents' Labor Market Experience on Juvenile Violence." Paper presented at the annual meeting of the American Society of Criminology, Phoenix, Arizona, November.

Desmond, Scott A., and Charis E. Kubrin. 2009. "Immigrant Communities and Adolescent Violence." *Sociological Quarterly* 50:581–607.

Elliot, James R. 1999. "Social Isolation and Labor Market Insulation: Network and Neighborhood Effects on Less Educated Workers." *Sociological Quarterly* 40 (2): 199–216.

Fagan, Jeffrey, and Richard B. Freeman. 1999. "Crime and Work." *Crime and Justice* 25:225–290.

Freeman, Richard B. 1983. "Crime and Unemployment." In James Q. Wilson, ed., *Crime and Public Policy*. San Francisco: ICS Press.

Gordon, David M. 1971. "Class, Productivity, and Class: A Study of Labor Market Stratification." Ph.D. diss., Harvard University.

Gould, Eric D., Bruce A. Weinberg, and David B. Mustard. 2002. "Crime Rates and Local Labor Market Opportunities in the United States: 1979–1997." *Review of Economics and Statistics* 84 (1): 45–61.

Greenberger, Ellen, and Laurence Steinberg. 1986. *When Teenagers Work: Psychological and Social Costs of Adolescent Employment*. New York: Basic Books.

Grogger, Jeff. 2006. "An Economic Model of Recent Trends in Violence." In *The Crime Drop in America*, 266–287. New York: Cambridge University Press.

Hindelang, Michael J., Trais Hirschi, and Joseph G. Weis. 1979. "Correlates of Delinquency: The Illusion of Discrepancy between Self-Report and Official Data." *American Sociological Review* 44:995–1014.

Hirschi, Travis. 1969. *Causes of Delinquency*. Berkeley: University of California Press.

Jenkins, Patricia H. 1997. "School Delinquency and the School Social Bond." *Journal of Research in Crime and Delinquency* 34:337–367.

Kozol, Jonathan. 1991. *Savage Inequalities: Children in America's Schools*. New York: Crown.

Krivo, Lauren J., and Ruth D. Peterson. 2004. "Labor Market Conditions and Violent Crime among Youth and Adults." *Sociological Perspectives* 47:485–505.

Lewis, Amanda E. 2003. *Race in the Schoolyard: Negotiating the Color Line in Classrooms and Communities*. New Brunswick: Rutgers University Press.

Martinez, Ramiro. 2002. *Latino Homicide: Immigration, Violence and Community*. New York: Routledge.

Massey, Douglas S., and Nancy A Denton. 1993 *American Apartheid: Segregation and the Making of the Underclass*. Cambridge: Harvard University Press.

Merton, Robert K. 1949. *Social Theory and Social Structure: Toward the Codification of Theory and Research*. New York: Free Press.

Parker, Robert Nash, and Allan V. Horwitz. 1986. "Unemployment, Crime, and Imprisonment: A Panel Approach." *Criminology* 24:751–773.

Paternoster, Raymond, Shawn Bushway, Robert Brame, and Robert Apel. 2003. "The Effect of Teenage Employment on Delinquency and Problem Behaviors." *Social Forces* 82:297–335.

Ploeger, Matthew. 1997. "Youth Employment and Delinquency: Reconsidering a Problematic Relationship." *Criminology* 35:659–675.

Rosenberg, S. 1975. "The Dual Labor Market: Its Existence and Consequences." Ph.D. diss., University of California at Berkeley.

Sampson, Robert J., and Walter Groves. 1989. "Community Structure and Crime: Testing Social Disorganization Theory." *American Journal of Sociology* 94:774–802.

Sampson, Robert J., and John Laub. 1993. *Crime in the Making*. Cambridge: Harvard University Press.

Sampson, Robert J., Jeffrey D. Morenoff, and Stephen Raudenbush. 2005. "Social Anatomy of Racial and Ethnic Disparities in Violence." *American Journal of Public Health* 95 (2): 224–232.

Staff, Jeremy, and Christopher Uggen. 2003. "The Fruits of Good Work: Early Work Experiences and Adolescent Deviance." *Journal of Research in Crime and Delinquency* 40 (3): 263–290.

Steinberg, Laurence, and Sanford M. Dornbusch. 1991. "Negative Correlates of Part-Time Employment during Adolescence: Replication and Elaboration." *Developmental Psychology* 27 (2): 304–313.

Sullivan, Mercer L. 1989. *"Getting Paid": Youth Crime and Work in the Inner City.* Ithaca: Cornell University Press.

Tittle, Charles R., Wayne J. Villemez, and Douglas A. Smith. 1978. "The Myth of Social Class and Criminality: An Empirical Assessment of the Empirical Evidence." *American Sociological Review* 43:643–656.

Toby, Jackson, 1957. "The Differential Impact of Family Disorganization." *American Sociological Review* 22:505–512.

Uggen, Christopher. 1999. "Ex-Offenders and the Conformist Alternative: A Job Quality Model of Work and Crime." *Social Problems* 46:127–151.

Wadsworth, Tim. 2000. "Labor Markets, Delinquency and Social Control Theory: An Empirical Assessment of the Mediating Process." *Social Forces* 78:1041–1066.

Wadsworth, Tim. 2004. "Industrial Composition, Labor Markets and Crime." *Sociological Focus* 37:1–24.

Wadsworth, Tim. 2006. "The Meaning of Work: Conceptualizing the Deterrent Effect of Employment on Crime." *Sociological Perspectives* 49:343–368.

Warren, John Robert, Paul C. LePore, and Robert Mare. 2000. "Employment during High School: Consequences for Students' Academic Achievement." *American Educational Research Journal* 37:943–969.

Wilson, William Julius. 1987. *The Truly Disadvantaged: The Inner City, the Underclass, and Public Policy.* Chicago: University of Chicago Press.

Wilson, William Julius. 1996. *When Work Disappears: The World of the Urban Poor.* New York: Knopf.

Wright, John Paul, Francis T. Cullen, and Nicolas Williams. 1997. "Working While in High School and Delinquent Involvement: Implications for Social Policy." *Crime & Delinquency* 43:203–221.

7

Street Markets, Adolescent Identity, and Violence

A Generative Dynamic

MARK EDBERG AND PHILIPPE BOURGOIS

Introduction

As for others in this volume, this chapter originated as part of a major effort sponsored by the Centers for Disease Control and Prevention (CDC)[1] to identify the linkages between macroeconomic factors and youth violence. The effort includes a significant review of the current scientific literature as well as the convening of a national, interdisciplinary panel of experts who have been addressing these issues from different social science and public health disciplinary perspectives. The primary purpose of the combined effort is (a) to understand what is currently known about the linkages between macroeconomic factors and youth violence linkages and to identify where gaps exist—including information related to potential prevention applications; and (b) to propose future directions for research and intervention. Two basic assumptions have framed the inquiry:

- A wide range of macroeconomic factors and indicators exist, and different factors (e.g., poverty, economic inequality, unemployment, ethnic/racial discrimination and inner-city segregation, economic growth and recessions) are likely to have varying effects on promoting youth violence.
- The effects of macroeconomic conditions on youth violence are rarely direct but are *mediated* and *moderated* by other processes, policies, and conditions.

An analytic framework has been proposed that includes both a temporal dimension (long- versus short-term impacts) as well as a matrix of social, psychosocial, cultural, and economic domains through which the impacts of macroeconomic factors are manifested. Some macroeconomic factors, such as levels of economic inequality, change slowly over time, and their impact on youth violence may occur over many years or decades; other factors may only have an impact on youth violence when they reach a critical threshold level, which may differ across communities; and still other macroeconomic conditions, such as unemployment, GDP growth, or consumer confidence, change more rapidly.

The mediating domains through which macroeconomic factors exert influence on youth violence have been organized into the following four: families, schools, community resources and social spending, and street markets. These intervening factors do not cover all possible connecting links between economic conditions and youth violence, but they do constitute major domains through which economic factors are likely to influence levels and patterns of youth violence. The working hypothesis regarding domains is that any given macroeconomic factor produces a number of pathways or *trajectories* of impact through these domains and that the ultimate impact on youth violence is an outcome of the ways in which the economic conditions are filtered, shaped, mediated, and moderated through these domains.

In this chapter, we focus on one particular mediating dynamic within the street market domain that we believe contributes significantly to the way in which street markets lead to increases in youth violence. It is not the only dynamic generated by street markets, but it is one that has not received sufficient attention in prevention efforts. *That dynamic involves the ways in which street markets, as a highly violent social-ecological context shaped by structural inequality and law enforcement policies, in turn affect the identity development process for adolescents who must negotiate their self-construction within that context.*

Street Markets and Youth Violence: General Issues

"Street markets" are by definition social spaces, typically within an urban context, centered around the distribution and public sale of illegal goods—drugs, stolen merchandise, and other goods. The common depiction is that they flourish within marginalized communities and social groups excluded from fruitful participation in the mainstream economy. Because such markets exist outside the formal social and regulatory systems of control, they are a site for the production of alternative ("informal") social structures, sociocultural codes, and practices. Moreover, because the mechanisms of social process and control are often neither institutionalized nor durable (with some exceptions), and the potential rewards lucrative, they are also situations of high risk (with respect to violence) and volatility.

The literature on street markets includes a long legacy of "street ethnographies," including more recent work specifically relevant to youth violence, as well as analyses of gun use and availability, neighborhood and population characteristics where street markets exist, gang involvement, drug markets, and "street codes" or behavioral norms arising out of street market contexts. Much of this literature is highly relevant with respect to the connection between macroeconomic factors and youth violence because (a) a range of macroeconomic factors contributes to social exclusion and marginalization which undergirds the creation of street markets; and (b) it is adolescent/young males who are most directly involved in the violence associated with these contexts. Generally, most research and literature on this issue focuses on the proximal connections between street markets and youth violence as opposed to the role of macroeconomic factors in creating/shaping street markets in the first place. The proximal links established in the literature between street markets and youth violence can be summarized as follows:

- Street markets focused on drug sales are the most prone to violence due to the concentrated presence and use of guns.

- Street markets increase perceived vulnerability and the perceived imperative to carry and use guns.
- As community social contexts, street markets intersect with, but are not necessarily coterminous with, youth gang activity.
- Although street markets may be a product of macroeconomic factors, risk behavior patterns that emerge within them may spread via endogenous processes, as a "social contagion," and by the creation of oppositional youth cultures.
- Street markets increase youth exposure to violence, which is developmentally and socially related to youth perpetration of violence.
- Street markets are sites for the creation and maintenance of "street codes" and social identities that contribute to violence and weapons use.
- Early exposure to juvenile incarceration normalizes the prison experience as a rite of passage and consolidates networks of gang-structured organized crime as well as independent petty crime (Bayer, Pintoff, & Pozen 2004; Dodge, Dishion, & Lansford 2006).

Literature concerned with the distal link—economic factors associated with the development of street markets—can be summarized as follows:

- Concentrated poverty and neighborhood disadvantage contribute to the development and maintenance of street markets (from W. Wilson 1987).
- At a distal level, and permeating other levels, "structural violence" creates the conditions for youth violence (Scheper-Hughes & Bourgois 2004; Bourgois 1996b; Farmer 2003; Galtung 1969, 1990).
- Concentration of unemployment, low income, and other marginalizing factors (race, discrimination) lead to alternative income-generating structures —with some variations for immigrant groups and historically segregated ethnic minorities (Hagedorn 2007; MacLeod 1987; Padilla 1992; Sullivan 1989; Venkatesh 2006; Vigil 2007; Wacquant 1998).

The focus of this chapter is on the specific proximal link between street markets and the development of identity through a social logic enmeshing youth in violence, weapons use, and oppositional street culture. Figure 7.1 illustrates the connection to be examined.

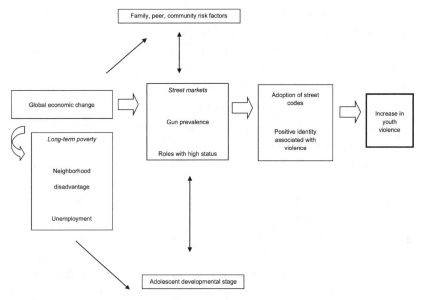

Fig. 7.1. Street markets, youth identity development, and violence—a model

Street Markets, Youth Violence, and Identity: Current Literature

Research concerning the impact of street market contexts on youth identities connected to violence has generally followed the William Julius Wilson thesis (1987) down to more micro levels, including classic work by Elijah Anderson on "codes of the street" and their origin (1990, 1992, 1999; Stewart & Simons 2006). Essentially, the argument is as follows: where economic opportunities are very limited and there is a historical pattern of disconnection from mainstream economic activity, drug selling and other aspects of the "street economy" become the dominant playing field for achievement, material gain, and status (see also Bourgois 1989, 1996b; Fagan 1992; Fagan and Wilkinson 1998; Edberg 1992, 1998, 2007) and thus have a strong role in the development and perpetuation of norms and attitudes about violence. Wilkinson's and Katz's rich data from interviews with violent offenders explore the ways in which violence—and gun violence in particular—becomes such an important tool for negotiating personal status (Wilkinson 2004;

Katz 1988; see also Harcourt 2006; Bourgois 1997). Street codes are also intrinsically tied to the attainment and performance of (primarily) male gender roles within a limited social ecology (Messerschmidt 1993, 1997), though female gender roles in the same settings intersect with these codes in complex ways (Miller & Decker 2001). There is also an important interaction between street codes and gang-related codes where gangs are prevalent, and gangs add an additional and salient dimension of identity (see Vigil 2007) that may coincide with turf- and market-control conflicts within street market contexts—though we caution that gang-related identity is not always connected to the sale of drugs or illegal goods. Many of these conclusions about violence involvement draw from classical sociology's strain theory (e.g., Merton 1938; Messner & Rosenfeld 1994) and from theories concerning the isolated and uniformly poverty-ridden nature of inner-city "underclass" communities (W. Wilson 1987; Sampson and Wilson 1995) as well as cultural reproduction theory (Bourdieu and Accardo 1999; Bourdieu and Wacquant 1992; Bourgois 2003; Bourgois, Prince & Moss 2004; Willis 1981). They also reflect the way in which violence involvement and victimization are outcomes of limited choices and constrained agency as an outcome of structural inequality (see Farmer 2003; Bourgois 2010).

Inescapably, the processual chain of youth identity development under conditions of structural inequality is tied to race. As Wilkinson, Beaty, and Lurry (2009) describe from extensive interviews, African American youth do not feel that it is possible to rely on police to obtain justice for violent crime they have experienced. These youth hold a widely shared belief that the police do not have their interests at heart and neither respect nor care about them. Thus, they are left to their own devices to take care of justice against violations, and their own personal reputations are tied up in their willingness and ability to do so —through the use of violence. Wilkinson's work here draws on Donald Black's theory of crime and violence as a form of "self-help" and social control, given limited access to other resources (Black 1983; Cannon & Wilkinson 2007).

While much of the literature on street codes has focused on African American or Latino youth, Chong et al. (2009) have documented a similar set of circumstances and street codes among young Southeast Asian men (ages 13–17) in the San Francisco Bay Area. As in the other literature, a social context shaped by alienation and discrimination has contributed to a situation in which violence becomes an important means of constructing racial/ethnic and gender identities. Moreover, while the street-code literature has focused on young males, Jones (2008) conducted an ethnographic study with inner-city girls, finding that they also come to organize their social world around three key aspects of the code: reputation, respect, and retaliation (also see Miller 2001; Miller & Decker 2001). Cross-culturally, research in Oslo, Norway (Sandberg 2009a, 2009b) highlights two discursive modes of self-presentation among minority drug dealers. One mode focuses on personal narratives of oppression, unemployment, racism, and other difficulties—utilized for personal justification of drug dealing and violence as well as during interaction with welfare agencies. The other, called "gangster discourse," presents the narrator as "thick-skinned, smart and sexually alluring" (Sandberg 2009a, 532) and is the dominant discourse on the street, used to gain respect. In other related work, Sandberg and colleagues have more generally examined the acquisition of symbolic capital among ethnic-minority/immigrant youth in urban Oslo, where such capital is tied to violent street culture (Sandberg & Peterson 2009).

One more aspect of "identity" that deserves exploration is the impact of high poverty and chronic violence on adolescent constructions of risk. This is a phenomenon that occurs with respect to other health risks (see Edberg 2004a, 2007). Essentially, beliefs about a limited future in such high-risk settings change the interpretation of risk, such that the benefits of immediate or short-term social recognition and the resources that may accompany that recognition outweigh concerns over incarceration, injury, or death. In support, DuRant et al. (1995) examined social and psychological factors associated with weapon carrying by African American adolescents in a community with extensive poverty and violence, finding that, among other factors, weapon carrying was significantly associated with a self-appraised probability of being alive at age 25.

There is also a body of work that addresses person-environment dynamics contributing to the kinds of resources youth have and choices youth are able to make in situations of high risk. Self-concept models have attempted to understand person-environment dynamics behind clusterings of risk behavior and risk factors, focusing on the construct of *self-concept* as an internal mechanism that provides the "incentives, standards, plans, rules, and scripts for behavior" and adjusts "in response to challenges from the social environment (Markus & Wurf 1987, pp. 299–300). Markus and Nurius (1986) further posit that an individual's array of self-representations includes *possible selves*—that is, representations of selves that could be, should be, are not desirable, and so on or that represent past, current, or future selves. These, according to Markus & Nurius (1986), serve as incentives or motivation for behavior. If a key task of adolescence is to experiment in order to resolve identity/social role (Erikson 1968), then the "possible selves" element of the self-concept is said to be highly salient, because adolescents can construct possible selves in "conventional domains" supporting positive behavioral outcomes, or if this does not occur, adolescents may seek alternative ways to self-define (Oyserman & Markus 1990), including violence and risk, if these are supported within the social context (Erikson 1968; Hirschi 1969; Sutherland & Cressey 1978; Oyserman & Packer 1996). Drawing from the theories of Ogbu (1991) and Bourdieu (1977, 1990), among others (Devine 1996; Fordham 1993, 1996), in high-poverty situations where academic success may not be perceived as related significantly to available life paths, it may in turn garner little social value.

Finally, although much of the current prevention programming addressing youth violence and delinquency has been based on the predictive *risk and protective factor* model (e.g., Hawkins, Catalano, & Miller 1992; Hawkins et al. 2000; Catalano & Hawkins 1995), which posits multiple levels of exposure to risks and protective factors as precursors of involvement in violence, some related approaches do make a link to identity-generating dynamics. *Problem behavior syndrome* theory, for example (Jessor & Jessor 1977; Donovan and Jessor 1985; Jessor, Donovan, & Costa 1991; Donovan et al. 1988; Catalano & Hawkins 1995; Oetting and Beauvais 1987; Elliott, Huizinga, & Ageton 1985; Elliott, Huizinga & Menard 1989; Hawkins and Weis 1985), views risk-factor patterns and trajectories of involvement in risk as clustered and as a reflection of shared attitudinal/worldview characteristics. The *resilience* (e.g., Pransky 1991; Benson, Galbraith, & Espeland 1994; Search Institute 1998; Benard 1991, 1996) and more recent *positive youth development* (PYD) approaches (Schwartz et al. 2007; Scales et al. 2000, 2005;

Theokas et al. 2005; Lerner et al. 2005) address the presence of protective factors in the youth environment as part of a person-context, developmental process.

The Link to Identity

Of key importance for this chapter, the compelling nature of street market conditions in concentrated poverty communities, *as a social ecology*, exerts a particular effect at the time adolescents are in a key phase of development—thus compounding the effect by linking the "imperatives of the street" to the development of personal identity. Street markets themselves become a unique, integrative social formation that *generates* identities connected to violence-supportive rationales, motivations, and behavior as an integrative process separate from the impact of exposure to identified risk or protective factors that may have preceded involvement in such contexts—a quality that will be referred to herein as *generative*.[2] There is a contrast between this approach and the risk/ protective-factors models, as well as a complementary aspect. Focusing on a context-based generative process implies less scrutiny of the specific micro-paths that lead to youth involvement in a street market setting and more on what happens when they are there—because of what street markets entail. Youth violence connected to street markets thus reflects a context-based *weltaunschuung* that may originate from exposure to risk factors yet is generative of behavior on its own terms.

A few examples may help illustrate the approach. In an ethnographic study recently conducted in the U.S.-Mexico border region—primarily in high-poverty urban areas such as Ciudad Juarez—investigating perceptions of the "narcotrafficker image" as portrayed in popular media (Edberg 2001, 2004a, 2004b), many youth in focus groups and interviews expressed a desire to have hero songs (in Mexican and border culture, these are called *corridos*) written and sung about them, like the songs sung about the exploits of popular narcotraffickers. The fact that the exploits described in these *narcocorridos* included violence and other "risk behaviors" did not deter that desire. By contrast, the violence and other risks foregrounded in these narratives were actually the key to understanding a social context in which the narcotrafficker-protagonists were positioned as individuals who *stood out, who possessed something special.* Risk, even risk of death, was viewed as the currency that could elevate a youth who lived in the dusty squalor of the border *colonias* into a kind of pantheon of the notable, to be among those who "made a dent in the cosmos," so to speak and were recognized for doing so—something that regular life in the *colonias* was not likely to offer. Even if the end result was death, the attainment of any notoriety was perceived as better than the poverty, facelessness, and lack of respect they expected otherwise. Thus, prevalent understandings about violence and related risk were inseparable from the context that generated them.

Current risk/protective-factor explanatory models take the form of exposure-output or "exposure-push" (to use the "cost-push" analogy from economics) explanations, in which the concomitant remedy is to reduce the exposure or to minimize the research-based set of factors "pushing" risk behavior, hence changing the behavioral output. It is almost certain, however, that no effort to address these "push" factors can eliminate them entirely, because they are too entwined with the broader environment of inequality and poverty. Yet it is also very likely, as noted here, that there are other mediating processes set in motion through exposure to risk or push factors, and these take on a life of their own that is no longer proximally related to such factors in a straightforward manner. Such mediating processes are themselves worthwhile points for intervention.[3]

Generative Context: Clarifying the Term

Street markets as a *generative context* for youth violence are an important step removed from the direct impact of exposure to risk factors yet are not unrelated to that exposure. Once youth are in a marginalized or oppositional (anticonventional, street culture) setting—which may be the result of exposure to multiple risk factors—they are often negotiating a unique social world[4] in which the calculus of risk, the structure of social goals, and values related to behavior are shaped primarily by the characteristics and imperatives of that social world as the dominant, proximal influence. That "high-risk" social world becomes the "customary" or governing social context, in the sense of Bourdieu's *habitus* and associated *doxa* (Bourdieu 1977, 1990). Previous exposure to specific risk factors as defined in the literature becomes less mean-ingful either in terms of behavioral influence or as an intervention tar-get. In a high-risk context, violence may have many positive attributes. It may be instrumentally useful, worth the risks involved, customarily practiced, and socially valued (even expected) as a means of gaining status, reputation, household support, material benefits, or partners (Bourgois 1989, 1996a; Karandinos 2010). More important, engaging in violent behavior is an integral part of the setting—not an outlier behav-ior. Thus, the characteristics of the context create or *generate* ongoing motivations and rationales for engaging in violence. This is qualita-tively different from a risk-factor, "exposure-push" process. Using the analogous term from economics, there is a "demand-pull" mechanism involved that comes from the aggregate impact of the social context and its motivational structure.

Furthermore, however tempting it may seem, "context" cannot prop-erly be construed as a risk factor itself in the manner that risk factors are typically treated in the literature. Context is not a discrete factor. It is an aggregate phenomenon, whose social force derives from the dynamic interaction of internal characteristics and their articulation with larger, external, socioeconomic and cultural patterns. While, as noted, there are context-based internal processes that motivate and sustain vio-lent behavior, these processes also interact—arguably primarily—with broader phenomena that transcend a given high-risk context. Violent behavior itself, for example, is not new, nor is it always proscribed. Sometimes it is broadly admired—and certainly so in the American cultural idiom. The interplay between a behavior that is socially valued in society as a whole—at least in certain forms—and its interpolation within high-risk contexts where there are fewer behavioral options to place it in perspective very likely amplifies the "demand-pull" effect.

Linking Generative Context, Adolescent Identity Development, and Violence

Because the discussion concerns *youth* violence, the relationship be-tween high-risk contexts and behavior must be considered in terms of one of the key developmental processes for youth and adolescents—the construction of an identity (or of a *self*). The generative role of these contexts may even exert greater force for youth/adolescents because of the importance of this stage and its inherent vulnerability.

Erikson (1968) has described the adolescent concern with establishing identity, noting, for example, that adolescents are "sometimes morbidly . . . preoccupied with what they appear to be in the eyes of others as compared to what they feel they are, and with the question of how to connect the roles and skills cultivated earlier with the ideal prototypes of the day" (p. 128). The concept of "ideal prototypes" in this sense offers a useful cross-disciplinary construct linking identity and risk behavior, since, by nature, "ideal prototypes" are public and thus sociocultural phenomena to which value is assigned, and the prototypes can be *appropriated by individuals as part of the formation of self-schemas, or identities*. Becoming a self involves a dialogue between individual, particular experience and collective representations for experience (Battaglia 1995; Bakhtin 1981; Holland et al. 1998). The assigning of social value to behavior occurs by definition in an environment in which at least some meaning is shared. Shared meaning, however, is *public* and intersubjective precisely because it is propagated among a group through the way specific behaviors are *represented* (see, for example, Geertz 1983; Sperber 1996). These representations form the basis for development of a self as well, because they include "available representations" of self from which individuals build their self-concept—for example, standards and processes by which individuals become full persons, gendered persons, admired persons, and so on (see Marsella, DeVos, & Hsu 1985; Carrithers, Collins, & Lukes 1985; Leenhardt 1979). Erikson (1968) has called such material the "resources of identity."

The social process of becoming a self also involves the *performance* of the "represented self" in day-to-day life (see Goffman 1959). This approach to understanding the self draws from the concept of the social "me" that has long roots in psychological theory (James 1892; Mead 1934). This includes the idea of the *performative self* (Goffman 1959), in which one's main task is to *manage the information* others have about you—a process of impression management in which the sociocultural environment provides the stages, scripts, characters/personas, and mise-en-scène by which to do that. Individuals constantly use this (social, cultural) material to create selves or identities and in doing so must provide the cues that let others know what identity is being presented. In addition, the individual must then *validate* the identity by "follow-up actions" that are in keeping with one's purported identity. Regarding youth violence, this dynamic is well described by Wilkinson (2004), Fagan & Wilkinson (1998), Anderson (1990, 1999), and Sandberg (2009a, 2009b) in terms of performance of self within the code of the street and within a set of opposing and value-laden identities—for example, the highly valued "tough" or "wild" identity versus the devalued "punk" and "herb" identities (Wilkinson 2004). There is a consistency across cultures with respect to such identity categories. The street identities just referred to are remarkably consonant with the requirements for a personal reputation within the "reputation versus respectability" identity continuum first identified by P. J. Wilson (1973) in the Caribbean and amplified by Whitehead (Whitehead 1992; Whitehead, Peterson, & Kaljee 1994) as a framework for understanding male-gendered risk behavior in a context of historical and structural constraints.

Thus, extensive involvement in violence and other risk behavior by adolescents is likely to be consistent with the construction and performance of a "risky self" (or "delinquent self" or "violent self," etc.) that is understood as such both by the individual taking on this identity and by others within the high-risk social context in which he or she enacts it. Performance, then, entails *encoding one's actions* such that they are consonant with that identity. Encoding occurs in the actions taken—the violence itself and specific symbolic aspects of its presentation. For example, turning the gun sideways is by now a well-known symbolic gesture that has become a part of what could be called "gangsta body language." The symbolic aspects of violence are also encoded in narrative representations about violence and other risk behavior that become part of the performance—having *stories to tell* that will have meaning and resonance with other adolescents in terms of creating a socially valued identity and through which feedback can be obtained.

Importantly with respect to the impact of context, one cannot invent out of whole cloth the material from which an acceptable identity can be constructed and the types of actions that need to be included. This material will come largely from public models, representations and narratives (public discourse) that exist within and across sociocultural groups and contexts, including narratives that have resonance with youth, including music, social media, blogging, YouTube, and so on. In this way, the development and enactment of a risky identity is in one sense a running series of stories or a staged narrative. The narrative process involved in performing and representing a violent or risky identity is a key part of its taking shape, and taking hold, within an individual,[5] acting within a specific social context.

The first author has recorded and observed this narrative aspect of self-performance in a number of research and programmatic efforts addressing populations involved in high-risk activities (see, for example, Edberg 1998, 2004a, 2004b):

- "Street" drug addicts who talk about the meaning of drug use as if it were a tool for demonstrating (to others) their willingness and ability to handle risk—a demonstration of *mastery*, as it were
- Runaway youth from high-poverty inner-city areas who sum up the meaning of involvement in drug dealing, petty theft, and other street economy activities with the phrase, "See, I know how to make money without carrying people's bags"—clearly referencing the meaning of these activities as a counter to subordinate social position
- Young people in the *colonias* of Ciudad Juarez, Mexico, who express a desire to be a narcotrafficker, to have a reputation that is disseminated via popular narrative, and thus to have some consequence as a human being

In these kinds of narratives, people are structuring the way in which various behaviors have meaning for them in their respective high-risk social worlds.

Returning to the earlier reference to a popular song genre (*narcocorridos*) about narcotraffickers (see Edberg 2001, 2004a, 2004b) as a case in point, these are narratives that include extensive descriptions of risk behavior including violence, drug use, drug selling, and sexual risk, typically presented as part of the life led by narcotraffickers. It is a life full of danger, treachery, and tragedy, but a life that also communicates a kind of unapologetic power and flaunting of structural restrictions based on class, race/ethnicity, or national power. The portrayals have a considerable, though complex, resonance with people who tend to be poor and otherwise shut out of powerful or esteemed social roles.

While listener interpretation of *narcocorridos* is not one-dimensional, these narco-tales reference at least one meaning-laden framework for organizing actions and provide a kind of narrative road map for becoming a "notable person."[6] Almost all the youth interviewed at a youth prison in Juarez, Mexico, for example, *wanted to have a corrido written about them.* Thus, the narratives were motivators and meaningful structuring agents for action. As narrative structures, *corridos* and *narcocorridos* link behavior and meaning in a kind of *semiotics of self.* While no one in any interview directly attributed any specific actions or activities that they were or had been involved in, or specific actions of others, to *narcocorridos* per se, they clearly provided sociocultural material—an *objectified self* through which an individual could personify the values represented. This is translated into clothes, body language, a physical presentation of self, an attitude toward death and risk, a preoccupation with projecting power and importance, and other ways in which the identity is articulated with daily life in the high-poverty, and high-risk, border setting.

It is important to emphasize here that understanding violence and risk behavior from this perspective offers a more holistic picture of the integration of attitudes and behaviors within a social setting, rather than treating those attitudes as distinct factors (e.g., "social norms"), subject to change outside of the context that gives them force.

Implications for Policy and Practice

If the function presented here of generative, structural context in framing, motivating, and sustaining youth violence in an interactive process with identity formation is accurate, then one key implication is that the many risk/protective-factor and related prevention approaches are likely to be most useful at an earlier stage, in preventing youth from involvement, or entrenchment, in a high-risk social context—although, as noted, none of these approaches addresses the structural context that underlies the co-occurrence of risk factors. Once youth are involved, however, the context and its imperatives may be more useful as defining points for intervention. Also, within a risk/protective-factors framework, even program models that address *community* risk factors such as gun and drug availability or *peer* risk factors such as *social norms supporting violence* have to be understood as important but incomplete insofar as these factors are—at least operationally—treated as distinct. Viewed as a risk factor, supportive norms are just one of many etiological precursors to violence not qualitatively distinguished from each other. Viewed from a generative perspective, however, "supportive norms" are no longer a distinct risk factor among others but an integrated element of a culture of risk behavior that is embedded within a pattern of living, such that one can no longer simply "change norms" as if they were discrete, fungible objects.

Attaining a valorized identity is a *generative* process in which individuals do what they understand to be appropriate in order to achieve contextually embedded goals. There is something about violence that forms a meaningful dimension of identity. It commands a moral valence. It may be a symbolic demonstration of power or of existential efficacy or of notoriety in a circumscribed world or of solidarity among peers (e.g., gang members). In order to intercede in that process, the syndemic (Singer 2006) contextual conditions that narrow or shape the identity-behavior possibilities for youth must change in the long run; while in the short run, interventions must be added to the current stock that are designed to expand the potential behavioral repertoire of these youth such that the expanded behavioral possibilities have identity value vis-à-vis the dimensions of personal status currently associated with violence.[7] In the short run, it could be said that new behaviors must "symbolically mimic" violence in certain essential ways—but with no actual violence. These expanded possibilities for a valorized identity may also effectively include links to role options outside the immediate social context.

There are multiple research and program implications for this perspective, in order to elucidate the nature of the violence-identity connection and to develop appropriate interventions:

- Research is needed to identify, in different street market and related high-risk contexts, those key dimensions of personal status and identity that are fulfilled through violence—identifying the "generative schema." Qualitative methods seeking attributes and ranked attributes connected to personal status within such contexts is one relevant research methodology.
- Research is needed to explore other identities, roles, and behaviors that would respond to the same or similar dimensions of identity and

status. A modified, exploratory use of the "possible selves" approach may be useful for this purpose, tied to the attributes elicited from the first research strategy.

- Interventions could employ a range of strategies to introduce non-violence-related roles[8] and behaviors (to the "inventory" of violence-related behaviors) that satisfy the generative schema as identified. Social-cognitive modeling and positive youth development (PYD) community participation approaches are two such strategies. Another, less tested approach may be to use workshops such as those implemented by the Alternatives to Violence Project (AVP),[9] originally a prison-based intervention model that seeks to develop personal mastery and responsibility without violence.

- Interventions could also identify the resources and contextual factors necessary to introduce non-violence-related roles/identities/behaviors as realistic possibilities for youth in high-violence communities. This may involve collaboration with schools, businesses, or nonprofit and other funders to support tailored positive youth development and particularly job-related options. The idea is to dilute the potency of violence as a socially validated component of identity by adding, over time, to the social fabric meaningful social roles and employment/economic possibilities that produce visible evidence of personal efficacy and gain and that share some aspects of the qualities identified as worthy of emulation.

- Interventions could identify modes of representation and channels of communication through which alternative identities (not dependent on violence) and behaviors identified from the formative research could be disseminated. From that step, social marketing and diffusion approaches could be employed to disseminate messages about these "status-worthy" alternative behaviors and identities.

A distinguishing characteristic of this kind of program approach is that the potential social roles/identities offered are context driven, structured around the complex of behavioral motivations characteristic of specific social contexts, based on an understanding that these motivations are now a product of the context itself, not just the designated risk factors that may have contributed to its existence. Thus, instead of implementing a preset school-based curriculum that teaches conflict-resolution skills based on a risk-factor assessment that identifies these skills as lacking, a generative approach understands that *conflict resolution* may not in fact be a meaningful goal in that particular context. The normative goal may be dominance, publicly asserted. The program solution would therefore focus on developing an intervention component that sought to *change the terms* by which dominance is defined.

A key principle for program development within this approach is the use of what can be called the *principle of substitution*, in which youth have opportunities to direct at least some of the motivational force connected to violence toward *substitute roles or activities* that meet the same or similar basic motivational needs. In such a case, other traditional violence-prevention modalities may not even be necessary, because a simple substitution of behavior is involved (relative to a schema) that may take a youth out of his or her risk situation. An important caveat is warranted here, however. Given the compelling nature of street markets and the potential for achieving status and reputation—and all that goes with it—relatively quickly in some cases, anything that is presented as a substitute will face a tough challenge. Simply put, alternative roles/actions will have to compete against what the street market offers. There have been some program attempts following a positive youth development (PYD) orientation (Kurtines et al. 2008a, 2008b; Delgado 2002) that center on supporting youth *agency*—the ability of youth to assess their own situation, to reframe goals, and to control personal change. These kinds of programs support youth involvement in political and community change, which can introduce roles/identities that gain social recognition and yet represent a community-based, oppositional stance. Indeed, this aspect of youth participation has been an increasingly common feature of global youth movements (for example, in Latin America—see Edberg 2008; Dowdney 2005). The SAFER Latinos program, a CDC-funded, community-level youth-violence-prevention intervention targeting Latino immigrant youth (Edberg et al. 2010a, 2010b), incorporates some components of this approach as well, particularly in its attempt to develop a cadre of (Latino immigrant) youth within the community and in the local high school who can gain status and represent personal efficacy through *visible* community change activities. However, comparatively little has been done to date to explore or test interventions that incorporate the approach presented here. It is an important area in need of further study as well as practice.

NOTES

1. National Center for Injury Prevention and Control (NCIPC), Division of Violence Prevention.

2. To engage with new developments in the social sciences (Bourdieu & Wacquant 1992; Bourdieu 2000; Foucault 1978), street markets contribute to the creation of a "*habitus*" (Bourdieu 1977) or a "subjectivity" (Foucault 1978), which refer to a conscious and preconscious "way of being in the world" that is best understood as being framed by one's larger historical era and social formation, including forms of "governability"—e.g., policies and institutions, nongovernment initiatives, structural and political forces (including markets), cultural ideological forces (including religion), and discourses that constitute a contingent field.

3. Sampson and colleagues (Sampson, Morenoff, & Raudenbush 2005; Sampson 2003) and findings from the Project on Human Development in Chicago Neighborhoods have been instrumental in highlighting neighborhood-level and social contextual mediating factors in violence and health risk and in calling for more research to understand these processes.

4. Anthropologist Dorothy Holland (Holland et al. 1998) uses the term "figured world" to refer to the constructed, imagined, meaning-laden, and relational aspects of particular sociocultural spaces—the idea of intersubjectivity.

5. The formative and cognitive role of narrative is well recognized in psychology, child development, and anthropological theory about the self—e.g., Budwig & Wiley 1995; Sperry & Sperry 1995; Mintz 1995; Miller et al. 1992; Ochs & Capp 1996; Bruner 1986). As Ochs and Capp (1996) have noted, "as narratives are apprehended, they give rise to the selves that apprehend them" (p. 22). Indeed the psychologist Jerome Bruner (1986) has called narrative one of the two fundamental modes of cognitive thinking.

6. According to Ochs and Capps (1996), "Narratives situate narrators, protagonists, and listeners/readers at the nexus of morally organized past, present, and possible experiences" (p. 22, also citing Guignon 1993; Heidegger 1962).

7. This has been described elsewhere as the "generative schema" associated with violence or other risk behavior (Edberg 2007).

8. In other words, "possible selves."

9. See the AVP website: http://www.avpusa.org.

REFERENCES

Anderson, E. (1990). *Streetwise: Race, class, and change in an urban community*. Chicago: University of Chicago Press.

Anderson, E. (1992). The story of John Turner. In A. V. Harrell & G. E. Peterson (Eds.), *Drugs, crime, and social isolation* (pp. 147–180). Washington, DC: Urban Institute Press.

Anderson, E. (1999). *Violence and the inner-city street code*. Chicago: University of Chicago Press.

Bakhtin, M. M. (1981). *The dialogic imagination* (M. Holquist, Ed. C. Emerson, Trans.). Austin: University of Texas Press.

Battaglia, D. (Ed). (1995). *Rhetorics of self-making*. Berkeley: University of California Press.

Bayer, P. J., Pintoff, R., & Pozen, D. E. (2004). *Building criminal capital behind bars: Peer effects in juvenile corrections* (Yale University Economic Growth Center Discussion Paper 684). Available at http://papers.ssrn.com/sol3/papers.

Benard, B. (1991). *Fostering resiliency in kids: Protective factors in the family, school, and community*. Unpublished paper.

Benard, B. (1996). *Mentoring: New study shows the power of relationship to make a difference* (Research report). Berkeley, CA: Resiliency Associates.

Benson, P., Galbraith, J., & Espeland, P. (1994). *What kids need to succeed*. Minneapolis, MN: Search Institute and Free Spirit.

Black, D. (1983). Crime as social control. *American Sociological Review, 48*, 34–45.

Bourdieu, P. (1977). *Outline of a theory of practice*. Cambridge: Cambridge University Press.

Bourdieu, P. (1990). *The logic of practice* (R. Nice, Trans.). Cambridge, UK: Polity. Originally published 1980.

Bourdieu, P. (2000). *Pascalian meditations* (R. Nice, Trans.). Stanford: Stanford University Press.

Bourdieu, P., & Accardo, A. (Eds.). (1999). *The weight of the world: Social suffering in contemporary society*. Stanford: Stanford University Press.

Bourdieu, P., & Wacquant, L. (1992). *An invitation to reflexive sociology*. Chicago: University of Chicago Press.

Bourgois, P. (1989). In search of Horatio Alger: Culture and ideology in the crack economy. *Contemporary Drug Problems, 16*, 619–650.

Bourgois, P. (1996a). In search of masculinity: Violence, respect and sexuality among Puerto Rican crack dealers in East Harlem. *British Journal of Criminology, 36*(3), 412–427.

Bourgois, P. (1996b). *In search of respect: Selling crack in el barrio*. Cambridge: Cambridge University Press.

Bourgois, P. (1997). Overachievement in the underground economy: The life story of a Puerto Rican stick-up artist in East Harlem. *Free Inquiry for Creative Sociology, 25*(1), 23–32.

Bourgois, P. (2003). *In search of respect: Selling crack in El Barrio*. New York: Cambridge University Press.

Bourgois, P. (2010). Recognizing invisible violence: A 30-year ethnographic retrospective. In B. Rylko-Bauer, P. Farmer, & L. Whiteford (Eds.), *Global health in times of violence* (pp. 17–40). Santa Fe, NM: School for Advanced Research Press.

Bourgois, P., Prince, B., & Moss, A. (2004). Everyday violence and the gender of hepatitis C among homeless drug-injecting youth in San Francisco. *Human Organization, 63*(3): 253–264.

Bruner, J. (1986). *Actual minds, possible worlds.* Cambridge: Harvard University Press.

Budwig, N., & Wiley, A. (1995). What language reveals about children's categories of personhood. In L. Sperry & P. Smiley (Eds.), *New directions for child development: Vol. 69. Exploring young children's concepts of self and other through conversation* (pp. 21–32). San Francisco, CA: Jossey-Bass.

Cannon, E., & Wilkinson, D. (2007, November 13). *Crime as self-help among violent adolescents in disadvantaged neighborhoods: a mode of preserving reputation.* Paper presented at the annual meeting of the American Society of Criminology, Atlanta, GA.

Carrithers, M., Collins, S., & Lukes, S. (Eds.). (1985). *The category of the person: Anthropology, philosophy, history.* Cambridge: Cambridge University Press.

Catalano, R. F., & Hawkins, J. D. (1995). *Risk-focused prevention: Using the social development strategy.* Seattle: Developmental Research and Programs.

Chong, Vincent, Khatharya Um, Monica Hahn, David Pheng, Clifford Yee, and Colette Auerswald. 2009. Toward an intersectional understanding of violence and resilience: An exploratory study of young Southeast Asian men in Alameda and Contra Costa County, California. *Aggression and Violent Behavior, 14*(6), 433–506.

Delgado, M. (2002). *New frontiers for youth development in the 21st century: Revitalizing and broadening youth development.* New York: Columbia University Press.

Devine, J. (1996). *Maximum security: The culture of violence in inner-city schools.* Chicago: University of Chicago Press.

Dodge, K. A., Dishion, T. J., & Lansford, J. E. (2006). *Deviant peer influences in programs for youth: Problems and solutions.* New York: Guilford.

Donovan, J. E., & Jessor, R. (1985). The structure of problem behavior in adolescence and young adulthood. *Journal of Consulting and Clinical Psychology, 53,* 890–904.

Donovan, J. E., Jessor, R., & Costa, F. M. (1988). Syndrome of problem behavior in adolescence: A replication. *Journal of Consulting and Clinical Psychology, 56*(5), 762–765.

Dowdney, L. (2005). *Neither war nor peace: International comparisons of children and youth in organized armed violence.* Rio de Janeiro, Brazil: 7 Letras.

DuRant, Robert H., et al. 1995. The association between weapon-carrying and the use of violence among adolescents living in or around public housing. *Journal of Adolescence 18*(5), 579–592.

Edberg, M. (1992). AIDS risk behavior among runaway youth in the Washington, DC–Baltimore Area. In *Report of multi-site runaway risk behavior study.* Rockville, MD: National Institute on Drug Abuse.

Edberg, M. (1998). Street cuts: Splices from project notebooks and other indelible impressions. *Anthropology and Humanism, 23*(1), 77–82.

Edberg, M. (2001). Drug traffickers as social bandits: Culture and drug trafficking in northern Mexico and the border region. *Journal of Contemporary Criminology, 17*(3), 259–277.

Edberg, M. (2004a). *El narcotraficante: Narcocorridos and the construction of a cultural persona on the U.S.-Mexico border.* Austin: University of Texas Press.

Edberg, M. (2004b). The narcotrafficker in representation and practice: A cultural persona from the Mexican border. *Ethos, 32*(2), 257–277.

Edberg, M. (2007). Application of theory: High-risk and special populations. In *Essentials of health behavior: Social and behavioral theory in public health* (pp. 137–150). Boston: Jones & Bartlett.

Edberg, M. (2008, December). *Development of UNICEF Latin America–Caribbean (LAC) adolescent well-being indicators: Background and proposed indicators.* Panama City, Panama: UNICEF LAC.

Edberg, M., Cleary, S., Andrade, E., et al. 2010a. "SAFER Latinos: A community partnership to address contributing factors for Latino youth violence." *Progress in Community Health Partnerships 4*(3), 221–233.

Edberg, M., Cleary, S., Klevens, J., Collins, E., Leiva, R., Bazurto, M., Rivera, I., Taylor, A., Montero, L., & Calderon, M. 2010b. "The SAFER Latinos project: Addressing a community ecology underlying Latino youth violence." *Journal of Primary Prevention 31*, 247–257.

Elliott, D. S., Huizinga, D., & Ageton, S. (1985). *Explaining delinquency and drug abuse.* Beverly Hills, CA: Sage.

Elliott, D. S., Huizinga, D., & Menard, S. (1989). *Multiple problem youth: Delinquency, substance use, and mental health problems.* New York: Springer-Verlag.

Erikson, E. H. (1968). *Identity: Youth and crisis.* New York: Norton.

Fagan, J. (1992). Drug selling and licit income in distressed neighborhoods: The economic lives of street-level drug users and dealers. In A. V. Harrell & G. E. Peterson (Eds.), *Drugs, crime, and social isolation* (pp. 99–146). Washington, DC: Urban Institute Press.

Fagan, J., & Wilkinson, D. L. (1998). Guns, youth violence and social identity in inner cities. In M. Tonry & M. H. Moore (Eds.), *Crime and Justice: Vol. 24. Youth violence* (pp. 105–188). Chicago: University of Chicago Press.

Farmer, P. (2003). *Pathologies of power: Health, human rights, and the new war on the poor.* Berkeley: University of California Press.

Fordham, S. (1993). "Those loud black girls": (Black) women, silence, and gender "passing" in the academy. *Anthropology & Education Quarterly, 24*(1), 3–32.

Fordham, S. (1996). *Blacked out: Dilemmas of race, identity, and success at Capital High.* Chicago: University of Chicago Press.

Foucault, M. (1978). *The history of sexuality* (R. Hurley, Trans.). New York: Pantheon Books.

Galtung, J. (1969). Violence, peace and peace research. *Journal of Peace Research, 6*(3), 167–191.

Galtung, J. (1990). Cultural violence. *Journal of Peace Research, 27*(3), 291–305.

Geertz, C. (1983). *Local knowledge: Further essays in interpretive anthropology.* New York: Basic Books.

Goffman, E. (1959). *The presentation of self in everyday life.* New York: Doubleday.

Guignon, C. (1993). *The Cambridge companion to Heidegger*. Cambridge: Cambridge University Press.

Hagedorn, J. (2007). *Gangs in the global city: Alternatives to traditional criminology*. Urbana: University of Illinois Press.

Harcourt, Bernard E. 2006. *Language of the gun: Youth, crime, and public policy*. Chicago: University of Chicago Press.

Hawkins, J. D., Catalano, R. F., & Miller, J. Y. (1992). Risk and protective factors for alcohol and other drug problems in adolescence and early adulthood: Implications for substance abuse prevention. *Psychological Bulletin, 112*, 64–105.

Hawkins, J. D., Herrenkohl, T. I., Farrington, D. P., Brewer, D., Catalano, R. F., Harachi, T. W., & Cothern, L. (2000). Predictors of youth violence. *Juvenile Justice Bulletin*. Washington, DC: Office of Juvenile Justice and Delinquency Prevention.

Hawkins, J. D., & Weis, J. G. (1985). The social development model: An integrated approach to delinquency prevention. *Journal of Primary Prevention, 6*, 73–97.

Heidegger, M. (1962). *Being and time*. New York: Harper & Row.

Hirschi, T. (1969). *Causes of delinquency*. Berkeley: University of California Press.

Holland, D., Lachicotte, W., Skinner, D., Cain, C. (1998). *Identity and agency in cultural worlds*. Cambridge: Harvard University Press.

James, W. (1892). *Psychology: The briefer course*. Notre Dame, IN: Notre Dame University Press.

Jessor, R., Donovan, J., & Costa, F. M. (1991). *Beyond adolescence: Problem behavior and young adult development*. New York: Cambridge University Press.

Jessor, R., & Jessor, S. L. (1977). *Problem behavior and psychosocial development: A longitudinal study of youth*. New York: Academic Press.

Jones, Nikki. 2008. Working 'the code': On girls, gender, and inner-city violence. *Australian & New Zealand Journal of Criminology 41*(1), 63–83.

Karandinos, G. (2010). *"You ridin'?" The moral economy of violence in North Philadelphia*. Undergraduate thesis, Department of History and Sociology of Science, Program in Health and Societies, University of Pennsylvania.

Katz, J. (1988). *Seductions of crime: Moral and sensual attractions in doing evil*. New York: Basic Books.

Kurtines, W. M., Ferrer-Wreder, L., Berman, S. L., Lorente, C. C., Silverman, W. K., & Montgomery, M. J. (2008a). Promoting positive youth development: New directions in developmental theory, methods, and research. *Journal of Adolescent Research, 23*, 233–244.

Kurtines, W. M., Montgomery, M. J., Eichas, K., Ritchie, R., Garcia, A., Albrecht, R., Berman, S., Ferrer-Wreder, L., & Lorente, C. C. (2008b). Promoting positive identity development in troubled youth: A developmental intervention science outreach research approach. *New directions for identity and intervention* [Special issue], *Identity: An International Journal of Theory and Research, 8*, 125–138.

Leenhardt, M. (1979). *Do Kamo: Person and myth in the Melanesian world*. Chicago: University of Chicago Press.

Lerner, R. M., Lerner, J. V., Almerigi, J. B., Theokas, C., Phelps, E., Gestsdottir, S., et al.

(2005). Positive youth development, participation in community youth development programs, and community contributions of fifth-grade adolescents: Findings from the first wave of the 4-H study of positive youth development. *Journal of Early Adolescence, 25,* 17–71.

MacLeod, J. (1987). *Ain't no makin' it: Leveled aspirations in a low-income neighborhood.* Boulder, CO: Westview.

Markus, H., & Nurius, P. (1986). Possible selves. *American Psychologist, 41,* 954–969.

Markus, H., & Wurf, E. (1987). The dynamic self-concept: A social-psychological perspective. *Annual Review of Psychology, 38,* 299–337.

Marsella, A. J., DeVos, G., & Hsu, F. K. (1985). *Culture and the self: Asian and Western perspectives.* New York: Tavistock.

Mead, G. H. (1934). *Mind, self and society.* Chicago: University of Chicago Press.

Merton R. K. (1938). *Social theory and social structure.* New York: Free Press.

Messerschmidt, J. W. (1993). *Masculinities and crime: Critique and reconceptualization of theory.* Lanham, MD: Rowman & Littlefield.

Messerschmidt, J. W. (1997). *Crime as structured action.* Thousand Oaks, CA: Sage.

Messner, S., & Rosenfeld, R. (1994). *Crime and the American dream.* Belmont, CA: Wadsworth.

Miller, J. (2001). *One of the guys: Girls, gangs, and gender.* New York: Oxford University Press.

Miller, J., & Decker, S. H. (2001). Young women and gang violence: Gender, street offending, and violent victimization in gangs. *Justice Quarterly, 18*(1), 115–140.

Miller, P. J., Mintz, J., Hoogstra, L., Fung, H., & Potts, R. (1992). The narrated self: Young children's construction of self in relation to others in conversational stories of personal experience. *Merrill-Palmer Quarterly, 38,* 45–68.

Mintz, J. (1995). Self in relation to other: Preschoolers' verbal social comparisons within narrative discourse. In L. Sperry and P. Smiley (Eds.), *New directions for child development: Vol. 69. Exploring young children's concepts of self and other through conversation* (pp. 61–74). San Francisco: Jossey-Bass.

Ochs, E., & Capps, L. (1996). Narrating the self. *Annual Review of Anthropology, 25,* 19–43.

Oetting, E. R., & Beauvais, F. (1987). Peer cluster theory, socialization characteristics and adolescent drug use: A path analysis. *Journal of Counseling Psychology, 34*(2), 205–220.

Ogbu, J. U. (1991). Minority coping responses and school experience. *Journal of Psychohistory, 18,* 433–456.

Oyserman, D., & Markus, H. (1990). Possible selves and delinquency. *Journal of Personality and Social Psychology, 59*(1), 112–125.

Oyserman, D., & Packer, M. J. (1996). Social cognition and self-concept: A socially contextualized model of identity. In J. L. Nye & A. M. Brower (Eds.), *What's social about social cognition? Research on socially shared cognition in small groups* (pp. 175–201). Thousand Oaks, CA: Sage.

Padilla, F. M. (1992). *The gang as an American enterprise.* New Brunswick: Rutgers University Press.

Pransky, J. (1991). *Prevention: The critical need.* Springfield, MO: Burrell Foundation and Paradigm.

Sampson, R. J. (2003). The neighborhood context of well-being. *Perspectives in Biology and Medicine, 46*(3S), S53–S64.

Sampson, R. J., Morenoff, J. D., & Raudenbush, S. (2005). Social anatomy of racial and ethnic disparities in violence. *American Journal of Public Health, 95*(2), 224–232.

Sampson R. J., & Wilson, W. J. (1995). Race, crime, and urban inequality. In J. Hagen & R. Peterson (Ed.), *Crime and inequality* (pp. 37–54). Stanford: Stanford University Press.

Sandberg, S. (2009a). Gangster, victim or both? The interdiscursive construction of sameness and difference in self-presentations. *British Journal of Sociology, 60*(3), 523–542.

Sandberg, S. (2009b). A narrative search for respect. *Deviant Behavior, 30*(6), 487–510.

Sandberg, S., & Peterson, W. (2009). *Street capital: Black cannabis dealers in a white welfare state.* Bristol, UK: Policy.

Scales, P. C., Benson, P. L., Leffert, N., and Blyth, D. (2000). Contribution of developmental assets to the prediction of thriving among adolescents. *Applied Developmental Science, 4*(1), 27–46.

Scales, P. C., Foster, K. C., Mannes, M., Horst, M. A., Pinto, K. C., and Rutherford, A. (2005). School-business partnerships, developmental assets, and positive outcomes among urban high school students: A mixed-methods study. *Urban Education, 40,* 144–189.

Scheper-Hughes, N., & Bourgois, P. (Eds.). (2004). *Violence in war and peace: An anthology.* Oxford, UK: Blackwell.

Schwartz, S. J., Pantin, H., Coatsworth, J. D., & Szapocznik, J. (2007). Addressing the challenges and opportunities for today's youth: Toward an integrative model and its implications for research and intervention. *Journal of Primary Prevention, 28*(2), 117–144.

Search Institute. (1998). *Developmental assets: An investment in youth.* http://www.search-institute.org/developmental-assets (accessed December 2012).

Singer, M. (2006). A dose of drugs, a touch of violence, a case of AIDS, part II: Further conceptualizing the SAVA syndemic. *Free Inquiry for Creative Sociology, 34*(1), 39–53.

Sperber, D. (1996). *Explaining culture: A naturalistic approach.* Oxford, UK: Blackwell.

Sperry, L. L., & Sperry, D. E. (1995). Young children's presentations of self in conversational narration. In L. Sperry and P. Smiley (Eds.), *New directions for child development: Vol. 69. Exploring young children's concepts of self and other through conversation* (pp. 47–60). San Francisco: Jossey-Bass.

Stewart, Eric A., and Ronald L. Simons. 2006. Structure and culture in African

American adolescent violence: A partial test of the "code of the street" thesis. *JQ: Justice Quarterly* 23(1), 1–33.

Sullivan, M. L. (1989). *"Getting paid": Youth crime and work in the inner city.* Ithaca: Cornell University Press.

Sutherland, E. H., & Cressey, D. R. (1978). *Criminology.* Philadelphia: Lippincott.

Theokas, C., Almerigi, J. B., Lerner, R. M., Dowling, E. M., Benson, P. L., and Scales, P. C., & von Eye, A. (2005). Conceptualizing and modeling individual and ecological asset components of thriving in early adolescence. *Journal of Early Adolescence,* 25, 113–143.

Venkatesh, S. A. (2006). *Off the books: The underground economy of the urban poor.* Cambridge: Harvard University Press.

Vigil, J. D. (2007). *The projects: Gang and non-gang families in East Los Angeles.* Austin: University of Texas Press.

Wacquant, L. (1998). Inside the zone: The social art of the hustler in the black American ghetto. *Theory, Culture, and Society,* 15, 1–36.

Whitehead, T. (1992). Expressions of masculinity in a Jamaican sugartown: Implications for family planning programs. In T. Whitehead & B. Reid (Eds.), *Gender constructs and social issues* (pp. 103–141). Chicago: University of Illinois Press.

Whitehead, T., Peterson, J., & Kaljee, L. (1994). The "hustle": Socioeconomic deprivation, urban drug trafficking, and low-income African American male gender identity. *Pediatrics,* 93, 1050–1054.

Wilkinson, D. L. (2004). *Guns, violence, and identity among African American and Latino youth.* New York: LFB.

Wilkinson, D. L., Beaty, C. C., & Lurry, R. M. (2009). Youth violence: Crime or self-help? Marginalized urban males' perspectives on the limited efficacy of the criminal justice system to stop youth violence. *Annals of the American Academy of Political and Social Science,* 623, 25–38.

Willis, P. (1981). *Learning to labor: How working class kids get working class jobs.* New York: Columbia University Press.

Wilson, P. J. (1973). *Crab antics: The social anthropology of English-speaking societies of the Caribbean.* New Haven: Yale University Press.

Wilson, W. J. (1987). *The truly disadvantaged: The inner city, the underclass, and public policy.* Chicago: University of Chicago Press.

8

Incarceration and the Economic Fortunes of Urban Neighborhoods

JEFFREY FAGAN AND VALERIE WEST

Introduction

Research on the growth in incarceration has focused on both the sources of incarceration and its public safety returns.[1] The incapacitative and deterrent effects of incarceration are fundamental rationales for the heavy fiscal burdens of mass incarceration, and legislators have used a wide range of policy instruments to increase both the number of persons sentenced to prison and the lengths of their sentences. Recent studies disagree on the impacts of incarceration on crime rates within states (see, for example, Spelman, 2000; Zimring, Hawkins, and Kamin, 2003; Levitt, 2004; Katz, Levitt, and Shustorovich, 2003) or smaller areas within cities (Clear et al., 2003; Lynch and Sabol, 2004; Fagan, West, and Holland, 2003).

While this debate continues, a parallel line of research has started to examine the impacts of the rise in incarceration on both inmates and the family members they left behind and to whom they return (Nagin, Cullen, and Jonson, 2009; Durlauf and Nagin, 2011). Recent studies have examined the intergenerational impacts of incarceration on the economic and social well-being of children and families (Geller, Garfinkel, and Western, 2011; Hagan and Dinovitzer, 1999; LeBlanc, 2003). Other research has examined the challenges facing newly released inmates to avoid crime and successfully return to community life (Visher and Travis, 2003; Travis, 2005; Petersilia, 2003). Prisoners' reentry is complicated by the specific effects of incarceration on work (Western, 2006; Pettit and Western, 2004), crime (Chen and Shapiro, 2007), and earnings (Lyons and Pettit, 2011). For example, incarceration suppresses future earnings, especially for young African American males, whether by diminishing their human capital that makes them marketable in the workplace (e.g., Freeman, 1996; Pettit and Lyons, 2007; Lyons and Pettit, 2011) or by attaching a stigma that discourages employers from hiring them even for low-paying, unskilled-labor jobs (Pager, 2003, 2007; Pettit and Lyons, 2007). Incarceration increases—or perhaps coerces—residential mobility, contributing to social instability and detachment from supportive social networks that in turn increases crime (Clear et al., 2003). Incarceration often is a developmental transitional turning point that diminishes the life prospects for stable marriage and employment (e.g., Sampson and Laub, 1993; Laub and Sampson, 2003, 290–292). Incarceration also excludes returning inmates from several forms of political participation and citizenship: jury service, the right to vote, and the right to hold elective office (Fletcher, 1998; Maurer, 2006; Manza and Uggen, 2006; but see Miles, 2004). The racial concentration of incarceration means that these effects are especially pronounced for African Americans (Maurer, 2006; Loury, 2008; Fagan, 2004, 2008).[2]

These studies show how the consequences of incarceration extend beyond individual effects to change the social organization and economic fortunes of neighborhoods. Incarceration is spatially concentrated, a consequence of the spatial clustering of crime, law enforcement, social structural risk, and racial residential segregation (Morenoff and Sampson, 1997; Fagan et al., 2010; Fagan and Davies, 2004; Sampson and Raudenbush, 2004).[3] A handful of studies have illustrated this spatial concentration of incarceration and examined whether this spatial concentration reduces or contributes to crime (e.g., Clear et al., 2003; Fagan, West, and Holland, 2003; Lynch and Sabol, 2004).

These studies examined the reciprocal effects of crime, incarceration, and neighborhood social and economic disadvantage that are bound together in complex neighborhood ecological dynamics. These neighborhood dynamics themselves exert secondary or one-off effects on a range of individual outcomes including crime, employment, school dropout, teenage pregnancy, and drug abuse, often swamping any individual effects (Sampson, Morenoff, and Gannon-Rowley, 2002; Sampson, Morenoff, and Raudenbush, 2005). In some neighborhoods, this racial-spatial concentration may accumulate to produce collective consequences for entire neighborhoods, consequences whose effects are well beyond what we might expect from the aggregation of individual effects of persons within neighborhoods.

Several researchers now are examining the effects of this spatial concentration of incarceration, including its effects on social and economic indicia of community life. Recent theoretical and empirical work has focused on the unintended consequences of incarceration not just for individuals or families but for the neighborhoods that experience the highest rates of incarceration (Lynch and Sabol, 2004). Much of this work has focused on the possibility that incarceration may increase neighborhood crime rates (Clear et al., 2003; Fagan, West, and Holland, 2003; Lynch et al., 2001; Lynch and Sabol, 2004). Few (Hagan and Dinovitzer, 1999; Sabol and Lynch, 2003) have looked at the effects of incarceration on the social and economic contexts—human capital, poverty, and family and child well-being—of neighborhoods that are intricately bound up with incarceration and crime (see Crutchfield and Wadsworth, chapter 6 in this volume). Because crime, incarceration, and neighborhood contexts are part of a complex ecological dynamic with reciprocal effects over time, unraveling these influences is a potentially important step in understanding the persistent spatial concentration of incarceration that seems to be orthogonal to local crime rates.[4]

In this chapter, we take another step in this direction. We analyze data from a panel study of New York City neighborhoods to examine the effects of incarceration on two indicia of the economic well-being of neighborhoods: median household income and human capital. The research setting is New York City in the years from 1985 to 1997, a period when there was a perfect storm of crime crises and their sequelae: epidemics of gun violence and highly addictive drugs (Fagan, Wilkinson, and Davies, 2007), economic instability (Drennan, 1992), a significant increase in incarceration per crime (Fagan, West, and Holland, 2003), and high rates of residential mobility (DeGiovanni and Minnite, 1992; Beveridge, 2008). These dynamics disproportionately affected the city's minority citizens (Fagan, West, and Holland, 2003; Fagan, 2004). In our earlier study in 2003, we showed that incarceration grew over time after controlling for the crime rate and for law enforcement. The stability of incarceration in the face of declining crime rates illustrated the endogeneity of incarceration in the most disadvantaged neighborhoods. But neighborhood economic strength was one of the factors that protectively insulated neighborhoods from the spiraling crime-incarceration dynamic.

Accordingly, we examine here whether in fact the dynamics of incarceration adversely affect the social and economic resources of New York City's neighborhoods and embed neighborhoods in the endogenous dynamics of crime, incarceration, and disadvantage. We examine whether incarceration exhibits negative effects on neighborhood well-being, using two dimensions of neighborhood economic status: median income and human capital. Both are robust predictors of elevated crime, enforcement, and incarceration rates. We use a panel design to examine the effects of incarceration on New York City census tracts over an 11-year period from 1985 to 1997, a period which saw crime rates rise and then fall (Karmen, 2000; Fagan, Zimring, and Kim, 1998; Bowling, 1999; Fagan et al., 2010; Zimring, 2006) but an era when incarceration rates rose steadily in concentrated areas throughout the city. We ask whether persistently high incarceration rates erode human capital and depress incomes, intensifying incarceration risks and threatening to create conditions where incarceration and economic disadvantage are endogenous features of certain neighborhoods.

Background

Neighborhoods exert strong effects on a wide range of social behaviors (for a review, see Sampson, Morenoff, and Gannon-Rowley, 2002), including crime (Fagan, 2008). These effects influence the social and economic behaviors not only of their residents but also of residents of the surrounding areas, through dynamics of diffusion or contagion of neighborhood effects (Reordan et al., 2008; Lee et al., 2008; Reordan and Sullivan, 2004; Grannis, 1998). Neighborhood effects capture the intricate interplay between social structure, social organization, and social control, which combine to influence individual behaviors. Interest in neighborhood effects has produced new research on small-area variations in child development and child maltreatment, domestic violence, teenage sexual behavior and childbearing, school dropout, home ownership, several indicia of health, suicide, social and physical disorder, drug use, and adolescent delinquency (see, for example, Coulton et al., 1995; Miles-Doan, 1998; Crane, 1991; Gould, Wallenstein, and Kleinman, 1990; Gould et al., 1990; Brooks-Gunn et al., 1993; Rowe and Rogers, 1994). Moreover, evidence of the spread of social behaviors from one neighborhood to the next suggests that elements of social contagion may also explain variation in crime rates over time (Fagan and Davies, 2004).

Here, we focus not on the neighborhood effects on individuals but instead on the effects of incarceration on the ecology of neighborhoods and their developmental trajectories over time. We assume that neighborhoods (like people) are dynamic entities that change over time and that these transformations are likely to lead to complex outcomes of crime and other indicia of social and economic life.

A small number of studies use panel methods to examine these interactions within neighborhoods over time, identifying complex interactions and (nonrecursive) feedback processes between crime and the social dynamics and compositional characteristics of neighborhoods (e.g., Bellair, 2000).[5] Some neighborhood-change studies have examined the reciprocal influence of adjacent neighborhoods on crime rates. For example, Taylor and Covington (1988), Morenoff and Sampson (1997), and Heitgerd and Bursik (1987) all identified dynamics in which crime or violence in one area influenced homicide rates in adjacent areas over time. Taylor and Covington examined gentrification as a trigger for crime, while Heitgerd and Bursik used a similar strategy to show that even stable, well-organized communities can have high rates of delinquency when the adjacent neighborhoods experienced rapid racial change. Other studies have identified turning points in neighborhoods that precede the onset or intensification of crime. Bursik and colleagues (Bursik and Webb, 1982; Bursik, 1984; Bursik and Grasmick, 1992, 1993) analyzed neighborhood change in Chicago's 74 planning areas to identify turning points in the natural history of neighborhood development to pinpoint when crime rates change and grow.

In this chapter, we are concerned with the effects of both endogenous social dynamics—including crime, economic activity, and stratification—and exogenous shocks to these systems through public policy choices. The fact that incarceration has elements of both—endogeneity with crime, exogeneity with policy choices—is both a conceptual and analytic challenge. That is, the specific question is how incarceration, which is both a response to crime within neighborhoods and also a public policy choice produced by factors exogenous to the neighborhoods, affects the developmental history of neighborhood economics. If the effects are salutary, then we might conclude that incarceration produces the ancillary benefits of promoting neighborhood resilience to crime while at the same time reducing one of the main sociological culprits in local crime rates. But we might also worry that if incarceration adversely affects neighborhoods, the criminal justice policies producing incarceration may actually worsen and reify the social and economic risks of crime and other social behaviors, creating an internal equilibrium that will sustain incarceration over time and resist incremental policy changes meant to disrupt it.

Incarceration and Neighborhood Crime

Three studies have shown that the risks of going to jail or prison grow over time for persons living in poor neighborhoods. In a panel study of New York City neighborhoods from 1985 to 1996, Fagan, West, and Holland (2003) showed that neighborhoods with high rates of incarceration invited closer and more punitive police enforcement and parole surveillance, contributing to the growing number of repeat admissions and the resilience of incarceration even as crime rates fall. The authors included measures of both prison and jail admissions, emphasizing how even short-term incarceration in local facilities contributed to further incarceration. Using growth curve models and controlling for the endogeneity of crime, incarceration, and social structural disadvantage, they concluded that incarceration produced more incarceration net of crime and that incarceration was associated with increasing crime. The engine for the growth in incarceration was drug enforcement, which continued to resupply incarceration (Fagan, West, and Holland, 2003, 2005). These dynamics spiraled over time in a reciprocal dynamic that at some tipping point is likely to reach equilibrium. The dynamic becomes self-sustaining and reinforcing and continues even as externalities such as labor market dynamics or population structure undergo significant change, as well as in the face of declining crime rates and receding drug epidemics.

In the second study, based on data from a two-wave study of neighborhoods in Tallahassee, Florida, Clear et al. (2003) showed a positive relationship between the rate of releases one year and the community's crime rates the following year. They showed a dose-response relationship between prison admissions and crime—low rates of prison admissions had nonsignificant effects on local crime rates, moderate prison admission rates produced modest effects on crime, and the neighborhoods with the highest rates had the strongest increase in crime. Provocative as this study may be, it overlooked endogeneity of crime and incarceration that would lead to intercept differences in the neighborhoods at the outset of the panel and weaken the causal claim. That is, higher incarceration rates may simply respond to higher crime rates, or the two may be spuriously related to the factors that produced these intercept differences (i.e., simultaneous equation bias).

The Tallahassee study was silent on causal mechanisms, such as incarceration impacts on informal social control or community organization. These mediating mechanisms were an explicit focus in a study by Lynch and Sabol (2004) of crime, incarceration, and social organization in 30 Baltimore communities. Lynch and Sabol examined the effects of neighborhood incarceration rates on community social cohesion and informal social control in the 30 neighborhoods and ultimately the effect of those rates on crime. They tested whether incarceration lessens the capacity of communities to engage in social control, which in turn could increase crime rates. They identified the discretionary component of law enforcement—one of the primary engines of incarceration (see also Fagan, West, and Holland 2003)—through an instrumental variables model to estimate the effects of law enforcement (arrest) on incarceration net of crime.[6] They showed that incarceration rates reduced feelings of community solidarity and undermined neighborhood residents' willingness to join in the types of neighborhood activities that are critical elements of collective actions to reduce crime. At the same time, incarceration seemed to promote informal social control, a neighborhood benefit that can produce an effective response to crime.[7] Their results leave complicated lessons, though perhaps these lessons could be unraveled by sorting out the effects on communities with different baselines of collective action and crime.

The common ground in both studies is the indictment of incarceration as a negative influence on community organization and informal social control, a perverse consequence that may produce more and not less crime. Rose and Clear (1998) hypothesize that concentrations of incarceration may disrupt social networks by damaging familial, economic, and political sources of informal social control, mortgaging the community's social capital and also the social ties of the persons living there (regardless of whether they had been to prison). In their 2003 study, Clear et al. identify *coercive mobility* as the mechanism for the erosion of social cohesion and social capital (also noted by Lynch and Sabol). Coercive mobility is a dynamic process of residential mobility that is induced by high rates of removal to and return from prison, as well as high rates of crime and victimization. Such mobility has long been implicated in higher crime rates in communities (e.g., Shaw and McKay, 1942), but more recent updates of this theory pinpoint the mechanisms by which mobility raises the risk of crime (see, for example, Bursik, 1988; Fagan and Davies, 2004, 2007). Rose and Clear suggest that coercive mobility undermines the less coercive and more influential institutions of social control, such as families and community associations and a community's capacity to enforce norms to defend against crime (see, for example, Bursik and Grasmick, 1993). These dynamics are compounded systemically by the mobility of citizens who are victims of crime,[8] citizens who might otherwise be participants in social regulation. Thus, the churning effects of prisoners coming and going with limited job prospects every time they return may contribute systemically to the mobility that increases the risks of crime.

High rates of incarceration may reduce incentives for citizens to participate in informal social control by reducing the communicative value of sanctions, delegitimizing law and legal actors, further inviting crime, and intensifying the crime-enforcement-incarceration-crime cycle (Fagan and Meares, 2008; Uggen and Manza, 2004). High rates of imprisonment raise questions of the legitimacy of government and potentially undermine incentives to comply with the law (Sherman, 1993; Tyler and Huo, 2002). The racial and neighborhood asymmetry in punishment offers a stark contrast to the claims of legal actors that law is fair and legitimate. If local residents reject the claim that prison sentences are fairly distributed across races and neighborhoods, they may conclude that the policy that produces the unfair distribution is illegitimate (Fagan, 2004).

Incarceration and Neighborhood Economic Well-Being

Much of what we know about the adverse effects of incarceration on individuals' prospects in the legal labor market come from large and small panel studies of former inmates. We were unable to locate studies of the effects of incarceration on the aggregate social or economic well-being of neighborhoods as a function of the rates of removal to prison or jail.

The panel studies agree that the prospects for stable employment and future earnings of former inmates are dim (Freeman, 1996; Fagan and Freeman, 1999; Western and Pettit, 2000; Western, 2006). As a person's time spent in prison increases, the subsequent likelihood of disengagement from the legal economy increases (Freeman, 1996; Grogger, 1995; Hagan, 1991). Once out of prison, a criminal record disadvantages low-skill and other workers who are attempting either to enter the labor force or to improve their earnings (Pager, 2003). Western and Beckett's (1999) study of incarceration and unemployment found that although growing levels of incarceration initially produced lower rates of conventional measures of unemployment, the recycling of these ex-offenders back into the job market with reduced job prospects had the effect of increasing unemployment in the long run. Western (2002) estimates that the earnings loss associated with prison ranges between 10% and 30%, and serving time in prison is also associated with decreased earnings growth.

Some studies have looked at the aggregation effects of concentrated incarceration on labor market outcomes. Western, Kling, and Weiman (2001) and Western (2006) showed not only that incarceration lowers the work prospects of former inmates but that the spatial concentration of incarceration may aggravate social and economic disadvantages by compounding individual barriers to meaningful employment for released prisoners and their peers (Western, Kling, and Weiman, 2001, 414). These aggregate effects become a collective problem in neighborhoods marked by high incarceration, decreasing the prospects for desistance by returning inmates (Western, 2002; Laub and Sampson, 2003), while increasing crime risks for others living in the same areas.

Incarceration potentially stigmatizes neighborhoods, complicating the ability of local residents to access job-hiring networks to enter and compete in labor markets (Granovetter, 1973, 1974) and deterring businesses from locating in those areas (Granovetter, 1974). The stigma evidently is not lost on employers. Holzer, Raphael, and Stoll (2004) show that employers are more reluctant to hire former prisoners than to hire welfare recipients. Both welfare recipients and inmates are spatially concentrated in poor minority neighborhoods, so the imbalance in employer preferences is even more striking. Thus, job scarcity, even for low-skill jobs, will likely add to the concentration of economic disadvantage in neighborhoods that already lag behind others in employment and earnings.

In Sabol and Lynch's (2003) Baltimore study, they examined labor force participation using releases from prison as a proxy for incarceration rates. Using race-specific models, they found that release rates were positively and significantly related to unemployment for blacks but that the opposite was the case for whites. Disruption of these local networks of social control and economic activity can mean that the long-run consequences of incarceration will be to increase crime (Lynch and Sabol, 2004). The secondary effects of incarceration are diffused to others in neighborhoods with spatially concentrated incarceration. Low earnings and employment by returning prisoners burden families since former inmates have less ability to bring money to families and less to spend on essential services in their communities.

Lynch and Sabol argue that incarceration "can also reduce the earning power of family left behind because they must tend to tasks formerly performed by the incarcerated family member. In the long run, incarceration will have negative effects on the economic life of the community by reducing the ability of returning inmates to obtain jobs and higher salaries" (2004, 273). This prediction is reinforced when we consider the employer preferences shown by Holzer and colleagues.

Incarceration and Family Integrity

One would expect incarceration to be a turning point in the lives of men in several ways that increase their crime risks. Not only are they disadvantaged in the workplace, but their ties to their children and families suffer, eroding an essential form of emotional and social support that has strong effects on criminal activity (Sampson and Laub, 1993; Laub and Sampson, 2003). Recent studies offer evidence that imprisonment damages the ties between incarcerated men and women, their families, and their communities (Hagan and Dinovitzer, 1999, 122; Geller et al., 2009, 2012). These effects further burden the efforts of former inmates to avoid crime once back in their communities but also diminish their capacity to supervise and raise children.

Researchers have focused on the fates of families and children, with inferences about communities based on the concentration of incarceration and the aggregation of individual effects. In *Random Family*, LeBlanc (2003) reports on a social and familial network of Latino families and neighbors. Her ethnography shows how incarceration can weaken families by removing men from existing families, by reducing the supply of marriageable men in the neighborhood, and in turn by attenuating or skewing family formation toward unstable couplings (see also Wilson, 1996). Her work shows the effects of incarceration on the capacities of families as socializing agents for children and on their ability to supervise teenage children.

Edin, Nelson, and Paranal (2004) show that incarceration influences the ties between imprisoned men and their children in several ways. In life-history studies with men with low job skills in two cities, they identify a group of men whose ties to their children—ties that were strong prior to incarceration—were disrupted by their imprisonment. Fathers in this group were less able to supervise their children and to maintain parental ties that are important to preventing children's involvement with the law (Geller et al., 2009, 2012). For some men, incarceration disrupted the destructive behaviors that had weakened their ties to their children in the years before prison. For this group, prison offered the chance for a different kind of turning point. For others, having children provided an incentive to avoid crime and raised the costs of crime and legal trouble. But incarceration also disrupted the economic role of those men whose criminal activities were an important income source for their children and partners. For these men, incarceration strained not only family ties but also family economic well-being. Fatherhood increased the pressure on men to provide materially for their children, not just with strollers and playpens when they are younger but for clothes and shoes when they become adolescents. Yet the workplace stigma of incarceration kept many of these men out of even low-wage legal work and contributed to their return to crime (Edin et al., 2004).

Several studies show that children of incarcerated parents have poorer emotional, behavioral, and psychological development than do other children (Wildeman, 2010; Murray et al., 2009; for a review of earlier work, see Johnson and Waldfogel, 2002). Even when parent behaviors prior to incarceration have had negative influences on child development, these studies show that the effects of incarceration are also observed once the parent leaves home for prison. One pathway to adverse child development is through children's removal to foster care. Children with an incarcerated parent are more likely to be placed in foster care, where developmental outcomes are uncertain, and the disruption of parental attachment can have serious developmental consequences (Johnson and Waldfogel, 2004; Geller et al. 2009, 2012).

These effects fall more heavily on nonwhite families and especially on African American families. Myers (2000) argues that the high rates of incarceration of African American males contribute to the higher prevalence of black families headed by single women in predominantly African American neighborhoods. Lynch and Sabol (2004) estimate that increases in incarceration of black men were associated with about 20% of the increase in the number of black families headed by single women during the 1980s. And when men go to prison in high rates in poor, minority neighborhoods, the supply of marriageable men declines, suppressing the marriage rate. As Wilson explains, "both inner-city black males and females believe that since most marriages will eventually break up and since marriages no longer represent meaningful relationships, it is better to avoid the entanglements of wedlock altogether" (1996, 104).

The children of African American incarcerated mothers are far more likely to be placed with another family member or in foster care compared to the children of white incarcerated mothers, even after controlling for differences in social position (Johnson and Waldfogel, 2004, 123). One consequence, then, of higher incarceration rates is strain on the child welfare system. The spatial concentration of incarceration will focus these systemic strains in small social areas with limited foster care resources and supervisory or regulatory capacities.

Incarceration and Local Social Control

Recent work with incarcerated males and the "fragile families" they leave behind suggests that incarceration disrupts family ties and social networks, aggravating vulnerabilities to crime through compromises to social control, in turn creating a churning effect on social networks (McLanahan and Sandefur, 1994; McLanahan and Bumpass, 1998; Wildeman, 2010). Social organization and social control are spatially embedded processes that influence neighborhood-level variations in violence (Morenoff, Sampson, and Raudenbush, 2001). Thus, rising and concentrated rates of incarceration not only become a part of the fabric of poor communities, already susceptible to crime, but they compromise the limited forms of social control that poor communities can mount.

Informal social control is essential in the regulation of crime (Bursik and Grasmick, 1993). But social control is intricately tied to social structure, supporting citizen activities—social regulation—that can sustain or inhibit crime (Sampson, Raudenbush, and Earls, 1997). When economic conditions are weak, the strains of everyday life can compromise the participation of local residents in social regulation. If these effects extend to neighborhood economic well-being, the strains on residents' capacity for social control reinforce the crime-incarceration dynamics well observed in other studies.

This Study

The negative consequences of concentrated incarceration in poor neighborhoods may offset its public-safety benefits (Fagan, West, and Holland, 2003). The cascade of negative consequences may corrode the ecological dynamics of neighborhood social control, in a way that actually may elevate crime risks over time (Lynch and Sabol, 2004; Clear et al., 2003; Fagan, West, and Holland, 2005). Here, we reverse the question and estimate the effects of incarceration on neighborhood economic fortunes as part of the influence of incarceration on the ecology of social control. We suspect that higher incarceration is associated with lower income and less human capital at the tract level.

We suggest that the spatial concentration of incarceration can attenuate a neighborhood's economic fortunes through three possible mechanisms (Fagan, West, and Holland, 2003): (1) incarceration complicates the efforts of individuals to forge links to legal work (Hagan and Palloni, 1990; Fagan and Freeman, 1999; Pager, 2003; Holzer, Raphael, and Stoll, 2004); (2) concentrated incarceration compromises social control in multiple ways, by increasing the number of single-parent households, by reducing the number of older males, and by straining citizens' relationships to law and social control (Lynch and Sabol, 2004; Myers, 2000); and (3) the concentration of incarceration in poor, predominantly minority communities can also lead to voter disenfranchisement, which may adversely affect the political economy of neighborhoods (Maurer, 2006; Uggen and Manza, 2002; Uggen, Behrens, and Manza, 2005. In addition, high rates of incarceration may mark a neighborhood as risky or high crime and may attract recurring and intensive police attention that sustains the elevated risks of police action.

With these mechanisms in mind, we present analyses on the effects of incarceration on the economic fortunes of neighborhoods. First, we present trends in incarceration and crime for New York City census tracts for the period 1985–1996, the most recent era of sharp increases in incarceration in New York City and New York State (Fagan, West, and Holland, 2003). Next, we show the effects of incarceration on two indicia of neighborhood economic well-being—median household income and human capital—in a series of regression models that take advantage of the panel structure of the data. We include jail populations in addition to prison populations, a dimension of incarceration that has been neglected in much of the research on incarceration. We use the homicide victimization rate as a proxy for the overall crime rate (see Maltz, 1998). We include a series of control variables that capture the dimensions of neighborhood social control and social structure and that themselves are bound up with both incarceration and crime. To estimate temporal effects, we include interactions of time with each of these predictors.

Research Setting and Methods

Crime and Incarceration in New York City

Trends in crime and incarceration in New York City from 1985 to 1997 provide the backdrop for understanding how incarceration shapes the economic fortunes of neighborhoods. Crime rates rose in New York beginning in 1985, concurrent with the onset of the crack epidemic and the emergence of street drug markets that themselves were flashpoints for violence and other crimes (Fagan, Zimring, and Kim, 1998; Karmen, 2000; Harcourt and Ludwig, 2006). Table 8.1 shows that violent crime rose 29.1% from 1985 to 1990, and the total index crime (i.e., major felonies) rate rose by 18%. Starting in 1991, crime fell sharply, by nearly 50% for index crimes and 46.7% for violent crimes.

Incarceration rates rose and fell concurrently with changes in crime rates, though the trajectories were quite different. Prison sentences rose 89% from 1985 to 1990, rising more quickly than the crime rates.[9] Prison sentences then declined by 19.2% through 1997, a rate slower than the decline in crime. The steadily increasing rates of prison sentences per reported crime, arrest, and conviction—during periods of both increase and decline in crime—showed the rise in the propensity for incarceration within the criminal justice system in New York City. The effect of these changes in punishment norms was sharp and sustained growth in New York State's prison population. The state prison population rose from 25,000 in 1985 to 55,000 in 1990 and then to nearly 70,000 in 1997 (Fagan, West, and Holland, 2003). Most—about 70%—of the state's inmates come from New York City.[10]

The jail population grew more slowly than did the prison population

Table 8.1. Crime and Punishment, New York City, 1985–1997

	1985	1990	1995	1997	% change 1985– 1990	% change 1985– 1997	% change 1990– 1997
Reported crime							
Total index crimes	602,945	711,556	442,532	356,573	18.0	(40.9)	(49.9)
Violent crimes	135,305	174,689	114,180	92,866	29.1	(31.4)	(46.8)
% violent crimes	22.4	24.6	25.9	26.0	9.8	16.1	5.7
Sentences							
Total	75,264	92,261	79,845	93,141	22.6	23.8	1.0
Prison	10,802	20,420	18,353	16,490	89.0	52.7	(19.2)
Jail	61,839	66,035	55,957	71,508	6.8	15.6	8.3
Jail + probation	2,623	5,806	5,535	5,143	121.3	96.1	(11.4)
Incarceration rates							
Prison sentences per 100 index crimes	1.79	2.86	4.15	4.62	59.8	158.1	61.5
Prison sentences per 100 felony prosecutions	35.50	37.20	42.90	44.50	4.8	25.4	19.6
Prison sentences per 100 convictions	7.20	12.80	10.50	8.80	77.8	22.2	(31.3)
Jail sentences per 100 misdemeanor arrests	50.70	60.60	33.90	37.40	19.5	(26.2)	(38.3)

Source: New York State Division of Criminal Justice Services, various years.

after 1985 but continued to grow as prison populations declined in the 1990s. The city's average daily jail-inmate population was 17,897 in 1999, a small decline from the population of 19,643 in 1990, when crime rates were twice as high (Zimring, 2006).[11]

The engine for the growth and stability of incarceration—in the face of declining crime rates—is aggressive enforcement of drug laws, especially street-level enforcement resulting in large numbers of felony arrests of retail drug sellers (Fagan, West, and Holland, 2003). Aggressive street enforcement and drug enforcement programs such as Operation Pressure Point, the Tactical Narcotics Teams, the Street Crime Unit, and Operation Condor produced consistently high rates of felony drug arrests since the mid-1980s (see, for example, Letwin, 1990; Herman, 1999; Smith et al., 1992; Belenko, Fagan, and Dumarovsky, 1994; Greene, 1999; Rashbaum, 2000; Fagan and Davies, 2000; Ketcham, 2002). Despite the dramatic decreases in crime in New York City, drug-related arrests continued to increase each year through the late 1990s.[12] For most of the 1990s, drug-related offenses accounted for an increasing proportion of New York State prison admissions: from just 12% of all New York State prison admissions in 1985 to 31% in 1990 to 38% in 1996.[13] Because these inmates are likely to serve long sentences under New York's "predicate felony" laws, drug offenders comprised a growing proportion of the city's and the state's incarcerated population (Fagan, West, and Holland, 2003).

Data

To estimate the effects of incarceration on neighborhood economic fortunes, we used a longitudinal panel of incarceration, crime, enforcement, and social structure in New York City census tracts for the period from 1985 to 1997 (Fagan, West, and Holland, 2003). We obtained a 25% sample of all individuals sentenced to prison and a 5% sample of all jail sentences for cases with dispositions in New York City for the years 1985, 1987, 1990, 1993, and 1996. This yielded an annual sample of prison sentences of 2,000 to 4,000 individuals and an annual sample of jail sentences of 3,000 to 4,000 individuals. Records of persons admitted to prisons or jails were geocoded by residential address of the incarcerated person. Geocoded cases and crime counts were aggregated to each census tract. Rates of crime and incarceration were then computed for each census tract.

We used homicide victimization rates as a proxy of crime generally (Maltz, 1998, 1999) and to account both for base rates of the supply of individuals available for incarceration and the endogeneity of crime with incarceration and neighborhood social organization (Morenoff, Sampson, and Raudenbush, 2001; Fagan and Davies, 2004). Unfortunately, the New York City Police Department does not make available crime data for geographically precise areas such as neighborhoods or census tracts.[14] Instead, we used data on homicide victimization from the Office of Vital Statistics of the New York City Department of Health and Mental Hygiene. Deaths are recorded by the Office of the Medical Examiner after classifying injuries as either intentional, accidental, or self-inflicted. Neighborhood rates were estimated by aggregating from individual cases that were geocoded to the census tract using residential address of the victim and by using a population denominator for each year in the time series.[15]

To address the specific and theoretically significant contribution of drug enforcement on incarceration, we constructed a time series on drug arrests as a measure of the intensity of drug enforcement and as a proxy for the locations and intensity of drug markets (Baumer et al., 1998; Ousey and Lee, 2002). This time series was created by obtaining a 10% sample of drug arrests from 1985 to 1997 from the New York State Division of Criminal Justice Services (see Fagan and Davies, 2002). Each arrest record was geocoded to the residential address of the arrestee and then assigned to each type of spatial unit. We aggregated arrests for drug possession, drug sales, and possession with intent to sell into a single measure of drug arrest as a measure of overall police aggressiveness in drug enforcement that was independent of the changing enforcement priorities that influenced the separate indicia over time.

Data on human capital, household income, and other measures of neighborhood social organization were obtained from the 1980, 1990, and 2000 census files (U.S. Bureau of the Census, Summery Tape File 3A). Census tract equivalencies were developed to adjust for changes in census tract configuration of the three census iterations. Data for between census years were linearly interpolated.

Measures

Neighborhood economic well-being is measured along two dimensions: median household income and human capital. Human capital is an index of three items, derived from principal components factor analysis of educational attainment (percentage high school graduates), labor force participation (weeks worked by persons 16 and over in past year), and job skills (percentage 16 and over with skilled occupation) (see Fagan, West, and Holland, 2003). These are indicia of work experience and labor market skills that tend to increase earnings (e.g., Becker, 1994) and are consistent with earlier indicia of human capital (e.g., Sanders and Nee, 1996). We used a Z-score for median household income, rather than applying uncertain cost-of-living or inflation estimators to this measure; we preferred to use the standardized measure that aligns each observation with other observations (tracts) in the panel in a consistent metric over time and that overcomes differences in the skew and variance within each panel.

We used propensity scores of incarceration to identify the "treatment effects" of incarceration on neighborhood economic status. Propensity scores are commonly used to adjust for biases resulting from the nonrandom allocation of subjects to treatment exposures (Rosenbaum and Rubin, 1983; Rosenbaum, 2002). In this case, incarceration is not randomly allocated across the city's census tracts, and the "dosages" of incarceration similarly reflect nonrandom differences in crime, social structure, and law enforcement (Fagan, West, and Holland, 2003). In this case, propensity scores for both prison and jail are the estimated probability of the allocation of the "treatment" to each neighborhood. Propensity scores thus control for the endogeneity of crime, social structure, and law enforcement, as well as other unobserved confounding variables. We used separate equations to estimate jail and prison propensity scores for each tract in each year of the panel.

Following Rubin (1997), we used a set of theoretical predictors to estimate the propensity scores that differed from those used to test the primary research questions. This allows for greater flexibility in model specification than the typical adjustments in regression-based model estimation techniques and more effectively reduces biases resulting from confounding among predictors that is a recurring problem with observational data (Rosenbaum, 2002). Ideally, we would want the functional form of the propensity score analysis to be determined by the data, but in this case, the extreme skew in incarceration rates by tract dictated that we use a log transformation and a linear model.

Accordingly, we estimated ordinary least squares regressions for logged jail and prison rates, with predictors including homicide, drug arrests, and a series of social structural factors that are well identified in criminological research on crime and punishment (e.g., Land, McCall, and Cohen, 1990; for a review, see Fagan and Davies, 2004). Following Land et al. (1990), we sorted 18 tract-level variables along seven dimensions—poverty, labor market, segregation, supervision, anonymity, immigration, and housing structure—that characterize the dimensions of concentrated disadvantage articulated in the theoretical and empirical literature linking neighborhood effects with indicia of social adversity and isolation including crime (see, for example, Sampson, Morenoff, and Gannon-Rowley, 2002; Bursik and Grasmick, 1993). For each census year, we used principal components analysis with varimax rotation to construct a factor score for each dimension. The appendix shows the item loads and factor scores for each dimension for 1990. We imputed factor scores for the between-census years to construct a score for each year.

From the regression models, we generated the predicted value for jail and prison rates for each period to estimate the effects of incarceration on neighborhood economic status over time. The results are not shown but are available from the authors. The explained variance in each model exceeds .60, a sign that a large fraction of the explanatory power of incarceration is attributable to other factors that are associated with incarceration. A strong factor efficiently isolates the effects of incarceration by removing the effects of potentially confounding variables.

To estimate the effects of concentrated prison incarceration, census tracts were sorted for each year into quartiles. First, for each year, we included all tracts with no incarceration events in a "no event" group. The remaining tracts were sorted into quartiles.[16] We also computed the percentage of population for African Americans and nonwhite Hispanics in each tract in each year. Alternate specifications of the estimation models included these measures to examine race-specific effects and also to control for the demographic concentration of incarceration in New York City within these two minority populations (Fagan, West, and Holland, 2003).

Analysis

We estimated growth curve models using random effects regression methods[17] to examine incarceration effects on neighborhoods (Gelman and Hill, 2006; Singer, 1998; Raudenbush, Bryk, and Congdon, 2002; Singer and Willett, 2003). We included the propensity scores for incarceration, with controls for the homicide rate (lagged one year and logged), the drug arrest rate (lagged one year and logged), the population over age 15 (logged), and the social control factor. Models were estimated with random intercepts. We emphasize social control because of its central role in theoretical and empirical work on the effects of incarceration on communities (Bursik and Grasmick, 1993; Rose and Clear, 1998; Lynch and Sabol, 2004). As shown in the appendix, this measure is a factor score that combines the concentration of youth population, the percentage of female-headed households with children under 15, and the ratio of youths to adults. The general model is

$$(Y_{it} - \theta \bar{Y}_i) = (1-\theta)a + (X_{it} - \theta \bar{X}_i)b + [(1-\theta)\alpha_1 + (\eta - \theta \bar{\eta}_i)],$$

where Y_{it} is economic measure of each census tract i for each time period t, Y_i is the mean of Y over time for each tract, and X is a vector including the incarceration propensity scores and other predictors.

We include time as both a fixed and random effect: time is included as a random effect to account for the panel structure of the data and as a fixed effect to account for the specific year within the panel. We include an interaction term of time by each predictor to estimate their specific longitudinal effects. In this form, the main effect represents the average effect of the predictor across the time series, with the interaction with time as the longitudinal effect. We focus on the latter to identify the cumulative longitudinal effects of incarceration.

Results

Patterns and Trends

We begin by showing the concentration of prison admissions and their relationship to income and human capital in New York City neighborhoods. Figures 8.1A and 8.1B compare prison admissions by median household income for two periods: 1985–1990 and 1993–1996, periods of increasing and then declining crime in New York City; figures 8.2A and 8.2B similarly compare incarceration with human capital. The patterns show the strong inverse correlation for each economic indicator with the rate of prison admissions: prison admissions are concentrated in neighborhoods with the lowest incomes and the lowest human capital. The figures also show the stability of incarceration by neighborhood during two distinctly different crime eras. Despite strong crime declines in New York City, prison admissions were concentrated in the same neighborhoods.

Tables 8.2 and 8.3 show change over time in household income and human capital using quartiles to group neighborhoods according to their concentration of prison incarceration.

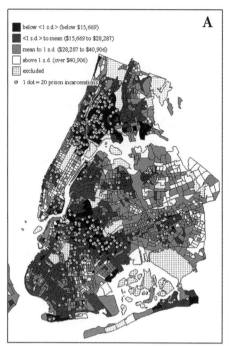

A

- below <1 s.d.> (below $15,669)
- <1 s.d.> to mean ($15,669 to $28,287)
- mean to 1 s.d. ($28,287 to $40,906)
- above 1 s.d. (over $40,906)
- excluded
- ⊙ 1 dot = 20 prison incarcerations

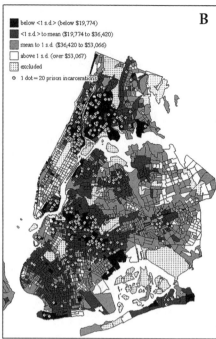

B

- below <1 s.d.> (below $19,774)
- <1 s.d.> to mean ($19,774 to $36,420)
- mean to 1 s.d. ($36,420 to $53,066)
- above 1 s.d. (over $53,067)
- excluded
- ⊙ 1 dot = 20 prison incarcerations

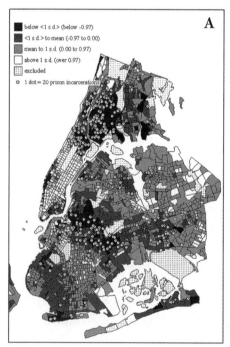

A

- below <1 s.d.> (below -0.97)
- <1 s.d.> to mean (-0.97 to 0.00)
- mean to 1 s.d. (0.00 to 0.97)
- above 1 s.d. (over 0.97)
- excluded
- ⊙ 1 dot = 20 prison incarcerations

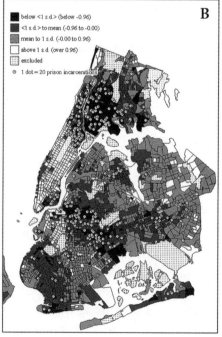

B

- below <1 s.d.> (below -0.96)
- <1 s.d.> to mean (-0.96 to -0.00)
- mean to 1 s.d. (-0.00 to 0.96)
- above 1 s.d. (over 0.96)
- excluded
- ⊙ 1 dot = 20 prison incarcerations

Table 8.2. Median Household Income by Incarceration Quintiles, 1986–1997, New York City Census Tracts (Means, Standard Deviations)

	Year				
Quintile	1986	1988	1991	1994	1997
No Events	28,523	32,740	38,354	41,890	44,039
	(10535)	(12241)	(14320)	(16197)	(16568)
1	24,022	28,917	34,389	36,720	40,047
	(8195)	(10597)	(12733)	(12280)	(17943)
2	21,706	25,186	31,171	33,250	34,654
	(8961)	(10888)	(10946)	(11361)	(12197)
3	17,709	21,058	24,704	26,162	28,715
	(8095)	(9550)	(10776)	(10988)	(13908)
4	14,832	17,621	18,790	20,066	22,198
	(7373)	(8977)	(10715)	(9816)	(14212)
Total	24,675	27,972	32,218	35,012	37,821
	(10815)	(12527)	(14584)	(15854)	(17526)

Source: Bureau of the Census, STF 3A, Interpolated for Reconciled Census Tracts 1980–2000

Table 8.3. Human Capital (Factor Score) by Incarceration Quintiles, 1986–1997, New York City Census Tracts (Means, Standard Deviations)

	Year				
Quintile	1986	1988	1991	1994	1997
No Events	0.261	0.283	0.316	0.335	0.302
	(0.854)	(0.870)	(0.841)	(0.800)	(0.826)
1	0.288	0.317	0.409	0.334	0.253
	(0.931)	(0.868)	(0.898)	(0.893)	(0.933)
2	−0.143	−0.096	0.051	0.037	−0.063
	(0.896)	(0.921)	(0.786)	(0.845)	(0.861)
3	−0.583	−0.485	−0.432	−0.483	−0.477
	(0.875)	(0.869)	(0.918)	(0.859)	(0.918)
4	−0.940	−0.870	−1.049	−1.053	−0.958
	(0.840)	(0.929)	(0.844)	(0.796)	(0.881)
Total	0.001	0.000	0.000	0.000	0.000
	(0.966)	(0.978)	(0.987)	(0.964)	(0.968)

Source: Bureau of the Census, STF 3A, Interpolated for Reconciled Census Tracts 1980–2000

FACING PAGE:

Top, Fig. 8.1, *A*, 1985–1990 median household income; *B*, 1993–1996 median household income

Bottom, Fig. 8.2, *A*, 1985–1990 human capital; *B*, 1993–1996 human capital

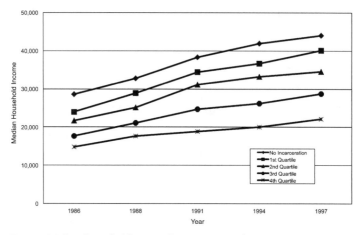

Fig. 8.3. Median household income by prison quartile, 1986–1997

The patterns for jail quartiles are similar (data not shown). The un-adjusted median household income rose over the study period in each of the quartiles and in the no-incarceration group; however, there is less fluctuation when the values for income are standardized. Figure 8.3 shows the adjusted median household income (Z-scores) over time, and table 8.2 show the general trend in income unadjusted for inflation.

Over the panel, neighborhoods with the highest incarceration have the lowest median household income. Although there is some fluctuation between the two highest and the lowest levels of household income, the neighborhoods with highest incarceration rates had lower household incomes over time. The concentration seems, at first glance, to be stable in the face of changing externalities such as declining homicide rates and changing property values. As expected, household income was greater in the neighborhoods with no incarceration and lowest in the areas with the highest rates of prison admissions. There are slight differences between the observed pattern in the two highest and lowest quartiles. But these differences in slope appear to be marginal.

The temporal patterns for human capital were less consistent across quartiles. As with household income, none of the lines cross, indicating stability in the relative position of neighborhoods over time in the distribution of human capital across the city, which seems invariant to changes in crime rates or other economic or social externalities. Table 8.3 shows a slight increase in human capital through 1991 for the neighborhoods with no incarceration and then a slight decline. For the first quartile, those neighborhoods with the lowest incarceration rates, human capital remained stable over time. In the second and third quartiles, human capital increased through 1991 before declining slightly through 1997. The trend in the fourth quartile differed: human capital rose slightly before declining sharply and then rising slightly again in the last period in the study interval.

Incarceration Effects: Model Estimation

Models were estimated in four ways to identify more specifically the effects of both jail and prison on neighborhood economic status. Models for jail and prison were estimated separately. Models with both jail and prison were then estimated to examine their additive effects on economic measures. The fourth model examined their conditional effects by including an interaction term that combined jail and prison admissions. We included race-specific measures of neighborhood demography. Each set of models included first-order interactions of each predictor with time to examine the effects over time of incarceration and the other predictors.[18] Descriptive statistics for the variables used in the models are shown in table 8.4 and also in the appendix.

Table 8.4. Descriptive Statistics

	Mean	Std. Dev.	Minimum	Maximum
Median household income	31,541	15,208	4,757	177,088
Population > 15	3018	2361	16	34079
% African American	26.2	32.1	0.0	100.0
% nonwhite Hispanic	22.6	21.9	0.0	100.0
Prison rate*	2.4	4.3	0.0	114.1
Jail rate*	7.9	18.2	0.0	421.1
Drug arrest rate*	9.6	19.9	0.0	619.8
Homicide victimization rate[†]	0.24	0.36	0.0	6.5
Poverty/inequality (factor)	0.0	1.0	−3.1	3.1
Human capital (factor)	0.0	1.0	−5.1	3.0
Segregation (factor)	0.0	1.0	−2.8	1.7
Social control (factor)	0.0	1.0	−5.2	4.9
Anonymity (factor)	0.0	1.0	−3.4	8.9
Immigration (factor)	0.0	1.0	−1.8	4.5
Housing structure (factor)	0.0	1.0	−3.4	13.7

* Rate per 10,000 persons
† Rate per 1,000 persons

Table 8.5. Random Effects Regression of Jail and Prison on Median Household Income (Z–score) by Census Tract, 1986–1997 (Coefficients, p(z))

	Prison only	Jail only	Addictive effects	Conditional effects
Main effects				
Prison (propensity)	−.448***		−.121	−.360***
Jail (propensity)		−.224***	−.188***	−.276***
Interaction				.065***
% black	−.078	−.057	−.005	.332***
% Hispanic	−1.037***	−.949***	−.918***	−.517***
Effects over time				
Prison (propensity)	.036***		.026	.058*
Jail (propensity)		.014***	.011**	.007
Interaction				−.000
% black	−.036***	−.024***	−.029***	−.036***
% Hispanic	.008	.015**	.012**	.001
Model statistics				
R^2	.648	.662	.662	.688
χ^2 (Wald)	3595.10	3694.45	3749.04	4742.71
$p\,(\chi^2)$	.000	.000	.000	.000
Rho	.928	.928	.926	.911

Note: All models include random effects for time, population size, social control, human capital, drug arrest rate (logged), homicide rate (logged). All models estimated with random intercepts and robust standard errors p(z): *** $p < .001$, ** $p < .01$, * $p < .05$

Incarceration Effects on Household Income

Table 8.5 shows incarceration effects across four model specifications for neighborhood (median) household income. In these, we pay attention both to the direct effect of incarceration and the interactions between the incarceration "treatment" and time. Incarceration in general, but jail more specifically, has an economically destabilizing effect on neighborhoods. When estimated separately, prison and jail have significant negative effects on communities' economic fortunes: higher rates of all forms of incarceration depress household incomes. When estimated together, jail continues to decrease a neighborhood's household income, but prison, while still negative, fails to reach significance. The positive interaction terms between time and incarceration suggest that over time these negative effects are significantly amplified.

In the first three models, there are no significant effects for blacks. Higher percentages of Hispanics in neighborhoods, however, are associated with lower household income, and the effects increase over time. The effect of race/ethnicity persists separately from its contributions through the propensity score estimations for jail and prison, perhaps owing to the scale of race effects on neighborhood economic status relative to highly variable incarceration rates by census tract.

In the conditional model, the coefficients for jail and prison are still negative and significant, while the interaction term is positive and significant. However, there is little change in the explanatory power of the additive and conditional models. There is no change in the R^2 between the jail-only model and the additive model and only a very modest gain in explained variance in the conditional model. In these data, then, there is little evidence of interactions between jail and prison: the effects appear to be neither conditional nor interdependent, nor are they additive in their effects on neighborhood incomes.

The opposing effects of jail and prison are not surprising as a matter of crime control and neighborhood ecology. Admissions to jail and prison are processes that occur concurrently, though they are perhaps sustained by distinct patterns of policing and enforcement. In New York, jail admissions result from enforcement of quality-of-life crimes and low-level misdemeanors, consistent with order-maintenance policing strategies (Harcourt, 2001; Greene, 1999), whereas drug enforcement and other anticrime activities are more likely to produce prison-generating felony arrests (Fagan, West, and Holland, 2003). Nevertheless, the models estimating the propensity scores suggest that the two incarceration processes are concentrated in similar, if not identical, neighborhoods. In fact, their bivariate correlation averaged over the study interval is .914. Including both prison and jail in the same model (table 8.5, columns 3 and 4) may conceptually more accurately capture the dynamics of incarceration within neighborhoods than is portrayed by separate models, but the coefficients are almost indistinguishable from other specifications. The additive and conditional models produce similar results, and in both estimations, the effects for jail and prison each decrease a community's economic outlook.

Incarceration Effects on Human Capital

The effects of prison and jail admissions on human capital follow a similar pattern. The main effects of prison and jail models (table 8.6, columns 1 and 2) are significant and negative. However, neither jail nor

Table 8.6. Random Effects Regression of Jail and Prison on Human Capital by Census Tract, 1986–1997 (Coefficients, p(t))

	Prison only	Jail only	Addictive effects	Conditional effects
Main effects				
Prison (propensity)	–.116*		–.002	–.092
Jail (propensity)		–.055*	–.058	–.070
Interaction				–.026
% black	.657***	.656***	.668***	.708***
% Hispanic	–.168	–.156	–.154	–.121
Effects over time				
Prison (propensity)	.026*		–.008	.028
Jail (propensity)		.004*	.006	.012**
Interaction				–.006**
% black	–.028***	–.028***	–.026***	–.038***
% Hispanic	–.032***	–.032***	–.030***	–.042***
Model statistics				
R^2	.732	.732	.733	.736
χ^2(Wald)	3123.05	3023.45	3392.95	3683.06
p (χ^2)	.000	.000	.000	.000
Rho	.892	.896	.886	.884

Note: All models estimated with fixed effects for time, population size, social control, drug arrest rate (lagged, logged), homicide rate (lagged, logged). All models estimated with random intercepts.
p(t): *** $p < .001$, ** $p < .01$, * $p < .05$

prison is significant in the additive and conditional models. We see that the effects of incarceration for both the jail and prison models are amplified over time. Again, combining measures of incarceration has no additional explanatory power.

There are positive and significant race effects for the proportion of the population that is black. This is distinct from the result predicting household income, where the influence of the proportion of the population that is black was negative but failed to reach statistical significance. Rather than suppressing human capital, when incarceration is controlled for, tracts with a higher proportion of the population that is black had more human capital. However, this effect is diminished over time. The proportion of the population that is Hispanic is not significantly associated with human capital.

Discussion

Recent work on the collateral effects of incarceration has focused on the fortunes of individuals returning from prison and on the social and psychological well-being of those left behind. Only a few studies have attended to the collective fates of neighborhoods with elevated incarceration rates, and most of these projects have examined how incarceration patterns contribute to the endogenous and spiraling relationship between crime and incarceration. Given prison's unique and heavy individual costs, the emphasis in incarceration research has been primarily on prisons, with little attention to frequent though shorter-term stays in local jails. Here, we address each of these dimensions of research on incarceration.

Loosely Coupled Enforcement

We find distinct, yet consistent, effects for prisons and jails, suggesting that these separate processes based on loosely coupled law enforcement priorities and penal strategies have a distinct impact on communities in New York City. Heterogeneous policing regimes in New York City have created separate streams of prisoners eligible for prison and jail. During much of the study period, prison populations were driven by street drug enforcement aimed at low-level dealers (Fagan, West, and Holland, 2003; Smith et al., 1992; Jacobson, 2005). This enforcement strategy was carried out by elite police units such as the Tactical Narcotics Teams, known locally as TNT (Smith et al., 1992; Fagan, 1994; Kleiman, 1992). TNT units were assigned to broad areas of the city rather than to specific precincts. They made tens of thousands of felony drug arrests each year beginning in 1988 and continuing through 1992, heavily populating prisons with felony drug offenders, changing the offense composition of prisons (Letwin, 1990; Herman, 1999; Fagan, West, and Holland, 2003). But jail populations were driven by enforcement of misdemeanor laws, including lesser drug crimes and local enforcement of incivilities and minor misdemeanors. Uniformed patrol officers assigned to precincts, without the organizational attention or status that was conferred on the specialized street drug details, were the front lines in this less visible but persistent enforcement strategy. However, it would seem that the jail removals have had the more profound and lasting impact on communities.

Only for the last of the waves in this panel—1996—had New York's Order Maintenance Policing (OMP) been implemented, which switched the priorities from felony drug enforcement to enforcement of a variety of forms of low-level disorder crimes, including tens of thousands of misdemeanor marijuana arrests (Maple and Mitchell, 2000). But the enforcement dichotomy remained. Like TNT, the elite Street Crime Unit under OMP searched for guns and violent offenders, while uniformed patrol officers emphasized misdemeanor arrests (Spitzer, 1999; Fagan et al., 2010).

So, even after the onset of OMP strategies, we still see loosely coupled police regimes producing different arrest streams that influence jail and prison populations separately. While the Street Crime Unit concentrated its efforts in high-crime areas, predominantly poor neighborhoods with higher crime rates and concentrations of nonwhite residents, lower-level enforcement of disorder was a citywide campaign that —although skewed somewhat toward poor areas—affected residents of neighborhoods across the city. The effects of race or ethnicity seem to work differently for different communities of color. After controlling for prison and jail removals, the size of the black population does not significantly influence the income outcome of communities, but the Hispanic population does. It is possible that there are a number of ecological forces at work, including enforcement strategies that disproportionately target certain Hispanic communities. Effects are different for human capital than for income. The size of the Hispanic population is unrelated to a community's human capital, but the black population is related in an unanticipated way. Since Hispanic communities in New York are heterogeneous with respect to the balance of immigrants and native-born residents, as well as differences by country of origin (Kasinitz et al., 2008), more research is needed on the effects of incarceration on neighborhood economics that account for subgroup differences among Hispanics.

Two Kinds of Poverty Traps

Incarceration effects are more pronounced for household income than for human capital, suggesting perhaps different ecological explanations and policy pathways. The negative effects of imprisonment rates on aggregate household income are illustrative of the complex but systemic relationship between persistent poverty, crime, and incarceration. Jail and prison have lasting effects on incomes, effects that persist over time. Incarceration in prison seems to give rise not only to more imprisonment (Fagan, West and Holland, 2003) but also to lower incomes. Jail serves not only as a pathway to prison but also as a profound destabilizing influence on communities. The reinforcing spiral of poverty, crime, and incarceration describes what Sampson and Morenoff (2006) characterize as a poverty trap (see also Fagan, 2008). High rates of neighborhood imprisonment can have multiple effects that sustain the downward pressure on local incomes: tainting nonoffender residents who seek jobs as crime risks, burdening returning inmates with reduced prospects in the workplace, and reducing the attractiveness of such neighborhoods for economic or housing investments.

The effect of jail on incomes is suggestive of the increasing reliance on the use of jail as an enforcement strategy across New York City's residential neighborhoods. Places with high jail rates are characterized if not by high rates of low-level crime, then by at least low-level social disorder of the kind that attracts law enforcement attention and a kind of enforcement that removes people for short but disruptive periods. The repetitive high rates of removal to jail of low-level offenders from poor communities, followed by their quick release, create a churning effect on neighborhoods that destabilizes social control and instills a sense of chaos and disorder more typical of a version of *broken windows* theory (Wilson and Kelling, 1982; Kelling and Cole, 1996; Livingston, 1997; Maple and Mitchell, 2000; Waldeck, 2000; Harcourt, 2001). Also, jail populations often are socially and psychologically troubled, and their interrupted presence in struggling communities is unlikely to aid the efforts of residents in those areas to develop economically or to become socially cohesive (Jacobson, 2005). Ex-inmates also have dim prospects in the workplace, but their diffusion across neighborhoods dilutes their concentrated effects on local incomes.

Race and ethnicity effects on income work in unanticipated ways and require further analyses. While prison and jail inmates come from predominantly poor and segregated communities, once incarceration is factored out of the equation, the difference in the proportions of African Americans was not related to incomes, but there was a lasting negative influence on neighborhood fortunes. We observed greater effects for neighborhoods with higher proportions of Hispanics, notwithstanding differences in Hispanics by country of origin. Still, Hispanics not only have a wider income distribution than African Americans in New York City, but they also tend to live in less segregated areas (Kasinitz et al., 2008). Immigrants in New York now represent a higher percentage of residents in Hispanic neighborhoods and of Hispanic populations than they represent in other ethnic groups, and their spatial spread and economic diversity may explain at least some of the story in this differential. Beyond these factors, more research is needed to further decompose the crime, incarceration, and economic conditions of Hispanics.

Human capital is less sensitive to incarceration effects than are incomes. Human capital, including both workplace activity and educational capital, may be more sensitive to education policy than to incarceration or crime policy, and that may explain the narrow effects of incarceration on human capital. Both educational status and workplace experience are components of our measure of human capital, and the effects of incarceration may be unequal for these separate dimensions. High rates of imprisonment or jail removal have the potential to diminish the workplace prospects both of those who have gone to prison or jail and of their neighbors (Pettit and Lyons, 2007; Lyons and Pettit, 2011). Again, the effects are direct as well indirect through adverse forms of neighbor network effects, as neighborhood stigma affects both former prisoners and others in high-incarceration places. Not only are those who are removed to jail or prison likely to have low educational attainment, but they also are unlikely to find remedial services in overcrowded and underfunded prison systems and jails.

Policy Linkages

Spatially targeted policies such as business microinvestment and housing development could potentially help offset the local embeddedness of poverty and disrupt its connections to incarceration and crime (Deutsch, 2006; Sen, 2011). Job creation is potentially the most productive step to disrupt poverty traps. Microinvestments typically are small business startups that employ fewer than 10 persons, often in economically deprived areas where business development and job creation lag. Because of their small size, these enterprises often fail to qualify for typical business loans from larger lenders and are too small to attract private investment capital (Sen, 2011). Microinvestment banks, as economic innovators, fill this gap and provide startup opportunities where other support is harder to access. Some governments also have experimented with this model to spur economic development and job creation in economically isolated areas (Deutsch, 2006). Locating these businesses in the neighborhoods where incarceration rates are higher could provide access to jobs for former inmates and remove some of the barriers to employment that seem to sustain these poverty traps (see, generally, Lyons and Pettit, 2011).

Housing issues also intersect with economic development in areas characterized by high rates of crime and incarceration (Schwartz, Susin, and Voicu, 2003). New York experienced a housing and real estate boom starting in the mid-1990s that was concurrent both temporally and spatially with crime declines that persisted through much of the following decade (Fagan and Davies, 2007; Fagan, 2008). At the same time that residential real estate rose in value, so too did the value of commercial real estate, suggesting potential demand for sustainable small businesses in the neighborhoods with high crime and incarceration rates. Abandoned or dilapidated housing was condemned and then transformed into affordable low-income units and made available to local families who qualified for housing assistance (van Ryzin and Genn, 1999). Beginning in 1990, at the outset of New York City's crime decline, the city created nearly 250,000 *in rem* housing units from abandoned properties in the city's poorest and highest crime and incarceration neighborhoods. These units were made available to families qualifying under a variety of low-income and affordable housing programs (van Ryzin and Genn, 1999; Fagan, 2008). The increase in affordable housing in high-crime areas such as the South Bronx, which transformed during that time into a stable, low-crime, and economically diverse neighborhood (Fagan, 2008), suggests the potential for housing to intervene in neighborhoods to disrupt the poverty traps that link crime, incarceration, and economic disadvantage (Sampson and Morenoff, 2006).

Human capital may also be sensitive to these types of economic-development policies, as well as to the linkage between education and crime-control policies. One connection may be in the use of Order Maintenance policing strategies in schools, which results in high rates of suspension and expulsion for both violations of school rules and low-level crimes (Dodge, 2008). Dodge (2008) suggests that any public-safety benefits of such a strategy are tempered by the risk of attenuated educational capital for older adolescents and young adults attempting to enter the workforce. While microinvestment may provide work opportunities in areas scarred by high crime and incarceration, the attenuation of educational capital in poor neighborhoods through school expulsion may offset newly created chances and block access to these new workplaces. And the deterioration of education and training programs in prisons—and their nonexistence in jails—may further compound the human capital deficits of those going to and returning from spells of incarceration. While these two policy options can leverage local resources to potentially help offset the adverse effects of incarceration, ignoring the economic consequences of incarceration has its own risks.

Appendix: Neighborhood Factor Composition, 1990

	Rotated coefficient	Eigenvalue	% explained variance
Poverty/Inequality		2.20	73.29
% households with public assistance income	0.97		
% households with income below poverty	0.95		
Gini for total household income	0.61		
Labor Market/Human Capital I		3.14	78.43
% college grads—persons 25 and over	0.88		
% labor force participation—persons 16 and over	0.88		
Employment rate—persons 16 and over	0.92		
Skilled occupation—persons 16 and over	0.86		
Segregation		1.51	75.62
Racial fragmentation index	0.87		
% nonwhite	0.87		
Social Control I—Supervision		2.34	77.88
% youth population (5–15)	0.94		
% female-headed households with children < 18	0.85		
Supervision ratio (25–64 | 5–24)	−0.86		
Social Control II—Anonymity		1.04	52.16
Population—1990	0.72		
Residential mobility—same house as 1985	0.72		
Immigration and Cultural Isolation		1.64	81.86
Foreign born	0.91		
Linguistic isolation	0.91		
Housing Structure		1.61	80.61
% rental housing	0.90		
Housing density (persons per room)	0.90		

NOTES

1. This research was supported by Grant 85-00-11 from the Russell Sage Foundation, Future of Work Program. All opinions are solely those of the authors, as are any errors. Additional support was provided by the Robert Wood Johnson Foundation, Substance Abuse Policy Research Program. We are grateful to the New York State Division of Criminal Justice Services, the New York State Department of Labor, the New York City Police Department, and the New York City Department of Health for generously supplying data for this research. Tamara Dumanovsky helped conceptualize and launch the project and supervised the assembly of the data sets. Jan Holland prepared the maps and supervised the geocoding of incarceration and arrest records. Steven Glickman, Nicole Mutter, and Carolyn Pinedo provided excellent research assistance.

2. Disenfranchisement disproportionately and severely affects African American males, consistent with their disproportionate presence in the incarcerated population: of the 3.9 million American felons who were disenfranchised in 1999, nearly 1.4 million were African American males, representing 13% of all black males (Maurer, 2006).

3. For example, neighborhood disadvantage may invite closer surveillance by law enforcement, well in excess of levels of surveillance and enforcement that would be predicted by crime rates alone (Fagan and Davies, 2000, 2002), increasing incarceration risks relative to crime rates. These reciprocal patterns of crime, enforcement, and social risk sustain the elevated rates of incarceration and appear to do so even when crime rates decline (Fagan, West, and Holland, 2003).

4. See, for example, Fagan, West, and Holland, 2005, showing the persistence over time of incarceration rates that are independent of local crime rates, even after accounting for the endogeneity of crime, incarceration, and social structural disadvantage in New York City neighborhoods.

5. Physical and social deterioration is a persistent theme of neighborhood change in several studies (Taub, Taylor, and Dunham, 1984; Schuerman and Kobrin, 1986; Harrell and Gouvis, 1994). Deterioration often cued citizens to leave previously stable areas on the basis of changes in their subjective evaluation of the likelihood of crime affecting them personally.

6. That is, they computed the portion of the rate of drug arrests in each neighborhood that was not explained by the index crime rate.

7. The positive effect of incarceration on informal social control may, at first glance, be unexpected. Lynch and Sabol suggest that changes (increases) in incarceration rates encourage informal social control through mechanisms such as fear reduction. Because they failed to find that incarceration promotes prosocial interactions among residents, they suggest that the incarceration–informal social control linkage operates through individuals: "Residents may see or know of persons being incarcerated for crime, and this may increase their confidence in engaging in informal social control. They may feel that the 'bad guys' are gone

and that the criminal justice system is working with them to increase safety" (Lynch and Sabol, 2004, 24).

8. See, for example, Laura Dugan and Robert Apel (2002) on the coerced mobility of women who flee from violent relationships with intimate partners.

9. Over the past decade, New York City has experienced a steady decline in crime rates that ranks among the largest decreases of any American city. The total number of homicides dropped from a record high of 2,262 in 1990 to 606 in 1998 —the lowest homicide count since 1964. As the number of homicides declined steadily, other serious crime was also dropping, but not at the same rate. From 1990 to 1995, reported index crimes declined by nearly 40%, from 711,556 to 442,532. Within two more years, index crimes dropped further to 356,573, an overall decline of nearly 50% from the peak in 1990. Overall, the total number of index crimes in New York City dropped by 50% between 1990 and 1997, and violent crimes dropped by 47% (Fagan, West, and Holland, 2003). However, felony arrests dropped by only 12%, and misdemeanor arrests increased by 73% in the same period, despite the dramatic decrease in overall crime numbers.

10. In 1987, 75% of all New York State prison admissions originated from cases disposed in New York City, 69% in 1990, and 69% in 1994. New York State Division of Criminal Justice Services (DCJS); and U.S. Department of Justice, Bureau of Justice Statistics, *National Corrections Reporting Program* (NCRP).

11. New York City Department of Correction (DOC), online data report, http://www.ci.nyc.ny.us/html/doc/html/avrdaily.html.

12. From 1990 to 1997, misdemeanor drug arrests in New York City were steadily increasing—accounting for 27% of all misdemeanor arrests in 1990 to 31% in 1997. During the same period, felony drug arrests remained relatively stable—accounting for approximately 32% of all felony arrests. New York State, Division of Criminal Justice Services, *Criminal Justice Indicators by Percent Change New York City: 1990–1997*, http://criminaljustice.state.ny.us/crimnet/ojsa/areastat/areast.htm (accessed May 30, 2003).

13. U.S. Department of Justice, Bureau of Justice Statistics, NCRP 1985, NCRP 1990, NCRP 1996.

14. Beginning in 1994, the New York City Police Department launched a computerized crime-mapping system, COMPSTAT (Bratton and Knobler, 1998). Crime data before 1994 cannot be located to specific addresses other than through manual geocoding of complaint and arrest records or manual coding of the records of arrestees. Even after the launch of COMPSTAT, these data were unavailable for research purposes but were used internally for strategic analysis of enforcement practices. One reason is that the spatial coordinates were obtained only for the initial crime complaint, which often was unverified at the time it was incorporated into the database. NYPD officials were reluctant to release these data, since many of the complaints had not been investigated. For example, a complaint of a gunshot might turn out on investigation to be a car

backfiring. Or a burglary could simply be a missing personal item that was later recovered. Once verified, complaints were entered into the city's crime counts, but for unstated reasons, the geographical coordinates of the crime location were not carried forward or aggregated.

15. Although using residential address in lieu of event location may distort the spatial estimates for violent events, we based this decision on prior work showing the close proximity of homicide events to the residences of victims. See, for example, Fagan and Wilkinson, 1998.

16. We estimated models with dummies for the two highest quartiles as "high incarceration" tracts and with the top quartile as "very high incarceration." Models were estimated substituting these indicia of prison for the actual prison rates. The results were robust to these specifications.

17. Separate models were estimated with either fixed and random effects, and a Hausman test was employed to test for the choice between the two kinds of models. Models with fixed versus random effects produced similar results, though coefficients varied in magnitude but not significance.

18. Alternate specifications included race-specific incarceration measures and models that included a dummy for whether the neighborhood was in the highest quartile of incarceration rates to identify whether effects were concentrated at the extremes of the distribution of jail or prison rates. The results were unchanged.

REFERENCES

Baumer, Eric, Janet L. Lauritsen, Richard Rosenfeld, and Richard Wright. 1998. "The Influence of Crack Cocaine on Robbery, Burglary, and Homicide Rates: A Cross-City, Longitudinal Analysis." *Journal of Research in Crime and Delinquency* 35 (3): 316–340.

Becker, Gary S. 1994. *Human Capital: A Theoretical and Empirical Analysis, with Special Reference to Education.* 3rd ed. Chicago: University of Chicago Press.

Belenko, Steven, Jeffrey Fagan, and Tamara Dumarovsky. 1994. "The Impact of Special Drug Courts on Recidivism of Felony Drug Offenders." *Justice System Journal* 17 (1): 53–82.

Bellair, Paul E. 2000. "Informal Surveillance and Street Crime: A Complex Relationship." *Criminology* 38 (1): 137–169.

Beveridge, Andrew A. 2008. "A Century of Harlem in New York City: Some Notes on Migration, Consolidation, Segregation, and Recent Developments." *City and Community* 7:358–365.

Bowling, Benjamin. 1999. "The Rise and Fall of New York Murder: Zero Tolerance or Crack's Decline?" *British Journal of Criminology* 39 (4): 531–554.

Bratton, William, and Peter Knobler. 1998. *The Turnaround: How America's Top Cop Reversed the Crime Epidemic.* New York: Random House.

Brooks-Gunn, J., G. J. Duncan, P. K. Klebanov, and N. Sealand. 1993. "Do Neighborhoods Influence Child and Adolescent Development?" *American Journal of Sociology* 99:353–395.

Bursik, Robert J., Jr. 1984. "Urban Dynamics and Ecological Studies of Delinquency." *Social Forces* 63 (2): 393–413.

Bursik, Robert J., Jr. 1988. "Social Disorganization and Theories of Crime and Delinquency: Problems and Prospects." *Criminology* 26 (4): 519–551.

Bursik, Robert J., Jr., and Harold G. Grasmick. 1992. "Longitudinal Neighborhood Profiles in Delinquency: The Decomposition of Change." *Journal of Quantitative Criminology* 8 (3): 247–263.

Bursik, Robert J., Jr., and Harold G. Grasmick. 1993. "Economic Deprivation and Neighborhood Crime Rates, 1960–1980." *Law & Society Review* 27 (2): 263–283.

Bursik, Robert J., Jr., and Jim Webb. 1982. "Community Change and Patterns of Delinquency." *American Journal of Sociology* 88 (1): 24–42.

Chen, M. Keith, and Jesse M. Shapiro. 2007. "Do Harsher Prison Conditions Reduce Recidivism? A Discontinuity-Based Approach." *American Law and Economics Review* 9 (1): 1–29.

Clear, Todd R., Dina R. Rose, Elin Waring, and Kristen Scully. 2003. "Coercive Mobility and Crime: A Preliminary Examination of Concentrated Incarceration and Social Disorganization." *Justice Quarterly* 20:33–64.

Coulton, Claudia J., Jill E. Korbin, Marilyn Su, and Julian Chow. 1995. "Community-Level Factors and Child Maltreatment Rates." *Child Development* 66:1262–1276.

Crane, Jonathan. 1991. "The Epidemic Theory of Ghettos and Neighborhood Effects on Dropping Out and Teenage Childbearing." *American Journal of Sociology* 96 (5): 1226–1259.

DeGiovanni, Frank F., and Lorraine C. Minnite. 1992. "Patterns of Neighborhood Change." In John H. Mollenkopf and Manuel Castells (eds.), *Dual City: Restructuring New York*, 267–315. New York: Russell Sage Foundation Press.

Deutsch, Ronald. 2006. New York State Legislature Joint Fiscal Committee Hearings on Economic Development Policy in the 2005–6 Executive Budget Proposal.

Dodge, Kenneth A. 2008. "Framing Public Policy and Prevention of Chronic Violence in American Youths." *American Psychologist* 63 (7): 573–590.

Drennan, Matthew. 1992. "The Decline and Rise of the New York Economy." In John H. Mollenkopf and Manuel Castells (eds.), *Dual City: Restructuring New York*, 25–42. New York: Russell Sage Foundation Press.

Dugan, Laura, and Robert Apel. 2002. "An Exploratory Study of the Violent Victimization of Women: Race/Ethnicity, Situational Context, and Injury." Paper prepared for the Workshop on Issues in Research on Violence Against Women, National Academies, Washington, DC, January 3–4.

Durlauf, Steven N., and Daniel S. Nagin. 2011. "The Deterrent Effect of Imprisonment." In Philip J. Cook, Jens Ludwig, and Justin McCrary (eds.), *Controlling Crime: Strategies and Tradeoffs*. Chicago: University of Chicago Press.

Edin, Kathryn, Timothy J. Nelson, and Rechelle Paranal. 2004. "Fatherhood and

Incarceration as Potential Turning Points in the Criminal Careers of Unskilled Men." In Mary Pattillo, David Weiman, and Bruce Western (eds.), *Imprisoning America: The Social Effects of Mass Incarceration*, 46–75. New York: Russell Sage Foundation Press.

Fagan, Jeffrey. 1994. "Do Criminal Sanctions Deter Drug Offenders?" In Doris MacKenzie and Craig Uchida (eds.), *Drugs and Criminal Justice: Evaluating Public Policy Initiatives*, 188–214. Newbury Park, CA: Sage.

Fagan, Jeffrey. 2004. "Crime, Law and Community: Dynamics of Incarceration in New York City." In Michael Tonry (ed.), *The Future of Imprisonment*, 27–60. New York: Oxford University Press.

Fagan, Jeffrey. 2008. "Crime and Neighborhood Change." In Arthur S. Goldberger and Richard Rosenfeld (eds.), *Understanding Crime Trends*, 81–126. Washington, DC: National Academy Press.

Fagan, Jeffrey, and Garth Davies. 2000. "Street Stops and Broken Windows: *Terry*, Race, and Disorder in New York City." *Fordham Urban Law Journal* 28:457–504.

Fagan, Jeffrey, and Garth Davies. 2002. *The Effects of Drug Enforcement on the Rise and Fall of Homicides in New York City, 1985–95*. Final Report, Grant 031675, Substance Abuse Policy Research Program, Robert Wood Johnson Foundation.

Fagan, Jeffrey, and Garth Davies. 2004. "The Natural History of Neighborhood Violence." *Journal of Contemporary Criminal Justice* 20 (2): 127–147.

Fagan, Jeffrey, and Garth Davies. 2007. "The Political Economy of the Crime Decline in New York City." Paper presented at the annual meeting of the American Association for the Advancement of Science, San Francisco, February.

Fagan, Jeffrey, and Richard B. Freeman. 1999. "Crime and Work." In Michael Tonry (ed.), *Crime and Justice*, vol. 25, *A Review of Research*, 113–178. Chicago: University of Chicago Press.

Fagan, Jeffrey, Amanda Geller, Garth Davies, and Valerie West. 2010. "Street Stops and Broken Windows Revisited: Race and Order Maintenance Policing in a Safe and Changing City." In Stephen K. Rice and Michael D. White (eds.), *Exploring Race, Ethnicity and Policing: Essential Readings*, 309–348. New York: NYU Press.

Fagan, Jeffrey, and Tracey L. Meares. 2008. "Punishment, Deterrence and Social Control: The Paradox of Punishment in Minority Communities." *Ohio State Journal of Criminal Law* 6:173–229.

Fagan, Jeffrey, Valerie West, and Jan Holland. 2003. "Reciprocal Effects of Crime and Incarceration in New York City Neighborhoods." *Fordham Urban Law Journal* 30:1551–1602.

Fagan, Jeffrey, Valerie West, and Jan Holland. 2005. "Neighborhood, Crime, and Incarceration in New York City." *Columbia Human Rights Law Review* 36:71–108.

Fagan, Jeffrey, and Deanna L. Wilkinson. 1998. "Guns, Youth Violence and Social Identity in Inner Cities." In Michael Tonry and Mark H. Moore (eds.), *Crime and Justice*, vol. 24, *Youth Violence*, 373–456. Chicago: University of Chicago Press.

Fagan, Jeffrey, Deanna L. Wllkinson, and Garth Davies. 2007. "Social Contagion of Violence." In Daniel J. Flannery, Alexander T. Vazsonyi, and Irwin D. Waldman (eds.), *The Cambridge Handbook of Violent Behavior*, 688–723. Cambridge: Cambridge University Press.

Fagan, Jeffrey, Franklin E. Zimring, and June Kim. 1998. "Declining Homicide in New York: A Tale of Two Trends." *Journal of Criminal Law and Criminology* 88: 1277–1324.

Fletcher, George P. 1998. "Disenfranchisement as Punishment: Reflections on the Racial Uses of Infamia." *UCLA Law Review* 46:1985–1908.

Freeman, Richard. 1996. "Why Do So Many Young American Men Commit Crimes and What Might We Do about It?" *Journal of Economic Perspectives* 10 (1): 25–42.

Geller, Amanda B., Carey E. Cooper, Irwin Garfinkel, Ofira Schwartz-Soicher, and Ronald B. Mincy. 2012. "Beyond Absenteeism: Father Incarceration and Child Development." *Demography* 49 (1): 49–76.

Geller, Amanda B., Irwin Garfinkel, Carey E. Cooper, and Ronald B. Mincy. 2009. "Parental Incarceration and Child Wellbeing: Implications for Urban Families." *Social Science Quarterly* 90 (5): 1186–1202.

Geller, Amanda B., Irwin Garfinkel, and Bruce Western. 2011. "Parental Incarceration and Support for Children in Fragile Families." *Demography* 48 (1): 25–47.

Gelman, Andrew, and Jennifer Hill. 2006. *Data Analysis Using Regression and Multilevel/Hierarchical Models*. New York: Cambridge University Press.

Gould, Madeline S., Sylvan Wallenstein, and Marjorie Kleinman. 1990. "Time-Space Clustering of Teenage Suicide." *American Journal of Epidemiology* 131 (1): 71–78.

Gould, Madeline S., Sylvan Wallenstein, Marjorie Kleinman, Patrick O'Carroll, and James Mercy. 1990. "Suicide Clusters: An Examination of Age-Specific Effects." *American Journal of Public Health* 80 (2): 211–212.

Grannis, Ric, 1998. "The Importance of Trivial Streets: Residential Streets and Residential Segregation." *American Journal of Sociology* 103 (6): 1530–1564.

Granovetter, Mark S. 1973. "The Strength of Weak Ties." *American Journal of Sociology* 78 (6): 1360–1380.

Granovetter, Mark S. 1974. *Getting a Job: A Study of Contacts and Careers*. Cambridge: Harvard University Press.

Greene, Judith. 1999. "Zero-Tolerance: A Case Study of Police Policies and Practices in New York City." *Crime & Delinquency* 45:171–199.

Grogger, Jeffrey. 1995. "The Effect of Arrests on the Employment and Earnings of Young Men." *Quarterly Journal of Economics* 110 (1): 51–71.

Hagan, John. 1991. "Destiny and Drift: Subcultural Preferences, Status Attainments, and the Risks and Rewards of Youth." *American Sociological Review* 56:567–582.

Hagan, John, and Ronit Dinovitzer. 1999. "Collateral Consequences of Imprisonment for Children, Communities, and Prisoners." In Michael Tonry and Joan Petersilia (eds.), *Crime and Justice*, vol. 26, *Prisons*, 121–162. Chicago: University of Chicago Press.

Hagan, John, and Alberto Palloni. 1990. "The Social Reproduction of a Criminal Class in Working-Class London, circa 1950–1980." *American Journal of Sociology* 96 (2): 265–299.

Harcourt, Bernard E. 2001. *Illusion of Order: The False Promise of Broken Windows Policing*. Cambridge: Harvard University Press.

Harcourt, Bernard E., and Jens Ludwig. 2006. "Broken Windows: New Evidence from New York City and a Five-City Social Experiment." *University of Chicago Law Review* 73:271–320.

Harrell, Adele, and Caterina Gouvis. 1994. *Predicting Neighborhood Risk of Crime*. Washington, DC: Urban Institute.

Heitgerd, Janet L., and Robert J. Bursik. 1987. "Extracommunity Dynamics and the Ecology of Delinquency." *American Journal of Sociology* 92 (4): 775–787.

Herman, Susan. 1999. "Measuring Culpability by Measuring Drugs? Three Reasons to Evaluate the Rockefeller Drug Laws." *Albany Law Review* 63:777–798.

Holzer, Harry J., Steven Raphael, and Michael Stoll. 2004. "Will Employers Hire Ex-Offenders? Employer Preferences, Background Checks, and Their Determinants." In Mary Patillo, David Weiman, and Bruce Western (eds.), *Imprisoning America: The Social Effects of Mass Incarceration*, 205–243. New York: Russell Sage Foundation Press.

Jacobson, Michael. 2005. *Downsizing Prisons: How to Reduce Crime and End Mass Incarceration*. New York: NYU Press.

Johnson, Elizabeth I., and Jane Waldfogel. 2002. "Parental Incarceration: Recent Trends and Implications for Child Welfare." *Social Service Review* 76 (3): 460–479.

Johnson, Elizabeth I., and Jane Waldfogel. 2004. "Children of Incarcerated Parents: Multiple Risks and Children's Living Arrangements." In Mary Pattillo, David Weiman, and Bruce Western (eds.), *Imprisoning America: The Social Effects of Mass Incarceration*, 97–131. New York: Russell Sage Foundation Press.

Karmen, Andrew. 2000. *New York Murder Mystery: The True Story behind the Crime Crash of the 1990s*. New York: NYU Press.

Kasinitz, Philip, John H. Mollenkopf, Mary C. Waters, and Jennifer Holdaway. 2008. *Inheriting the City: Children of Immigrants Come of Age*. New York: Russell Sage Foundation Press.

Katz, Lawrence, Steven D. Levitt, and Ellen Shustorovich. 2003. "Prison Conditions, Capital Punishment, and Deterrence." *American Law and Economics Review* 5:318–343.

Kelling, George, and Catherine Cole. 1996. *Fixing Broken Windows*. New York: Free Press.

Ketcham, Christopher. 2002. "Roach Motel." *Salon*, October 17. http://archive.salon.com/mwt/feature/2002/10/17/jail_time/index_np.html.

Kleiman, Mark. 1992. *Against Excess: Drug Policy for Results*. New York: Basic Books.

Land, Kenneth, Patricia McCall, and Lawrence Cohen. 1990. "Structural Covariates of Homicide Rates: Are There Any Invariances across Time and Space?" *American Journal of Sociology* 95:922–963.

Laub, John H., and Robert J. Sampson. 2003. *Shared Beginnings, Divergent Lives: Delinquent Boys to Age 70*. Cambridge: Harvard University Press.

LeBlanc, Adrian Nicole. 2003. *Random Family: Love, Drugs, Trouble, and Coming of Age in the Bronx*. New York: Scribner.

Lee, Barrett A., Glenn Firebaugh, Stephen A. Matthews, Sean F. Reordan, Chadd Farrell, and David O'Sullivan. 2008. "Beyond the Census Tract: Patterns and Determinants of Racial Segregation at Multiple Geographic Scales." *American Sociological Review* 73:766–791.

Letwin, Michael. 1990. "Report from the Front Line: The Bennett Plan, Street-Level Drug Enforcement in New York City, and the Legalization Debate." *Hofstra Law Review* 18:795–835.

Levitt, Steven. 2004. "Understanding Why Crime Fell in the 1990s: Four Factors That Explain the Decline and Six That Do Not." *Journal of Economic Perspectives* 18 (1): 163–190.

Livingston, Debra. 1997. "Police Discretion and the Quality of Life in Public Places: Courts, Communities, and the New Policing." *Columbia Law Review* 97:551–625.

Loury, Glenn C. 2008. *Race, Incarceration, and American Values*. Cambridge: MIT Press.

Lynch, James P., and William J. Sabol. 2004. "Assessing the Effects of Mass Incarceration on Informal Social Control in Communities." *Criminology & Public Policy* 3:267–294.

Lynch, James P., William J. Sabol, Michael Planty, and Mary Shelley. 2001. *Crime, Coercion, and Community: The Effects of Arrest and Incarceration Policies on Informal Social Control in Neighborhoods*. Report to the National Institute of Justice. Washington, DC: Urban Institute Justice Policy Center.

Lyons, Christopher J., and Becky Pettit. 2011. "Compounded Disadvantage: Race, Incarceration, and Wage Growth." *Social Problems* 58 (2): 257–280.

Maltz, Michael D. 1998. "Which Homicides Decreased? Why?" *Journal of Criminal Law & Criminology* 88:1489–1496.

Maltz, Michael D. 1999. *Bridging Gaps in Police Crime Data*. Bureau of Justice Statistics, NCJ-177615. Available at http://www.ojp.usdoj.gov/bjs/pub/pdf/bgpcd.pdf.

Manza, Jeff, and Christopher Uggen. 2006. *Locked Out: Felon Disenfranchisement and American Democracy*. New York: Oxford University Press.

Maple, Jack, and Christopher Mitchell. 2000. *The Crime Fighter: How You Can Make Your Community Safe*. New York: Broadway Books.

Mauer, Marc. 2006. *Race to Incarcerate*. 2nd ed. New York: New Press.

McLanahan, Sara, and Larry Bumpass. 1988. "Intergenerational Consequences of Family Disruption." *American Journal of Sociology* 93 (2): 130–152.

McLanahan, Sara, and Gary D. Sandefur. 1994. *Growing Up with a Single Parent: What Hurts, What Helps*. Cambridge: Harvard University Press.

Miles, Thomas J. 2004. "Felon Disenfranchisement and Voter Turnout." *Journal of Legal Studies* 33:85–129.

Miles-Doan, Rebecca. 1998. "Violence between Spouses and Intimates: Does Neighborhood Context Matter?" *Social Forces* 77 (2): 623–645.

Morenoff, Jeffrey D., and Robert J. Sampson. 1997. "Violent Crime and the Spatial

Dynamics of Neighborhood Transition: Chicago, 1970–1990." *Social Forces* 76 (1): 31–64.

Morenoff, Jeffrey D., Robert J. Sampson, and Stephen Raudenbush. 2001. "Neighborhood Inequality, Collective Efficacy, and the Spatial Dynamics of Urban Violence." *Criminology* 39:517–553.

Murray, Joseph, David P. Farrington, Ivana Sekol, and Rikke F. Olsen. 2009. "Effects of Parental Imprisonment on Child Antisocial Behaviour and Mental Health: A Systematic Review." *Campbell Systematic Reviews* 4.

Myers, Samuel L., Jr. 2000. "The Unintended Impacts of Sentencing Guidelines on Family Structure." Paper presented at the annual meeting of the American Sociological Association, Washington, DC, August.

Nagin, Daniel S., Francis T. Cullen, and Cheryl Lero Jonson. 2009. "Imprisonment and Reoffending." In Michael Tonry (ed.), *Crime and Justice*, vol. 38, *A Review of Research*, 115–200. Chicago: University of Chicago Press.

Ousey, Graham C., and Matthew R. Lee. 2002. "Examining the Conditional Nature of the Illicit Drug Market–Homicide Relationship: A Partial Test of the Theory of Contingent Causation." *Criminology* 40:73–102.

Pager, Devah. 2003. "The Mark of a Criminal Record." *American Journal of Sociology* 108 (5): 937–975.

Pager, Devah. 2007. *Marked: Race, Crime, and Finding Work in an Era of Mass Incarceration.* Chicago: University of Chicago Press.

Petersilia, Joan. 2003. *When Prisoners Come Home: Parole and Prisoner Reentry.* New York: Oxford University Press.

Pettit, Becky, and Christopher J. Lyons. 2007. "Status and the Stigma of Incarceration: The Labor Market Effects of Incarceration by Race, Class, and Criminal Involvement." In Shawn Bushway, Michael Stoll, and David Weiman (eds.), *Barriers to Reentry? The Labor Market for Released Prisoners in Post-industrial America*, 203–226. New York: Russell Sage Foundation Press.

Pettit, Becky, and Bruce D. Western. 2004. "Mass Imprisonment and the Life Course: Race and Class Inequality in U.S. Incarceration." *American Sociological Review* 69 (2): 151–169.

Rashbaum, William. 2000. "Police Suspend Extra Patrols for 10 Days." *New York Times*, Oct. 12, B1.

Raudenbush, Stephen W., Anthony Bryk, and Richard Congdon. 2002. *Hierarchical Linear Modeling.* Thousand Oaks, CA: Sage.

Reordan, Sean F., Chadd R. Farrell, Stephen A. Matthews, Daniel O'Sullivan, and Kenneth Bischoff. 2008. "The Geographical Scale of Metropolitan Racial Segregation." *Demography* 45:489–514.

Reordan, Sean F., and Daniel O'Sullivan. 2004. "Measures of Spatial Segregation." *Sociological Methodology* 34:121–162.

Rose, Dina R., and Todd R. Clear. 1998. "Incarceration, Social Capital, and Crime: Implications for Social Disorganization Theory." *Criminology* 36:441–480.

Rosenbaum, Paul R. 2002. *Observational Studies.* 2nd ed. New York: Springer-Verlag.

Rosenbaum, Paul R., and Donald B. Rubin. 1983. "The Central Role of the Propensity Score in Observational Studies for Causal Effects." *Biometrika* 70 (1): 41–55.

Rowe, David C., and Joseph Lee Rogers. 1994. "A Social Contagion Model of Adolescent Sexual Behavior: Explaining Race Differences." *Social Biology* 41:1–18.

Rubin, Donald. B. 1997. "Estimating Causal Effects from Large Data Sets Using Propensity Scores." *Annals of Internal Medicine* 127 (8, part 2): 757–763.

Sabol, William J., and James P. Lynch. 2003. "Assessing the Longer-Run Consequences of Incarceration: Effects on Families and Employment." In Darnell Hawkins, Samuel L. Myers, Jr., and Randolph N. Stone (eds.), *Crime Control and Social Justice: The Delicate Balance*. Westport, CT: Greenwood.

Sampson, Robert J., and John Laub. 1993. *Crime in the Making*. Cambridge: Harvard University Press.

Sampson, Robert J., and Jeffrey Morenoff. 2006. "Durable Inequality: Spatial Dynamics, Social Processes, and the Persistence of Poverty in Chicago Neighborhoods." In Samuel Bowles, Steven Durlauf, and Karla Hoff (eds.), *Poverty Traps*, 176–203. Princeton: Princeton University Press.

Sampson, Robert J., Jeffrey Morenoff, and Thomas Gannon-Rowley. 2002. "Assessing 'Neighborhood Effects': Social Processes and New Directions in Research." *Annual Review of Sociology* 28:443–478.

Sampson, Robert J., Jeffrey Morenoff, and Stephen Raudenbush. 2005. "Social Anatomy of Racial and Ethnic Disparities in Violence." *American Journal of Public Health* 95:224–232.

Sampson, Robert J., and Stephen Raudenbush. 2004. "Seeing Disorder: Neighborhood Stigma and the Social Construction of 'Broken Windows.'" *Social Psychology Quarterly* 67:319–342.

Sampson, Robert J., Stephen Raudenbush, and Felton Earls. 1997. "Neighborhoods and Violent Crime: A Multilevel Study of Collective Efficacy." *Science* 277 (5328): 918–924.

Sanders, Jimmy M., and Victor Nee. 1996. "Immigrant Self-Employment: The Family as Social Capital and the Value of Human Capital." *American Sociological Review* 61:231–249.

Schuerman, Leo, and Soloman Kobrin. 1986. "Community Careers in Crime." In Albert J. Reiss, Jr., and Michael Tonry (eds.), *Communities and Crime*, 67–100. Chicago: University of Chicago Press.

Schwartz, Amy Ellen, Scott Susin, and Ivan Voicu. 2003. "Have Falling Crime Rates Driven New York's Real Estate Boom?" *Journal of Housing Research* 14:101–135.

Sen, Arup K. 2011. "Micro Enterprises in Inner-City Communities: Current Challenges and Viability." *Journal of Business Case Studies* 7 (3): 55–62.

Shaw, Clifford R., and Henry D. McKay. 1942. *Juvenile Delinquency in Urban Areas*. Chicago: University of Chicago Press.

Sherman, Lawrence W. 1993. "Defiance, Deterrence, and Irrelevance: A Theory of the Criminal Sanction." *Journal of Research in Crime and Delinquency* 30 (4): 445–473.

Singer, Judith D. 1998. "Using SAS PROC MIXED to Fit Multilevel Models,

Hierarchical Models, and Individual Growth Models." *Journal of Educational and Behavioral Statistics* 24 (4): 323–355.

Singer, Judith D., and John B. Willett. 2003. *Applied Longitudinal Data Analysis: Modeling Change and Event Occurrence.* New York: Oxford University Press.

Smith, Michael E., Michele Sviridoff, Susan Sadd, Ric Curtis, and Randy Grinc. 1992. *The Neighborhood Effects of Street-Level Drug Enforcement–Tactical Narcotic Teams in New York: An Evaluation of TNT.* New York: Vera Institute.

Spelman, William. 2000. "What Recent Studies Do (and Don't) Tell Us about Imprisonment and Crime." *Crime and Justice* 27:419–494.

Spitzer, Elliott. 1999. "The New York City Police Department's 'Stop and Frisk' Practices." Office of the New York State Attorney General. Available at http://www.oag.state.ny.us/bureaus/civil_rights/pdfs/stp_frsk.pdf.

Taub, Richard P., Garth D. Taylor, and Jan D. Dunham. 1984. *Paths of Neighborhood Change: Race and Crime in Urban America.* Chicago: University of Chicago Press.

Taylor, Ralph B., and Jeanette Covington. 1988. "Neighborhood Changes in Ecology and Violence." *Criminology* 26:553–589.

Travis, Jeremy. 2005. *But They All Come Back: Facing the Challenges of Prisoner Reentry.* Washington, DC: Urban Institute Press.

Tyler, Tom R., and Yuen J. Huo. 2002. *Trust in the Law: Encouraging Public Cooperation with the Police and Courts.* Vol. 5. New York: Russell Sage Foundation Press.

Uggen, Christopher, Angela Behrens, and Jeff Manza. 2005. "Criminal Disenfranchisement." *Annual Review of Law and Social Science* 1:307–322.

Uggen, Christopher, and Jeff Manza. 2002. "Democratic Contraction? Political Consequences of Felon Disenfranchisement in the United States." *American Sociological Review* 67:777–803.

Uggen, Christopher, and Jeff Manza. 2004. "Lost Voices: The Civic and Political Views of Disenfranchised Felons." In Mary Patillo, David Weiman, and Bruce Western (eds.), *Imprisoning America: The Social Effects of Mass Incarceration*, 165–204. New York: Russell Sage Foundation Press.

van Ryzin, Gregg G., and Andrew Genn. 1999. "Neighborhood Change and the City of New York's Ten-Year Housing Plan." *Housing Policy Debate* 10 (4): 799–838.

Visher, Christy A., and Jeremy Travis. 2003. "Transitions from Prison to Community: Understanding Individual Pathways." *Annual Review of Sociology* 29:89–113.

Waldeck, Sarah. 2000. "Cops, Community Policing, and the Social Norms Approach to Crime Control: Should One Make Us More Comfortable with the Others?" *Georgia Law Review* 34:1253–1297.

Western, Bruce D. 2002. "The Impact of Incarceration on Wage Mobility and Inequality." *American Sociological Review* 64:526–546.

Western, Bruce D. 2006. *Punishment and Inequality in America.* New York: Russell Sage Foundation Press

Western, Bruce D., and Katherine Beckett. 1999. "How Unregulated Is the U.S. Labor Market? The Penal System as a Labor Market Institution." *American Journal of Sociology* 104:1030–1060.

Western, Bruce D., Jeffrey R. Kling, and David F. Weiman. 2001. "The Labor Market Consequences of Incarceration." *Crime & Delinquency* 47:410–427.

Western, Bruce D., and Becky Pettit. 2000. "Incarceration and Racial Inequality in Men's Employment." *Industrial and Labor Relations Review* 2000:3–16.

Wildeman, Chris. 2010. "Parental Incarceration and Children's Physically Aggressive Behaviors: Evidence from the Fragile Families and Child Wellbeing Study." *Social Forces* 89 (1): 285–310.

Wilson, James Q., and George L. Kelling. 1982. "Broken Windows: The Police and Neighborhood Safety." *Atlantic Monthly*, March, 29–38.

Wilson, William J. 1996. *When Work Disappears: The World of the Urban Poor*. New York: Knopf.

Zimring, Franklin E. 2006. *The Great American Crime Decline*. New York: Oxford University Press.

Zimring, Franklin E., Gordon Hawkins, and Sam Kamin. 2003. *Punishment and Democracy: Three Strikes and You're Out in California*. New York: Oxford University Press.

PART III

Child Development, Families, and Youth Violence

9

Macroeconomic Factors, Youth Violence, and the Developing Child

NANCY G. GUERRA

Introduction

A substantial literature has shown an association between violence rates and macroeconomic conditions such as poverty, economic downturns, unemployment, and income inequality (Pratt & Cullen, 2005). In general, poor developing nations have higher violence rates than do wealthier industrialized countries, and violence rates typically are highest in the most economically disadvantaged urban communities worldwide (Moser & Holland, 1997). For example, Japan, which is ranked second worldwide in gross domestic product (GDP), had an overall homicide rate of 0.5 per 100,000 population in the late 2000s, with similarly low rates among youth (United Nations Office on Drugs and Crime, 2009). In contrast, Jamaica, ranked 105 in GDP, witnessed recent homicide rates of approximately 60 per 100,000 islandwide, reaching over 140 per 100,000 in poor communities of inner-city Kingston (Jamaica

Constabulatory Force, 2009). Serious violence rates also are highest when prosperity is unequal, even in developed nations (Wilkinson & Pickett, 2009). In this regard, the relatively high violence rates in the United States have been linked to the disengagement and marginalization of the most vulnerable populations from the economic fabric of social life (Currie, 1998).

Still, poverty, inequality, and other macroeconomic factors do not directly lead to increased violence. Most poor people do not engage in violence, and low-paying occupations such as clergy have not swelled the ranks of violent criminals (Jencks, 1993). Indeed, much of the scholarly work examining the contribution of macroeconomic factors to violence has emphasized how these effects are filtered and shaped through multiple contexts. A large literature in sociology has emphasized their impact on structural conditions of communities that, in turn, impact more proximal contexts such as families and schools. In examining how macroeconomic conditions impact *youth violence*, the focus of this volume, it is particularly important to understand their impact on relevant developmental contexts that influence the learning of aggression and violence from birth through adolescence.

One strategy to unpack the mediating processes within distinct developmental contexts is to focus on a particular context and to empirically examine hypothesized relations between contextual processes and outcomes linked to violence. Several of the chapters in this volume provide important insights into potential mechanisms of influence, with a particular focus on those most proximal to late adolescence and early adulthood, the peak ages for youth violence. For example, Matjasko, Barnett, and Mercy (chapter 10) examine how macroeconomic conditions and macroeconomic shocks can increase youth violence as a byproduct of elevated family stress and compromised family functioning. Crutchfield and Wadsworth (chapter 6) consider how economic disadvantage at the neighborhood level can lead to adolescent delinquency via its detrimental effects on attachment and bonding to school. Edberg and Bourgois (chapter 7) emphasize how macroeconomic factors impact neighborhood street markets that contribute to youth violence via their role in shaping adolescent identities linked to violence and reputation.

A complementary strategy used in the present chapter is to consider how macroeconomic factors influence the developing child across multiple contexts that are differentially salient at different developmental stages and can increase or decrease risk for violence. For young children, the most relevant developmental contexts are families and communities, with families clearly embedded in communities. As children enter school, the school and peer context become important as well. During adolescence, the influence of peers in shaping deviant behavior increases, and more direct macroeconomic impacts linked to opportunities for employment and productive engagement may come into play.

The purpose of this chapter is to examine potential linkages between macroeconomic conditions, developmental processes, and youth violence from the prenatal period through adolescence. Much of the developmental literature has examined biological, psychological, and social processes related to aggression and violence, with some studies considering how these processes are impacted by macroeconomic conditions. Most typically the focus has been on how chronic and extreme poverty impact development, although some studies have examined other factors such as economic downturns (Elder, 1999) and unemployment or underemployment (Yoshikawa, Weisner, & Lowe, 2006). In this chapter, the focus is on macroeconomic conditions most likely to disrupt relevant contextual processes at different developmental stages and, consequently, to increase risk for aggression and violence. This includes a discussion of how biological development can be compromised as well as how these processes impact psychological development and the learning of aggression and violence over time. Emphasis is placed on early neurological development and the child's emerging cognitive system, including social-information-processing skills, attitudes, and beliefs that have been associated with higher levels of childhood aggression and youth violence (Crick & Dodge, 1994). Specification of these risk factors associated with violence and linked to macroeconomic conditions also provides directions for policy and interventions to prevent youth violence under adverse economic circumstances.

A developmental perspective also provides a unique lens to examine inconclusive or inconsistent evidence regarding the effects of economic downturns on youth violence. Although there is general support for a relation between economic downturns and increases in some indices of youth violence, even the chapters in this book reveal different relations depending on the specific indices used (e.g., consumer sentiment versus unemployment), outcomes measured by subgroup (e.g., effects on males versus females and by ethnicity), and historical time period studied. It is also the case that most studies examine changes in violence rates within a defined period during or immediately following economic downturns. Yet many of the impacts on youth violence may affect children even before they are born, translating into changes in youth violence rates a decade or more in the future. As such, efforts to document the impact of macroeconomic factors on youth violence are incomplete without considering their effects on the developing child.

Indeed, there is a robust literature examining risk for youth violence across developmental stages that can be discussed in terms of the distinct contributions of macroeconomic conditions during each period. As mentioned previously, much of this literature emphasizes the effects of neighborhood stressors, disrupted family processes, and negative childhood experiences typically associated with chronic and/or extreme poverty. Overall, regardless of the predictors used (e.g., family income, household dysfunction), children raised under conditions of adversity associated with poverty evidence a range of problematic developmental outcomes including higher rates of violence and delinquency (Bradley & Corwyn, 2002; McCord, 1997). Even within poor populations, it is the most disadvantaged children, the poorest of the poor, who face the greatest risks of violence and delinquency (Farrington, 1995; Krivo & Peterson, 1996). Although conditions of chronic poverty are unlikely to change, it may also be the case that economic downturns can have similar effects if they impact risk factors most relevant to violence during a particular developmental stage.

The Cumulative Nature of Risk across Development

Risk factors that are affected early in development may set in motion a cascade of negative events that close the doors of future opportunity and increase the likelihood of aggressive and violent behavior during adolescence and beyond. The cumulative nature of risk across development has given rise to an emerging area of study known as developmental or life-course criminology (Farrington, 2010). This is particularly relevant for the smaller percentage of "early starter" violent youth whose troubled behavior is evident early in development and persists over time (Moffitt, 2003). Still, within each developmental stage, macroeconomic factors are most likely to compromise children's development and possibly increase risk for youth violence via their effects on key developmental contexts and processes. Let us now turn to a review of risk factors likely to be impacted by macroeconomic conditions across specific developmental stages: the prenatal period through age 5; the early school years (ages 6–11); adolescence (ages 12–18).

The Prenatal Period through Age 5

During this developmental stage, communities and families are the most relevant context for child development. A number of scholars have proposed that community conditions related to low socioeconomic status and/or poverty primarily influence child development via their influence on parental behavior (e.g., Linver, Brooks-Gunn, & Kohen, 2002; Mistry, Vandewater, Huston, & McLoyd, 2002). Limited resources and services in a community can translate into blunted opportunities for adequate prenatal and postnatal care and compromised parenting due to high levels of family stress. Direct effects of community poverty that can operate independent of their influence on families also are evident, including increased exposure to environmental toxins, lack of opportunities for early enrichment, and psychological trauma linked to witnessing community violence. Children growing up in poor families living in economically disadvantaged communities thus experience a double whammy of community-level stressors that affect both children and families and that parents are unlikely to be able to buffer adequately. Each of these factors can increase risk for childhood aggression and youth violence.

Maternal behavior has direct bearing on children's development during the prenatal period, and a number of maternal characteristics and behaviors can lead to higher levels of biological and neuropsychological vulnerability associated with later aggression. Chronic poverty has long been associated with inadequate prenatal care and a higher likelihood of fetal exposure to toxic agents, possibly leading to impaired brain development, lower birth weight, nutritional deficiencies, and greater risk for assorted neurological problems. Even birth complications associated with poor-quality health care (e.g., brain insult during delivery) may increase risk for later violent behavior (Kandel & Mednick, 1991). Although these conditions are likely to co-occur in poor communities, they may also result from economic shocks that translate into reduced access to quality health care, poor nutrition, and inadequate prenatal care and education. During economic downturns, unemployed parents can lose health insurance, and governmental subsidies for access to health care may wane—in either case potentially leading to increased prenatal and infant vulnerability and risk.

Still, when vulnerability co-occurs with ongoing family disadvantage and chronic poverty, risk is likely to be exacerbated over time. More difficult infants may strain the already overtaxed capacity of their families to cope with their problems. Parents who themselves have been raised in disadvantaged environments may have fewer psychological, social, and financial resources to help them create optimal environments for their children (McLeod & Kaiser, 2004) and may suffer from mental health problems of their own that interfere with effective parenting (Leadbeater & Bishop, 1994). On the other hand, parents who experience short-term economic hardships may also experience heightened levels of stress that makes it more difficult for them to cope with their children's problems, coupled with limited financial resources to access potentially helpful services.

During the early childhood period, the establishment of a secure attachment relationship with a caregiver is a key developmental task with implications for future behavior. Both retrospective and longitudinal studies have identified an association between *insecure* attachment and subsequent aggression and violence. For example, in a recent meta-analysis of 69 studies involving almost 6,000 children age 12 and younger, Fearon and colleagues (2010) found that children (particularly boys) with insecure maternal attachments and difficulty coping with separation were at elevated risk for later behavior problems and aggression. This may result from a number of different but related processes that are more likely under conditions of economic adversity. First, children with neuropsychological vulnerabilities may be more difficult for parents to connect with, disrupting the formation of parent-child bonds, especially when parents live in disadvantaged neighborhoods with few supportive relationships (Crockenberg, 1981). In turn, young children who are not engaged in securely attached relationships with parents or caregivers may escalate their angry and aggressive behavior in order to elicit a response from them. Parents who are ill equipped to manage this behavior, whether due to a history of disadvantage or immediate stressors, may respond with increased punishment and retaliation. This pattern of insecure attachment can lead to problematic *internal working models* reflecting cognitive representations of relationships that may compromise the developing child's ability to develop trusting and stable friendships and long-term intimate relationships later in life (Bowlby, 1973).

In addition to problems associated with weak and insecure attachment bonds, harsh parenting and corporal punishment can increase the likelihood of child aggression and youth violence. The use of corporal punishment is greatest toward young children age 5 and under and among low-socioeconomic-status parents (Straus & Stewart, 1999). There are several reasons for the relation between early corporal punishment and subsequent aggression and violence. First, corporal punishment communicates to the child that aggression and acting-out behaviors are normative, acceptable, and effective ways to gain compliance (Bandura, 1986). Second, corporal punishment often leads children to avoid the disciplinary figure, reducing available opportunities for parents to direct and influence their child (which already may be limited under adverse economic conditions). Third, corporal punishment leads children to be hypervigilant to hostile cues, to attribute hostile intent to others, to access more aggressive potential responses, and to view aggression as a way to attain social benefits (Dodge, Pettit, McClaskey, & Brown, 1986). Fourth, corporal punishment can motivate children to avoid future punishment but does not teach children the responsibility to behave independently in morally and socially acceptable ways (Gershoff, 2002). Thus, not only are children developing characteristic patterns of behavior that include aggression (and facilitate later violence), but they are also forming early patterns of social cognition—and what they are learning is that aggression and violence are integral parts of social relationships.

The evidence linking physical abuse, aggression, and later violence also is compelling (Luntz & Widom, 1994). In many cases, this abuse begins as corporal punishment and is then taken to the extreme. In other words, many cases of physical abuse begin when parents try to impact children's behavior or "teach them a lesson" (Gershoff, 2002). Just as corporal punishment is associated with economic disadvantage, most all of the conditions associated with child physical abuse are more frequent within poor communities, often linked to associated social stress, isolation, and lack of support services.

In addition, children growing up in economically disadvantaged communities, particularly high-violence inner-city neighborhoods, are more likely to witness violence in the community. Multiple empirical studies have found an association between witnessing community violence and increased aggressive and violent behavior, particularly for boys (Attar, Guerra, & Tolan, 1994; Morales & Guerra, 2006). From a neuropsychological perspective, heightened exposure to violence early in development can lead to a persistently active stress-response apparatus in the central nervous system in response to perceived threat, including an increased startle response. In other words, it is adaptive for children who grow up witnessing violence to be hypervigilant to external stimuli and potential threats (Perry, 1997). A climate of fear can also lead children to be more attentive to aggressive cues and to interpret ambiguous situations as threats, similar to the concept of hostile attribution bias (Crick & Dodge 1994). Further, children who witness violence more regularly come to see it as acceptable behavior and internalize normative beliefs supporting aggression (Guerra, Huesmann, & Spindler, 2003).

The link between poverty, child abuse, and aggressive behavior also has been extended to child neglect—that is, both abused and neglected children are more likely to engage in subsequent aggression with peers (Dodge, Bates, & Pettit, 1990). Early parental rejection and neglect also have been found in longitudinal studies to be robust predictors of adolescent delinquency and later criminal careers (Loeber & Stouthamer-Loeber, 1986). One pathway of influence on early development is through the effects of neglect on brain development in young children. Specifically, emotional neglect has been shown to decrease the strength of the subcortical and cortical impulse-modulating capacity, leading to lower levels of empathy. Further, neglected children (or even chronically understimulated children) also are likely to experience lower levels of sensory-motor and cognitive experiences, leading to an underdevelopment of the cortex. Because the cortex plays a major role in regulating the lower parts of the central nervous system, increased cortical capacity should be expected to decrease propensity for violence over the course of development (Perry, 1997).

The importance of early experience for the child's neurological and psychological development cannot be understated. Although the human brain continues to mature well into early adulthood, the early years are a particularly sensitive period for "wiring" the developing brain, and compromised development during this time can increase the likelihood of aggression and violence. As illustrated, problematic development is more likely under conditions of extreme economic and social adversity. For some children, these early experiences can serve as stepping stones to an ill-fated course of habitual aggression and later violence, particularly if they are exacerbated by subsequent interactions at home, in school, and with peers. As Moffitt (1997) notes, "for poor urban children, the snowball of cumulative continuity is anticipated to begin rolling earlier, and it rolls faster downhill" (p. 150).

The Early School Years (Ages 6–11)

Many of the difficulties that begin before birth and through age 5 can be compounded by experiences when children enter school. Not only do educational opportunities and the structure of the school impact children's development, but the influence of the peer group is heightened as children begin to learn rules for social engagement. Early school experiences can lead to academic problems, lack of engagement or "bonding" to school, and peer difficulties, all of which can increase risk for aggression and violence.

In addition to the continued influence of communities and families, school entry opens (or shuts) new doors to academic and social development and can exacerbate the negative effects of earlier problems. For some children, new challenges may be particularly acute in light of earlier disadvantage. For example, children with early neuropsychological or IQ impairments associated with living in chronic poverty are likely to have difficulty learning basic academic skills. Schools in low-income communities with limited resources may not provide remedial education services, further limiting these children's academic progress. In turn, academic delays can disengage children from the school experience and, in some cases, increase the likelihood of early aggression (Miles & Stipek, 2006). On the other hand, children who begin school with behavioral and attention problems including aggression and ADHD also have more difficulty learning basic academic skills. Just as aggression can result from academic difficulties, cognitive development can also be impeded by aggressive behavior. Under the worst conditions, these influences occur reciprocally and over time (Hinshaw, 1992).

Research on teacher practices within disadvantaged communities has demonstrated a number of mechanisms that can potentially interfere with academic progress and reinforce aggression, particularly among urban minority children. For example, Raudenbush (1983) found that teachers of low-income students were more likely than teachers of middle-income students to minimize discussion and interaction and to rely on rote learning. Other studies have found that teachers are less likely to praise low-income minority students. Further, teachers' expectations about students they see as aggressive and potentially violent can result in self-fulfilling prophecies (Fleischner & VanAcker, 1990).

Consider a 3-year-old boy with modest neurological impairment and poor verbal skills. Imagine that the neighborhood preschool for low-income children had recently closed due to lack of funding, and the boy is left in the care of his aunt. The boy's mother is working long hours for low wages and is too tired to read to him when she gets home. Clearly, she does not have extra money to purchase educational toys or games. When he enters elementary school, he is not ready to learn. Unfortunately, his school has few resources, high student-teacher ratios, and high turnover rates, rendering remediation of his difficulties unlikely. His language development is delayed, and he has difficulty communicating effectively with peers and teachers. After repeated academic failure, he is older than his peers and is easily disengaged from school. He is assigned to a special education class with other children who have behavior problems. His lack of verbal skills and present-oriented cognitive style make it difficult for him to delay gratification, and he learns to use aggression for personal gain. School becomes a venue for acting out rather than learning, and he quickly becomes disconnected from academic tasks—and he now is only 10 years old.

Children learn both academic skills and social behavior at school. Although academic skills are linked to specific curriculum guidelines, a child's social world is more likely to be regulated by the peer group. By the time children are 8 or 9 years old, peers demand more social competence and control of aggression. Aggressive children who are easily agitated and cannot solve social problems often are rejected by their peers, which can lead to increased aggression (Bierman, Smoot, & Aumiller, 1993). However, aggression does not always lead to peer rejection. In settings where aggression is normative and adaptive, aggression can lead to increased popularity and social status (Rodkin, Farmer, Pearl, & VanAcker, 2000). In economically disadvantaged communities with high rates of violence, being "tough" and ready to fight may be seen as an important quality from an early age, particularly for boys.

During this time period, children become active agents in navigating and interpreting their social worlds. They acquire a cognitive understanding of the meaning of social interactions and develop characteristic styles of thinking that influence their behavior. In recent years, there has been an increased emphasis on the importance of the cognitive underpinnings of aggression and violence, particularly within psychology (Bandura, 1986; Crick & Dodge, 1994; Huesmann & Guerra, 1997). This line of research draws heavily from cognitive-information-processing theory, emphasizing both discrete social-information-processing skills as well as the "database" in memory that individuals develop over time. Much of the work in this area has emphasized sequential social-information-processing skills that involve encoding and interpretation of cues, response search, evaluation, decision, and action. Aggression has been associated with hostile attributional bias, attention to aggressive cues, generation of more aggressive solutions, and anticipation of positive outcomes (Crick & Dodge, 1994).

However, a child's choice of an appropriate response also hinges on what is encoded in memory as a normative standard for acceptable behavior. These standards develop from observation of one's own behavior and the behavior of influential models as well as from direct instruction across contexts. As children get older, normative beliefs about aggression become increasingly stable and predictive of their own aggressive behavior (Huesmann & Guerra, 1997). In this regard, aggressive behavior in school, particularly when reinforced within this context, can quickly become a characteristic style of responding that is guided by an increasingly stable understanding of social relationships and social interactions. Over time, associated cognitive biases and beliefs are encoded in memory and can be invoked automatically without deliberate attention. Expected events and actions often are linked together in *scripts* to guide behavior in everyday situations. Because scripts also simplify cognitive processing, in many cases a particular scripted response becomes dominant or automatic. More aggressive children presumably have more well-connected and dominant aggressive scripts encoded in memory (Huesmann, 1998).

Linking the early school years to prior experiences in the family and community, neuropsychological deficits coupled with insecure attachment, poor parenting, and exposure to violence and followed by aggressive peer interactions in school can quickly lead to aggressive and violent scripts. As mentioned previously, the social-cognitive foundations of aggression begin early in development. For example, insecurely attached infants are likely to develop internal working models of relationships as unreliable and untrustworthy. Children who are severely physically punished or abused by parents and whose aggressive interactions continue on the playground are likely to learn that aggression is an acceptable response to problems. Further, children who grow up in economically disadvantaged urban neighborhoods with high levels of violence are likely to perceive the world as dangerous and threatening, leading to cognitive distortions such as hostile attribution bias. Absent a positive learning experience in school, a child's social ties and connections with conventional norms are less likely, paving the way for engagement in antisocial and violent behavior during adolescence.

Adolescence (Ages 12–18)

Because youth violence peaks during adolescence and into early adulthood (from ages 16 to 24), much of the work on macroeconomic factors and risk for youth violence has focused on this age group. Several of the chapters in this volume examine specific developmental processes during adolescence that can increase violence, including low levels of bonding to school and the development of deviant identities. As the developmental focus of the present chapter suggests, it is important to consider the cumulative effects of early experience on adolescent risk. In addition to a child's being disengaged from school and forging an identity based on violence, the snowball of disadvantage can limit opportunities for career development and gainful employment, facilitate involvement in antisocial peer networks that require bravado rather than skill for personal and economic gain (particularly for males), and underscore the importance of the present over the future. It is here that the developmental tasks of adolescence intersect with age-specific and contextually bound constraints to solidify a path toward youth violence. Even for youth without an early history of aggression, the demands of adolescence coupled with limited opportunities for self-expression and advancement in poor neighborhoods may propel them to experiment with risky behaviors such as violence.

Of course, adolescence is a time of increased engagement in risky behaviors for all youth. Recent advances in cognitive neuroscience have highlighted the role of brain maturation during adolescence in the etiology of these behaviors. From an evolutionary perspective, this is understandable. During this developmental stage, individuals must leave their families and seek out mates and opportunities for productive engagement—which require a certain degree of sensation seeking and risk taking. Distinct features of brain development that emerge in middle adolescence have been linked to increased reward seeking, specifically the rapid rise in dopaminergic activity around puberty. Simultaneously, self-regulation and coordination of affect and cognition are more problematic, linked to the slower maturation of the prefrontal cortex and its connection to other brain regions. At the same time, adolescence also is a time of considerable brain plasticity linked to experience (Steinberg, 2010).

The developmental mandate to "leave the nest" also is accompanied by a psychological quest for a coherent identity. Identity includes a sense of uniqueness, a sense of continuity, and a sense of affiliation. Identity achievement has been heralded as a key task of adolescence, providing a link between past experience, present activities, and future goals (Erikson, 1968). Identity development is facilitated by advances in cognitive abilities during adolescence but is also impacted by available opportunities for productive engagement. In other words, who one *will* become is contingent on who one *can* become. Not only do extremely poor environments constrain opportunities for a legitimate future, but they frequently offer rewarding opportunities in the illegal or underground economy that require limited academic or vocational skills. For youth who have been marginalized over the course of development, possibly as a result of academic or behavioral difficulties, who experience inequality as a result of ethnic background or income, and who live in communities where the prospects for long-term, meaningful, and well-paid work are few or nonexistent, a deviant identity may be one of the few viable options available.

The lure of a deviant identity is amplified when it is solidified through negative group affiliations. During adolescence, the influence of peers increases, and peer groups provide validation and support for the standards of behavior they are defined by. Aggressive, antisocial, or delinquent peer groups tend to attract like-minded youth, and being in a deviant peer group tends to increase antisocial behavior (Dobkin, Tremblay, Masse, & Vitaro, 1995). When aggressive or violent youth band together, the peer group can provide an organizational context for enacting violence, attracting more aggressive youth, and legitimizing their behavior as normative. In the extreme, organized groups such as high-violence juvenile gangs provide a structured developmental context with clear mandates for violent behavior. They also provide opportunities to regularly rehearse cognitive scripts for social interactions that not only include but often require aggression and violence.

Although family influences may wane slightly as peers become more prominent, parents can buffer the potentially negative effects of peers by carefully monitoring their children's behavior. Parents who effectively monitor their teenagers know where they are, who they are with, and what they are doing. Effective supervision allows parents to respond appropriately to youth misbehavior and can minimize an adolescent's involvement with risky situations (Pettit, Laird, Dodge, Bates, & Criss, 2001). Yet a key feature of socioeconomic disadvantage is its corrosive effect on family functioning from before birth through adolescence. Although short-term economic shocks can significantly affect parents' abilities to monitor and supervise their teenagers, the effects of chronic poverty and joblessness are likely to be magnified greatly and compounded over time. Parents who cannot provide a secure base for their infants or leverage resources for academic enrichment are unlikely to have the time, skills, and fortitude to adequately supervise their children as they get older and become more independent.

In addition to the effects of chronic poverty and short-term economic shocks, the effects of income inequality may be more pronounced for poor teenagers who grow up in a context of easily visible wealth. As their cognitive capacity for abstract thinking matures, inequalities become more salient, particularly for lower-social-status youth. Simultaneously, the need to stand out and be unique is amplified during this developmental stage, and possessions take on new meaning. In the United States and internationally, the lure of material wealth, strongly reflected in magazines, television, music, and the Internet, can further reinforce the sense of injustice experienced by many youth. Not only does inequality produce a type of cognitive disequilibrium, it has also been shown to increase chronic stress. Long-term exposure to this type of chronic stress shifts physiological priorities from those that maintain function to those that improve reaction times and provide quick energy for activity (Marmot & Wilkinson, 2006). As this illustrates, a cascade of events in poor, marginalized communities can create physiological and cognitive reactions that foster hypersensitivity to threat and danger from birth onward.

It is easy to see how a spiral of cumulative disadvantage linked to socioeconomic factors can leave some youth unprepared for the developmental tasks of adolescence and increase risk for violence. Teenagers who have fallen behind academically are unlikely to have basic skills needed for advanced courses and to compete in a competitive job market. They are likely to be disconnected from school as a social institution, potentially limiting their social ties with conventional opportunities. Youth who do not find their niche in the school setting may seek out other like-minded youth and discover alternate opportunities in the underground or criminal economy. In neighborhoods where illegal opportunities are readily available and highly rewarding, the lure of easy money, camaraderie, and belonging may easily offset any negative consequences of this behavior. The focus on short-term rewards at the expense of long-term consequences characteristic of adolescent brain development is particularly acute for youth growing up in settings where long-term opportunities are few and far between. Under conditions of chronic poverty, many parents cannot serve as role models for the merits of hard work, and the lack of productive work inhibits a family's ability to achieve informal social control and to adequately monitor their children. Further, under conditions of inequality, teenagers are likely to be sensitive to this marginalization and to experience a type of chronic stress that favors physiological processes typically involved in responding to immediate threat or danger.

Moving Forward: A Developmental Perspective on Macroeconomic Influences and Youth Violence Prevention

As discussed in this chapter, a number of macroeconomic factors that can increase risk for youth violence impact children from before they are born through adolescence. These factors can operate independently at each developmental stage, but they also accumulate over time to exacerbate risk. Some of these factors can have direct effects on development by truncating opportunities, creating toxic conditions, or shaping children's emerging cognitive understanding of social interactions. Other macroeconomic influences operate indirectly by negatively impacting developmental contexts such as families, schools, and communities and hampering their ability to raise healthy (and nonviolent) children. Among diverse macroeconomic factors, the most lethal mix for development seems to be growing up under conditions of extreme and persistent poverty in marginalized urban communities.

Still, the urban poor are not a homogeneous group equally disposed to violence and ineffective parenting but rather a heterogeneous group of citizens trying to make ends meet and to raise families under extremely difficult conditions. Most are law-abiding and employed, although often at or below the minimum wage. As parents, they try to provide the best education and training for their children and often go to great lengths to leverage resources for their families. Although all children growing up under these difficult circumstances could be considered "at risk," most children do not become violent delinquents but rather become productive adults. Similarly, even in gang-occupied neighborhoods, studies shown that between 6 and 30 percent of youth from these neighborhoods actually affiliate with and/or join a gang during their lifetime, and most gang members only stay involved for about one year (Esbensen, Huizinga, & Weiher, 1993).

What can be done to prevent youth violence under these difficult conditions? Absent the obvious shift to policies that engender a more equitable distribution of wealth (something which seems increasingly less likely in countries such as the United States), much still can be accomplished. This requires raising the floor of social inclusion, making critical services for healthy development universal, providing a more stable and equitable funding base for schools and training teachers to serve the needs of poor students, building opportunities and social connections in communities, teaching parents effective strategies for child rearing under adverse circumstances, and teaching children effective social-problem-solving skills from an early age.

From a developmental perspective, early interventions that engage families and communities hold great promise for setting a strong foundation for child well-being and risk prevention. However, these efforts must be sustained, as the effects of early programs can easily wash out over time under harsh conditions. In addition to an early start, children also need boosters and "developmental cushions" along the way that protect them from the cumulative consequences of earlier mistakes. For children growing up under harsh conditions, relatively minor problems can easily initiate a downward spiral of person-environment interactions that can permanently foreclose future opportunities, absent their ability to bounce back from these events.

Further, although there is general consensus that it is "never too early," there is also a growing recognition that it is "never too late." Indeed, remedial and second-chance programs for at-risk children and youth can work, even under conditions of extreme and chronic poverty and marginalization (Guerra, Williams, Walker, & Meeks-Gardner, 2010). Although much has been made of the importance of the early years for brain development, most studies point to "sensitive" rather than "critical" periods in the maturation of the brain (Knudsen, 2004), and the brain remains remarkably plastic into early adolescence (Steinberg, 2010).

There are numerous examples of programs and policies that have improved children's lives and have been effective in preventing aggression and violence. Many of these programs have been developed specifically for economically disadvantaged parents and their children. One of the most effective programs is the Home Visitation Program, providing educational and support services to at-risk mothers of newborns. Similarly, well-known preschool enrichment programs such as the Perry Preschool Project and the Houston Parent-Child Development Center, which provided enriched educational experiences and engaged parents through regular meetings and home visits, have demonstrated long-lasting effects on prevention of violence (for a detailed review, see Guerra, 1997).

In addition to programs that support families of newborns, infants, and toddlers through multiple services, a range of focused parent-training programs have been developed to help parents promote healthy development and prevent child behavior problems for both children and adolescents. Many of these programs are tailored specifically to address the needs of disadvantaged and ethnically diverse urban families. In some cases, this requires including program content that focuses on the unique challenges of the urban poor. In other cases, this requires adaptive implementation strategies. For example, a recent universal program, ParentCorps, yielded statistically significant and medium-size effects on effective parenting practices and child behavior problems in school among poor, urban, Latino and African American families. This relatively brief program provided a series of 13 group sessions for parents and children during early evening hours and facilitated by trained school staff and mental health professionals (Brotman et al., 2011). Programs for parents of adolescents have also been successful across a range of community and ethnic contexts—for example, Multisystemic Family Therapy (MST) is a well-documented and effective prevention program for delinquents and their families (Schaeffer & Borduin, 2005).

Preventive interventions that focus on classrooms and schools can also be effective in enhancing student achievement and preventing associated behavioral problems. As noted, the effects of early learning problems quickly multiply if left unchecked. A number of classroom-management and teacher-training programs have yielded benefits in terms of student performance and behavioral outcomes. For example, cooperative learning is a well-regarded classroom-management and teaching strategy that promotes student motivation and mastery of tasks as well as tolerance and understanding across diverse student groups

(Slavin, 1995). Large-scale projects such as the Comer project (Comer, 1998) have emphasized the importance of school reorganization in the most distressed urban settings in order to empower students, teachers, and parents to work together to maximize positive outcomes.

A number of broader "social experiments" have demonstrated positive effects on child development and prevention of aggression and violence. Many of these community-based programs have involved relatively modest efforts to provide a safety net for poor families. For example, the New Hope project, operating in some of the poorest areas of Milwaukee, Wisconsin, in the 1990s, was designed to increase the benefits and to reduce the barriers of work by providing a range of available supports. These included an earnings supplement to raise income above the poverty line, subsidized child care, health insurance, temporary employment, and support from project staff. Among the most relevant findings, children from New Hope families, particularly boys, did better in school and displayed more prosocial and fewer aggressive behaviors than did comparison children (Duncan, Huston, & Weisner, 2006).

Unfortunately, just as macroeconomic factors can lead to an array of community stressors and family disruptions that can impact child vulnerability and increase risk for childhood aggression and youth violence, resource constraints also can limit the availability of services to counteract or buffer the effects of these risk factors. Although programs such as home visitation and preschool enrichment historically have received high levels of governmental and private support, the infusion of funds into these programs may wane during difficult economic times. This may particularly impact early childhood programs during periods of heightened crime and violence, when benefits of these programs may not appear for many years. In spite of increasing support for the importance of early intervention, the politics of funding may preclude long-term investments in the face of problems requiring immediate solutions. On the other hand, skepticism about the effectiveness of remedial and second-chance programs can lead to an overall frustration with prevention programs and a default to punishment and suppression strategies. It is hoped that this chapter highlights the need to provide universal and targeted supports for the most at-risk children, supports that begin early in development and continue through adolescence.

Although the costs may be high, the costs of not promoting healthy development among the most vulnerable are infinitely higher.

REFERENCES

Attar, B., Guerra, N. G., & Tolan, P. (1994). Neighborhood disadvantage, stressful life events, and adjustment in elementary school children. *Journal of Clinical Child Psychology, 23*, 394–400.

Bandura, A. (1986). *Social foundations of thought and action: A social-cognitive theory.* Englewood-Cliffs, NJ: Prentice-Hall.

Bierman, K. L., Smoot, D. L., & Aumiller, K. (1993). Characteristics of aggressive-rejected, aggressive-nonrejected, and rejected-nonaggressive boys. *Child Development, 64*, 139–151.

Bowlby, J. (1973). *Attachment and loss: Vol. 2. Separation.* New York: Basic Books.

Bradley, R. H., & Corwyn, R. F. (2002). Socioeconomic status and child development. *Annual Review of Psychology, 53*, 371–399.

Brotman, L., Calzada, E., Huang, K.-Y., Kingston, S., Dawson-McClure, S., Kamboukos, D., et al. (2011). Promoting effective parenting practices and preventing child behavior problems in school among ethnically diverse families from underserved, urban communities. *Child Development, 82*, 258–276.

Comer, J. P. (1988). Educating poor minority children. *Scientific American, 256*, 42–48.

Crick, N. R., & Dodge, K. A. (1994). A review and reformulation of social information-processing mechanisms in children's social adjustment. *Psychological Bulletin, 115*, 74–101.

Crockenberg, S. (1981). Infant irritability, mother responsiveness and social support influences on the security of infant/mother attachment. *Child Development, 52*, 857–865.

Currie, E. (1998). *Crime and punishment in America.* New York: Holt.

Dobkin, P., Tremblay, R., Masse, L., & Vitaro, F. (1995). Individual and peer characteristics in predicting boys' early onset of substance abuse: A seven-year longitudinal study. *Child Development, 66*, 1198–1214.

Dodge, K. A., Bates, J. E., & Pettit, G. S. (1990). Mechanisms in the cycle of violence. *Science, 250*, 1678–1683.

Dodge, K. A., Pettit, G. S., McClaskey, C. L., & Brown, M. M. (1986). Social competence in children. *Monographs of the Society for Research in Child Development, 51*(2, Serial No. 213).

Duncan, G. J., Huston, A. C., & Weisner, T. S. (2006). *Higher ground: New hope for the working poor and their children.* New York: Russell Sage Foundation.

Elder, G. (1999). *Children of the Great Depression: Social change in life experience.* Boulder, CO: Westview.

Erikson, E. E. (1968). *Identity: Youth and crisis.* New York: Norton.

Esbensen, F., Huizinga, D., & Weiher, A. W. (1993). Gang and non-gang youth:

Differences in explanatory variables. *Journal of Contemporary Criminal Justice, 9*, 94–116.

Farrington, D. P. (1995). The development of offending and antisocial behavior from childhood: Key findings from the Cambridge study in delinquent development. *Journal of Child Psychology and Psychiatry, 360*, 929–964.

Farrington, D. P. (2010). Developmental and life-course criminology: Key theoretical and empirical issues. *Criminology, 41*, 221–225.

Fearon, R. P., Bakermans-Kranenburg, M. J., Van Ijzendoorn, M. H., Lapsley, A. M., & Roisman, G. I. (2010). The significance of insecure attachment and disorganization in the development of children's externalizing behavior: A meta-analytic study. *Child Development, 81*, 435–456.

Fleischner, J. E., & VanAcker, R. (1990). *Monograph on critical issues in special education.* Denton: University of North Texas Press.

Gershoff, E. T. (2002). Corporal punishment by parents and associated child behaviors and experiences: A meta-analytic and theoretical review. *Psychological Bulletin, 128*, 539–579.

Guerra, N. G. (1997). Intervening to prevent childhood aggression in the inner city. In J. McCord (Ed.), *Violence and childhood in the inner city* (pp. 256–312). New York: Cambridge University Press.

Guerra, N. G., Huesmann, L. R., & Spindler, A. (2003). Community violence exposure, social cognition, and aggression among urban elementary-school children. *Child Development, 74*, 1507–1522.

Guerra, N. G., Williams, K. R., Walker, I., & Meeks-Gardner, J. (2010). *Building an ecology of peace in urban Jamaica.* Washington, DC: World Bank.

Hinshaw, S. P. (1992). Externalizing behavior problems and academic achievement in childhood and adolescence: Causal relationships and underlying mechanisms. *Psychological Bulletin, 111*, 127–155.

Huesmann, L. R. (1998). The role of social information processing and cognitive schema in the acquisition and maintenance of habitual aggressive behavior. In R. Geen & E. Donnerstein (Eds.), *Human aggression* (pp. 73–109). San Diego, CA: Academic Press.

Huesmann, L. R., & Guerra, N. G. (1997). Social norms and children's aggressive behavior. *Journal of Personality and Social Psychology, 72*, 408–419.

Jamaica Constabulary Force. (2009). *Island-wide violence trends.* Ministry of National Security, Kingston, Jamaica.

Jencks, C. (1993). *Rethinking social policy: Race, poverty, and the underclass.* New York: HarperCollins.

Kandel, E., & Mednick, S. A. (1991). Perinatal complications predicts violent offending. *Criminology, 29*, 519–530.

Knudsen, E. I. (2004). Sensitive periods in the development of the brain and behavior. *Journal of Cognitive Neuroscience, 16*, 1412–1425.

Krivo, L. D., & Peterson, R. D. (1996). Extremely disadvantaged neighborhoods and urban crime. *Social Forces, 75*, 619–650.

Leadbeater, B., & Bishop, S. J. (1994). Predictors of behavior problems in preschool children of inner-city Afro-American and Puerto Rican adolescent mothers, *Child Development, 65,* 638–648.

Linver, M. R., Brooks-Gunn, J., & Kohen, D. (2002). Family processes as pathways from income to young children's development. *Developmental Psychology, 38,* 719–734.

Loeber, R., & Stouthamer-Loeber, M. (1986). Family factors as correlates and predictors of juvenile conduct problems and delinquency. In M. Tonry & N. Morris (Eds.), *Crime and justice: Vol. 7. A Review of Research* (pp. 29–150). Chicago: University of Chicago Press.

Luntz, B. K., & Widom, C. S. (1994). Antisocial personality disorders in abused and neglected children grown up. *American Journal of Psychiatry, 151,* 670–674.

Marmot, M., & Wilkinson, R. (2006). *Social determinants of health.* Oxford: Oxford University Press.

McCord, J. (1997). *Violence and childhood in the inner city.* New York: Cambridge.

McLeod, J. D., & Kaiser, K. (2004). Childhood emotional and behavioral problems and educational attainment. *American Sociological Review, 69,* 636–658.

Miles, S. B., & Stipek, D. (2006). Contemporaneous and longitudinal associations between social behavior and literacy achievement in low-income elementary school children. *Child Development, 77,* 103–117.

Mistry, R. S., Vandewater, E. A., Huston, A. C., & McLoyd, V. C. (2002). Economic well-being and children's social adjustment. *Child Development, 73,* 935–951.

Moffitt, T. E. (1997). Neuropsychology, antisocial behavior, and neighborhood context. In J. McCord (Ed.). *Violence and childhood in the inner city* (pp. 116–170). New York: Cambridge University Press.

Moffitt, T. E. (2003). Life-course persistent and adolescence-limited antisocial behavior: A 10-year research review and a research agenda. In B. Lahey, T. E. Moffitt, & A. Caspi (Eds.), *The causes of conduct disorder and serious juvenile delinquency* (pp. 49–75). New York: Guilford.

Morales, J., & Guerra, N. G. (2006). Effects of multiple context and cumulative stress on urban children's adjustment in elementary school. *Child Development, 77,* 907–923.

Moser, C., & Holland, J. (1997). *Urban poverty and violence in Jamaica.* Washington, DC: World Bank.

Perry, B. D. (1997). Incubated in terror: Neurodevelopmental factors in the "cycle of violence." In J. Osofsky (Ed.), *Children, youth and violence: The search for solutions* (pp. 124–148). New York: Guilford.

Pettit, G. S., Laird, R. D., Dodge, K. A., Bates, J. E., & Criss, M. M. (2001). Antecedents and behavior-problem outcomes of parental monitoring and psychological control in early adolescence. *Child Development, 72,* 583–598.

Pratt, T., C., & Cullen. F. T. (2005). Assessing macro-level predictors and theories of crime: A meta-analysis. In Michael Tonry (Ed.), *Crime and justice: Vol. 32. A review of research* (pp. 373–450). Chicago: University of Chicago Press.

Raudenbush, S. W. (1983). Utilizing controversy as a source of hypotheses for meta-analysis: The case of teacher expectancy's effect on pupil IQ. *Urban Education, 28,* 114–131.

Rodkin, P. C., Farmer, T. W., Pearl, R., & VanAcker, R. (2000). Heterogeneity of popular boys: Antisocial and prosocial configurations. *Developmental Psychology, 36,* 14–24.

Schaeffer, C. M., & Borduin, C. M. (2005). Long-term follow-up to a randomized clinical trial of multisystemic therapy with serious and violent juvenile offenders. *Journal of Consulting and Clinical Psychology, 63,* 569–578.

Slavin, R. E. (1995). *Cooperative learning.* Boston: Allyn & Bacon.

Steinberg, L. (2010). A behavioral scientist looks at the science of adolescent brain development. *Brain and Cognition, 72,* 160–164.

Straus, M., & Stewart, J. (1999). Corporal punishment by American parents: National data on prevalence, chronicity, severity, and duration, in relation to child and family characteristics. *Clinical Child and Family Psychology Review, 2,* 55–70.

United Nations Office on Drug and Crime. (2009). International homicide statistics. Retrieved October 24, 2009, from http://www.unodc.org/documents/data-and-analysis/IHS-rates-05012009.pdf.

Wilkinson, R. G., & Pickett, K. E. (2009). Income inequality and social dysfunction. *American Sociological Review, 35,* 493–511.

Yoshikawa, H., Weisner, T. S., & Lowe, E. D. (2006). *Making it work: Low-wage employment, family life, and child development.* New York: Russell Sage Foundation.

10

Macroeconomic Factors and Inequities in Youth Violence

The Cyclical Relationship between Community Conditions, Family Factors, and Youth Violence

JENNIFER L. MATJASKO, SARAH BETH BARNETT,
AND JAMES A. MERCY

One of the central questions of this volume is whether there is a relationship between broader macroeconomic factors and youth violence.[1] Macroeconomic fluctuations, or a deviation in the growth of gross domestic product (GDP) around a long-term trend, can cause systemic changes in institutions and macroeconomic conditions and at the same time cause stress or strain on local and regional economies, communities, families, and individuals. These economic fluctuations at the macro and local levels have differential effects on individuals that may depend on their community conditions as well as their families' socioeconomic status (Moen, 1979). Research on the risk factors for youth violence involvement, for example, points to the importance of the community and family contexts in predicting long-term involvement in violence (e.g., Sampson, Wilson, & Petersilia 1995). Furthermore, communities that are differentially affected by economic fluctuations often have higher rates of crime and youth violence involvement (Bursik & Grasmick, 1993). Oftentimes, these communities have persistently high rates of violence that may be driven by long-term inequities in youth violence that can occur over many years and many generations (Land, McCall, & Cohen, 1990). Based on existing theory and research, we posit theory that specifies a cyclical relationship between community economic factors and youth violence that may explain why racial inequities in youth violence exist and persist in the United States. This theory is described in this chapter.

Racial inequities in rates of youth violence, especially in its more severe forms (e.g., homicide), have existed for as long as data on this phenomenon have been collected. Because of the high correlation between race and socioeconomic status, family and community economic conditions may partially explain these inequities. There are stark racial differences in youth arrests, differences that are persistent over time (Elliott, 2009). In the National Youth Survey, the African American–Caucasian race gap in those who report serious violence is the greatest between the ages of 14 and 17 (Elliott, 2009). The rate of African American involvement with serious violence is 50% higher than the rate of serious violence involvement among Caucasian youth (U.S. Department of Health and Human Services, 2001). In addition, in 1998, there were approximately five African American youths arrested for homicide for every Caucasian youth. This racial gap is much greater for arrests compared to self-reported violence (U.S. Department of Health and Human Services, 2001). Nevertheless, the gap in arrests has persisted over time.

An important question is why these inequities have persisted. On the surface, one may surmise that since they have persisted over a wide range of macroeconomic fluctuations, these fluctuations may have little to do with them. However, there may be a dynamic relationship between more localized community and family economic conditions and youth violence, in which both types of economic conditions and youth violence replicate one another. One explanation for the racial inequities in youth violence is neighborhood-concentrated disadvantage (Pratt & Cullen, 2005). African Americans are more likely to live in disadvantaged neighborhoods due to community conditions such as racial segregation, housing discrimination, and socioeconomic-status-related outmigration from the inner city (Sampson et al., 1995). In addition, poor Caucasians live in relatively more advantaged neighborhoods compared to poor African Americans, in that they tend not to live in areas of concentrated poverty (Jargowsky, 1997). Sampson et al. (1995) argued that residential segregation explained the race differences in youth violence, in that African American youth tended to reside in neighborhoods with more risk factors for violence compared to Caucasian youth. In particular, Sampson et al. (1995) found that those neighborhoods that had a higher proportion of adults who held professional or managerial jobs were protective against violence. Furthermore, early and persistent exposure to disadvantaged community and family conditions increases the likelihood that individuals will become involved with youth violence (Sampson et al., 1995).

The aim of this chapter is to propose a theory that links macroeconomic fluctuations to community and family economic conditions and inequities in youth violence. The main elements of our theory are the following: First, the interaction between macroeconomic fluctuations and the extant economic environment causes strain on communities and families. Second, the experience of prolonged and substantial economic strain within a community and a family disrupts healthy patterns of child development by contributing to family instability and undermining a family's ability to protect and nurture its children. Third, when a family's stability and ability to protect and nurture its children are compromised, the likelihood that its children will be exposed to risk factors for youth violence increases. These conditions also decrease the probability that children will be exposed to protective factors for youth violence. Finally, the consequences of involvement as either a victim or perpetrator of youth violence can compromise an adolescent's or young adult's ability to take advantage of life opportunities and move up the economic ladder. These individual and family systems of disadvantage tend to be geographically concentrated in certain communities. Hence there is a dynamic system that, in essence, tends to lock poorer communities into perpetually high rates of youth violence relative to higher-income communities.

In this chapter, we (a) provide definitions for macroeconomic fluctuations and economic conditions; (b) present some existing theoretical models that link macroeconomic fluctuations and community economic conditions with child development; (c) describe the impact of stress on child development; (d) describe how the social environment is linked to developmental pathways of youth violence; (e) show how youth violence affects the economic conditions of a community; (f) posit a cyclical model of economic factors and youth violence; and (g) end with some modeling, policy, and program implications of this cyclical model. The purpose of this chapter is to review existing theory and research in order to construct a plausible theoretical model that helps to explain the persistence of racial and socioeconomic inequities in youth violence by linking macroeconomic factors with community and family factors known to be associated with youth violence.

Defining Macroeconomic Fluctuations and Conditions

A macroeconomic fluctuation is a deviation in the growth of gross domestic product around a long-term trend. There are several types of macroeconomic fluctuations, including business cycles, shocks, bubbles and crises. Although the main outcomes of fluctuations are changes in GDP, the way they impact people's lives and their root causes are different; therefore, policies aimed at mitigating the effects of fluctuations on the propensity of youth to commit violence must be catered to the type and determinants of fluctuations. For that reason, it is important to define and draw the distinction between differing types of macroeconomic fluctuations. The business cycle is a source of common macroeconomic fluctuations, because the economy is continually in one of four phases of GDP growth: expansion, peak, recession, and trough.

Expansions are periods of growth in real (adjusted for inflation) GDP, and recessions are defined as two consecutive quarters of negative GDP growth (O'Sullivan & Sheffrin, 2003). Shocks are events that are unexpected or unpredictable, and in economic modeling terms, they are exogenous, or external to the economic system. Shocks subsequently push the economy into disequilibrium and result in changes in macroeconomic factors and outcomes. Shocks happen frequently, though the severity of their effects on markets and the economy vary widely. A prime example is the terrorist attacks that took place on 9/11, which were unpredictable and had numerous effects on the economy, particularly in the airline sector and stock market. Economic or financial crises, regardless of whether they are internal or external to the economic system, are similar to shocks in that they result in disequilibrium and have detrimental effects, though oftentimes it takes the economy longer to recover from a crisis than a shock. Economic or financial crises are events in which currency, institutions, or assets lose a significant portion of their value. A related phenomenon that results in the loss of value is a speculative bubble, which is a sharp rise in the price of an asset that is not in tandem with the intrinsic value of the asset; this is what occurred in the technology stock market bubble of the late 1990s. From 1995 to 2000, the NASDAQ average went from 800 to over 5,000 at its peak, significantly outpacing other economic indicators, and after the bubble burst, the NASDAQ plummeted to below 2,000 within a year (http://finance.yahoo.com/q/hp?s=%5EIXIC+Historical+Prices).

Apart from these macroeconomic fluctuations, the economy typically behaves around a long-term trend and returns to a steady state or equilibrium. This path is often summarized by the average growth rate of the economy over time. The United States has grown about 3% a year over the past 50 years (Bureau of Economic Analysis, 2010), resulting in substantial gains in living standards across several generations. Despite the fact that an economy may be growing, it may not be performing as well as it could be due to market failures, imperfect government intervention, weak institutions, and imbalanced trade. One non-optimal trend is that although the United States has been experiencing rising median income per capita, there is greater income inequality. The bottom fifth of households owned 4.2% of aggregate income in 1968 and 3.4% in 2008, whereas the top fifth of households owned 42.6% of aggregate income in 1968 and 50% in 2008 (U.S. Census Bureau, 2010).

Regional and local economies also have all the qualities of the larger national economic system, in that they have steady rates of growth and market imperfections, and they sometimes operate independently from the broader macroeconomy. Smaller economies often have concentrated industries, and the effects of fluctuations in the macroeconomy on a local economy are partially dependent on the structure and conditions of the local economy as well as the type and cause of the macro-level fluctuation. For example, Silicon Valley, located in the southern part of the San Francisco Bay Area, is home to some of the largest technology companies and was affected by the many dot-com companies that went under in the early 2000s. We refer to the economic factors and environment that individuals and families interact with at the local level as *community economic conditions*.

We turn our attention to the impact of macroeconomic fluctuations, local economy fluctuations, and community economic conditions on youth violence. The primary mechanism through which macroeconomic fluctuations may influence youth violence involvement may be through community and family economic conditions. Community economic conditions include local job opportunities, local sectors and industries, credit markets, local policies related to small businesses, taxes, and community resources such as nonprofit organizations. Family economic conditions include family income and benefits, assets (home ownership, retirement or college savings), and access to credit (borrowing and indebtedness). Families and youth in lower socioeconomic strata may be more severely disrupted by macroeconomic fluctuations than are those in higher strata because they are more likely to lack the familial and community resources to buffer the impact of such fluctuations. In other words, macroeconomic fluctuations may contribute to community and familial environments that are disadvantaged and strained. Community and family strain are related to stressors such as family disruption and harsh parenting (Webster-Stratton, 1990). When such stressors on children are chronic, uncontrollable, and experienced without the support of caring adults, they can influence brain development in ways that may contribute to risk for youth violence (National Scientific Council on the Developing Child, 2005). In a very real sense, macroeconomic fluctuations and community and family economic conditions, therefore, may alter children's developmental trajectories and result in a cycle of disadvantage. This cycle of disadvantage may also be associated with a cycle of relatively higher rates of youth violence in disadvantaged communities, compared to the rates in communities with greater economic resources. In the next section, we present some theoretical models that describe the relationship between macroeconomic factors, communities, families, and child development.

Economic Factors, Communities, Families, and Child Development

In terms of the body of evidence that exists at the intersection of the fields of psychology and economics, research has explored the relationship between poverty (i.e., a generally long-term family economic condition) and family functioning (e.g., Smith, Brooks-Gunn, & Klebanov, 1997). Studies have also shown that the stress of parental unemployment can spill over into the home in the form of intimate-partner violence (Benson & Fox, 2004) as well as harsh and inconsistent parenting (McLoyd, Jayaratne, Ceballo, & Borquez, 1994). In addition, when parents work nonstandard hours, there is often a lack of quality child care options, which may also be a stressor for families and children (Strazdins, Korda, Lim, Broom, & D'Souza, 2004).

Elder's (1999) study on the children of the Great Depression demonstrated how macroeconomic fluctuations are filtered through the family to affect children and adolescents. The extent to which macroeconomic fluctuations, such as the Great Depression, influence child and adolescent functioning depends on the severity of the fluctuation, how the family system copes, and the time in the child's development when these fluctuations occur. Elder's study illustrated that adolescents, who were likely to seek work in order to help their families make ends meet, did not do as well, in terms of their behavioral and emotional functioning, as younger children. He also found that middle-class children, compared to working-class children, were better able to adapt to change, and this increased the social and economic inequities between the middle and working class.

Prior research has identified two primary theoretical models that depict the relationship between family economic conditions, family factors, and child and adolescent adjustment: (1) the family stress model (Conger et al., 1992) and (2) the family investment model (Becker & Thomes, 1986; Bradley & Corwyn, 2002; Corcoran & Adams, 1997; Duncan & Magnuson, 2003; Haveman & Wolfe, 1994; Linver, Brooks-Gunn, & Kohen, 2002; Mayer, 1997). A third model, Agnew's (1999) general strain theory, specifies the relationship between community economic conditions and crime. Our depictions of these models are shown in figures 10.1–10.3 and include factors across levels of the social ecology

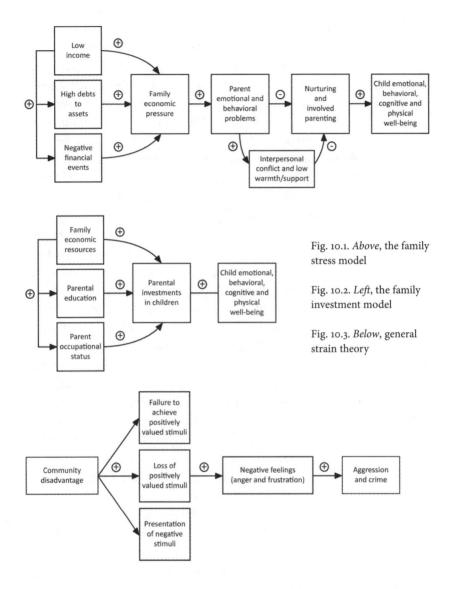

Fig. 10.1. *Above*, the family stress model

Fig. 10.2. *Left*, the family investment model

Fig. 10.3. *Below*, general strain theory

(Bronfenbrenner, 1979). The social ecological model (Bronfenbrenner, 1979) is a model wherein the individual is nested within relationships, the community, and the larger society. In this case, the macroeconomic fluctuations are part of the "outer levels" of the social ecology, in that these fluctuations occur at city, state, or national levels.

Elder's study (1999) is an illustration of the family stress model, which describes how macroeconomic fluctuations can affect families and children. It describes the circumstances that families face when their incomes fall as a result of a recession (and, at times, depression). When parents are unable to pay bills, they may experience distress in the form of depression, anxiety, irritability, anger, or even substance abuse. Parental emotional and behavioral problems, in turn, are also related to less nurturing and involved parenting (Cummings, Keller, & Davies, 2005). Compared to children who do not experience family economic hardships, children of families that do experience such hardships have difficulties in social, academic, and psychological functioning, including overt aggression and physical fighting, which are predictors of youth violence (Conger et al., 1992). Similar findings have been replicated among different populations, including African Americans; poor, urban, ethnic minorities with single parents; early adolescent Finnish children; and European Americans and Mexican Americans living in urban California (Conger et al., 2002; Mistry, Vandewater, Huston, & McLoyd, 2002; Yeung, Linver, & Brooks-Gunn, 2002; Solantaus, Leinonen, & Punamaki, 2004; Parke et al., 2004). Thus, the family stress model posits that there is an indirect relationship between macroeconomic fluctuations and child and adolescent functioning, a relationship that is mediated by family economic pressure, parent emotional and behavior problems, and parenting. In other words, according to the family stress model, macroeconomic fluctuations affect family economic factors (e.g., family debt-to-asset ratio, negative family financial events), which, in turn, affect family economic pressure, parent emotional and behavioral problems, and parenting.

The family investment model states that families who are economically disadvantaged face tough decisions about where to spend their limited resources (Becker & Thomes, 1986; Bradley & Corwyn, 2002; Corcoran & Adams, 1997; Duncan & Magnuson, 2003; Haveman & Wolfe, 1994; Linver et al., 2002; Mayer, 1997), whereas families with more resources are able to invest in the development of their children through access to greater financial, social, and human capital. Investments include several different types of support, including learning materials in the home and parental stimulation as well as living in a neighborhood with more resources and better schools. The family investment model may be more relevant for families that face more persistently poor family economic conditions, such as poverty. Evidence for this model comes from studies that document that family income during childhood and adolescence is positively correlated with academic, financial, and occupational success in adulthood (Bradley & Corwyn, 2002; Corcoran & Adams, 1997; Mayer, 1997; Teachman, Paasch, Day, & Carver, 1997). Perhaps the strongest evidence comes from researchers who used several waves of the National Longitudinal Survey of Youth (Bureau of Labor Statistics, 2002) and found significant differences related to family investments in enriching home environments among families living above versus below the poverty line (Bradley, Corwyn, McAdoo, & Garcia Coll, 2001). These investments included both social and physical resources such as the quality of parent-child relationships and the provision of cognitively enriching activities. Income and investment are expected to translate to developmental success through these family processes. Researchers have found an association between child cognitive development at ages 3 and 5 and family income, controlling for parental education and intelligence, establishing a relationship between income and child functioning over and above these parental characteristics (Linver et al., 2002).

Both the family stress and family investment models contain some assumptions about the nature of family economic conditions. The family stress model frames economic stressors as decreases in income, presumably from a macroeconomic fluctuation since the model was developed based on a downturn in the agricultural economy in the 1980s (Conger et al., 1992). The family investment model usually defines the family economic condition as family disadvantage or poverty, a term often used to describe a state that is persistent. When families are in poverty, they tend to face constant economic stress and financial strain. Macroeconomic fluctuations such as recessions that result in unemployment may place further strain on families who are already unemployed and living below the poverty line. The family investment model posits that families exposed to long-term economic disadvantage already face chronic economic stressors, and macroeconomic fluctuations may result in additional strain on them. These two models appear to be pointing to two distinct experiences when it comes to macroeconomic factors—one subset of families may be influenced by macroeconomic fluctuations, while others may be entrenched in long-term economic conditions that were shaped by inequality in opportunities for gainful employment and the acquisition of assets.

Unlike the family stress and investment models, Agnew's general strain model (1999) focuses more on how individuals react to disadvantaged community conditions. The theory posits that community disadvantage results in three possible types of strain: (1) failure to achieve positively valued stimuli, (2) loss of positively valued stimuli, and (3) presentation of negative stimuli. According to Agnew, positively valued stimuli include money, status, and autonomy. Individuals in chronically disadvantaged communities are unlikely to have these positively valued stimuli. Furthermore, individuals in communities that are experiencing the effects of a macroeconomic fluctuation may lose positively valued stimuli, in addition to the loss of important relationships. Finally, negative stimuli include important family processes (e.g., harsh parenting, child abuse), school experiences (e.g., failure, suspensions), peer relationships, and neighborhood conditions. When individuals are faced with such strain, they are likely to experience feelings of anger and frustration because they cannot attain money, status, and autonomy in their communities while they are simultaneously feeling the effects of loss and other stressors at various levels of the social ecology (Agnew, 1999). These feelings of anger and frustration can result in aggression and crime.

All three of these models highlight the importance of developmental considerations in the characterization of economic stressors and their potential influence on youth violence involvement. The family stress model demonstrates that the developmental timing of the stressor is important, while the family investment and general strain models show that it is also important to consider the severity of the economic stressor on the family, school, peers, and neighborhoods. The family plays a role in each of the models primarily through family strain and parenting. Although not illustrated in the figures, the severity, persistence, and developmental timing of these events can have both short- and long-term consequences for individuals. Based on this evidence, it is critical to account for three conditions in order to understand whether macroeconomic fluctuations affect youth violence: (1) the nature of the economic stressor (i.e., how severe is the stressor?), (2) the persistence of the economic stressor (i.e., is it a short- or a long-term event?), and (3) the timing of the economic stressor (i.e., at what point in development does it occur?). With short-term macroeconomic fluctuations, all three of these considerations are sources of variability that can elucidate the relationship between macroeconomic fluctuations, community and family economic conditions, and youth violence. On the other hand, the concept of long-term or chronic economic conditions assumes that there is persistence to the stressor and that it occurs throughout development. However, the nature of that stressor can vary. In addition, there can be variation over time in the nature of this stressor, so it is also important to tie the nature of the stressor to developmental periods over the course of childhood and adolescence. When economic conditions are severe, occur early in development, and are persistent over time, it is likely that the conditions will negatively influence development and increase the likelihood of youth violence involvement. In the following section, we describe the developmental literature on youth violence involvement.

Social Environment, Child Development, and Youth Violence

Macroeconomic fluctuations can contribute to youth violence in at least two key ways. First, they can impact families and increase children's exposure to key risk factors for youth violence, such as harsh parenting. Second, they can contribute to community conditions that lead to greater social disorganization and youth violence in communities by, for example, creating communities with larger numbers of delinquent and antisocial youth. The developmental literature on youth violence involvement has identified developmental-stage-specific risk factors for youth violence as well as various developmental trajectories of youth violence. Most of this work is based on longitudinal studies of youth violence involvement. In this volume, Guerra (chapter 9) provides an excellent summary of the developmental-stage-specific risk factors for youth violence for the prenatal period (through age 5), the early school years (ages 6–11), and adolescence (ages 12–18). We present a summary of these developmental stage risk factors in table 10.1. Guerra emphasizes the cumulative nature of stress throughout development and that macroeconomic stressors are typically filtered through families

Table 10.1. Developmental-Stage-Specific Risk Factors for Youth Violence

Risk factor	Early childhood (prenatal–age 5)	Early school years (ages 6–11)	Adolescence (ages 12–18)
Individual	Neuropsychological vulnerabilities	Neuropsychological/IQ impairments Attention problems Hostile attribution bias Normative beliefs about aggression Gender	Deviant identities Cumulative adverse early experiences Limited opportunities for self-expression Attention problems Substance use Gender
Family	Inadequate prenatal care Harsh parenting/ corporal punishment Insecure attachments Child maltreatment	Harsh parenting Antisocial parents	Parental monitoring Antisocial parents
Peer		Peer rejection Peer norms of aggression	Deviant peer groups Gang involvement
School		Low school resources Suboptimal teacher practices Low teacher expectations	School disengagement
Neighborhood	Poor quality health care Witnessing community violence	Witnessing community violence	Witnessing community violence Marginalized communities

and communities to influence youth violence. Furthermore, Guerra presents evidence that risk factors for youth violence (e.g., harsh parenting, insecure attachments) are more likely to occur in impoverished environments.

High levels of youth violence in a community can also have an important influence on the economic conditions of a community. For example, high levels of community violence have been demonstrated to influence the viability of service-related business establishments and the value of the housing market (Greenbaum & Tita, 2004; Tita, Petras, & Greenbaum, 2006). In addition, individuals involved in youth violence may compromise their ability to secure meaningful employment or otherwise achieve higher socioeconomic status (Guerra, chapter 9 in this volume). As a result, communities also tend to be locked in a cycle of economic disadvantage.

A Cyclical Model of Economic Factors and Youth Violence

Based on the theory and research just presented, we posit a cyclical, or recursive, relationship between community and family economic factors and youth violence. In essence, we are suggesting that a dynamic system exists that maintains and sustains a relationship between community and family economic factors and youth violence and that resists disruption. This theory seeks to explain why racial and socioeconomic inequities in youth violence have persisted over a long period of time in the United States. Figure 10.4 depicts this model.

The main elements of the model are (1) economic fluctuations are filtered through community and family economic conditions, and this predicts parenting, strain, and school/peer risk factors; (2) the extent to which economic fluctuation influences parenting, strain, and school/ peer risk factors depends on the extant community and family economic conditions (represented by the dashed line in figure 10.4); (3) the experience of prolonged and substantial economic strain within communities and families disrupts healthy patterns of child development by contributing to family instability and undermining a family's ability to

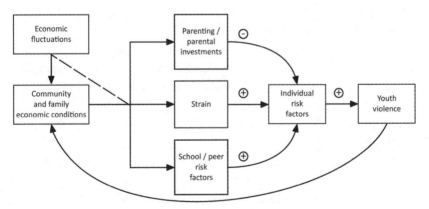

Fig. 10.4. Community and family economic conditions and youth violence: a cyclical model

protect and nurture its children within a broader community context of disadvantage with higher rates of school and peer risk factors; (4) when a family's stability and ability to protect and nurture its children is compromised, this increases the likelihood that its children will experience individual risk factors for violence (e.g., anger/frustration, neurological impairments, attention problems, hostile attribution bias), especially within disadvantaged communities; (5) these individual risk factors may, then, lead to youth violence involvement; and (6) the youth violence involvement compromises an adolescent's or young adult's ability to take advantage of life opportunities and to move up the economic ladder and move away from disadvantaged environments. In figure 10.4, this dynamic is represented by the arrow from youth violence to community and family economic conditions. These individual and family systems of disadvantage tend to be geographically concentrated in certain communities. Hence there is a dynamic system that, in essence, locks poorer communities into perpetually higher rates of youth violence relative to higher-income communities that have resources to soften the blow of macroeconomic shocks. The model is cyclical, in that youth violence predicts community and family economic conditions.

Modeling Considerations

Our cyclical model can be characterized as a conceptual model that can be empirically tested. The cyclical framework is a complex model—it calls for longitudinal data with broader macroeconomic fluctuations, community and family economic conditions, parenting and school/ peer factors, individual factors, and indicators of youth violence. There is a paucity of available data sets that include all of these variables. There are some promising nationally representative data sets that can be used to test some parts of the model (e.g., the National Longitudinal Study of Adolescent Health; Harris & Udry, 2010), though they have their limitations.

The conceptual model can be tested using multilevel structural equation models. In the model, a macroeconomic shock is an exogenous variable, and youth violence is a single latent variable outcome. Here, the assumption is that macroeconomic shocks at time t will be significantly related to youth violence at time t. This may not be an accurate assumption; if there is a hypothesized lag between a larger macroeconomic fluctuation and youth violence, the model can be estimated with a lagged measure of macroeconomic shocks. The community and family economic conditions variables can be added in a separate model to test their strength as a mediator and a moderator. In other words, community and family economic conditions may mediate the relationship between macroeconomic fluctuations and parenting, strain, and school/peer risk factors, which are related to individual risk factors and youth violence. In order to accurately test mediation, the other mediating variables—parenting/parental investments, strain, and school/peer risk factors—can also be added in separate models. Furthermore, the extent to which macroeconomic fluctuations affect parenting, strain, and school/peer risk factors depends on the community and family economic conditions at the time the fluctuation occurs. Thus, the interaction between macroeconomic fluctuations and community/family economic conditions in predicting those mediating variables would also be included in the model. Finally, individual risk factors can then be added to the model. Evidence of mediation can be shown by significant paths to and from the mediating variables, as well as a reduction in the direct effects of the exogenous variable on the outcome. Finally, a structural equation model can be used to test whether youth violence at time t is significantly related to community and family economic conditions at time $t + 1$.

Prevention and Policy Implications

In this chapter, we made the distinction between two types of economic factors—ones that are a result of short-term macroeconomic fluctuations and long-term economic conditions that are manifested at the community and family levels in the form of community and family economic conditions. We presented the family stress and investment models as well as general strain theory—three models that have been used to explain how macroeconomic fluctuations within local economies influence communities and families, which, in turn, are thought to influence youth violence. We integrated these three models and proposed a cyclical model that specifies the relationship between macroeconomic fluctuations, community and family economic conditions, and youth violence involvement and describes how some communities may be locked into economic disadvantage because of high rates of violence. These models included community, family, and individual factors that are hypothesized to mediate the relationship between macroeconomic fluctuations and youth violence. Finally, we proposed some empirical strategies that can be employed in order to estimate the relationship between macroeconomic fluctuations, community and family economic conditions, and youth violence. While there is likely a complex relationship between macroeconomic fluctuations and youth violence, there are prevention and policy implications based on the proposed cyclical model. From the theoretical perspective that we have outlined, policies that interrupt the cycle of economic disadvantage and youth violence are keys to prevention. Unless the cycle is interrupted, the racial inequities in youth violence are likely to persist. We describe some viable prevention and policy options in the following sections.

Strategies That Differ by Type of Economic Factors

Our model suggests that at least two types of policy approaches are necessary in order to reduce the level of stress that families experience due to macroeconomic fluctuations: one set of policies shortens the duration of the impact of macroeconomic fluctuations, while another aims to alleviate the impact that macroeconomic fluctuations have on community and family economic conditions. With regard to the former, multiple approaches are necessary to reduce the number and severity of macroeconomic fluctuations. Policy approaches designed to alleviate short-term macroeconomic fluctuations include tax deductions and the extension of unemployment benefits to stimulate spending, job creation, and increased support in the form of extensions to government programs (Romer, 2009). By decreasing the duration and severity of short-term macroeconomic fluctuations, communities and families are less likely to experience severe and prolonged periods of economic stress, unemployment, and so on.

In addition, low-income assistance or poverty-reduction policies have been suggested by scholars in the field as a strategy to alleviate long-term community and family economic conditions such as poverty and inequality (Ames, Brown, Devarajan, & Izquierdo, 2001). Some poverty-reduction policies transfer income and wealth from some individuals to others, often through taxing individuals with higher incomes and distributing the revenue to low-income individuals (Alesina & La Ferrara, 2005). Another potentially viable strategy to alleviate disadvantaged community and family economic conditions and perhaps vulnerability to macroeconomic fluctuations is the establishment of business improvement districts (BIDs) or other strategies to create a more viable community economic environment in distressed communities (Levy, 2001). Existing research is inconclusive about the effectiveness of BIDs in reducing youth violence. It is clear that BIDs alone cannot create and sustain neighborhood change, but some research has suggested that many BIDs have invested in private security measures (MacDonald, Golinelli, Stokes, & Bluthenthal, 2010). In addition, BIDs have been found to have significant positive effects on reducing rates of crime and, in particular, robberies (MacDonald et al., 2009). Other ways to reduce long-term community and family economic conditions include job training, living-wage policies, and policies that reduce discriminatory lending practices (e.g., higher-interest-rate loans to minorities) so that low-income individuals can acquire higher earnings and property, respectively. It is also important to evaluate whether these economic policy approaches are effective at shortening the duration of macroeconomic fluctuations and reducing their impact on community and family economic conditions and youth violence.

Developmental Considerations for Youth Violence Prevention

Despite policies aimed to alleviate macroeconomic fluctuations and long-term community and family economic conditions, some income inequity within the United States is probably inevitable. Therefore, it is also important to bolster families' ability to cope with disadvantaged economic conditions in order to reduce the likelihood that youth will become involved with violence. First, for macroeconomic fluctuations, it might be necessary to focus on families that may be economically vulnerable or at the margin, since those are the families that are likely to feel the impact of such fluctuations (Stiglitz, 1999). For both economically vulnerable families and those that have experienced long-term poverty and inequality, it is important to provide supports that bolster family members' ability to engage in healthy family processes (e.g., appropriate monitoring, nurturing, and positive, nonviolent relationships). Behavioral parent-training programs, such as Triple P, encourage positive parenting practices and have been shown to slow the rates of child maltreatment, which is a risk factor for youth violence involvement (Prinz, Sanders, Shapiro, Whitaker, & Lutzker, 2009). Healthy parenting practices are also related to children's lower likelihood of being involved with youth violence (Capaldi & Patterson, 1996). In addition to parenting programs, there are several promising youth-violence-prevention interventions for adolescents at the individual, school, and community levels (for a review of these interventions, see Limbos et al., 2007).

Furthermore, it may also be necessary to target families with children of certain ages. Studies on risk and resilience have demonstrated that promoting resiliency early in life is a better use of resources than treating behavior problems later in development (Cowen, 1991, 1994, 1999; Knitzer, 2000a, 2000b; Luthar, Cicchetti, & Becker, 2000; Rutter, 2000; Werner, 2000). Cumulative adverse early experiences are also a risk factor for youth violence involvement (Guerra, chapter 9 in this volume). Furthermore, economic analyses have demonstrated the cost-effectiveness of intervening earlier rather than later in development (Greenwood, 1999). Hence, in order to reduce the likelihood of an individual becoming involved with violence during adolescence, an increased emphasis should be placed on supports to alleviate adverse community and family economic conditions that occur early in development and continue throughout childhood and adolescence. Supports will also be necessary for children and youth who had adverse childhood experiences and, hence, may be more likely to become involved in youth violence.

In addition, in times of economic crisis, many localities face tight budgets and are forced to cut services in schools and in communities. During the economic crisis that began in 2008, for example, many states have required teacher furlough days that may leave many children and youth with a lack of adult supervision (Johnson, Williams, & Oliff, 2010), a situation that may increase the opportunities for youth to become involved with delinquent peer networks and to engage in delinquent and violent behavior. This may be especially likely to occur in communities that have also been forced to scale back on the services available to youth and their families because of budget cuts. When this combination of events occurs, vulnerable families have fewer resources and sources of support to help them cope with macroeconomic fluctuations and disadvantaged economic conditions. Decisions to cut school and local budgets in such ways may thus have unintended consequences on youth violence, making the availability of prevention programs at multiple levels of the social ecology even more vital (for a review, see Limbos et al., 2007). In sum, a multifaceted effort at multiple levels is necessary in order to break the cycle of disadvantage and to reduce inequities in youth violence.

NOTES

1. Disclaimer: The findings and conclusions of this report are those of the authors and do not necessarily represent the official position of the Centers for Disease Control and Prevention.

REFERENCES

Agnew, R. (1999). A general strain theory of community differences in crime rates. *Journal of Research on Crime and Delinquency, 36*, 123–155.

Alesina, A., & La Ferrara, E. (2005). Preferences for redistribution in the land of opportunities. *Journal of Public Economics, 89*, 897–931.

Ames, B., Brown, W., Devarajan, S., & Izquierdo, A. (2001). *Macroeconomic policy and poverty reduction*. Washington, DC: International Monetary Fund.

Becker, G., & Thomes, N. (1986). Human capital and the rise and fall of families. *Journal of Labor Economics, 4*, S1–S139.

Benson, M. L., & Fox, G. L. (2004). *When violence hits home: How economics and neighborhood play a role* (Research in Brief). Rockville, MD: National Institute of Justice.

Bradley, R. H., & Corwyn, R. F. (2002). Socioeconomic status and child development. *Annual Review of Psychology, 53*, 371–399.

Bradley, R. H., Corwyn, R. F., McAdoo, H. P., & Garcia Coll, C. (2001). The home environments of children in the United States: Part I, Variations by age, ethnicity, and poverty status. *Child Development, 72*, 1844–1867.

Bronfenbrenner, U. (1979). *The ecology of human development*. Cambridge: Harvard University Press.

Bureau of Economic Analysis. (2010). *Gross domestic product: Percent change from preceding period*. http://www.bea.gov/national/index.htm#gdp.

Bureau of Labor Statistics. (2002). National Longitudinal Survey of Youth 1979 cohort, 1979–2002 (rounds 1–20). Produced and distributed for the U.S. Department of

Labor by the Center for Human Resource Research, The Ohio State University, Columbus.

Bursik, R. J., & Grasmick, H. G. (1993). Economic deprivation and neighborhood crime rates, 1960–1980. *Law and Society Review, 27*, 263–283.

Capaldi, D. M., & Patterson, G. S. (1996). Can violent offenders be predicted from frequent offenders? Prediction from childhood to adolescence. *Journal of Research on Crime and Delinquency, 33*, 206–231.

Conger, R. D., Conger, K. J., Elder, G. H., Lorenz, F. O., Simons, R. L., & Whitbeck, L. B. (1992). A family process model of economic hardship and adjustment of early adolescent boys. *Child Development, 63*, 526–541.

Conger, R. D., Wallace, L. E., et al. (2002). Economic pressure in African American families: A replication and extension of the family stress model. *Developmental Psychology, 38*, 179–193.

Corcoran, M., & Adams, T. (1997). Race, sex, and the intergenerational transmission of poverty. In G. J. Duncan and J. Brooks-Gunn (Eds.), *Consequences of growing up poor* (pp. 461–517). New York: Russell Sage Foundation.

Cowen, E. L. (1991). In pursuit of wellness. *American Psychologist, 46*, 404–408.

Cowen, E. L. (1994). The enhancement of psychological wellness: Challenges and opportunities. *American Journal of Community Psychology, 22*, 149–179.

Cowen, E. L. (1999). In sickness and in health: Primary prevention's vow revisited. In D. Cicchetti & S. L. Toth (Eds.), *Rochester symposium on developmental psychopathology: Vol. 9, Developmental approaches to prevention and intervention* (pp. 1–24). Rochester, NY: University of Rochester Press.

Cummings, E. M., Keller, P. S., & Davies, P. T. (2005). Towards a family process model of maternal and paternal depressive symptoms: Exploring multiple relations with child and family functioning. *Journal of Child Psychology and Psychiatry, 46*, 479–489.

Duncan, G. J., & Magnuson, K. A. (2003). Off with Hollingshead: Socioeconomic resources, parenting and child development. In M. H. Bornstein & R. H. Bradley (Eds.), *Socioeconomic status, parenting, and child development* (pp. 83–106). Mahwah, NJ: Erlbaum.

Elder, G. H. (1999). *Children of the Great Depression: Social change in life experience* (25th Anniversary Edition). Boulder, CO: Westview. Originally published 1974.

Elliott, D. (2009). *National Youth Survey [United States]*. Ann Arbor, MI: Inter-university Consortium for Political and Social Research [distributor].

Greenbaum, R. T., & Tita, G. E. (2004). The impact of violence surges on neighbourhood business activity. *Urban Studies, 41*, 2495–2514.

Greenwood, P. W. (1999). The cost-effectiveness of early intervention as a strategy for reducing violent crime. In E. L. Rubin (Ed.), *Minimizing harm: A new crime policy for modern America* (pp. 67–89). Boulder, CO: Westview.

Harris, K. M., & Udry, J. R. (2010). *National Longitudinal Study of Adolescent Health (Add Health), 1994–2002*. Ann Arbor, MI: Inter-university Consortium for Political and Social Research [distributor].

Haveman, R. B., & Wolfe, B. (1994). *Succeeding generations: On the effects of investments in children.* New York: Russell Sage Foundation.

Jargowsky, P. A. (1997). *Poverty and place: Ghettos, barrios, and the American city.* New York: Russell Sage Foundation.

Johnson, N., Williams, E., & Oliff, P. (2010). *Governors' new budgets indicate loss of many jobs if federal aid expires.* Washington, DC: Center on Budget and Policy Priorities.

Knitzer, J. (2000a). Early childhood mental health services: A policy and systems development perspective. In J. P. Shonkoff & S. J. Meisels (Eds.), *Handbook of early childhood intervention* (2nd ed., pp. 416–438). New York: Cambridge University Press.

Knitzer, J. (2000b). *Promoting resilience: Helping young children and families affected by substance abuse, domestic violence, and depression in the context of welfare reform* (Children and Welfare Reform Issue Brief No. 8). New York: National Center for Children in Poverty.

Land, K. C., McCall, P. L., & Cohen, L. E. (1990). Structural covariates of homicide rates: Are there any invariances across time and social space? *American Journal of Sociology, 95,* 922–963.

Levy, P. (2001). Paying for the public life. *Economic Development Quarterly, 15,* 124–131.

Limbos, M. A., Chan, L. S., Warf, C., Schneir, A., Iverson, E., Shekelle, P., & Kipke, M. D. (2007). Effectiveness of interventions to prevent youth violence: A systematic review. *American Journal of Preventive Medicine, 33,* 65–74.

Linver, M. R., Brooks-Gunn, J., & Kohen, D. (2002). Family processes as pathways from income to young children's development. *Developmental Psychology, 38,* 719–734.

Luthar, S., Cicchetti, D., & Becker, B. (2000). The construct of resilience: A critical evaluation and guidelines for future work. *Child Development, 71,* 543–562.

MacDonald, J., Blumenthal, R. N., Golinelli, D., Kofner, A., Stokes, R. J., Sehgal, A., Fain, T., & Beletsky, L. (2009). *Neighborhood effects on crime and youth violence: The role of business improvement districts in Los Angeles.* Santa Monica, CA: RAND.

MacDonald, J., Golinelli, D., Stokes, R. J., & Bluthenthal, R. (2010). The effect of business improvement districts on the incidence of violent crimes. *Injury Prevention.*

Mayer, S. (1997). *What money can't buy: Family income and children's life chances.* Cambridge: Harvard University Press.

McLoyd, V. C., Jayaratne, T. E., Ceballo, R., & Borquez, J. (1994). Unemployment and work interruption among African American single mothers: Effect on parenting and adolescent socioemotional functioning. *Child Development, 65,* 562–589.

Mistry, R. S., Vandewater, E. A., Huston, A. C., & McLoyd, V. C. (2002). Economic well-being and children's social adjustment. *Child Development, 73,* 935–951.

Moen, P. (1979). Family impacts of the 1975 recession: Duration of unemployment. *Journal of Marriage and the Family, 41,* 561–572.

National Scientific Council on the Developing Child. (2005). *Excessive stress disrupts the architecture of the developing brain* (Working Paper #3). http://www.developingchild.net.

O'Sullivan, A., & Sheffrin, S. M. (2003). *Economics: Principles in action.* Upper Saddle River, NJ: Pearson Prentice Hall.

Parke, R. D., Coltrane, S., Duffy, S., Buriel, R., Dennis, J., Powers, J., et al. (2004). Economic stress, parenting, and child adjustment in Mexican American and European American families. *Child Development, 75,* 1632–1656.

Pratt, T. C., & Cullen, F. T. (2005). Assessing macro-level predictors and theories of crime: A meta-analysis. In M. Tonry (Ed.), *Crime and justice: Vol. 32. A review of research* (pp. 373–450). Chicago: University of Chicago Press.

Prinz, R. J., Sanders, M. R., Shapiro, C. J., Whitaker, D. J., & Lutzker, J. R. (2009). Population-based prevention of child maltreatment: The U.S. Triple P system population trial. *Prevention Science, 10,* 1–12.

Romer, C. D. (2009). Fiscal policy and economic recovery. *Business Economics, 44,* 132–135.

Rutter, M. (2000). Resilience reconsidered: Conceptual considerations, empirical findings, and policy implications. In J. P. Shonkoff & S. J. Meisels (Eds.), *Handbook of early childhood interventions* (2nd ed., pp. 651–682). New York: Cambridge University Press.

Sampson, R. J., Wilson, J. Q., & Petersilia, J. (1995). The community. In J. Q. Wilson & J. Petersilia (Eds.), *Crime* (pp. 193–219). San Francisco: Institute for Contemporary Studies Press.

Smith, J. R., Brooks-Gunn, J., & Klebanov, P. K. (1997). Consequences of living in poverty for young children's cognitive and verbal ability and early school achievement. In G. J. Duncan & J. Brooks-Gunn (Eds.), *Consequences of growing up poor* (pp. 132–189). New York: Russell Sage Foundation.

Solantaus, T., Leinonen, J., & Punamaki, R. L. (2004). Children's mental health in times of economic recession: Replication and extension of the family economic stress model in Finland. *Developmental Psychology, 40,* 214–429.

Stiglitz, J. (1999). Responding to economic crises: Policy alternatives for equitable recovery and development. *Manchester School, 67,* 409–427.

Strazdins, L., Korda, R. L., Lim, L. L., Broom, D. H., & D'Souza, R. M. (2004). Around-the-clock: Parent work schedules and children's well-being in a 24-h economy. *Social Science & Medicine, 57,* 1517–1527.

Teachman, J. D., Paasch, K. M., Day, R. D., & Carver, K. P. (1997). Poverty during adolescence and subsequent educational attainment. In G. J. Duncan & J. Brooks-Gunn (Eds.), *Consequences of growing up poor* (pp. 382–418). New York: Russell Sage Foundation.

Tita, G. W., Petras, T. L., & Greenbaum, R. T. (2006). Crime and residential choice: A neighborhood level analysis of the impact of crime on housing prices. *Journal of Quantitative Criminology, 22,* 299–317.

U.S. Census Bureau. (2010). *Table H-2: Share of aggregate income received by each fifth and top 5 percent of households, all races: 1967 to 2008.* http://www.census.gov/hhes/www/income/data/historical/household/index.html.

U.S. Department of Health and Human Services. (2001). *Youth violence: A report of the*

Surgeon General. Rockville, MD: U.S. Department of Health and Human Services, Centers for Disease Control and Prevention, National Center for Injury Prevention and Control; Substance Abuse and Mental Health Services Administration, Center for Mental Health Services; and National Institutes of Health, National Institute of Mental Health.

Webster-Stratton, C. (1990). Stress: A potential disruptor of parent perceptions and family interactions. *Journal of Clinical Child and Adolescent Psychology, 19,* 302–312.

Werner, E. E. (2000). Protective factors and individual resilience. In J. P. Shonkoff & S. J. Meisels (Eds.), *Handbook of early childhood interventions* (2nd ed., pp. 115–132). New York: Cambridge University Press.

Yeung, W. J., Linver, M. R., & Brooks-Gunn, J. (2002). How money matters for young children's development: Parental investment and family process. *Child Development, 73,* 1861–1879.

PART IV

Looking to the Future

11

Economic Opportunity and Youth Violence

Conclusions and Implications for Future Research

CURTIS S. FLORENCE AND SARAH BETH BARNETT

In this volume, the authors have sought to identify macroeconomic factors that are associated with youth violence (defined as violence where the victim or perpetrator is 10 to 24 years old) and to explore aspects of the relationship between economic conditions and violence that can be useful in developing interventions to prevent violence.[1] In conducting the project, we departed from the standard textbook definition of macroeconomics—economic factors at the national, regional, or international level. Instead, we include economic factors across all levels of aggregation, from the national to the family level. Our reason for doing this was to examine economic factors that can potentially affect individual behavior via their impact on neighborhoods, schools, street markets, and family functioning. Thus, we examine factors that are likely to influence violence at the level of society and community—the higher levels of the organizing framework presented by Rosenfeld and also the "outer rings" of the social-ecological model used by the CDC's National Center for Injury Prevention and Control to describe the various levels of influence on violent behavior (Dahlberg & Krug, 2002). A primary motivation in examining economic factors at these levels is that, if they are strongly associated with violent behavior, the potential exists to develop interventions to prevent violent behavior that are likely to affect a broad number of individuals by addressing the economic conditions that influence violence. Given the research that has been presented in this volume, it is appropriate to ask, *What have we learned that can be useful in preventing violence?*

In order to answer this question, it is necessary to outline the information that would be necessary in order to prevent violence by changing economic conditions. First, *it must be established that violence is strongly associated with economic conditions, net of other factors that are also associated with violence.* Second, *if economic factors are associated with violence, policies, programs, or strategies developed to address these conditions must be able to identify the appropriate economic characteristics and be effective in improving them.* Third, *the improvement in these factors must be large enough that they can lead to a reduction in violence.* Ideally, this reduction in violence due to improved economic conditions would be demonstrated in multiple high-quality studies and could be recommended for prevention by organizations such as the Community Preventive Services Task Force, an independent, nonfederal group of public health and prevention experts who review evidence and make recommendations for community-based prevention programs and policies through the Guide to Community Preventive Services (the "Community Guide").[2]

Currently, none of the programs recommended by the Community Guide addresses violence prevention through improving economic conditions. However, some research has been conducted on programs that aim to improve neighborhood or family economic conditions, with one of the aims being the prevention of violence. Two examples are housing voucher programs and business improvement districts. However, either rigorous evaluation of those programs has not demonstrated reductions in violence, or there is not yet a sufficient evidence base for completion of a Community Guide review. Given the lack of effective programs that prevent violence through the improvement of economic conditions, this project can provide valuable information for understanding the evaluation of current programs and the development of future programs. We will review and synthesize the results of the chapters in this volume by viewing them in the context of the three issues raised in the preceding paragraph. While it has not been the purpose of this project to evaluate specific programs or policies to prevent violence by improving economic conditions, the findings reviewed here can help lay the groundwork for developing and evaluating those interventions in the future.

The Connection between Economics and Violence

There has been a large literature produced that examines the relationship between economic factors and crime. This literature has examined a wide variety of criminal outcomes and economic variables but generally attempts to establish whether crime is "countercyclical"—that is, whether crime goes up when economic activity declines and decreases when economic activity increases. In general, this literature focuses on the temporal associations between economic factors and crime in order to examine the effects of economic conditions net of the impact of confounding variables that may be associated with the levels of economic variables and crime. One of the seminal studies in this area was Cook and Zarkin (1985), which studied the relationship between recessions and property crime (auto theft and burglary) and violent crime (robbery and homicide). This study used national crime statistics published by the FBI and found a significant countercyclical relationship between both burglary and robbery and recessions but not a significant relationship with homicide. In this study, each recession since the 1940s was treated as its own experiment, and the relationship between the onset of the recession and the growth rates of crimes was tested. Additional tests were conducted with regression models that estimated crime as a function of either the unemployment rate or the employment ratio (the percentage of the total population employed), and the results were very similar to the associations of crime with recessions. The Cook and Zarkin studies focus on unemployment as an indicator of overall macroeconomic conditions; this work has subsequently been reexamined by a large number of studies which focus on the unemployment and crime relationship. The findings have generally been consistent with Cook and Zarkin's results (see, for example, Raphael and Winter-Ebmer, 2001). Most studies find a strong countercyclical relationship between unemployment and property crime but generally weak or no relationship between unemployment and violent crime.

Since the time of the original Cook and Zarkin study, there have been two additional recessions experienced by the United States, and Bushway, Cook, and Phillips, in their chapter in this volume, have updated the initial study by examining additional years of data and additional violence outcomes (e.g., femicide, multiple measures of homicide). The authors also include analysis of an additional economic variable, real GDP per capita, which measures the level of economic output per person in inflation-adjusted dollars. The new results presented by Bushway, Cook, and Phillips using only the relationship between national crime rates and recessions are essentially the same as the original Cook and Zarkin (1985) study. Recessions are significantly and countercyclically associated with burglary and robbery but not with several measures of homicide. However, the story changes somewhat when the authors disaggregate the data by age of the victim (using U.S. Vital Statistics data) and age of the perpetrator (using FBI data). They find a strong association between violence for certain age ranges and certain economic conditions. For example, the estimates using Vital Statistics data show a significant countercyclical relationship between GDP per capita and the age of homicide victims for ages 15 to 24. The analysis with the Uniform Crime Reports (UCR) arrest data shows a significant and countercyclical relationship between arrest rates for robbery and murder for perpetrators ages 18 to 24 but interestingly not for those under 18. The results for the unemployment rate and employment ratio do not show a significant relationship between those economic factors and violence.

The case for a strong, countercyclical relationship between robbery and economic conditions is robust across the original Cook and Zarkin study and the Bushway, Cook, and Phillips study. However, in the latter, the case for a relationship between economic conditions and homicide is only found for GDP per capita, and then only for certain age groups. The results that are disaggregated by age suggest that there may be a stronger connection between homicide and GDP per capita for victims and perpetrators below age 25, who are at particularly high risk for violence.

This raises an interesting possibility. The lack of a significant relationship between economic conditions and homicide found in Cook and Zarkin (1985) (as well as more recent studies such as Arvanites & Defina, 2006) could be driven by a combination of differential impacts of changes in employment status and income on violence, a combination that depends on the age of the victims and perpetrators. Therefore, it is a possibility that changes in income have a different impact on youth homicide than on homicide in other age ranges. Given the interesting possibility raised by these results, it is fortuitous that these issues are examined in two other studies in this volume.

Baumer, Rosenfeld, and Wolff extend the research on economic factors and crime along several dimensions. A particularly interesting aspect of their study is that they use data that is disaggregated from the national level, by collecting data on property crime and homicide from 82 metropolitan areas around the country. A notable strength of their study is that they include data for the most recent economic downturn. The authors control simultaneously for several economic conditions, including the unemployment rate, the mean wage rate, real GDP, and an index of consumer sentiment. They also measure the homicide rate for perpetrators under 18, 18 to 25, and over 25, so outcomes are examined for youth homicide as well as overall homicide. A key advantage of this approach is that the authors examine violence outcomes at a lower level of aggregation, so the economic factors examined should not suffer the same amount of collinearity as the national data examined by Bushway, Cook, and Phillips. The more recent data allows for examination of the most recent recession. While a key focus of the chapter is the moderating effects of inflation and policy variables on the effects of economic conditions, this chapter will focus on the linear effects found for the various economic factors.

Baumer, Rosenfeld, and Wolff's results show that higher real wages are associated with lower homicide rates overall and for youth under 18. However, higher real wages are also positively associated with higher rates of homicide for youth 18 to 24. Higher real GDP is associated with lower homicide rates overall and for youth 18 to 24 and adults over 25. Higher consumer sentiment (a measure of how positively the public views economic conditions) is associated with lower rates of homicide overall but only for those under 18 in the age-specific results. There is no significant association between the homicide rate and the unemployment rate.

Overall, the strongest and most consistent relationship between economic conditions and homicide is found by measures of income (real wages and real GDP), while there is no significant association between the unemployment rate and homicide. Both of these results are consistent with the results of Bushway, Cook, and Phillips, although they examine different time periods and measure violence at a different level of aggregation. This strengthens the case that homicide is more strongly related to income than to other economic factors, but both of these studies face a similar data limitation—they are unable to disaggregate violence by factors other than age, such as race and ethnicity and the socioeconomic status of the victim.

Lauritsen, Gorislavsky, and Heimer address a key limitation of the two previous studies by examining the relationship between economic conditions and violent victimization using self-reports from the National Crime Victimization Survey and police-reported homicide data. They compare trends in youth violence victimization to trends in consumer sentiment, poverty, and unemployment. Given the nature of their data, they are able to examine violence rates by gender and ethnicity (non-Latino whites, non-Latino blacks, and Latinos).

Their findings show that increasing youth poverty is significantly associated with homicide and gun violence for males 12 to 17 and significantly associated with homicide and serious violence for males 18 to 24. Increasing youth poverty is also associated with higher rates of gun and serious violence for females of all ages studied. Increasing youth unemployment, on the other hand, is not significantly associated with any of the violence measures for males and is only significantly associated with serious violence for females 12 to 17. Overall, these results are consistent with those found by Bushway, Cook, and Phillips and Baumer, Rosenfeld, and Wolff. The measure of income, youth poverty, is generally significantly and countercyclically associated with youth violence, while unemployment is generally not significantly associated with violence.

By comparing the results across these three studies, some common themes are apparent. First, examining the relationship between macroeconomic conditions and violence is much more complicated than asking whether a bad economy results in more violence. Previously published studies of this relationship have generally examined data collected at a high level of aggregation (e.g., national or state) and have not examined youth violence specifically. However, when the data begin to be disaggregated from the national level and measures of income are included among the economic factors examined, a clearer picture of the relationship between macroeconomic factors and youth violence begins to emerge. Measures of income are more likely to be associated with violence than are measures of employment. In some cases, these measures of income are more closely associated with violence among youth than they are with adults. These studies are also consistent with results that have examined the relationship between wages and violence (Gould, Weinberg, & Mustard, 2002). The strikingly consistent results across the three studies points to a future area of research that could be useful for violence prevention: why does there appear to be a specific relationship between income and violence that is not seen between violence and other economic variables? If there is a direct connection between income and violence, interventions to increase income and wages may be effective in preventing violence.

Neighborhoods, Schools, and Street Markets

While the studies in this volume have documented the connection between certain macroeconomic conditions and violence, this raises the question of how economic factors such as income at a national, state, or local level relate to individual violent behaviors. We will now review the studies in this volume that examine the effect of economic conditions through the mediating domains of neighborhoods, schools, and street markets to examine factors that are still macroeconomic in the sense that they measure conditions at a higher level than the individual or family. These factors are still broadly experienced by a large group of people and, therefore, fall under the societal and community levels of our explanatory framework.

Considerable research has been conducted on the effects of neighborhood disadvantage on violent behavior. However, Fang et al. highlighted in their chapter in this volume that there is considerable debate about whether the studies that examine the impact of neighborhood conditions truly measure the impact of the neighborhood and not compositional effects of the individual characteristics of those who make up the neighborhood. In addition, there is considerable evidence that neighborhood effects on violence mainly impact violence in the neighborhoods that are the most disadvantaged, which implies that there many be a nonlinear relationship between neighborhood disadvantage and violence.

Fang et al.'s study uses the National Longitudinal Survey of Adolescent Health to combine data on several self-reported violence outcomes (any violent behavior, serious fighting, and using a weapon) with census-track-level data on neighborhood characteristics (the proportion of nonelderly with income below the poverty line, the proportion of family households receiving public assistance income, the unemployment rate, the proportion of family households that are female headed with children under 18 years of age, and the proportion of the population aged 25 and over without a high school diploma or equivalency), as well as a detailed list of individual and family characteristics, to examine the nonlinear relationship between neighborhood disadvantage and violence. The results from this study reveal a complicated but intuitively plausible relationship. At low levels of neighborhood disadvantage (the 40 percent of neighborhoods with the lowest levels of disadvantage), there is no significant effect of neighborhood disadvantage on violent behavior, and a similar relationship is found for neighborhoods with the *most* disadvantage (the lower 40 percent of the distribution), as well. Changes in violent behavior are only observed for neighborhoods between the fortieth and sixtieth percentiles of disadvantage. The implication is that if a program or policy was implemented that attempts to prevent violence by improving levels of neighborhood disadvantage, it might improve neighborhood conditions without reducing violence, depending on the level of neighborhood disadvantage.

While interventions to prevent violence do not usually specifically attempt to improve the components of the disadvantage index used here, these results could help explain the mixed results of programs that have moved families from public housing to areas of less concentrated poverty. The Moving to Opportunity (MTO) demonstration project provided housing vouchers to low-income families living in areas of concentrated poverty to allow them to move to areas of less-concentrated poverty. Studies of the effects of this program found a significant reduction of violence by girls, but after initially positive results for boys, the effects on violence became negative (although nonsignificant; Kling, Ludwig, & Katz, 2005). The Fang et al. results suggest that these mixed results could arise because the improvement in neighborhood conditions induced by MTO may not have been sufficient to reduce violent behavior on the part of boys. This is consistent with the conclusions of the final report on the MTO evaluation, which stated that "a more comprehensive approach is needed [than housing vouchers] to reverse the negative consequences of living in neighborhoods with heavily concentrated poverty" (U.S. Department of Housing and Urban Development, 2011, p. 7).

The results of Fang et al.'s study also have implications for other interventions that attempt to improve neighborhood conditions to reduce crime and violence, such as business improvement districts (BIDs). BIDs allow local business owners to vote to collect from local businesses fees that are used to invest in neighborhood improvements in the district where they are collected (examples of BID investments in Los Angeles include security patrols, maintenance of sidewalks, graffiti removal, marketing of local businesses, parking and transportation management, and capital improvements, such as improved lighting).[3] This strategy has been shown to lead to a significant reduction in assaults following implementation of BIDs in Los Angeles districts (Cook & MacDonald, 2011). As this program is adopted in other locations, it will be important to view the Los Angeles experience in the context of the Fang et al.'s results. Did the BID program allow highly disadvantaged neighborhoods to improve substantially in ways that led to reduced violence? Was the program implemented in districts that were on the verge of moving into the middle ranges of disadvantage? Addressing these questions will be important to understand how the BID program has led to the improvements demonstrated.

An additional study included in this volume, by Crutchfield and Wadsworth, also examines the effects of neighborhood disadvantage on the protective effect of school performance on youth delinquency, a substantial risk factor for youth violence. In general, youth with higher grades are less likely to be delinquent. However, it is unclear how this relationship may be moderated by high levels of neighborhood disadvantage. The authors address this question by using data from the National Longitudinal Survey of Youth to estimate the effect of school grades and neighborhood disadvantage on delinquency. The authors find that neighborhood disadvantage moderates the protective impact of higher grades on delinquent behavior. In fact, in highly disadvantaged neighborhoods (those one standard deviation below the mean), the effect of good grades is actually reversed and is associated with *higher* rates of delinquency.

The implications of this finding, if it is confirmed by further research, suggest that interventions that attempt to prevent violence by improving performance in school may have their effects overwhelmed by the neighborhood conditions in areas of high disadvantage. It will also be important for future research to examine the interaction of neighborhood conditions with other individual- and family-level characteristics that may be associated with lower levels of violence. Interventions that are based on improving individual- or family-level factors may be adversely affected by the neighborhood context.

The unintended consequences of programs and policies are also important to understand, and Fagan and West examine in their chapter in this volume whether increasing incarceration rates in New York City from 1985 to 1997 had a negative impact on neighborhood economic conditions. They find that higher incarceration rates are associated with lower levels of neighborhood income but not neighborhood human capital (measured by percentage of high school graduates, labor force participation rate, and percentage of neighborhood residents with a skilled job). While it is not possible to determine from these results whether the impact of decreased income is substantial enough to cause a deterioration in neighborhood conditions that leads to more violent behavior, it does show that policies implemented, in part, to address violent behavior can have adverse consequences on neighborhoods. In a full accounting of the costs and benefits of any program or policy, it is important to include the full range of costs and benefits. If Fagan and

West's result is confirmed by further research, it will add an important component to the evaluation of crime control policies.

Finally, the relationship between neighborhood conditions and street markets is potentially an important pathway for macroeconomic conditions to influence violent behavior. For example, some researchers have linked the dramatic decline in homicide in the 1990s to the waning of the crack-cocaine market, which was characterized by a high level of violence (Blumstein & Wallman, 2000). Edberg and Bourgois present the results of a qualitative study that examines the relationship between the identity formation of adolescents and the violent imagery surrounding narcotraffickers in the U.S.-Mexico border region. It is clear that the positive portrayal of participants in the drug trade who are engaged in violent behavior strongly influences the self-image of the participants in the study. However, it remains an open question how much the presence of drug trafficking affects adolescent development and violence outcomes when other factors are held constant. In addition, it is not clear that this phenomenon experienced in the U.S.-Mexico border region generalizes to the rest of the United States.

Given the illegal nature of most street markets, it remains a very difficult area to address with the type of quantitative analysis that is necessary to establish the net effect of street market activity on violence. The data-collection challenges are daunting and will likely involve substantial resources to accomplish. For example, Ihlanfeldt (2007) examined the effect of the distance to available jobs on illegal drug sales in Atlanta, Georgia, neighborhoods. However, violence associated with the drug trade was not specifically examined. This study involved geocoding thousands of crime records from multiple law enforcement agencies compiled over a two-county area for four years. The author states that the difficulty in collecting data precluded examining additional years of data. This shortcoming will need to be addressed if the effect of street markets on violent behavior is to be evaluated and effective interventions are to be developed. The work in this volume illustrates that neighborhood, school, and street markets are important mediators that filter broader macroeconomic conditions down to the individual behavior. While the causal links among these three conditions are complex and not easily teased out in a research setting, understanding the nature of their effects is important to violence prevention. The non-linear nature of neighborhood effects and the interaction between neighborhoods and other violence risk factors is important to understand for the development of community- and society-level violence-prevention initiatives.

A Long-Term View of Youth Violence: The Role of the Family and Economic Factors

The final mediating domain between economic conditions and violence examined in this volume is family functioning. There are numerous potential ways that adverse economic conditions could affect family functioning that could lead to increases in the likelihood of violent behavior among youth. The chapters in this volume focus on the relationship between child development and economic conditions. The reason for this focus is a large and rapidly growing science base that demonstrates the impact of adverse conditions in a child's early life that contribute to a wide range of negative outcomes later in life. The implications of these developmental effects for the study of violence and for the development of effective interventions to prevent violence are profound.

In this volume, Guerra discusses the contributions of macroeconomic conditions to risk for youth violence within developmental stages, from prenatal through adolescence. The developmental-stage-specific risks include neurological and biological impairment and the learning of aggression and violence, which are associated with chronic poverty but may also be related to family economic shocks. Guerra describes these risks as cumulative, and the implication is that earlier detriments or assaults on development have the potential to be more harmful. For example, job loss by a parent of young children could increase family stress and increase episodes of harsh parenting, which will negatively affect the child's development and can increase aggressive tendencies in the child.

This finding is consistent with research by the National Scientific Council on the Developing Child (2005) and Shonkoff et al. (2012) showing that negative experiences which elicit a toxic stress response for prolonged periods of time in children have lasting impacts. Recently, the American Academy of Pediatrics published a policy statement in which it supports leveraging science and early childhood policies and services to reduce the precipitants of toxic stress and to mitigate their impact (Garner et al., 2012). Since both chronic poverty and economic shocks can contribute to developmental risks and toxic stress, it is important to study the impact of economic fluctuations on youth violence rates many years after the economic change. Guerra states, "most studies examine changes in violence rates within the defined period during or immediately following economic downturns. Yet many of the impacts on youth violence may affect children even before they are born, translating into changes in youth violence rates a decade or more in the future" (this volume, p. 258).

Despite the large body of evidence that demonstrates the impact of early life stress on child development, there have been very few studies that have examined the long-term impacts of severe economic downturns on child health and behavior. One exception is Elder (1999), which examined the impact of the Great Depression on children's life course. Elder's study found that the Depression negatively affected working-class children more than middle-income children. Economic downturns may disproportionately impact families that are living in poverty or are financially unstable. Future studies must document both the impact of economic conditions on families and their long-term impacts on children and youth violence rates.

Matjasko et al. discuss existing child development theory and propose a framework for explaining the interworking of macro, community, and family economic factors and their impact on family functioning. An existing model, the family stress model (Conger et al., 1992), posits that macroeconomic factors affect family economic factors that then alter family stress, parental emotion and behavior, and parenting practices. The family economic factors that could be affected include debt accumulation, asset loss, damage to property (e.g., the inability to pay for car repairs), housing transition (e.g., foreclosure or eviction), loss of medical coverage, food insecurity, and so on. These types of strain affect both chronically poor families as well as families that do not have the resources to withstand disruptions, including families that are near poverty. The family investment model (Becker & Thomes, 1986) underscores the relative differences in families' ability to promote the healthy development of their children; thus, families exposed to long-term economic disadvantage may be in a chronic state of suffering from the family stress described in the family stress model. Finally, individuals from low-socioeconomic-status backgrounds have a disproportionate amount of early adverse experiences, and a disproportionate number of individuals from these backgrounds are involved with youth violence. Matjasko et al. posit that "a dynamic system exists that maintains and sustains a relationship between community and family economic factors and youth violence and that resists disruption" (this volume, 291). Their chapter underscores the opportunities for preventing youth violence through strengthening families' abilities to endure poverty or economic shocks.

Prevention Strategies within the Family Context

Most youth violence prevention programs either do not attempt to prevent violence by improving the economic factors that may adversely impact family functioning, or the potential positive impacts of the programs on family economic conditions have not been examined. However, one pathway by which existing programs may reduce adverse events and promote child and adolescent development may be through stabilizing families' economic circumstances or providing families with resources that assist them in coping with difficult economic circumstances. Buffering families against the adverse economic conditions they face, whether due to economic fluctuations or persistent community economic disadvantage and poverty, may be one of the mechanisms through which programs could prevent youth violence. This stabilization may come in many forms—such as providing families with coping mechanisms for economic hardship, providing a space for struggling families to support each other emotionally, connecting families to services, providing child care, or assisting families in job searching or training. Here we discuss two early childhood programs which have been shown to reduce youth-violence-related behavior later in life, and we highlight the ways in which the programs address family economic factors directly or indirectly.

Nurse-Family Partnership (NFP) is a maternal and early childhood intervention program that has been designated a model program by Blueprints for Violence Prevention (Mihalic et al., 2001). The program sends trained registered nurses to visit first-time mothers on an ongoing basis while they are pregnant through the second year of the child's life. The nurses promote positive health-related behaviors during pregnancy and the early years of the child's life, competent care of the children, and maternal personal development. The nurses help women envision a future consistent with their values and aspirations (Olds, 2002). These aspects of the program reduce negative childhood experiences, promote children's resilience and development, and support positive family functioning in the face of economic strain. Since most participants are low income, these skills may be especially salient in the setting of economic instability or poverty. Furthermore, nurses also help mothers with family planning, connect them to government services, and help women continue their education and find employment. NFP acknowledges the gravity of economic factors and integrates economic factors into the program. Economic self-sufficiency for the family is one of NFP's three stated goals (NFP, 2012).

The program has demonstrated some long-term effects on youth-violence-related behaviors. In a 15-year follow-up of the first randomized control trial in Elmira, New York, children in the experimental group reported fewer arrests and convictions (Olds et al., 1998). However, in a 19-year follow-up, it appears that this effect only continued for girls (Eckenrode et al., 2010). Some of the long-term benefits of NFP may result from the way in which the program incorporates economic factors. For example, mothers who participate in NFP are more likely to be employed over time (Olds et al., 1988; Kitzman et al., 1997; Olds, 2009) and have longer intervals between first and second children due to family planning (Olds et al., 1988; Kitzman et al., 2000; Olds et al., 2004). Economic evaluations of both the Elmira and Memphis pilots show that the program is cost saving to society. Most of the benefits of the program come from mothers in the treatment groups using less government services including AFDC or TANF, food stamps, and Medicaid (Karoly et al., 1998; Olds et al., 2010).

In addition to early home-visitation programs, there is also evidence that early childhood education programs can reduce violence later in life. Rigorous evaluations of high-quality, center-based preschool programs for three- and four-year-old low-income children that include an intensive family component have been shown to demonstrate positive effects on a range of outcomes including reduced delinquent and violent behavior later in life. Preschool participation in the Chicago Child-Parent Centers program was associated with significantly fewer violent arrests at ages 20 and 24 (Reynolds et al., 2001, 2007). Two mechanisms by which high-quality preschool programs may be affecting youth violence behavior later in life are promoting healthy child development and supporting family functioning in the face of economic strain. The Chicago Child-Parent Centers program, which is still implemented today, provides half-day center-based preschool with low child-to-teacher ratios and family services through third grade. The program includes home visits upon enrollment (and as needed) and provides families in need with transportation to the center, health screenings for children by an on-site nurse, and breakfast and lunch for children. Staff members also connect families to employment training, mental health services, and public assistance (Reynolds, 2000). By providing the family with health screenings and food assistance and connecting families to outside resources, the program may be alleviating economic strain or may be assisting families so that they can better protect themselves from the negative effects of economic fluctuations.

Economic Opportunity and Youth Violence: Where Do We Go from Here?

The research presented in this volume has produced a wealth of new information that can be valuable in understanding the relationship between macroeconomic factors and youth violence. The information may also be useful in developing and implementing programs, policies, and strategies for preventing youth violence. Given what has been learned, then, what recommendations can we draw from these results for future research and prevention efforts? In order to develop these recommendations, we will return to the three conditions that need to be met for violence prevention through improving economic conditions to be successful.

First, *it must be established that violence is strongly associated with economic conditions, net of other factors that are also associated with violence.* The studies in this volume that examine the relationship between economic conditions and violence all identified significant relationships. The nature of these relationships, however, is not consistent across all economic conditions or all age groups. These findings point to a strong countercyclical relationship between income, wages, and youth violence. None of the studies identified a significant relationship between unemployment and youth violence, although this has been the primary focus of much of the prior research on economic conditions and crime. Given the relative void in the research literature on the relationships between income and youth violence, this is an area where future research can be helpful in describing the nature of this relationship can and provide information that can be useful in the development of preventive interventions that focus on this economic factor. It would be useful to know whose income is important. Is it family income? Income earned by youth and young adults? Addressing these questions will assist in designing programs and policies that can reduce violence by increasing income.

Second, *if economic factors are associated with violence, policies, programs, or strategies developed to address these conditions must be able to identify the appropriate economic characteristics and be effective in improving them.* While the studies in this volume did not directly examine the effectiveness of particular preventive intervention in improving economic conditions, they did examine several mediating domains that are potential pathways between higher-level macroeconomic conditions and youth violence outcomes. In particular, the nature of the relationship between neighborhood economic and societal conditions and youth violence was shown to be complex but extremely vital in understanding the relationships between macroeconomics and violence. Neighborhood disadvantage was shown to be associated with violent behavior by youth, but the relationship is not the same for all neighborhoods. In order to decrease violence in severely disadvantaged neighborhoods, it is likely that the necessary improvements in economic conditions would need to be large.

There is also a complex relationship between neighborhood conditions and grades in school. While higher grades in school are generally associated with less delinquency by youth, the results presented in this volume suggest that for youth in severely disadvantaged neighborhoods, this is not the case. It will be important for future research to continue to examine the relationship between neighborhood conditions and risk and protective factors for violence. This finding also has implications for evaluating prevention programs. For example, if school-based prevention programs are evaluated in neighborhoods of moderate disadvantage and found to be effective, will that same result hold true when the programs are implemented in neighborhoods of more severe disadvantage?

The final mediating pathway between macroeconomic conditions and youth violence considered in this volume is family functioning. Both of the chapters on family functioning and child development demonstrate that family factors have the potential to mediate the effects of adverse macroeconomic conditions and youth violence. Research has also shown that intervening with families can have long-term effects on youth violence (Spoth, Redmond, & Shin, 2000). Most research on the relationship between macroeconomics and violence is contemporaneous; economic conditions today, or in the recent past, are examined for their relationship with violence today. The science base in child development, as well as the evidence base for early childhood intervention programs, suggests that the effects of current economic conditions on violence can be seen years later. For example, while the recent "Great Recession" has not been associated with a contemporaneous increase in violence (at least as shown through FBI arrest rates; U.S. Department of Justice, 2011), there could be substantial effects on violent behavior for children in certain age ranges during or in the years following the recession. Future research should consider developmental-stage-dependent models of the relationship between the Great Recession and youth violence.

Third, *the improvement in these factors must be large enough that they can lead to a reduction in violence.* In general, the current volume sheds some light on this question, but more work needs to be done. For example, the early childhood programs described here attempt to improve the circumstances of disadvantaged families. Providing families with professional support and resources can assist families when they are experiencing economic difficulty and can reduce the probability that these difficulties will result in youth violence in the future. Given the positive impacts demonstrated in these programs on youth violence for children in their adolescent and young adult years, some preventive effect may be due to a substantial improvement in family economic conditions. This is an important preventive pathway for future program evaluations to examine.

In summary, the research presented here provides strong evidence of a relationship between certain macroeconomic conditions and youth violence. The associations between economic conditions and violence are likely mediated by several domains and in complex ways. However, violence is preventable, and the prevention of violence through improving economic conditions is a promising pathway. In the future, it will be important to better understand the short- and long-term relationships between macroeconomics and violence and to evaluate prevention programs for their effect on economic outcomes.

NOTES

1. Disclaimer: The findings and conclusions of this chapter are those of the authors and do not necessarily represent the official position of the Centers for Disease Control and Prevention.
2. Guide to Community Preventive Services, http://www.thecommunityguide.org/index.html.
3. Office of Justice Programs, "Program Profile: Business Improvement Districts (BIDs), Los Angeles (Calif.)," http://www.crimesolutions.gov/ProgramDetails .aspx?ID=67.

REFERENCES

Arvanites, T. M. & Defina, R. H. (2006). Business cycles and street crime. *Criminology, 44*(1), 139–164.

Becker, G., & Thomes, N. (1986). Human capital and the rise and fall of families. *Journal of Labor Economics, 4*, S1–S139.

Blumstein, A., & Wallman, J. (2000). The recent rise and fall of American violence. In A. Blumstein & J. Wallman (Eds.), *Crime drop in America* (pp. 1–12). Cambridge: Cambridge University Press.

Conger, R. D., Conger, K. J., Elder, G. H., Lorenz, F. O., Simons, R. L., & Whitbeck, L. B. (1992). A family process model of economic hardship and adjustment of early adolescent boys. *Child Development, 63*, 526–541.

Cook, P. J. & MacDonald, J. (2011). Public safety through private action: An economic assessment of BIDs. *Economic Journal, 121*(552), 445–462.

Cook, P. J., & Zarkin, G. A. (1985). Crime and the business-cycle. *Journal of Legal Studies, 14*(1), 115–128.

Dahlberg, L. L., & Krug, E. G. (2002). Violence—a global public health problem. In E.

Krug, L. L. Dahlberg, J. A. Mercy, A. B. Zwi, & R. Lozano (Eds.), *World report on violence and health* (pp. 1–56). Geneva: World Health Organization.

Eckenrode, J., Campa, M., Luckey, D. W., Henderson, C. R., Cole, R., Kitzman, H., et al. (2010). Long-term effects of prenatal and infancy nurse home visitation on the life course of youths. *Archives of Pediatrics & Adolescent Medicine, 164*(1), 9–15.

Elder, G. H. (1999). *Children of the Great Depression: Social change in life experience* (25th Anniversary Edition). Boulder, CO: Westview. Originally published 1974.

Garner, A. S., Shonkoff, J. P., Siegel, B. S., Dobbins, M. I., Earls, M. F., McGuinn, L., Pascoe, J., & Wood, D. L. Early childhood adversity, toxic stress, and the role of the pediatrician: Translating developmental science into lifelong health. *Pediatrics, 129*(1), 224–231.

Gould, E. D., Weinberg, B. A., & Mustard, D. B. (2002). Crime rates and local labor market opportunities in the United States: 1979–1997. *Review of Economics and Statistics, 84*(1), 45–61.

Ihlanfeldt, K. R. (2007). Neighborhood drug crime and young males' job accessibility. *Review of Economics and Statistics, 89*(1), 151–164.

Karoly, L. A., Greenwood, P. W., Everingham, S. S., Hoube, J., Kilburn, M. R., Rydell, C. P., et al. (1998). *Investing in our children: What we know and what we don't know about the costs and benefits of early childhood interventions.* Santa Monica, CA: Rand.

Kitzman, H., Olds, D. L., Henderson, C. R., Hanks, C., Cole, R., Tatelbaum, R., et al. (1997). Effect of prenatal and infancy home visitation by nurses on pregnancy outcomes, childhood injuries, and repeated child-bearing: A randomized controlled trial. *Journal of the American Medical Association, 278*, 644–652.

Kitzman H., Olds, D. L., Sidora, K., Henderson, C. R., Hanks, C., Cole, R. et al. (2000). Enduring effects of nurse home visitation on maternal life course: A 3-year follow-up of a randomized trial. *JAMA, 283*(15), 1983–1989.

Kling, J. R., Ludwig, J., & Katz, L. F. (2005). Neighborhood effects on crime for female and male youth: Evidence from a randomized housing voucher experiment. *Quarterly Journal of Economics, 120*(1), 87–130.

Mihalic, S., Irwin, K., Elliot, D., Fagan, A., & Hansen, D. (2001). *Blueprints for violence prevention.* Washington, DC: U.S. Department of Justice, Office of Justice Programs, Offices of Juvenile Justice and Delinquency Prevention.

National Scientific Council on the Developing Child. (2005). *Excessive stress disrupts the architecture of the developing brain* (Working Paper #3). Available at http://developingchild.harvard.edu.

Nurse-Family Partnership. (2012). *Changes in the mother's life course.* Available at http://www.nursefamilypartnership.org/proven-results/Changes-in-mother-s-life-course.

Olds, D. L. (2002). Prenatal and infancy home visiting by nurses: From randomized trials to community replication. *Prevention Science, 3*(3), 153–172.

Olds, D. L. (2009). *Impact of Nurse-Family Partnership on neighborhood context, government expenditures, and children's school functioning.* Final report, grant 2005-MU-MU-0001. U.S. Department of Justice.

Olds, D. L., Henderson, C. R., Cole, R., Eckenrode, J., Kitzman, H., Luckey, D., et al. (1998). Long-term effects of nurse home visitation on children's criminal and anti-social behavior. *JAMA, 280*(14), 1238–1244.

Olds, D. L., Henderson, C. R., Tatelbaum, R., & Chamberlin, R. (1988). Improving the life-course development of socially disadvantaged mothers: A randomized trial of nurse home visitation. *American Journal of Public Health, 78*(11), 1436–1445.

Olds, D. L., Kitzman, H., Cole, R., Hanks, C. A., Arcoleo, K. J., Anson, E. A., et al. (2010). Enduring effects of prenatal and infancy home visiting by nurses on maternal life course and government spending. *Archives of Pediatrics & Adolescent Medicine, 164*(5), 419–424.

Olds, D. L., Kitzman, H., Cole, R., Robinson, J. Sidora, K., Luckey, D., et al. (2004). Effects of nurse home visiting on maternal life-course and child development: Age-six follow-up of a randomized control trial. *Pediatrics, 114*(6), 1550–1559.

Raphael, S., & Winter-Ebmer, R. (2001). Identifying the effect of unemployment on crime. *Journal of Law & Economics, 44*(1), 259–283.

Reynolds, Arthur J. (2000). *Success in early intervention: The Chicago Child-Parent Centers.* Lincoln: University of Nebraska Press.

Reynolds, A. J., Temple, J. A., Robertson, D. L., & Mann, E. A. (2001). Long-term effects of an early childhood intervention on educational achievement and juvenile arrest. *JAMA, 285*(18), 2339–2346.

Reynolds, A. J., Temple, J. A., Suh-Ruu, O., Robertson, D. L. Mersky, J. P., Topitzes, J. W., & Niles, M. D. (2007). Effects of a school-based, early childhood intervention on adult health and well-being. *Archives of Pediatrics & Adolescent Medicine, 161*(8), 730–739.

Shonkoff, J. P., Garner, A. S., Committee on Psychosocial Aspects of Child and Family Health, American Pediatric Association Committee on Early Childhood, Adoption, and Dependent Care, and Section on Developmental and Behavioral Pediatrics. (2012). The lifelong effects of early childhood adversity and toxic stress. *Pediatrics, 129*(1), 232–246.

Spoth, R. L., Redmond, C., & Shin, C. (2000). Reducing adolescents' aggressive and hostile behaviors: Randomized trial effects of a brief family intervention 4 years past baseline. *Archives of Pediatrics & Adolescent Medicine, 154*(12), 1248–1257.

U.S. Department of Housing and Urban Development. (2011, October 14). *Moving to Opportunity for Fair Housing demonstration program: Final impacts evaluation.* Office of Policy Development and Research. Available at http://www.huduser.org/publications/pdf/MTOFHD_fullreport.pdf.

U.S. Department of Justice. (2011, September). *Arrests in the United States: 1980 to 2009.* NCJ 234319. Office of Justice Programs, Bureau of Justice Statistics.

Sarah Beth Barnett is Project Officer for the Health Economics and Policy Research and Analysis Team within the Prevention Development and Evaluation Branch in the Division of Violence Prevention at the Centers for Disease Control and Prevention.

Eric P. Baumer is Allen E. Liska Professor of Criminology in the College of Criminology and Criminal Justice at Florida State University.

Philippe Bourgois is Richard Perry University Professor of Anthropology and Family and Community Medicine at the University of Pennsylvania.

Shawn Bushway is Professor of Criminal Justice and Professor of Public Administration and Policy at the University at Albany. His research interests include the economics of crime, desistance, and decision making in the criminal justice system.

Philip J. Cook is ITT/Sanford Professor of Public Policy at Duke University. Recent books include *Controlling Crime: Strategies and Tradeoffs* (coedited) and *Paying the Tab: The Economics of Alcohol Policy*.

Robert D. Crutchfield is Professor and Chair of Sociology at the University of Washington.

Linda L. Dahlberg is the associate director for science in the Division of Violence Prevention at the U.S. Centers for Disease Control and Prevention. Dr. Dahlberg has spent much of the past 15 years working in the area of violence prevention—specifically on the efficacy of interventions to reduce violence.

Mark Edberg is Associate Professor at the George Washington University School of Public Health and Health Services, with secondary appointments in the Department of Anthropology and the Elliott School of International Affairs. His work on this volume was conducted under his concurrent role as Director of Qualitative Research for Development Services Group, Inc. (DSG). He has directed or codirected numerous research and intervention efforts focusing on at-risk youth, in both domestic and global contexts.

Jeffrey Fagan is Isidor and Seville Sulzbacher Professor of Law at Columbia Law School and Professor of Epidemiology in the Mailman School of Public Health at Columbia University. He also is Director of the Center for Crime, Community and Law at Columbia Law School. His research and scholarship examines policing, the legitimacy of the criminal law, capital punishment, legal socialization of adolescents, neighborhoods and crime, and juvenile crime and punishment. He is a Fellow of the American Society of Criminology and a National Associate of the National Academy of Science and the Institute of Medicine.

Xiangming Fang is Professor of Economics and Director of the International Center for Applied Economics and Policy in the College of Economics and Management at China Agricultural University. Prior to his current position, he was a Senior Health Economist with the Division of Violence Prevention at the Centers for Disease Control and Prevention (CDC). He has published in *American Journal of Preventive Medicine, Journal of Development Studies, Journal of Family Violence,* and *Journal of Pediatrics,* among others.

Curtis S. Florence is the lead health economist for the National Center for Injury Prevention and Control (NCIPC). Prior to joining NCIPC, Dr. Florence served as a faculty member in the Rollins School of Public Health at Emory University and the Tulane University School of Public Health and Tropical Medicine. His articles have appeared in journals such as the *American Journal of Public Health,* the *British Medical Journal, Health Affairs,* and *Inquiry.*

Ekaterina Gorislavsky is a PhD student in criminology and criminal justice at the University of Missouri–St. Louis. Her dissertation research examines race and ethnic differences in rape and sexual assault victimization among U.S. women.

Nancy G. Guerra is Professor of Psychology and Associate Dean for Research in the College of Arts and Sciences at the University of Delaware. She also serves as Director of the Global Research Consortium and Editor of the *Journal of Research on Adolescence*.

Karen Heimer is Professor of Sociology and Women's Studies at the University of Iowa. She conducts research on gender, race, victimization, and offending, as well as on gender and race differences in imprisonment over time.

Janet L. Lauritsen is Professor of Criminology and Criminal Justice at the University of Missouri–St. Louis and a visiting research fellow at the Bureau of Justice Statistics, U.S. Department of Justice. Her research is focused on the causes and consequences of victimization and the strengths and limitations of victimization methodologies.

Jennifer L. Matjasko is Acting Lead Behavioral Scientist for the Sexual and Youth Violence Evaluation Team within the Prevention Development and Evaluation Branch in the Division of Violence Prevention at the Centers for Disease Control and Prevention.

James A. Mercy is Special Advisor in the Division of Violence Prevention at the Centers for Disease Control and Prevention.

Matthew Phillips recently received his PhD in criminal justice from the University at Albany. His research interests include drug trafficking, drug-related violence, and quantitative methods.

Richard Rosenfeld is Curators Professor of Criminology and Criminal Justice at the University of Missouri–St. Louis. He is past president of the American Society of Criminology, and his current research focuses on the impact of the economy and policing on crime.

Tim Wadsworth is Associate Professor at the University of Colorado at Boulder. Much of his work focuses on explaining changing rates of violence in the United States.

Valerie West is Assistant Professor in the Department of Criminal Justice at John Jay College.

Kevin T. Wolff is a PhD candidate in the College of Criminology and Criminal Justice at Florida State University.

INDEX

The letter *t* following a page number denotes a table; the letter *f* denotes a figure.

DATE DUE